The Matter of Disability

Corporealities: Discourses of Disability

Series editors: David T. Mitchell and Sharon L. Snyder

Recent Titles

A complete list of titles in the series can be found at www.press.umich.edu

The Matter of Disability

Materiality, Biopolitics, Crip Affect

David T. Mitchell, Susan Antebi,
and Sharon L. Snyder, Editors

UNIVERSITY OF MICHIGAN PRESS

Ann Arbor

Published in the United States of America by the
University of Michigan Press

First published May 2019

A CIP catalog record for this book is available from the British Library.

Library of Congress Cataloging-in-Publication Data

Names: Mitchell, David T., 1962– editor. | Antebi, Susan, editor. | Snyder, Sharon L., 1963– editor.
Title: The matter of disability : materiality, biopolitics, crip affect / David T. Mitchell, Susan Antebi, and Sharon L. Snyder, editors.
Description: Ann Arbor : University of Michigan Press, 2019. | Includes bibliographical references and index. |
Identifiers: LCCN 2018052340 (print) | LCCN 2019007453 (ebook) | ISBN 9780472125098 (E-book) | ISBN 9780472074112 (hardcover : alk. paper) | ISBN 9780472054114 (pbk. : alk. paper)
Subjects: LCSH: People with disabilities in mass media. | People with disabilities. | Disabilities—Social aspects.
Classification: LCC P94.5.P46 (ebook) | LCC P94.5.P46 M38 2019 | DDC 302.23087—dc23
LC record available at https://lccn.loc.gov/2018052340

Cover image: Tom Lieber, *Red Loop*, 2012, oil on canvas. Courtesy of Dolby Chadwick Gallery.

Cover description: A frame of gold, maroon, and black square off a rectangular abstract image with white skeletal digits hanging over the edge of a round horizon with a jungle-tangle of warm, lively forms below. Centered in the upper plane is the title of the book in white lettering; the lower plane contains the names of the volume editors in smaller white type.

Contents

Digital materials related to this title can be found on
the Fulcrum platform via the following citable URL:
https://doi.org/10.3998/mpub.9365129

Preface and Acknowledgments

Every act of creating a new theory involves a process of deliberate overcorrection. To actively fashion theory otherwise requires one to privilege some mode of investigation that has been artificially underprivileged thus far, while more well-traveled routes are intentionally underutilized. In this way alternative theorizations help to expose how theory is a living, breathing agentive organism operating fully within the limits and possibilities of its own historical moment.

This volume is no different, as the editors and contributors attempt to think disability materiality more agentially. Such an effort works counter to prevailing disability methodologies in that the social model of disability set aside impairment on behalf of the more pressing matter of policy and politics to live in the world. Inevitably, working self-consciously in this manner involved us in actively suppressing some of the interpretive and methodological moves so characteristic of our prior work within social model, deconstructive, and cultural studies contexts. Not that the contributors to this volume did not continue to have a stake in exposing the political coordinates of disability, such as the exposé of barriers and forms of exclusion, the formation of expendable populations, and those bodies that could be rationally sacrificed as instances of *homo sacer*. Rather, we attempted to think through disabled bodies (human, nonhuman, organic, inorganic, and environmental) to as great an extent as possible.

Consequently, this project involved us in a radical application of posthumanism to disability in its most phenomenological orientations. And it is in this pursuit of a deeper level of engagement with how disabled bodies respond to and actively reshape worlds that the contributors are most in debt to forebears largely not involved with questions of disability—or, at least not explicitly as a subject of their study. In their approach to this volume, the editors believe that no employment of disability as a diagnostic measure of discrimination can unravel that foundational devaluation of disability from its culturally wrought stigmas, sexual prohibitions, or deviance. Such an approach forces us, we believe, to exceed scripts of aberrancy based on the assessment of distance placed between disability and desirable embodiments of normative capacity.

To front-load this shared approach, our work begins in an acknowledgment of the foundational work of mid-20th-century French philosopher Maurice Merleau-Ponty. Phenomenology at its most basic level fashions ways of approaching our alternative models of engagement with the material vibrancy of disability. Yet Merleau-Ponty's work makes few explicit appearances in this volume, and, in some ways we must recognize that later generations of phenomenological investigation exceed approaches that merely situate phenomena as separate from the nature of being—particularly those of neomaterialists such as Diana Coole, Samantha Frost, Karen Barad, Rosi Braidotti, Rey Chow, Sara Ahmed, William E. Connolly, Elizabeth Grosz, Jane Bennett, Pheng Cheah—so-often cited in this volume. The work of the neomaterialists (also known as new materialism and nonnormative positivism) serves as a second-or third-generation approach to phenomenological traditions before us. Specifically, wherein Merleau-Ponty's work tends to end at the intersections of human bodies and environments, this volume also follows key works in animal studies, environmental studies, animacy studies, critical race studies, queer theory, and body studies, to name just a few. Perhaps, most importantly the volume pursues some of the ramifications in disability studies that follow on the heels of Carol Thomas and Margrit Shildrick in their key investigations of "impairment-effects" and "leaky bodies." These disabled body-based approaches sat dormant for too long as productive sites where disability studies and other cultural studies scholarship have left experiences of impairment behind almost as an embarrassment in order to pursue a more radical politics of disability. While we all believe in the importance of this radical political potentiality of disability, we also argue that not engaging with what Canadian disability studies writer Rod Michalko called "the difference that disability makes" left scholars in the field incapable of engaging with the materiality of difference in more meaningful ways.

Perhaps most pointedly, and contemporaneous to our interests, all the contributors in this volume owe a debt to the disability studies theorist Tobin Siebers, who, in many of the essays he wrote before he died in 2015, took up the concept of "critical embodiment" as a key tool for development. Siebers's interest in pursuing this methodological innovation sprang from his close relationship to work on the "cultural model of disability," as he once commented to one of us while eating lunch in a café in downtown

Ann Arbor. In many ways, what he said at that time drives this volume, as Siebers extended his observation into the following argument: "The problem in disability studies is not that it engages identity as a foundational tool in its investigations of difference, but rather that is has not done so with respect to the alternative knowledge disabled people bring to our shared cultural experiences." What he meant in making this comment is that disability can only contest its consignment to the "dustbin of history" by showing that experiences of the nonnormative body are more than just degrees of what the novelist Stanley Elkins calls "falling away from true." In other words, Siebers believed as a disabled man who used a wheelchair that he knew things about the world that others could not. His words help to explicate the standpoint position of Nancy Mairs's famous disability-phenomenological phrase "waist-high in the world" as a key form of knowing that is not available to most walkies and other upright citizens. This comment was not an overvaluing of the importance of his own point of view so much as it was a means by which to argue that disability had its own laws and potentialities of insight that would be lost without cultural forums such as disability studies to create space for this uniquely embodied worldview.

Thus, the editors want to acknowledge our unique debts in this regard while also intending to push what Siebers and others delineated as "the embodied turn" in disability studies to further posthumanist ends. The alternative agential materiality of disability on display in this volume remains in transition to a significant extent in that one can still feel the pull of social model expositions and explorations running throughout these essays; they do not "break away" from the methodologies and domains of insight so critical to disability studies formulations since the early 1970s. Disability studies sociologist Harlan Hahn once argued that "Disability Studies was nothing other than the surprising encounter with the alternate world-making view of disabled people as their perspectives have been suppressed for so long and so dramatically." We believe in many ways that this contention is a helpful gloss on how to think about the content of the essays in this volume and their cross-disciplinary shaking approaches to the articulation of alternative knowledge bases. However, what has most struck us in the creation of this volume is the degree to which Disability Studies has postponed that encounter with the visceral, material basis of Hahn's insightful gloss on disability as an absented way of knowing and the unique innovations evolved by non-normative embodiments as they navigate environments built for others.

As we worked on this volume over the course of several years (2014–

2017), another group held bimonthly meetings in Washington, DC: the Disability Studies Reading Group. While none of this volume was vetted for comment directly with this group, their insightful observations on other work relevant to the questions addressed in this one and on the essay about posthumanist T4 memory that concludes this volume make this collective an important influence. Thus, we want to acknowledge our great friends and colleagues at George Washington University, Georgetown University, Gallaudet University, and Loyola Maryland University: Robert McRuer, Jeff Brune, Jonathan Hsy, Julia Watts Belser, Sara Scalenghe. This collective has exerted an enormous amount of influence on our thinking and played a more instrumental role in how this collection came to take shape than they will ever know.

Further, we would like to acknowledge the graduate students in the George Washington Fall 2015 seminar Disability New Materialisms who read and actively commented on the theory, fiction, journalism, and films that play such a central role in the essays that follow: Fawwaz Alfares, Victoria Aloupis, Grace Bailey, Raymond Budelman, Jamie Cohn-Stacey, Chelsea Faloona, Fowzia Farah, Brady Forest, Leah Grisham-Webber, Erik Hollis, Lilit Makaryan, Alan Montroso, Elizabeth Moser, Sarai Reed, and Samuel Yates (one of the contributors to this collection). Additionally, graduate students in the GW Fall 2017 seminar Globalization of Necropolitics also contributed to some of final thinking that went into this volume as it finally came to fruition. Those individuals include Alexandra Anastasia, Emma Cassabaum, Turni Chakrabarti, Nancy Chung, Oni Crawford, Jennifer Henderson, Michaela Kleppinger, Soo-Jin Kweon, Ling Liu, Rachel Lynch, Shawn Meddock, Ashley Miller, and Zahari Richter. Their enthusiasm for thinking alternatively about disability materiality made them some of the ideal readers for whom this volume is intended.

The development of this volume has also benefited from the dynamic community of disability studies scholars at the University of Toronto. Thanks are due in particular to Tanya Titchkosky and Anne McGuire, founders of the Unsettling Normalcy working group, and their students and collaborators. Their dynamic engagement with disability as a way of being in the world, and their ongoing facilitation of new spaces to approach the shifting questions of our discipline, have impacted the shaping of this project. Our colleague at the University of Rochester, Beth Jörgensen, coeditor of a previous project, has been an invaluable interlocutor over a number of years; her energy, generosity, and transdisciplinary approach to disability in the global South have contributed to many aspects of this project.

We also wish to acknowledge Ximena Berecochea and Salvador Alanis, codirectors of the Toronto Institute for Creative Exchange, and their collaborators Mario Bellatin and Daniel Canty, coleaders of the January 2017 workshop Art and Orthopaedics. The opportunity to collaboratively conduct this unique workshop with academics and artists, including Emily Hind, Eva-Lynn Jagoe, and Jeannine Pitas, was key in the reflective process through which this work developed. Graduate students from the fall 2017 University of Toronto seminar Disability, Biopolitics and Eugenic Futures in Latin America, including Catia Corriveau-Dignard, Petre Ene, Nae Hanashiro Avila, Daniela Maldonado Castañeda, Carlos Antonio Pajuelo, Jesús Porras Vielma, Josette Rosenzweig Espinal, Alejandro Soifer, and Ross Swanson, offered surprising and challenging insight on the theories that informed this volume. This research was supported by the Social Sciences and Humanities Research Council of Canada.

Finally, we thank the artist Tom Lieber for permission to use his artwork on the cover of this volume. The abstract painting, "Red Loop" (2012), captures the focus on shifting content in the essays collected in *The Matter of Disability* by exploring the interfolding of human, nature, environment, toxicities, and blood as an ever-merging mutation of intersecting agents. As the artist explains his objective, "My work is centered on human energy . . . experiencing, feeling, receiving, expressing," and this capture of entangling libidinal forces erupts here as a not completely unperilous mixture. The work might be characterized in Sharon Snyder's words as an amalgam of bamboo, wheat grass, sage, skeletal forms, and ghostly remnants nourished with the blood of ancients who leave behind whips, questions, and more brambles, bodies besotted and humming to the milky surface. This being in and among things—a world imprinted by bodies as well as forces which press themselves on embodiments—swirls in a more agential interaction than Disability Studies and deconstructionist-based criticism has been able to adequately capture and which this volume seeks to address. The painting came at the end of Lieber's experience of caregiving for his partner who had terminal illness and later died after great struggle. For the editors this work captures the irresolution of that engagement with dynamic forces and the ways in which their meanings, identities, shapes, expressions, and forms cannot be adequately separated from each other. Lieber's work is widely collected and featured in the permanent collections of the Guggenheim and Modern Art Museums in New York City, the San Francisco Modern Art Museum, and the Tate Gallery in London among many others. Lieber now splits his time between Kauai and Los Angeles and his paintings are significantly influenced by the environments of the Hawaiian islands.

In closing, we want to return to the matter of theory-making and over-correction with which we began. This volume explicitly foregrounded two things that all contributors were asked to address: first, an unabashed commitment to thinking disability and crip/queer materialities in the most lively manner possible—essentially a foregrounding of impairment but without the pathologizing baggage of diagnostic and normative determinations of deviance; second, a visceral engagement with embodiment as it marks the world and is, in turn, marked by it. In other words, we asked to our contributors to engage readers in the task of thinking the world through disability rather than the more customary way of thinking disability through the world. This dual task was no simple request, and all of the essays in this volume went through multiple vettings with editors and our most helpful anonymous, outside readers. While multiauthored collections are highly devalued in the academic publishing world, this volume took years to develop and cultivate as interactive series of engagements and iterations that each contribution made to the larger work as a whole. Thus, as each essay stands on its own and will interest readers with specific interests and particular investment in more singular objects of study, we hope many will read the entirety, as we believe the argument unfolds most forcefully at the level of the whole.

Of course, both tactics identified above are on display, and the collection can only hope to situate itself as a transitional one at best—straddling yawning gaps that exist somewhere between thought systems—but one that ultimately actively privileges the agency of materiality rather than the inscriptive forces of culture. Thus, we join Brian Massumi, Jeffrey Cohen, Mel Chen, and others in finding out whether or not disability can assist in locating an agency not entirely eclipsed by language and the workings of culture while, nonetheless, using words as our only route to the agentive materiality we seek. We believe overcorrecting in this direction will orient us toward ways in which materialities recognized as disabilities might reconfigure worlds rather than primarily serve as failures of capacitation demanded by neoliberal orders.

David T. Mitchell, Washington, DC
Susan Antebi, Toronto, Canada
Sharon L. Snyder, Washington, DC

Introduction

David T. Mitchell, Susan Antebi, and Sharon L. Snyder

Giving (Disability) Materiality Its Due

Over the past two decades, theorizations of posthumanism and neomate-rialist philosophy have begun to radically reshape our understanding of what counts as materiality. Matter itself begins to take on a complex, inter-active role in the configuration of knowledge and the world, and is in turn shaped by that universe of interactions. According to the posthumanist philosopher of agential realism Karen Barad, "Matter is a dynamic intra-active becoming that is implicated and enfolded in its iterative becom-ing. . . . In other words, materiality is discursive . . . just as discursive prac-tices are always already material" (151–52). For this reason, it is "matter(ing)" rather than matter that most effectively defines the scenes of posthuman-ist philosophical intervention. And it is this "matter(ing)," too, that occu-pies our attention in the present volume, as we seek to elucidate the key role of disability's ongoing potentiality in the reshaping of the world.

For many readers, the notion of matter will still tend to conjure exam-ples with more clearly delimited boundaries, from the primacy of the atom, to the fleshiness of human and nonhuman bodies, to broader con-figurations of environment and world. Within this more familiar terrain, matter appears either to promise greater solidity to its discursive counter-part, or to serve as a purely overdetermined product of discourse, as in the tradition of social constructivism.

The urgency of posthumanist attention to materiality thus lies in its challenge to the boundaries that have traditionally posited matter as either given and separate from historical, cultural, and discursive processes, or as the constructed end-product of such processes. This bounded and lin-ear reading of matter that is integral to social constructivism continues to permeate disability studies, thanks in large part to the significance and longevity of the social model. The result is that disability is construed primarily through a discursive fate as synonymous with consignment to biological classifications of undesirable embodiment. Therefore disability studies now must encounter something amiss in social constructivism itself. This edited collection, titled *The Matter of Disability*, contends that such a critique opens up space for an alternative, neomaterialist, posthumanist basis to encounter disability more viscerally.

Posthumanist disability theory offers an opportunity to provide a substantive theoretical reworking of the repetitive employment of impaired—read: socially marked and biologically determined as undesirable—bodies as diagnostic tools of things gone awry in their social and environmental contexts. As Tobin Siebers points out in his essay on rebuilding the social model of disability in this volume, it is within the terrain of diagnosis that the medical and social models share a common objective in fixing things gone awry.[1] Within the scope of the medical model, disability is diagnosed as dysfunction and the impaired individual as incapacitated, thus, in need of fixing through supplementation, surgical intervention, therapy, and training. Alternatively, the social model of disability engages the social difficulties encountered by nonnormative bodies as opportunities to diagnose barriers in the environment forged around narrow norms of aesthetics, capacity, and functionality. While these two diagnostic approaches have profound differences when it comes to their findings (one diagnoses deviant embodiment, the other diagnoses exclusionary social and built environments) they both tend to empty disability materiality of its active participation in fashioning alternative biologies, alternative subjectivities, and viable nonnormative modes of life (human, animal, organic, inorganic). Social model thought also tends to keep in place the barrier between human and nonhuman animals, as the latter continues to resonate as a slander on the former. A posthumanist disability approach provides an opportunity to encounter disability more viscerally as an active participant in the transhistorical, intraspecies, and cross-cultural interactions of materiality, sociality, structures, and environments.

If, as posthumanist neomaterialism proposes, there is an interrelationship between matter and discursive meaning, we need to more tangibly recognize the materiality of disability's active participation in the processes of meaning-making itself.[2] This is not simply because disability must be resignified in more positive, affirming ways; but rather that disability provides the evidence of embodiment's shifting, kaleidoscopic, dynamically unfolding agency. If materiality's excess agency beyond the discursive proves incredibly difficult to capture, disability, with its un-characteristic morphing rearrangements of matter, makes that task a bit more tangible than it might prove otherwise. Bodies matter, but more than in the influential "citationally iterative" sense that Judith Butler theorizes in *Bodies That Matter* (6). For Butler both sex and gender are culturally constructed (there is no material essence to their meaning), and this production of the discursive realm opens their meanings up for reinscription. The ability of sex/gender norms to pass as "natural" serves as the product of cultural repetitions that deeply ingrain social meaning in materialities. Gender performativity (i.e., the "gender trouble" created by the defining instability of sexual identity), then, helps destabilize the cultural status of these "ostensibl[e] categories of ontology" (xxvii). Their discursive overdetermination offers up opportunities for the de-stabilizing play of resignification: the citationality of sameness can be used against itself to make the sex/gender terrain of meaning more elas-tic. However, such formulas of citationality (even in their most radical subversive applications) rely upon a passive substrate subject rather than a more fully agentive corporeality. Such a practice essentially subordi-nates materiality's agency to the whims of cultural iterations that func-tion as law. In contrast, posthumanist approaches are bound up in the material, discursive interplay that continually reconfigures the world. One does not precede or eclipse the other.

The posthumanist approaches undertaken by the contributors to this collection recognize that matter itself exerts influence and agency that ul-timately outstrips any human ability to deterministically channel its sub-stantiality into false discursive singularities. It makes the diagnostic im-perative that reduces disability to a mere barometer of cultural insufficiencies less determinative. It returns disability to its proper place as an ongoing historical process of materiality's dynamic interactionism. It situates disability not as deviant, but rather as evidence for the "excess" that marks materiality's agency and reaches beyond the realm of the cul-tural while shaping its formulations. *The Matter of Disability*, in other words, does not pursue representational, rehabilitative meanings for dis-ability, but rather takes as a starting point the fact that disability is already a part of the process of materiality's active, unfolding participation in the world. It is "world-making" in the cultural sense that queer theory intends (Berlant and Warner 558), but it is also the *world-making* of difference through matter as neomaterialist posthumanism contends. Elizabeth Grosz puts this process in Darwinistic terms as "life as the ever more com-plex elaboration of difference" (66–67).

No Mere Prosthetic Relation

Disability participates in this "complex elaboration of difference" rather than solidifies something gone awry in an otherwise stable process. Embodiment's defining precarity and surprising unfoldings turn disabilities into productive, proactive expressive capacities within matter itself. This alternative approach to materiality intends to "give materiality its due" by avoiding the purely inscription-based models of most social constructivist theory (Coole and Frost 7). Bodies are not "dumb material" upon which sociality simply writes; rather they actively participate in their own shapings and the shaping of the world of which they are a part (Massumi 1). Yet, at the same time, posthumanist disability theory is not to be confused with transhumanism. Transhumanism effectively extends the most dangerous inclinations within humanism in that proponents invest in the capacity of a human-directed escape from disability and other late eugenical dreams of an exceptionally capacitated humanity beyond our current one.[3] Posthumanism is an opposition to this belief, perhaps, even, as Cary Wolfe argues it, the "opposite of transhumanism" (*What Is Posthumanism?* xv).

This foundational distinction exists at the heart of what theorists in this volume refer to variously as neomaterialism, nonnormative positivism, or posthumanist disability theory. The attempt is to think more deeply about materiality's agential capacities without continuing to consign disability to a reductively pathologized and thus wholly human discursive fate. In part our collective attempt is to dislodge the human-centric foundation upon which humanist, liberal philosophy rests; in the next section of the introduction we expand on the destabilization of the foundations of this figure of hypercapacitated, homogenizing Western man. At this juncture, the roles of materiality in general, and disability materiality in particular, have reached their limit within liberal humanist philosophical formulas of material differences.

Disability therefore must be rescued as the more active, dynamic, and substantive materialization that it is. Or, rather, posthumanist disability theory assists the social model in surrendering its inability to give an ever-mutating materiality its due.

While social constructivism has largely consigned materiality to a minimalist-made product of discourse, posthumanism seeks to decenter this human-centric understanding by recognizing matter "not as iterative citationality [Butler] but as *iterative intra-activity*" (Barad 184). Matter makes new worlds of possibility surface even as it often seems statistically deterministic in its evident-ness. Disability, which the social model of disability has tasked as social disadvantage "constructed on top of impairment" (Corker 8), provides one of the best examples of an overdetermined, constructed, and socially sequestered materiality upon which normative social orders inscribe pathology, undesirability, even nonviability. Whereas difference has now been significantly refashioned as the potentiality of alternative modes of being, social constructivism continues to resist including disability as an alternate becoming. The majority of our extant critical theories have continued to ignore disability in their theories of queer, gender, racialized, classed, sexualized, environmentalist, and intersectionalist approaches to questions of embodiment. This tendency has continued despite active attempts to reverse this telling omission from social justice approaches, such as those of Robert McRuer (queer theory), Carol Thomas (feminist theory), Nirmala Erevelles (critical race theory), Jim Charlton (neo-Marxist theory), and Alison Kafer (sexuality studies), among many others.

We think that we know disability when we see it and that seeing, itself a privileging of an ableist capacity of a singular form of interactionism, involves encountering a limit with which most disciplines about materialist embodiment would rather not associate. Even the social model's culturally constructivist emphasis puts aside the question of direct encounters with the substantiality of nonnormative embodiment. As the authors of the Union of the Physically Impaired Against Segregation (UPIAS) put it in their 1972 white paper on disability: "It is only the actual impairment which we must accept, the additional and totally unnecessary problems caused by the way we are treated are essentially to be overcome and not accepted" (UPIAS). While it may at first appear that UPIAS anticipates a material encounter with disability ("It is only the impairment we must accept"), the admission dispenses with the need and moves immediately to an analysis of the sources of cultural oppression: "the additional and totally unnecessary boundaries" of socially constructed exclusions. The application of disability as the product of oppression situates nonnormative materiality as somehow inappropriate for, even threatening to, and certainly beside the point of, political discourse.[4] It must be accepted and immediately set aside as a private matter in order to deal with the exposé of the public forces of oppression. Within this formulation and its many offspring, disability, then, could be argued to serve as a holdover from antiquity. Impaired bodies continue to provide the illusion of ways to reliably anticipate less viable forms of embodiment and thus determine in the language of contemporary cost/risk analyses those bodies in which society should not invest. The payoff appears too meager, and, thus, the investors likely unrequited.

Yet, as studies in the sociology of medicine recently show, what appears to be a body's discordant sidestepping of a more stable program—one organisms only possess as an illusory investment in their own nonmorphing capacitation into the future—is actually the historical unfolding of a mutating, adaptive materiality responding to alterations in environmental conditions, internal stresses, inorganic/organic entanglements, fluctuating stimuli, and historical conditions of cultural practice. While mutations recognized as impairments might appear undesirable and "incapacitating," the conditions to which they respond are often far more deleterious. Examples of this insufficiency of predictive capacities abound: from the iron overloads of hemachromatosis to counteract bubonic plague (Moslem 18), to red blood cell mutations that render malarial infestations less effective (Neese and Williams 6), to esophageal atresia in order to protect the fetus from ingestion of high iron or mercury content (Mitchell and Snyder, "The Matter of Disability" 488), to name just three. Thus, many contemporary societies continue to treat the alternative responses of nonnormative materiality as discordant, while, in fact, our understanding of these alternative routings remains inexact at best, and deleteriously dehumanizing at worst.

This practice of using disability as predictive of life-forms in which we should *not* invest allows a certain confidence in the slippery concept of difference as undesirable to creep back into our social justice investments. Within this scenario of deviant matter, disability has little to offer beyond functioning as a vehicle for exposing certain arrays of disadvantageous material expressions, or at most, an embodiment through which to know the world's exclusions, intolerances, and inhumane discriminations. This is disability's dual diagnostic function in the medical and social models that many essays in this collection expose, reconnoiter, and rewrite. Disability, within these limited formulas, has nothing to tell us about the alternative agencies of becoming. It offers no ethical map to productive divergences of being-in-the-world from which we may learn, adopt, and adapt. It refuses crossings of the species barrier, where, for instance, Dawn Prince-Hughes argues gorillas helped her become more human (4), or where Temple Grandin argues her participation on the autistic spectrum enables her to go when imagining the perspective of cattle (20).[5] For both Prince-Hughes and Grandin, this "freedom" to cross species boundaries provides an opportunity in posthumanist disability studies to pursue alternative applications of ethical behaviors that may have nothing to do with a more typical normative exchange quotient where everything is undertaken in order to receive some form of reciprocity. These are human/nonhuman relations that do not depend on an exchange of the nonhuman animal's return of feeling for the experience of connectedness.

Consequently, through a variety of animal crossings and intra-agential encounters with organic and even inorganic life, this collection participates in what Cary Wolfe describes as a view of matter that is not "posthuman" in the sense of being "after embodiment," but rather is critical of the "fantasies of disembodiment and autonomy, inherited from humanism itself" (*What Is Posthumanism?*). In the first instance, impairment surfaces as a serious question that feminist disability studies originally introduced to disability studies' own fantasies of disembodiment through the concept of "impairment-effects" (Thomas 42). According to Carol Thomas, impairment-effects are those aspects of disability embodiments that cause disabled people to struggle with incapacity and often prohibit them from pursuing lives of robust political citizenry as the result of being what Asma Abbas refers to as "agency-impaired" (133). To be "agency-impaired" is to fall short of a leftist political investment in bodies actively pursuing their rights as a display of the agency-fetishizing signs of fully capacitated, even while marginalized, citizens. As Spike Lee memorably put it in his film of racial unrest, *Do the Right Thing*: "Fight the powers that be." Yet what Abbas points out is that such an idealization of citizenry neglects the lives of those who must labor to scrape out their basic needs on a daily basis, those bodies who, by definition, do not promise transcendence to a transhumanist overcoming, but rather are fully posthumanist in their composition, behaviors, and tactical alternatives of living. Many disabled lives can be found beneath this category and, in ignoring it by idealizing the rights-slinging alternative, we miss what these lives that matter have to teach us. Disability artist Micah Bizant creates portraits of those killed by police violence in the Black Lives Matter movement by emphasizing their deaths as an outcome of the compounding intersections of race, gender, and disability.

Consequently, the posthuman turn participates in the decentering of liberal classical man from the equation of the demands of materiality as in the above examples of Abbas's "low-level agency" participants and Bizant's intersecting identity portraits. Posthumanist approaches provide alternative pathways for investigating nonnormative and nonhuman embodiments as a source of insight and the alternative agential participation of materiality in knowledge production. It is no longer possible in this formulation to see disability as a deviance from able-bodiedness. Instead, posthumanist disability theory actively avoids thinking about disability as

JUSTICE FOR MARIO WOODS

OVER 50% of People KILLED by POLICE are DISABLED.*

* No comprehensive federal data is collected, but available reports show at least half of those killed by police have psych disabilities. These statistics do not include people with mobility, sensory, or developmental impairments or people who are autistic or sick/chronically ill.

DISABILITY JUSTICE NOW

#BLACK DISABLED LIVES MATTER

SINS INVALID + MICAH BAZANT

Fig. 1. *Justice for Mario Woods* by Micah Bazant and Sins Invalid (watercolor, 2015). According to the joint creators: "On Dec. 2 2015, San Francisco police executed Mario Woods, a young Black disabled man, in the SF Bayview neighborhood. Over 50% of police killings in SF and nationally are of people with disabilities, especially Black and Brown people with psych impairments (often referred to as 'mentally ill'.)" Image available at https://www.micahbazant.com/mario-woods/

some preexisting, external force that throws instability into a stable pattern or code. Rather, mutation (particularly when characterized as disability) names "the randomness which is always already immanent in the processes by which both material bodies and cultural patterns replicate themselves" (Rutsky 111).

Disability, then, is matter in motion and the exposure of the lie through which we think materiality as a stable baseline of limited plenitude. Borrowing from these recent traditions that feed into posthumanist neomaterialisms, the contributors in this volume seek to explore how the matter of disability *matters* beyond its diagnostic positioning since at least the fifteenth century as a depreciated socially inscribed deviant surface. As Foucault points out, the concept of man is rather recent (386). Rather than continue to accept the assumption of disability studies that disability primarily organizes our exposés of oppression, contributors to this volume argue that bodily variations discursively mapped as "impairments" do not merely mirror prejudicial interpretations of contra-aesthetic, dysfunctional, unexamined lessons of those living in undercapacitated bodies. Instead we collectively take as a starting point the idea that matter is neither inert nor simply inscribed by cultural forces against its interests. In order to derive this alternative approach we pursue disability as the space of possibilities opened up by the "indeterminacies entailed by exclusions" (Barad 230). In other words, the alternative modes of becoming that even the most severe impairments offer involve the promise of an alternative agency that reshapes the world and opens it up to other modes of (nonnormative) being.

Thus, we begin to return full circle from our starting point in contesting the notion that disability is *only* capable of being resignified, as this would be the constructivist end point. Even more significantly, we insist on the ways in which the materiality of impairment opens up new worlds of potentiality. Materiality's mattering is an active participant in the resignification process, as knowledge has to keep shifting in order to keep up with mutating matter and vice versa. As Lynn Huffer argues for queer lives, disability alternatives make available "an ethical frame that can actually be used as a map for living" (48). Able-bodiedness is a boundary-making process that relies on pejorative concepts of disability to see itself as privileged and desirably capacitated (Diedrich 219). In this sense, able-bodiedness needs disability to embody devalued states of existence in which to showcase its own capacitated desirability. Robert McRuer refers to this centrality of disability to ability as the latter's provision of a "mutually constitutive" inside for heteronormative able-bodiedness (4). Within able-bodiedness's parasitism exists a disability host. One cannot exist without the other, but to yield only to exposés of this interdependency of binaries further erodes disability's material promise. This is a primary degenerative relationship promoted by social constructivist thought that *The Matter of Disability* intends to throw into question.

What might a posthumanist disability theory tangibly offer to our understanding of materiality's agential participation in the world? This is a key question addressed by all of the essays to follow. However, here let us explore how disability has played a key role in the critique of Newtonian-ism by quantum physics based on a sequence of disability insights. Karen Barad points out that Newtonian physics argues one cannot both gauge the materiality of the measuring instrument and, at the same time, use the instrument to gauge the properties of the object/field to be measured. This separation helps Newtonian physicists in arguing that a "cut" (a distinct separation exists) between measurer and measurement device that makes neutral observation of the properties of another possible. In order to cri-tique this reigning distinction of faith in scientific neutrality, Barad takes up the formulations of quantum physics (particularly those of Niels Bohr), who critiqued Newtonianism through an elaboration of the inextricability of matter and measurement. One of Bohr's nodal points of entry for ar-ticulating a critique of Newtonianism is a man holding a cane and stand-ing in a dark room—first sensing its "weightiness" and then employing the cane to sense the immediate environment around him. In this arrange-ment, as Newtonian physics premises, a cut between observer and ob-served erupts as the experimenter is consigned to either paying attention to the materiality of the instrument of measurement or engaging in the act of measuring an external materiality. This either/or partition creates the Newtonian foundation for claims that the observer can be separated out from that which is observed. This subtraction of the observer from the observed produces the prized product of neutrality.[6]

Many disability studies scholars will recognize (as did the philosopher of phenomenology Maurice Merleau-Ponty) Bohr's description above as one akin to the use of a blind cane by those with visual impairments (144). "Travel caning" involves the arc-like swings of a white cane with a ball on the end of it to "feel" out the terrain before one. It also involves holding the rubberized handle in one's hand with a slackened grip to produce the most sensitive read of the topography ahead. In fact, the feel of the materiality of the cane and its interaction with the environment are simultaneously pivotal to a successful blind navigation of the world. In contrast, Newton's formulation erects a separateness in that one is either sensing the weight of the stick, the stickiness of the handgrip, the bounce of the ball, the flex-ing weight of the cane, or taking a reading of the surface of a sidewalk, for instance, in order to pick the least barrier-ridden route. The latter activity involves the displacement of the former and vice versa.

But through Bohr's alternative argumentative pathway that explains materiality as an active participate in measurement, posthumanist disabil-ity theory allows us to recognize that impairment is not separable from interaction with the environment in the ways Newtonianism posits; this contention exists at the heart of agential realism. Attention shifts back and forth between materiality and measurement, and neither can be held in a distinct partition as definitively separable from the other. To extend this disability insight at the heart of her book, Barad draws from the disability studies analysis of Lisa Diedrich to argue that late disability memoirist Nancy Mairs's intra-agential relationship to her Quickie P100 power wheelchair shows that the machine cannot be separated from the person (158). When the machine goes down, so does Mairs's body, and thus one is not simply the conveyance vehicle of the other (fleshy) occupant. This is no mere prosthetic relation.

Additionally, we would argue that the assertion made by Donna Haraway in her eponymous "Cyborg Manifesto" helps critique Newton's either/or argument in this regard: when one uses prosthetic equipment, one has to both sense its materiality and navigate an environment, as the lack of ease of detachable parts makes the difficult merger of materiality and machine chronically enmeshed. When a wheelchair user, for example, sits on a cushion placed on top of a metal platform, one will, at first, sense the cushion, the feel of its surface—hard, soft, narrow, ripped, ribbed, and then, not long in the future, increasingly come to sense the unforgiving materiality of the metal platform mattering beneath the foam. Over the course of use, through the daily positioning in a power wheelchair, one realizes that the wheelchair's navigation of surfaces—its measuring function—certainly coexists with some sense of the materiality of the metal platform on top of which one sits; the joystick that one manipulates to navigate the environment; the whir of the wheels and motors as they canvas various surfaces; screen readouts on the control pad that interact with the visual and audio inputs of cognition; the pressing of the plastic arm rests into the fleshy arms that create an indent in the foam cushion beneath and wear a groove in the bone above; the movement of one's body based on a pace set by the machine to which one is connected and other machines to which one is not, and so on. Awarenesses of the device, one's body, and the surface traversed by all occur simultaneously and do not exist in a Newtonian "cut" as separable from each other. This is one of the alternative ways that disability materiality holds a heightened sense of materiality's intra-agency with various forms of what is often euphemistically called "human enhancement."

Further, at the core of the neomaterialist argument is the interrogation of an assumption about the "vital, self-organizing, and non-naturalistic structure of living matter itself" (Braidotti 2). Posthumanism's alternative enjambment of "naturalcultural" is gradually replacing the stricter binary partitioning model of a nature-culture divide that has so dominated our conversations about materiality in general (King 2).[7] Stacy Alaimo's influential concept of transcorporeality, with its emphasis on the intermeshed qualities of human and "more-than-human nature" also resonates here (*Bodily Natures* 2). A critique of the assumed "cut" between the binary terms of disability and ability enables a further movement into encounters with multiplicity as the "diffraction pattern" they represent. An opposition to normative ability no longer proves tenable as a simple dualism. Those results that fall outside of the norm and, therefore, cannot be explained (or normed) and thus, discounted as mistakes, now provide an opportunity to focus on variance as a way to read the noncompliance of matter with measurement's standardization within disciplines of alternative embodiment, including quantum physics, posthumanism, black feminist materialisms, disability studies, and queer theory.

Nonnormative ability can no longer reliably operate as an expression of mere deviance from baseline normativity. As Jane Bennett puts it in her analysis of Lucretius's imaginings of bodies falling in a void: "Bodies . . . are not lifeless stuff but matter on the go, entering and leaving assemblages, swerving into each other" (18). Deviations in all measuring systems exist, yet posthumanist disability theory recognizes these waverings from a fictional normative baseline as, in fact, the activity of materiality's continuous reconfiguration, or materialization, of the world itself. The rearrangement of these concepts becomes one of the critical means by which we tailor more suitable schemes for scrutinizing the present and its historical relations with, for instance, the now crumbling project of Western man.

Western Man: A Productive Failure

> The colonized subject cannot experience her or his nonbeing outside the particular ideology of western Man as synonymous with human. (Weheliye 26)

To fashion the collective alternative methodological approaches that comprise this volume, posthumanist disability theory draws upon the insights of neomaterialism as a way to imagine materiality as enacting its own demands upon the social and discursively overdetermined world of poststructuralism. This is not to dispense with the semiotic slippage so central to post-Derridean analytical techniques, but rather to deprivilege the role of discursivity in relation to material agencies. As explained in the previous section, posthumanist methodologies foreground disability's "strange agencies of natural-cultural processes" as offering multiple pathways for reimagining the alternative flows of dynamic embodiment (Alaimo, *Exposed* 107). This approach allows us to analyze what we refer to as the fundamental instability of the post-Enlightenment project of classical man.

First, posthumanist disability theory positions the Western humanist project, classically represented in Leonardo da Vinci's model "Vitruvian Man" (1487–90; see figure 2), as incommensurate with contemporary approaches to materiality and embodiment. In *The Biopolitics of Disability*, Mitchell and Snyder refigure classical man by offering an alternative disability vision of "Vitruvian Man with CP" on their book's cover (see figure 3). This figuration further exposes the privileged contours of Leonardo's classical ideal as one that is thoroughly racialized (white), gendered (male), sexualized (heteronormative), aesthetic (symmetrically proportioned), and capacitated (hyperable). The classical "Vitruvian Man" features standards of capacitation that distance him from other embodiments as they are hypermarked by difference and denigrated based on the absence of the unmarked qualities attributed to any historical period's specific universalized concepts of normativity (Mitchell with Snyder, *Biopolitics of Disability* iii). Posthumanist disability theory, then, exposes the historically and socially particular constellation of embodied properties that have gone into the making of Western man as a culturally centric, time-bound, and now failing product of the post-Enlightenment. Its quantitative and qualitative proportions have accompanied the ongoing upsurge of territorial and cultural expansions informing the realization of a European world system of global imperialism over other(ed) bodies since the eruption of the "Age of Discovery."

For instance, in Christopher Columbus's "Letter to the Sovereigns" of March 4, 1493, he describes his New World anthropological encounters through a series of embodied displacements of racialized, gendered fantasies onto the indigenous islanders of what is now mapped as the Caribbean Islands (Zamora 3). One island (Matenino) has a population of all women "without a single man" who "use military weapons and other masculine practices" (Zamora 8); another island (Caribo) is populated by "those who eat human flesh" and grow their "hair very full, like women" and are willing to copulate with Matenino women, while other men fear bodily mutilation from such encounters; there is an island (Jamaica) with all bald inhabitants; and an island (Cuba) of people "who are born with

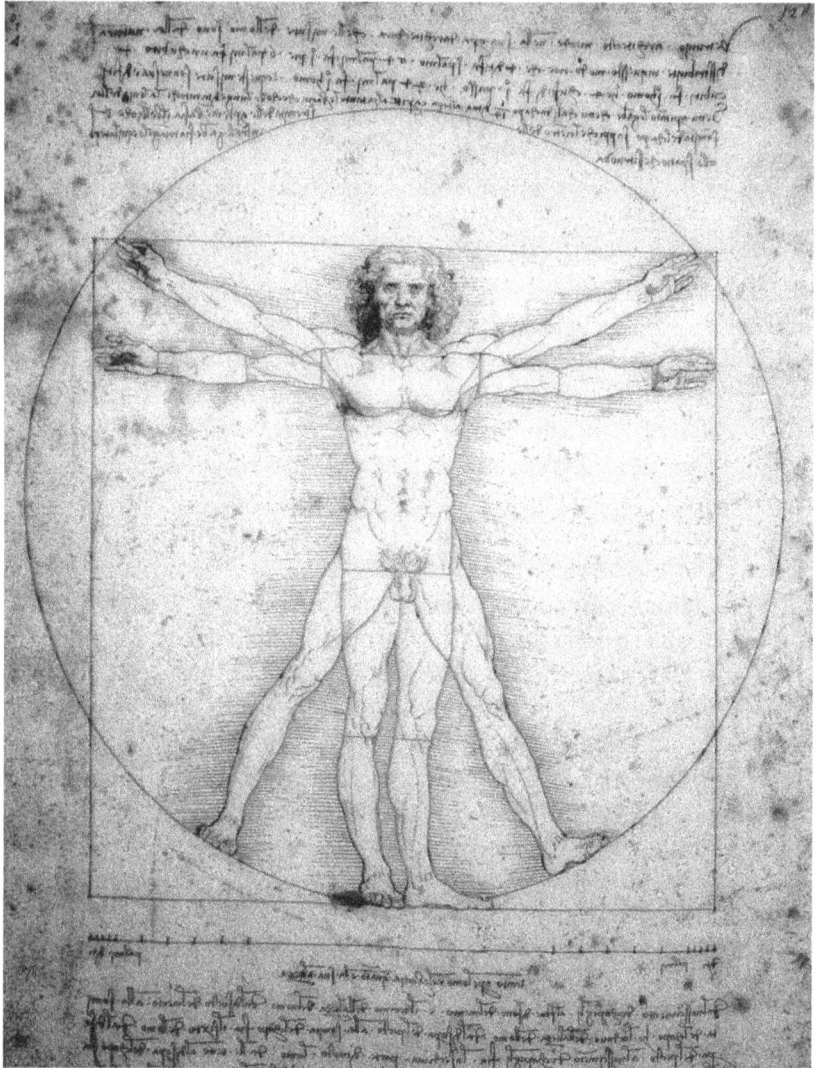

Fig. 2. "Vitruvian Man" by Leonardo da Vinci (pen and ink on paper, circa 1490). Leonardo daVinci developed his image of a classically proportioned man based on the calculations of Roman architect Vitruvius in Book III of *De Architectura*. The image is identified as representing the ideal human proportions of a body that is eight heads tall or twenty-four palms high and serves as the standard for deriving the classical orders of all architecture.

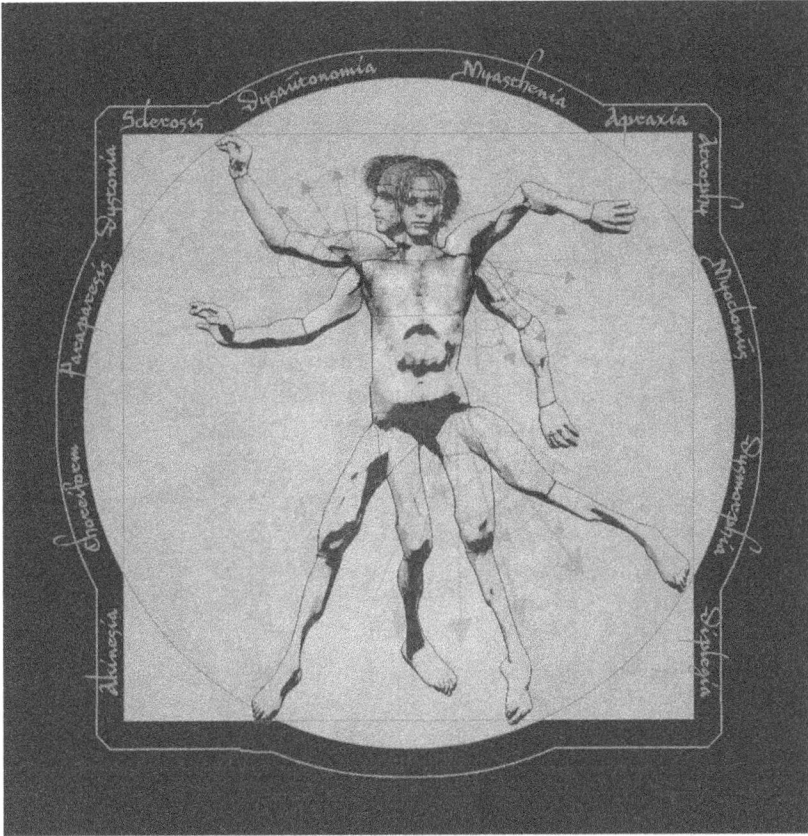

Fig. 3. "Vitruvian Man with CP" realization by Selene dePackh based on a design by David T. Mitchell and Sharon L. Snyder (mixed digital media, 2015). As the cover art on *The Biopolitics of Disability: Neoliberalism, Ablenationalism, and Peripheral Embodiment*, the image is described as follows: "disabled bodies . . . have been traditionally narrated as divisive, pathological, and in need of a heavily enforced grid of surveillance to limit their alternative flourishings. Their mere inclusion is not enough . . . without an active encounter with the alternative materialities such bodies and minds bring into being."

tails" (Zamora 8). The description arrives despite the fact that Columbus explains he has had little commerce with the indigenous peoples because they run away when his Spanish caravels approach. In *Carnal Inscriptions*, Susan Antebi argues that Columbus's lack of actual contact with indigenous people bearing the traits he describes allows for a European notion of monstrosity to function as a metaphor for indigenous alterity that is always projected and displaced. Corporeal otherness thus becomes a justification for exploitation and conquest, but also a site of absence—a flight from a more intra-agential encounter with the materiality of those encountered—that will continue to impact the network of material and discursive relations between imperial and colonial locales (26–28).[8]

In the same letter containing these demographic fantasies of nonnormatively embodied islanders, Columbus argues that the discovery holds particular promise for the Spanish king and queen who financed the endeavor because a militarized force could dominate such multiplicitous embodiments with its own superior regularity in a matter of weeks. Once colonized, the island resources and slave labor could be extracted and sent back to Spain to boost its coffers. Another key goal of this imperial project was to begin the expansion of a "world system" of colonialism that had the reconquest of Jerusalem from its Muslim inhabitants as the penultimate future objective (Zamora 7). As Aníbal Quijano argues, the colonization of the Americas produces the modern notion of racial difference and global capitalism as intertwined, mutually dependent processes. The resulting and ongoing "coloniality of power" is thus defined through labor exploitation as continuous with racialization, or differentiated and denigrated embodiment (536–40).[9]

Thus, colonialism, projected fantasies of nonnormative embodiment, Christian crusading, the rise of capitalism, and global conquest form the support pillars of European imperial fantasies from 1493 onward. The figure of classical man in relation to which this imperialist project is imagined situates Leonardo's "Vitruvian Man" as the instantiation of a biologically superior basis for a justification of conquest. The project of Western man, as black materialist feminist theorists such as Alex Weheliye (2014) and Sylvia Wynter (2014) point out, is eroding in Ozymandias-like ways because of the slow historical decay of properties that have proven increasingly biased based on their emphasis on the deficiency of some bodies. Both Weheliye and Wynters argue that the articulation of the project of Western man can be nothing but incomplete, as it excludes the historical, cultural, and material particularity of people of color from its colorless presentation. In Weheliye's terms, the principal goal of black studies is "to disrupt the governing conception of humanity as synonymous with Western Man" (5). Likewise, according to Katherine McKittrick, Sylvia Wynters notes that the "correlations in this image ["Vitruvian Man"] between the Human body and the universe hide the fact that the body depicted and the experience upon which Leonardo was relying was a Greco-Roman concept of the human figure" (109). Such a project proves inherently disqualifying for most, and for crip/queer/racialized people in particular as their radically diverse and evolving embodiments challenge the static vision of desirability that Vitruvian Man imposes. Alternatively, posthumanist disability theory positions the spastic, racially hybrid, polymorphously sexualized, androgynous, arms-and-legs-akimbo multiplicity of "Vitruvian Man with CP" in its place.

Consequently, in the incomplete and now increasingly abandoned project of Western man, disability can claim some contribution to bringing about this "productive failure." Halberstam points out in *The Queer Art of Failure* that what has been historically understood as queer people's inability to achieve a heteronormative baseline of adulthood in fact represents the unfolding of their alternative cultural and material agencies (31). Such divergent expressions of adulthood are based in the productive eruptive potential of queerness itself. Likewise, Rosi Braidotti points out that "the allegedly abstract ideal of Man as a symbol of Classical Humanity is very much a male of the species; it is a he. Moreover, he is white, European, handsome, and able-bodied" (24). To counter monistic celebrations of Leonardo's Vitruvian Man as the basis of the project of imagining Western Man, Braidotti offers up the image of "New Vitruvian Woman" (see figure 4) as an alternative to the representation of male embodiment.

While whiteness and maleness have long dominated critiques of classical humanism, "handsomeness" and "able-bodiedness" arrive as a startling eruption in Braidotti's philosophical formulation. This twining of aesthetic with able-bodiedness augments the racialized and engendered coordinates in the realization of Western man's classical contours. We rarely think of masculine appearance and bodily capacity as qualities of Enlightenment embodiment; likewise, disability, both aesthetic and functional, rarely impresses itself as necessary to exclude so specifically.

What is the meaning behind this inclusion of ability in the classical formula of "the human" that Braidotti so tellingly cites without further elaboration? Why might disability prove central to alternative formulations of "the posthuman"? First, in addition to heteronormative masculinity, the creature that Braidotti cites also comes with its class privileges intact. Her analysis borrows from Cary Wolfe's description of the "Cartesian subject of the cogito" defined as the "subject as citizen, rights-holder, property holder and so on" ("Posthumanities"). As a product of the convergence of gendered, racialized, sexualized, and class characteristics, the classical body of humanism has grown necessarily endangered as a unit of common belonging for the human (and, Wolf would add, nonhuman) species. Braidotti's calling out of the figure as a "he" brings attention to the fact that the Vitruvian is also excessively able-bodied in presentation.

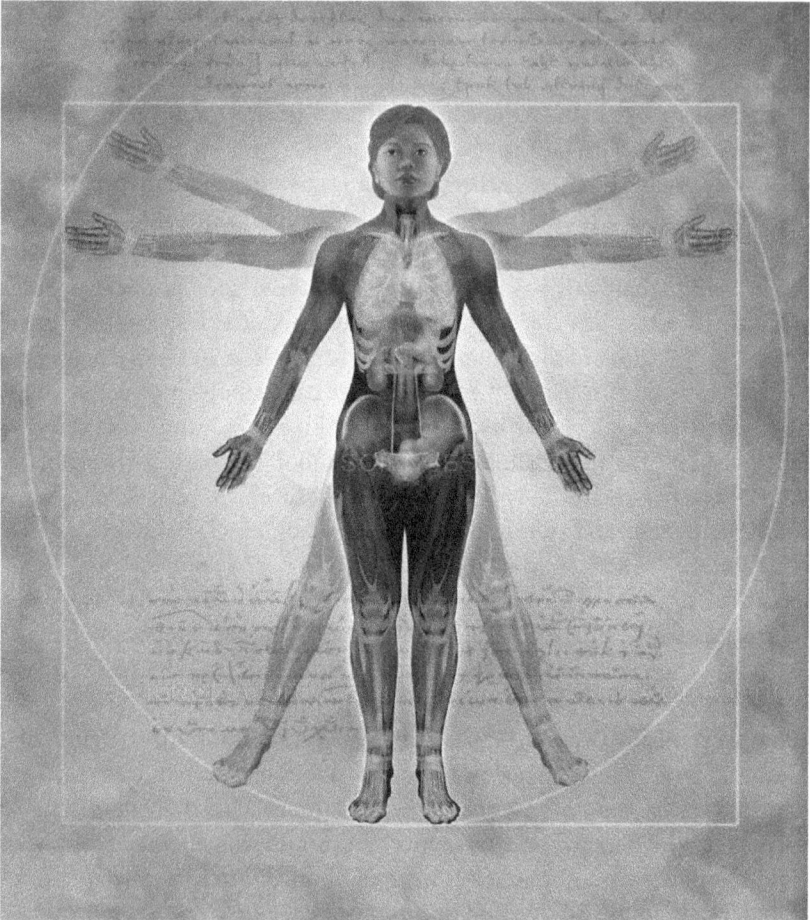

Fig. 4. "New Vitruvian Woman" by Jim Dowdalls (digital photograph, 2012). According to the artist: "This illustration pays homage to the famous drawing 'Vitruvian Man' by Leonardo Da Vinci . . . In this illustration, the figure of a man is replaced by that of a woman and the major organs of the female body are shown." Image credit, Jim Dowdalls/Science Source, used by permission.

Seven and a half heads tall, four-limbed (if we allow for its display of range of motion that creates an appearance of eight limbs), a fully flexible range of motion in each appendage, sculptured musculature, symmetrically proportioned, and well balanced on one or two legs, the Vitruvian Man defies all specificity of corporeal variation.

Such impossible coordination of parts conceals any apparent embodied idiosyncrasy, and thus proves a "pure product" of the kind of human exceptionalism that posthumanist disability theory critiques. Particularly as the world grows increasingly toxic, as medical science harbors the capacity to keep more kinds of bodies alive, and as disabled bodies expand their material presence as participatory subjects in exclusionary human-made environments, posthumanist disability theory asks how variation might serve as the foundation for modes of reconfiguring, reimagining, and renavigating the world.

Posthumanist disability theory thus attempts to reverse this Eurocentric foundational insight by joining in an outpouring of racial/gendered/trans/classed/disability critiques of the classical humanistic concept of Western man as based on a form of domination over othered bodies that deviate from its zero-degree game of sameness. As Wynter's philosophy explains, "Once the universality of the Human has been postulated—and we encounter this formulation in many official documents telling us that humans are 'are all born equal'—hierarchies are needed and put into place to establish differences between all who were 'born equal'" (McKittrick 109). Specifically for disability, the formula of Western man treats cognitive, physical, sensory, and psychiatric differences as faults localized in individual bodies rather than as revelatory of materiality's defining multiplicity.

Posthumanist philosophers commonly cite "human enhancement" as one cornerstone of this pursuit to seriously decenter the individual figure of Western man as self-contained and biologically intact. Much of this discussion is based on a contemporary technological fetishism of products (or potential products) that take disabled people as their test market in the hopes of moving adaptive devices out into the wider consumer market. As a formidable test market, disabled people are commonly considered to possess materiality in "obvious" need of supplementation, and thus, the direction of "human enhancement" takes on a "helping aura" formerly associated almost exclusively with the rehabilitation therapies (physical, occupational, speech, and others). Donna Haraway famously identifies "paraplegics and severely handicapped people" as having "the most intense experiences of complex hybridization with other communication devices" ("Cyborg Manifesto" 315–16).

Many disabled individuals we know describe their relationship to their assistive devices (communication or otherwise) in terms that resonate with "complex hybridization," but nevertheless Haraway's definition suggests a relationship of human and machine that comes off as a bit too breezy. These interactions between material bodies and machines generally prove anything but comfort ridden and usually signal the degree to which one arrives, at best, in a détente with supplementary equipment.[10]

Vitruvian Man has no adaptive technology on his person, and, thus, any prosthetic encumbrance draws crip/queer figures outside the lines of the enfolding circle of symmetrical normalcy in which he finds himself buffered from harm.

Like its new materialist predecessors, posthumanist disability theory certainly emerges from recognitions that the Anthropocene has engendered the agency of humanity to such a degree that the human now functions as akin to a geological force capable of affecting all life on the planet (Braidotti 5; Alaimo, *Exposed* 1). This force has marshaled significant destructive impact on what we know as the material world from the fifteenth century to the present day. Because the dominating figure of Western man has been key to the consolidation of this destructive and anthropocentric framework, posthumanist disability theory has to participate in collapsing the stability of fantasies of embodied normative power. A key challenge is to contest the imposition of a stable mode of desirability and functioning over forms of materiality that are devalued because of their excessive differentiation. The essays included in *The Matter of Disability* all participate in towing the chain that bends the figure of classical European normative masculinity at the ankles and drags it to the ground.

Posthumanist disability theory elaborates on the specific modes of differentiated embodiment materialized and impacted through relations between human and nonhuman, organic and inorganic bodies and environments, and in particular through agricultural and military forms of toxicity that give rise to biopolitical notions of sacrificial subjects such as Mbembe's "necropolitics" and Giorgio Agamben's "bare life." Both of these consciously pursued devaluation schemes are defined as the state-sanctioned material destruction and intentional disablement of human bodies and populations deemed expendable (14, 6). Alexander Weheliye champions Mbembe's approach and depreciates that of Agamben, based on the former's inclusion of targeted colonized subjects and the latter's emphasis on a universalized, abstracted concept of subjection to power-knowledge as in the Foucauldian tradition of European philosophy (63). Yet, to be fair, Agamben deals directly with disability populations in his analysis of Nazi eugenic formulations of "life unworthy of life," while Mbembe and Weheliye leave disablement as a material imposition of violence on bodies. Posthumanist disability theory straddles each of these terrains, as it neither avoids a Marxist tradition of employing disability as proof of industrial capitalism's destructive power nor eschews attention to materiality's morphing corporeal rearrangements.

Further, part of the reformulation of Western man involves a radical reassessment of the relationality between animal and human bodies (that which Wolfe refers to as "the animal turn" [*What Is Posthumanism?*]). Whereas humanism has aggressively promoted the controlled breeding of animal and plant bodies in order to increase yield, deny decay, and expand profits, such schemes of genetic direction have produced enormous disability-relevant alterations in human, nonhuman, organic, and inorganic environmental conditions. Pesticide development, for instance, not only alters the nature of what one ingests, but also threatens the migrant, lower-class bodies that clear, maintain, prune, and harvest the fields. In these agrarian locales capacitated labor power is extracted and worn into disabled bodies as a nearly inevitable outcome of the ways in which repetitious movements ultimately deny the very capacities on which they are initially valued. They are also those bodies that get "dusted" by pesticides sprayed across environments by "crop dusters" circling above (Rich 3).

Thus, racialized, devalued embodiments become excessively open to exposures that presumably keep the post-Enlightenment body safe. Privilege operates as an ability to seal off one's body from deleterious encounters with toxicity. Falsely buffered from his own carcinogenic products, Western man gradually ingests a productive portion of the "slow death" he sows and can only fantasize an escape hatch from such hazardous exposures (Berlant 754). His positioning at appropriate distances from the site of production for safekeeping does not prevent the animacies of such toxins from incorporation into his own bodily domain (Chen 218). Additionally, industrial farming has erased the presence of farmers and farmworkers across northern and southern hemispheres and, in moves reminiscent of the dust bowl 1930s, keep extended families adrift, and without access to the education, affiliation, health care, employment tenure, or organization requisite for empowering allies.

To a significant extent, this inability to buffer the farmer's or migrant worker's exposure to materiality's rewriting at the core of all being drifts from zones of agricultural production to necropolitical zones of conflict where expendable bodies are defined by forms of state-imposed immobility. The techno-military proliferation of microconflicts on a global scale has given way (largely via drone strikes and the arresting of refugee and immigrant movements) to new levels of administered violence. These new geographical displacements of populations result in a physical dislocation on the outskirts of a more bounded and desirable humanity. Mbembe refers to this placement across a long *dureé* in abjected physical space as a key characteristic of "the postcolony" (103). The material locations of such bodies position them as targets and thus their expendable peripherality coincides with their immobilizations in various fenced-off elsewheres. Aerial thanatic delivery systems merge artificial intelligence, cybernetic gaming, and human operators in a new formula of death with distance (Braidotti 44–45). As Jasbir Puar points out, the Gaza Strip can be recognized as a physical collection point that defines all bodies within it as expendable with respect to their peripheral location outside and within the borders of Israel (2). Their excessive exposure to death and disability are justified as a result of their immobilized, extreme localization in the occupied territories.

While militarized militias use civilian populations as their cover and as governments consciously place those defined as expendable at a physical distance in temporal, makeshift detention camps for the excessively diasporic, those same peripheral citizenries find themselves increasingly subject to what Elaine Scarry describes as the two primary products of war: death and disability (12). Thus, posthumanist disability theory encompasses an extraordinarily complex nexus of mutating bodies, including semipermeable interactions between human, nonhuman, and inorganic animacies; environmental toxicities and the mutating bodies they produce; quantitative and qualitative measurements of capacities, functionalities, and aesthetics; pharmaceutical and cybernetic trafficking in ways of rewriting material subjectivities; a preponderance of blind vendors in a Mexico City subway as the engine of an embodied, affective informal economy; eugenic lineups that take cognitively, psychiatrically, sensorily, and physically disabled bodies to psychiatric killing centers; the advent of tactile poetry that expresses the visceral nature of schizophrenic mindsets; the economic unfoldings of profit where products cause disease and then the same corporate producers provide the therapies to treat the impaired bodies their runoffs produce; amputee fantasies of incapacitated bodies performed by able-bodied actors that retain all but the material specificity of the bodies in question; "tropological confusions" between nonhuman and human animals cross-referenced as mutually devalued and, therefore, euthanasia-worthy; militarized productions of maimed human and nonhuman bodies in fabulations of sexualized hypercapacity; forms of mobility and environmental sensitivity that preclude a more robust participation in "natural" landscapes; as well as the targeting of disabled racialized bodies as unarmed threats to an excessively militarized police force. All of these topics posit the "unique mattering" of posthumanist disability embodiments that reveal uncanny capacities where only unproductive incapacity was imagined to reign.

All of these mutated locations can be found and plumbed in the essays that comprise this volume. There is no end to the exhaustive requirements placed upon developing posthumanist disability theory to engage more meaningful global encounters with the intra-active material-discursive agencies unleashed by such developments at the fall of the project of Western man.

The Posthumanist Disability to Come

Part I, "The Matter of Subjectivity," organizes contributions around the growing suspicion of posthumanist disability theory with the overdetermined constructivist bent of the social model of disability. The opening essay by Tobin Siebers critiques the social model for its overemphasis on diagnosing shortcomings in the environment. In order to nuance the insights of disability studies further Siebers proposes that any reformulation of the social model must include disabled people's subjective knowledge of their own experience of embodiment as a key part of their productive participation in the world. Disability as a phenomenon that delivers its own particular understanding and demands on subjectivity formation in and of itself involves an adaptation. Siebers calls the fruits of this interaction between body, mind, and environment: "complex embodiment."

Siebers bases his approach to disability as "complex embodiment" on the argument that disabled bodies incorporate their environments and internalize their discriminatory effects. This common insight in disability studies situates the body as a relatively passive recipient of inaccessibility with little ability to change it. Posthumanist disability theory, in Siebers's terms, has to reverse this course of assumptions by first undoing the tendency to position the relationship between embodiment and environment as a one-way street and also in refusing to explore the ways disabled people possess valuable knowledge about embodiment itself. The transformation of these two assumptions provides the basis for a rebuilding of the social model. To exemplify his point of what posthumanist theory has to offer, Siebers offers a close reading of Shakespeare's hefty, gout-impaired Falstaff in *Henry IV, Parts 1 and 2*, as a characterization based on embodiment that produces an alternative relationship of materiality to subjectivity. Falstaff's methodical negotiation of mobility establishes his materiality as the foreground of his disability subjectivity in ways that others might overlook or take for granted. Thus, complex embodiment sets a more intra-active circuit of relations between body and environment into motion. This is why we begin with this essay as a starting point for the articulation of the posthumanist disability theory to come.

Following on the heels of Sieberss's articulation of complex embodiment, Joshua Kupetz probes the intra-active processes at work in what he terms "disability ecologies." Kupetz's essay explores how disability materiality reacts back and shapes—as well as being shaped by—social, environmental, and economic forces. There is something more to be sought after in the co-constitutive relationships of human subjects and material objects/actors. As a result, all of the essays in this volume seek to take various posthuman pathways to breaking apart the boundedness of impairment. For instance, Kupetz's analysis of Richard Powers's novel *Gain* explores how personal impairment and corporate personhood intersect as exemplary of transnational flows of chemicals, medical practices, and capital. Whereas medical model approaches to disability might seem to operate closer to questions of materiality and embodiment, *Gain* demonstrates how a history of capitalist production interflows with forms of toxicity to which bodies respond and reformulate themselves.

As with all forms of adaptation these mutating responses do not prove fully advantageous to the organism undertaking the effort. Mutation is partial, ongoing, and inevitably flawed in its own productive alternative manifestations. Rather than position chemical production as an incursion into otherwise normative, stabile matter, Kupetz's analysis foregrounds how the runoff from product development at corporate headquarters proves anything but an inscription on the passive surface of its protagonist's body. When Laura Bodey, a real estate agent on her way up the corporate chain, is suddenly diagnosed with uterine cancer, her terminal condition becomes a means by which her experience is reimagined. As the corporation responsible for rising cancer rates in Lacewood, Illinois, Clare International's toxic environmental despoliation over the course of a morphing corporate history of soap maker, candlemaker, and household cleanser manufacturer, becomes a doorway revealing the complex interdependencies of persons and products. For example, the corporation contributes charitable donations to the local hospital at which Laura is treated and also supplies many of the ineffective treatment products used on cancer patients. Thus, Kupetz analyzes Powers's novelistic rendition of Clare International as first producing disability and then profiting from its treatment.

As with the rewiring of Laura Bodey's subjectivity through her experience of altered materiality as a cancer survivor, this model of fluid intra-action between disability materiality and organic/inorganic environmental forces has a significant impact on the formation of human subjectivities and on sensory experience. Olga Tarapata terms this emergence of the self "unique mattering," in her reading of William Gibson's science fiction novel *Pattern Recognition*. Tarapata reads disability in Gibson's work in a posthumanist key, as a process of evolving, symmetrical relations between bodies and environments. Turning specifically to examples of embodiment in Gibson's novel, Tarapata addresses the nonnormative corporeality and subjectivities of the two heroines, Cayce Pollard and Nora Volkova. Cayce's allergy to particular commercial logos or brands manifests through painful symptoms, but at the same time allows for her unusual skill in identifying market tendencies. Unique mattering, in this case, marks the character as embedded in her environment, in a complex corporeal and interdependent sensory relationship.

Nora, a paraplegic character, has a piece of shrapnel lodged in her brain, both dividing and connecting the two lobes. This unusual condition causes the character pain, but also makes possible her creative production of a series of reedited film clips, which are central to the development of the novelistic plot. Nora's existence and subjectivity is defined by this creative activity, and by its international dissemination through complex, intersubjective networks. "Unique mattering," in Tarapata's reading of Gibson's novel and of contemporary neomaterialist and posthumanist theories, emphasizes the dynamic and changing processes through which nonnormative bodies exist and interact, moving not toward wholeness or resolution, but rather toward new understandings and expressions of sensory experience.

The essays in Part II, "The Matter of Meaning," address questions of representation and the tactics of integrating materiality into the production of meaning-making itself. Patrick Durgin's essay, "Hannah Weiner's Transversal Poetics," further explores new materialist modes of intersubjectivity as a way to explain how Deleuze and Guattari's controversial concept of "schizo" upsets the binary relation between discordant identities. The essay employs the concept of "transversality" as that which entails "intersubjectivity" insofar as it is "engaged by non-subjective arrangements, extra-human and nonorganic components not necessarily available for interpretation" (Genosko 48). Consequently, Durgin proposes a critical rethinking of diagnosis as a compound object that has lost several of the relational properties that created such material impositions in the first place. In other words, all that's left in a diagnosis is the oppressive ableism of the reductive object it references. Here is some of the serious potential of posthumanist disability theory in that it can continue with the social model's exposé of prejudicial impositions while simultaneously showing how the materiality of the subject exists in the location of its displacement. In other words, posthumanist disability theory can show the workings of nonnormative materiality itself as the action of relational interactions. That which is repressed from its identity in social relations of diagnosis is, actually, the operations of the agency of alternative materiality.

To concretize this insight Durgin moves to an analysis of fashion designer-turned-wordsmith Hannah Weiner. Weiner's schizophrenia (that which she refers to as clairvoyance) resulted in the creation of a tactile language poetry that sought to attend to the materiality of words themselves. Weiner's primary intention was to create poetry with words that ought to be looked at as well as read—that is, their materiality should command attention as well as their conceptuality. In addition to experimenting in various sound and visual media, she wrote her poetry and prose in experimental typefaces. As a creative means by which to describe the material process of "schizophrenic" embodiment that Weiner's art captures, Durgin shows how the poet's mind was layered with each palimpsestic activity creating its own environment. Thus, in one of the most ethereal and seemingly nonembodied intersections of expression—poetry and clairvoyance—Weiner invents an art that exposes rather than expresses her alternative cognitive mind-set and material interactions with the world. This is not a confusion, as Durgin explains in his application of Guattari and Deleuze to the work in question, but rather an embodiment of the material nature of her mind in art.

The complex and interactive agency of disability materiality emerges through Durgin's reading of this moment of exposure of the mind in its poetic process. Such instances of disability exposure or recognition are key throughout the essays in this volume for the way they reconfigure the notion of impairment as fluid, shifting and expansive. This is the case, for example, in Angela Smith's interpretation of the popular phenomenon of amputee bodies in film. As she notes, despite the use of special effects to simulate disability in able-bodied actors on screen, continuity errors leave a residue or trace of the immateriality of disability on the screen, as when an unedited shadow betrays the presence of an actor's complete leg even after the character has experienced a fictionalized amputation. Such visual exposures demonstrate the incapacity of film to invent a seamless disability embodiment; they also betray filmmakers' and viewers' overinvestment in the simulacra of disability by nondisabled bodies. Alternatively, the failure of special effects to fully cover over the able-bodiedness of such portrayals opens up the nonnormative materiality of disability agency.

As the vast majority of amputee bodies are adjudged insufficient by casting directors to star in the role of amputee, otherwise able-bodies are staged as incapacitated with all of the revelry of mainstream special effects and prosthetic add-ons and takeaways. Thus, a "disability drag" is at stake according to Smith, and these media vehicles allow a certain material proximity to disabled bodies that, in fact, only solidifies a distance already instantiated in our public relations with amputees. The point is not a call for an impossible alignment of essentialisms between roles and bodies, but rather the ways in which disability materiality cultivates certain forms of identification that cannot be simulated (or are radically altered) through special effects-based artifice. Yet, as Smith argues, even the portrayal of these fictive amputee agencies results in a more flexible encounter with nonnormative embodiment and such encounters expand the range of cultural imaginaries and the subjectivities they might inhabit.

The essays in Part III, "The Matter of Mortality," take up questions of genetic hypercapacitation, militarization, reproductive futurity, and euthanasia as ways to approach questions of the relationship of disability to determinations of expendability. In "Spider-Man's Designer Genes: Hypercapacity and Transhumanism in a 'DIY World,'" Samuel Yates argues that while the notorious Broadway theatrical production by Julie Taymor resulted in disablement to multiple actors in the high-flying production, the play insists on a posthumanist utopianism as its explanatory framework. Yates takes up the distinction between transhumanism and posthumanism in order to mediate between two competing models of human adaptation. *Spider-Man: Turn Off the Dark* takes up its central argument about the possibility of designer genes as evidence of the potential for a successful human-directed escape from materiality's miscoding errors and thus places itself squarely in the tradition of transhumanism. While the lyrics ring out with references to posthumanism, Yates shows how such an interpretive contextualization would, in fact, materialize an opposition to the production's very premise.

The essay ultimately sets up a new materialist-based argument about the productive combinatory contingency and haphazard nature of human evolution to which the theatrical adaptation cannot adhere. Thus, posthuman is not a harnessing of nonhuman capacities (ownership), but rather a dynamic interplay of genetic development that cannot be consciously culturally harnessed, as that would kill the creative agency of materiality rather than improve it. By showing how the production can integrate one genetic mutation—Peter Parker's morphing genetic composition due to a spider bite—it fails to accommodate his mutated evil alter ego, the Green Goblin. Yates argues that Goblin's lack of integration is replete with disability, racialized, and queer meanings that cause a celebration of hetero-normative white masculinity's hypercapacitation while denigrating the other's more "freakish" nonnormative aesthetic presentation. By constructing a stage set that violated practices of workplace safety, the production disabled its laborers while simultaneously promoting a vision of a world in which they would ultimately be scapegoated and stigmatized.

In addition to theatrical productions such as *Spider-Man: Turn Off the Dark*, the contemporary cinematic turn toward amputee bodies—appendages flying off into space—and the techno rejuvenation of impaired materialities displayed for audience consumption, discussed previously in Angela Smith's chapter, also finds an echo in Chris Ewart's approach to prosthetized female characters in disability avenger films. Yet while Smith emphasizes special effects that allow able-bodied actors to play amputees, Ewart focuses specifically on a campy fetishization of militarized violence in the grindhouse genre film. In this case, special effects exaggerate the on-screen presence of prosthetic limbs, which serve as both weapons and human appendages, converting the hypersexualized, Japanese and Latina disabled female characters into human war machines. For Ewart, these disability-avenger narratives represent a kind of "overwriting" of disability, with reference to the work of Sarah Jain, in which embodied weaponization projects an ableist idealization of disability without any effort to capture the complexity of lived cyborgian experiences.

Consequently, through the pop-cultural use of violent prostheses in the Japanese *Machine Girl* and the US Latino *Planet Terror*, the materiality of weaponized disability emerges as specific to the geopolitics of postatomic Japan and of the US-Mexican borderlands. Posthumanist approaches to disability materiality, as in Ewart's reading, reveal a great deal about the cultural anxiety underpinning representations of human enhancement, violence, injury, and disease. Moreover, such scenes, and their proliferation in literature and film, transcend a merely symptomatic role, emerging as continuous with the regional and global biopolitical networks they illustrate. As Ewart argues, such fetishistic spectacles of violence by disabled women are almost entirely absent in the contemporary cultures to which they refer (Japan and the US-Mexico borderlands). The risk of these prosthetic fantasies is further escalated in that they claim to "empower" their disabled female characters with the props of masculine military weaponry. Thus, a false feminist agency of resistance buttresses their plotlines with the technological gimmickry common in popular narratives of prostheticized disabled bodies.

In a similar sense, Matt Frank's chapter, "Breeding Aliens, Breeding

AIDS: Male Pregnancy, Disability, and Viral Materialism in 'Bloodchild,'" approaches the African American writer Octavia Butler's short story as an allegory of HIV/AIDS biopolitics, but also as a literal evocation of state-controlled population management. In the story, an alien species known as the Tlic use human males as reproductive hosts, impregnating them and caring for their health in order to insure the survival of subsequent Tlic generations. Franks focuses on the materiality of male pregnancy as a representation of HIV/AIDS biopolitics from the 1980s to the present. The compulsory impregnation of black male hosts in Butler's narrative mirrors coercive state practices of population management, through which "crip/queer/black" bodies are unequally exposed to viral infection and subsequently compelled to function as debilitated health-care consumers, depending on antiretroviral pharmaceuticals for their survival, while at once offering their lives and bodies in the service of the health-care and pharmaceutical industries.

Male pregnancy in Butler's story, like the circulation of HIV/AIDS and its prevention and treatment, functions as a form of disability materialism because the aliens materially produce dependency and ensure their own survival through interspecies insemination. Similarly, the state and health-care industries materially produce docile, medicalized populations, in particular through discourses and practices surrounding the prevention and treatment of HIV/AIDS. Crucially, in the biopolitics of HIV/AIDS as in other areas of public health, people of color are overrepresented as disabled and stigmatized for failing to access methods of prevention and treatment. Franks reads the racialization of disability in the HIV/AIDS crisis and in Butler's story as a version of the "biopolitical afterlife of slavery," since in each case, the material production of disability—whether through forced insemination, rape, violent abuse, or coercive, unequally distributed health-care risk management—creates or exacerbates economic dependency, while generating ongoing supplies of labor and consumption. Franks's analysis thus offers a posthumanist reading of the biopolitics of HIV/AIDS, in which racialized disability materialism circulates through the metaphor of interspecies reproduction, and is made literal through compulsory economic and corporeal dependency on state and market forces.

If interspecies dependency, collaboration, and reproduction are familiar themes to readers of science fiction, critical focus on the crossover or blur between conventional categories of human and nonhuman animals has also emerged in the fields of posthumanist disability studies and animal studies in recent years. As David Oswald argues in his essay, "Why

Lennie Can Teach Us New Tricks: Reading for Idiocy, Caninity, and Tropological Confusion in *Of Mice and Men*," attention to the instability and interweaving of species' categories, along with the "unstable matters of dis/ability, sex/gender, and race" requires closer conversation between disability studies and animal studies. Oswald reads links between Lennie's mental disability and his "caninity," or doglike characteristics and narrative role, as producing "tropological confusion," suggesting that the novella produces both associations and distinctions between human and nonhuman categories. The result is an "interdependent contingency," as well as the creation of "affective relationships that cross the species line." As Oswald notes, with reference to Donna Haraway, in the eugenic-era context in which the novella was written, practices of dog breeding and human reproductive politics underpin racist fears of contamination or impure populations. Although both dogs and idiots may be said to function in binary opposition to normative and desirable human subjectivity, instability remains, thanks in large part to the novella's construction of a humanitarian sentimentalism, one dependent on interspecies affect.

In Steinbeck's classic text, Lennie, a mentally disabled character who accidentally kills a young woman, is euthanized by his friend George in a kind of "mercy killing" that parallels the prior killing of an old, infirm dog. As familiar literary figure, Lennie has also made his appearance in the Texas courts, in which capital punishment sentencing against cognitively disabled people of color has directly referenced Steinbeck's character as a test case for whether convicts should meet the criteria of mental disability as exemption. Most of these cases of execution, in which, as Oswald describes, convicts did not meet the criteria for exemption, involved African American men. Lennie's legal afterlife thus reveals the extent to which sovereign state power employs a racialized biopolitics to justify killing some bodies, even while paradoxically conceiving of itself as humanely positioned, via a complex literary affect that mixes idiot and canine tropes. Oswald's analysis insists on the fantasy underpinning the construction of the human, as well as the uncertainty of the human as moral category, while at once paying close attention to the inscriptions of animality, dis/ability, sex/gender, and racialization within the ongoing workings of US biopower.

Most of the essays in this volume take up forms of Anglo-American cultural production as their primary subject matter, with reference to works of literature and film that may be familiar to US-based readers. Yet as the posthumanist disability methodology of these essays suggests, material-discursive categories of region or nation, like those of human subjectivity or corporeality, are difficult to isolate from the fluidity of their contexts, the processes through which they come to matter. This is also, paradoxically the case in readings emphasizing state-centered biopower, as Oswald's analysis of Steinbeck's text argues, in which discourses of eugenics and racialized fears of population contamination point both to nationalist identification and to its multiple ruptures and boundaries.

In the final part of the volume, "The Matter of Memory," the coeditors contribute analyses that address questions of historical erasure and the material traces of forgotten global disability populations operating below the radar of cultural consciousness. A contemporary geopolitics of disability in a posthumanist key cannot fail to consider the complex transnational pathways through which disability materiality emerges on a global scale, strongly inflected by economic and political disparities that produce higher levels of environmental contamination, poverty, and war in global South regions, as well as among specific racialized populations in the North. Susan Antebi addresses one instance of the biopolitical framework of global and local inequalities in her reading of the Mexico City subway as a space of informal economic transactions strongly associated with the presence and participation of disabled people.

In Guadalupe Nettel's novel *El huésped*, the Mexico City subway is home to a community of disabled people, who operate as vendors, beggars, and political activists. Disability materiality in the novel emerges through the structure of "hosting," an activity that implies receiving another within oneself, in a relationship of economic dependency, but also, paradoxically, due to the double meaning of the term in Spanish, being a guest, parasite, or intruder in the space or body of another. This structure reflects the protagonist's experience as she develops a sense of her internalized disability as new subjectivity, and at the same time reflects the economic and affective relationships between disabled and able-bodied people in the Mexico City transit system within Nettel's novel.

The political and economic contexts of public transit, disability and the informal sector to which this novel refers have been marked in recent years by conflicts regarding the regulation of commercial activity, cost of transit, and the desirability of diverse, nonnormative bodies in public spaces. An increase in transit cost was accompanied by an ad campaign featuring the slogan "Don't buy from them and they will disappear," with the image of a music CD vendor with dark sunglasses. This campaign evokes both a charged national political climate in which numerous, racialized disappeared bodies are unaccounted for, and the notably high percentage of disabled, particularly blind, vendors, among those selling music on the subway. Antebi's reading of the subway as intercorporeal space of material and affective exchange emphasizes the fluid demarcations between transit and financial transaction, as well as between physical embodiment and economic survival. The framework of intercorporeality structuring this reading of disability materialism also suggests an unmooring of the clearly demarcated, individual subject, and an opening towards embodiment as affective exchange.

One of the key contributions of posthumanist materialism to our work in disability studies is in fact precisely its willingness to relinquish strict adherence to the figure of the coherently defined subject of political resistance. In their concluding chapter to this volume, "Posthumanist T4 Memory," David Mitchell and Sharon Snyder take up the concept of "low-level agency" as central to their reading of disabled lives, with specific reference to psychiatric patients and other disabled people murdered by the Nazis during World War II, in what is known as Operation T4. Key to this analysis, and with reference to the work of Asma Abbas and Alex Weheliye, is a questioning of the liberal model of exclusive attention to resistant subjects or "politically sturdy citizens" as those who display full agency and coherent opposition to oppression. Because this liberal model tends to operate at the expense of lives and bodies that are not necessarily recognizable within its definitions of agency and personhood, the task of posthumanist disability theory, as undertaken here by Mitchell and Snyder, is to emphasize material, visceral encounters with nonnormative embodiment, and thus to move toward a more expansive terrain of recognition and valorization of crip/queer lives.

As Mitchell and Snyder reveal, a central issue at stake in the study of T4 is the continuity between T4 and the Holocaust. Despite clearly established evidence linking the murders of disabled people under T4 to the murders of Jewish people and those of other groups targeted by the Final Solution, contemporary German euthanasia memorial centers have tended to avoid exploring this connection. Alternatively, insistence on reading these genocides through a common framework means insistence on the inclusion of those with low-level agency, at the risk of exposing a mainstream discomfort with a revised version of the history, and the blurring of familiar categories of victimization. Documentation of contemporary memorialization practices at the euthanasia memorial centers also demonstrates the expanding role of posthumanist disability theoretical approaches to materiality and memory. Examples include displays of victims' names and personal keepsakes—in contrast to cases where names are kept secret, based on an association with stigma of genetic lineage—

and the use of interactive digital media to increase access to historical documents. Attention to these practices allows for a closer engagement with the materiality of loss, and of broadly conceived nonnormative embodiment, without reliance on exemplary subjects of individual political agency.

Mitchell and Snyder's project of engaging the material, historical weight and meanings of lives of low-level agency finds echoes throughout the essays comprising this volume. Disability, as an intra-active, material, and discursive matter, shapes and is reshaped by the world, in an ongoing process of "mattering," though which human and nonhuman embodiments navigate their histories, vulnerabilities, and inequalities. This process is frequently constituted by the risk or reality of suffering or annihilation. The posthumanist inflection in our work emerges in part as recognition of the long oversaturated social model, which has left little room for consideration of disability materiality as active, transformative, agential, and in many instances, under threat. As the stories and histories explored in our essays make clear, this urgent attention to disability as matter is not simply intended to signpost a more celebratory materialist reading, though this may at times be the case. Instead, the exposure of material agency and interactivity in its multiple forms suggests the need for more nuanced understandings of what constitutes materiality, complexly imbricated in organic, inorganic, material, and discursive terrain, and of nonnormative embodiment as transformative, yet still vulnerable to the many worlds through which it comes to matter.

NOTES

1. Tobin Siebers died in 2015 from complications due to cancer. His essay in this volume is an unfinished composition that we're honored to include as one of his final contributions to the field of disability studies. Siebers's transitional efforts to theorize his notion of "complex embodiment" exemplifies the ways in which disability studies scholars are moving toward a more materialist encounter with disability and impairment.

2. "The neologism 'intra-action' signifies the mutual constitution of entangled agencies. That is, in contrast to the usual 'interaction,' which assumes that there are separate individual agencies that precede their relationship, the notion of intra-action recognizes that distinct agencies do not precede, but rather emerge through, their intra-action" (Barad 33).

3. The 2013 documentary film *Fixed: The Science/Fiction of Human Enhancement* offers an excellent elaboration of debates surrounding transhumanism, disability, and ableism.

4. In *The Biopolitics of Disability: Neoliberalism, Ablenationalism, and Peripheral Embodiment*, David Mitchell and Sharon Snyder call this neomaterialist methodology

within disability studies "nonnormative positivisms." The definition offered of this alternative approach to imagining disability runs as follows: "Disability Studies scholars are caught in their lives and their theories between two zones of negativity without something akin to 'nonnormative posivitisms.' Without alternative materialist approaches there exist few ways to identify the creative interdependencies at the foundations of disability alternatives for living addressed in our existing traditions of thought. Disability studies, in the years to come, must be able to address what crip/queer bodies bring to the table of imagining the value of alternative lives, particularly lives that exist at the fraught intersections of marginalized identities such as disability, race, gender, sexuality, and class. . . . There is a great need for an ethical methodology from which disabled people can articulate how their lives bring something new into the world that may otherwise go unrecognized. Nonnormative positivisms provide alternative spaces from which to discuss options for living within alternative embodiments (those designated here by lives lived in peripheral embodiments) as a critical third rail of disability experience" (5–6).

5. There have been a number of disability memoir-related works published within the last few years wherein disabled narrators (particularly those on the autistic spectrum) argue that their "oversensitivity" to touch and lowered reliance on vision allow them to cross the species barrier and enter into the worlds of animals with a greater degree of sensitivity and identification. One of the most significant examples of this claim occurs in Mark Haddon's novel *The Curious Incident of the Dog in the Night-Time.* The novel explores the narrator, Christopher Boone's, uncanny transspecies crossings with the neighbor's dead dog and his own hamster.

6. Other new materialist scholars in addition to Barad have emphasized the significant impact of quantum physics on philosophical approaches to materiality. For example, as Diana Coole and Samantha Frost write in their indispensable introduction to *New Materialisms: Ontology, Agency, Politics,* "Theoretical physics' understanding of matter is now a long way from the material world we inhabit in our everyday lives, and . . . it is no longer tenable to rely on the obsolete certainties of classical physics as earlier materialists did" (12).

7. Katie King argues that one way to evaluate the effectiveness of a feminist transdisciplinary practice is to index how "well it opens up unexpected elements of one's own elements in lively and re-sensitizing worlds." The essays in this volume all attempt to approach disability materiality in "ways of participating in multispecies learning or self-organization across ecologies, mattering without owning the action" (2).

8. Also see Palencia-Roth for further discussion of monstrosity as a trope within the project of European conquest.

9. Shaun Grech's work on disability in the global South effectively contextualizes Quijano's discussion of coloniality in relation to disability and contemporary global capitalism (94).

10. Vivian Sobchack's discussion of her experience of embodiment with a prosthetic leg offers detailed and complex insight on the lived materiality of human enhancement and disability. See her chapter "A Leg to Stand on" (205–25).

WORKS CITED

Abbas, Asma. *Liberalism and Human Suffering: Materialist Reflections on Politics, Ethics, and Aesthetics*. Palgrave Macmillan, 2010.

Alaimo, Stacy. *Bodily Natures: Science, Environment, and the Material Self*. U of Indiana P, 2010.

Alaimo, Stacy. *Exposed: Environmental Politics and Pleasures in Posthuman Times*. Minneapolis: U of Minnesota P, 2016.

Antebi, Susan. *Carnal Inscriptions: Spanish American Narratives of Corporeal Difference and Disability*. Palgrave Macmillan, 2009.

Barad, Karen. *Meeting the Universe Halfway: Quantum Physics and the Entanglement of Matter and Meaning*. Duke UP, 2007.

Bennett, Jane. *Vibrant Matter: A Political Ecology of Things*. Duke UP, 2010.

Berlant, Lauren. "Slow Death (Sovereignty, Obesity, Lateral Agency). *Critical Inquiry*, vol. 33, Summer 2007, pp. 754–80.

Berlant, Lauren, and Michael Warner. "Sex in Public." *Critical Inquiry*, vol. 24, no. 2, 1998, pp. 547–66.

Braidotti, Rosi. *The Posthuman*. Polity P, 2013.

Brashear, Regan Pretlow, dir. *Fixed: The Science/Fiction of Human Enhancement*. Making Change Media, 2013.

Butler, Judith. *Bodies That Matter: On the Discursive Limits of "Sex"*. Routledge, 2011.

Butler, Judith. *Gender Trouble*. Routledge, 2006.

Chen, Mel Y. *Animacies: Biopolitics, Racial Mattering, and Queer Affect*. Duke UP, 2012.

Coole, Diane H., and Samantha Frost, editors. *New Materialisms: Ontology, Agency, Politics*. Duke UP, 2010.

Corker, Marian. "Deafness/Disability—Problematising Notions of Identity, Culture, and Structure." Leeds Centre for Disability Studies. 2002. https://www.disability.co.uk/sites/default/files/resources/Deafness.pdf

Diedrich, Lisa. "Breaking Down: A Phenomenology of Disability." *Literature and Medicine*, vol. 20, no. 2, 2001, pp. 209–30.

Foucault, Michel. *The Order of Things: An Archeology of the Human Sciences*. Vintage Books, 1994.

Genosko, Gary. "Introduction." In *The Guattari Reader*. Blackwell, 1996.

Grandin, Temple, and Catherine Johnson. *Animals in Translation: Using the Mysteries of Autism to Decode Animal Behavior*. Scribner, 2005.

Grech, Shaun. "Recolonizing Debates or Perpetuated Coloniality: Decentring the Spaces of Disability, Community and Coloniality in the Global South." *International Journal of Inclusive Education*, vol 15, no. 1, 2011, pp. 87–100.

Grosz, Elizabeth. *The Nick of Time: Politics, Evolution, and the Untimely*. Duke UP, 2004.

Haddon, Mark. *The Curious Incident of the Dog in the Night-Time*. Vintage, 2004.

Halberstam, Judith. *The Queer Art of Failure*. Duke UP, 2011.

Haraway, Donna. *Simians Cyborgs and Women: The Reinvention of Women*. Routledge, 1990.

Huffer, Lynn. *Mad For Foucault: Rethinking the Foundations of Queer Theory*. Columbia UP, 2009.

King, Katie. "A Naturalcultural Collection of Affections: Transdisciplinary Stories of Transmedia Ecologies." *S&F Online*, vol. 10, no. 3, 2003, pp. 1–18.

Massumi, Brian. *Parables for the Virtual: Movement, Affect, Sensation.* Duke UP, 2002.

Mbembe, Achilles. "Necropolitics." Trans. L. Meintjes. *Public Culture*, vol, 15, no. 1, 2003, pp. 11–40.

Mbembe, Achilles. *On the Postcolony.* U of California P, 2001.

McKittrick, Katherine, editor. *Sylvia Wynter: On Being Human as Praxis.* Duke UP, 2014.

McRuer, Robert. *Crip Theory: Cultural Signs of Queerness and Disability.* New York UP, 2006.

Merleau-Ponty, Maurice. *The Phenomenology of Perception.* Translated by Donald A. Landes. Routledge, 2014.

Mitchell, David T., with Sharon L. Snyder. "The Matter of Disability." *Bioethical Inquiry*, vol. 13, 2016, pp. 487–92.

Mitchell, David T., with Sharon L. Snyder. *The Biopolitics of Disability: Neoliberalism, Ablenationalism, and Peripheral Embodiment.* U of Michigan P, 2015.

Moalem, Sharon. *Survival of the Sickest: The Surprising Connections between Disease and Longevity.* HarperCollins, 2007.

Neese, Randolph M., and George C. Williams. *Why We Get Sick: The New Science of Darwinian Medicine.* Vintage, 2012.

Palencia-Roth, Michael. "Enemies of God: Monsters and the Theology of Conquest." *Monsters, Tricksters, and Sacred Cows: Animal Tales and American Identities*, edited by A. James, UP of Virginia, 1996, pp. 23–49.

Prince-Hughes, Dawn. *Songs of the Gorilla Nation: My Journey through Autism.* Broadway Books, 2010.

Puar, Jasbir. "The Right to Maim: Disablement and Inhuman Biopolitics in Palestine." *Borderlands*, vol. 14, no. 1, 2015, pp. 1–26.

Quijano, Aníbal. "Coloniality of Power, Eurocentrism and Latin America." *Nepantla: Views from the South*, vol. 1, no. 3, 2000, pp. 533–80.

Rich, Adrienne. *An Atlas of the Difficult World: Poems 1988–1991.* Norton, 1991.

Rutsky, R. L. "Mutation, History, and Fantasy in the Posthuman." In "Posthuman Conditions," edited by Neil Badminton, special issue, *Subject Matters: A Journal of Communication and the Self*, vol. 3, no. 2, 2007, pp. 99–112.

Scarry, Elaine. *The Body in Pain: The Making and Unmaking of the World.* Oxford UP, 1987.

Sobchack, Vivian. *Carnal Thoughts: Embodiment and Moving Image Culture.* U of California P, 2004.

Thomas, Carol. *Female Forms: Experiencing and Understanding Disability.* Open UP, 1999.

UPIAS (Union of the Physically Impaired Against Segregation). Centre for Disability Studies, Leeds U. http://disability-studies.leeds.ac.uk/files/library/UPIAS-UPIAS.pdf

Weheliye, Alexander G. *Habeas Viscus: Racializing Assemblages, Biopolitics, and Black Feminist Theories of the Human.* Duke UP, 2014.

Wolfe, Cary. "Posthumanities." 2010. www.carywolfe.com/post_about.html

Wolfe, Cary. *What Is Posthumanism?* U of Minnesota P, 2013.

Zamora, Margarita. "Christopher Columbus's 'Letter to the Sovereigns': Announcing the Discovery." *New World Encounters*, edited by Stephen Greenblatt, U of California P, 1993, pp. 1–11.

Part I

The Matter of Subjectivity

Returning the Social to the Social Model

Tobin Siebers

Introduction: A Diagnostic Impasse

Despite the criticisms of the social model—and there are many—it is hard to imagine the field of disability studies without it. For one thing, its elimination would leave us without a strong sense of context and history. I propose to rebuild the social model by reconsidering it in terms of the theory of complex embodiment, with four consequences: (1) return of the body to the social model where the body and environment are seen as mutually transformative; (2) the social model no longer uses disabled people to diagnose aspects of a disabling environment; disabled people embody knowledge of the environment; (3) disabled people identify themselves and others as disabled, not based on mental and physical difference, or environmental incapacity, but based on the possession and use of embodied knowledge; (4) the social model is an epistemological model—it not only incorporates agency; it cannot exist without active subjects who

Siebers, one of the early influencers of disability studies in the humanities and author of two key works in the field, *Disability Theory* and *Disability Aesthetics*, was working on this essay before his death from cancer in 2015. He had been working to more fully elucidate his theory of "complex embodiment," locating disability identity at the crossroads of aesthetic, attitudinal, environmental, and material interactions. Shakespeare's Falstaff provided Siebers a literary example of his theory: the gout-ridden, hobbled, and over-large figure focuses on the factors of girth, mobility impairment, geography, and the abuse he takes about his body from others, as he explicitly calculates his moves. "Complex embodiment" argues for a mode of standpoint knowledge that disability brings to the world and helps to exemplify how Siebers was moving toward an engagement with neomaterialist, posthumanist disability theory. We include this unfinished work as evidence of that philosophical development and also as a textual memorial to Tobin's influential contributions to the field of disability studies. We miss him greatly.

are defined by their ability to produce and share knowledge. The "social" in the social model refers to what disabled people know about society as a consequence of embodying it.

There are two antithetical models at the heart of disability studies. The medical model changes people with disabilities into objects, steals their agency, and channels any findings into diagnosis. Here physical or mental impairments identify disabled people. The medical model views the cause of disability as lodged in the body, and only the removal of disability restores the person to health. The social model began as a tactic to remove barriers, but it became identified rather quickly with disability studies itself. The social model is supposed to save disabled people from medicalization with its almost exclusive emphasis on the environment. Here disabled people are identified by their inability to fit into the environment. The social model becomes in effect the theoretical model, but it sows confusion because no one knows what the theoretical properties of the social model actually are. Three problems soon become apparent:

A. The social model ignores the body for the environment.
B. The social model continues to objectify disabled people because they are targets of disabling environments, discovered by diagnosis.
C. The social model does not allow agency because the environment is everything. Consider the definition of social construction in the humanities. Here the strong emphasis on structural linguistics makes it easy to understand that determinism in languages equals lack of agency in society.

By the way, you can see how well certain characters work with these two models. The medical model, of which there is no better example than Freud, represents people with disabilities as biologically inferior to nondisabled people, and it assigns to medical experts the job of curing or eliminating disability. The principal method of the medical model is a diagnosis in which the doctor examines the disabled person, looking for "abnormalities," causes for symptoms, and signs of illness. The social model opposes the medical model by defining disability as the product of disabling social and built environments. Disabilities, according to the social model, do not require medical treatments but social justice.

The dependence of the medical model on diagnosis is obvious, but diagnosis supposedly has no place in the social model because it takes as its focus the environments in which people live. However, there is no way to uncover what is wrong in the environment without a diagnosis of people's bodies and minds. My point is not that the social model is the same as the medical model. The social model has reversed many years of medical interpretation and negative social beliefs in which disabled people are viewed as different, dangerous, inhuman, and without value. My point is that current methods of interpreting disability, of which the medical and social models are pillars, almost always diagnose symptoms of disability in the person: features attributed to disability are not seen, defined, criticized, claimed, or cured, unless there is a person to represent them.

Rebuilding the Social Model?

Do we throw out the social model or rebuild it? It is clear to me that we must rebuild it. Otherwise, we risk theorizing disability without any attention to either the environment or to history. Social constructionism in the humanities and occasionally strains of the social model in disability studies see the effect of the environment in terms of *embodiment*. According to these theories, the body is influenced by environmental factors in a way that changes what the body is. The body *incorporates* the outside environment, language effects, and so on, however you define the "outside." This is perhaps easiest to see in the case of negative attitudes. The person of color living in racist society internalizes racism, becoming his or her own victim. Most theories of internalized racism understand that negative attitudes change the body.

What disability studies makes clear, with its emphasis on the built environment, is that the body incorporates its environment, becoming a different body. In the strong versions of social construction, what becomes very evident is that this embodiment takes place beyond the realm of consciousness or self-consciousness. While environmental factors affect subjectivity, subjects for the most part do not understand how, why, or when. The "social" in the social model refers to what disabled people know about society as a consequence of embodying it. The other point worth stressing is that the body itself, while changed by the environment, has little power to influence the environment. This is why social constructionism is often thought to be apolitical—or adverse to politics. Both of these trends—that embodiment is a one-way street in which the environment impacts the body and that subjects have no self-consciousness of embodiment—have to change if the social model is to be rebuilt.

Complex Embodiment

This theory considers the influence of the environment and the body to be reciprocal. Since the body is the place where the environment is read, the body bears the markers of the environment, but the variety of bodies has the power to change these markers. The identity of people with disabilities presents itself as an awareness of a complex embodiment involving the reciprocal transformation between the body and its environment—a reciprocity that provides for change in each term within an otherwise constant equation, the content of which is embodied and thus known in and as the body.

In effect, complex embodiment, because it occurs under conditions of persons having lived for a long time in an environment, has self-consciousness as one of its most critical dimensions. Being made to embody what others hate and seeing what others love give one both self-consciousness and the ability to embody diverse positions in society. The social model is an epistemological model—it not only incorporates agency; it cannot exist without active subjects who are defined by their ability to produce and share knowledge.

Complex embodiment thus changes the identity of people with disabilities. They are no longer identified by physical differences or by environmental unfitness. Rather, they are recognized by the use of knowledge acquired by embodiment. Disability is a body of knowledge. Here the "social" in the social model refers to what disabled people know about society as a consequence of embodying it. Let me sum up where we are before turning to how we might understand the relationship of people with disabilities to the knowledge base. How does complex embodiment help to return the social to the social model?

    A. The social model no longer ignores the body for the environment. Complex embodiment theorizes the body and environment as mutually transformative.

    B. People with disabilities are no longer objectified by the social model. Diagnosis is of no use in identifying them; they are not only targets of the environment; they actively transform it.

    C. The social model, under the influence of complex embodiment, is an epistemological model. It not only incorporates agency; it cannot exist without active subjects who are defined by their ability to produce and share knowledge.

If people with disabilities know themselves and others as disabled, based on the possession and use of embodied knowledge, we should be able to find evidence of the fact. Here is where Shakespeare solved the problem for me of seeing the presence of disability as knowledge. I claimed for many years that we needed to argue the merits of minority disability identity epistemologically. I developed a limited conception of complex embodiment to account for the changing interaction between disabled bodies, environments, and individual consciousness. But I had not yet figured out the connection between knowledge and complex embodiment—for one thing because I really had no concrete examples of complex embodiment, and I did not know where to look for them, that is, until Shakespeare entered the picture. Then two things happened. First, I recognized disability for the first time based on the knowledge being gathered and exercised by disabled people. This knowledge was synonymous neither with gaps in the social model nor with advances in the medical model. Second, I figured out where to look for complex embodiment. Moreover, I discovered practices, known to most people, though greatly misunderstood by them, that were in fact forms of complex embodiment.

Let me cite and interpret a few passages from Shakespeare's *Henry IV, Parts 1 and 2* to show what I mean. Here Prince Hal and Poins steal Falstaff's horse:

> FALSTAFF: The rascal hath removed my horse, and tied him I know not where. If I travel but four foot by the square further afoot, I shall break my wind. . . .
> Eight yards of uneven ground is threescore-and-ten miles afoot with me, and the stony-hearted villains know it well enough. . . . Whew! A plague upon you all! Give me my horse, you rogues, give me horse, and be hanged! (2.2.10–28)

Old age? No! This is the kind of behavior learned over a long time—an indicator of disability. With more looking, I found this other passage in *Henry IV, Part 2*:

> FALSTAFF: A pox of this gout, or a gout of this pox, for the one or the other plays the rogue with my great toe. 'Tis no matter if I do halt; I have the wars for my colour, and my pension shall seem the more reasonable. A good wit will make use of anything. I will turn diseases to commodity. (1.2.238–43)

Falstaff limps. He seems to have gout affecting his big toe, and this disability explains why the theft of his horse injures him. But in many ways Falstaff's disability is immaterial. We cannot name gout as Falstaff's disability any more than we can say that it is the cause of his pretend death at the Battle of Shrewsbury.

In fact, critics have largely ignored gout as a factor in Falstaff's actions. The point, however, is not to assign a correct diagnosis but to reveal its inutility. There is no need for diagnosis. Those of us who notice that Falstaff is disabled know it, and know it instantly, not because he shows biological signs of a disability or withdraws from a disabling environment. We know it because he embodies the knowledge of what it means to be a disabled person. He calculates walking distances relative to an awareness of the ground: "Eight yards of uneven ground is threescore-and-ten miles afoot with me." Disabled embodiment holds a different knowledge of society, and this knowledge, not his "great toe," identifies Falstaff as disabled. Disability for Falstaff appears not in the body or even in a disabling environment but as another form of embodiment—a complex embodiment, the experience of which teaches that disability is both affected by environments and changed by the diversity of bodies, resulting in specific knowledge about the ways that environment and bodies mutually transform one another.

My second discovery came through the tendency in the critical literature to see Falstaff as "theatrical." Referring to "unfixed subjectivity," the characteristic that led some critics to name Falstaff as the first modern subject, Hugh Grady states that this "playfulness, this ability to subvert ideological interpellation through theatricality, is Falstaff's crucial characteristic, both as foil to Prince Hal and as thematic embodiment of resistance to power in all the plays of the Prince Hal trilogy" (611).

The ability of Falstaff to pass as nondisabled and disabled compels critics to define him as theatrical—theatricality has only this meaning with reference to him. People with a disability understand better than others the relation between disability and ability in any given situation. These two facets are not the frozen binaries of complex embodiment; nor is passing as nondisabled superior to passing as disabled. The desire to pass is central to how disabled people think about their identity. Passing, not coming out, defines the breathless moment when disabled persons first come to consciousness as disabled. In fact, they first recognize themselves as disabled when they know to pass. Those who pass treat social situations that others consider natural and normal as calculated, artificial, and subject to manipulation, thereby demonstrating their knowledge about the relation of human difference to social organization and human perception. Passing as disabled may involve playing roles, but its essential character is less a matter of deception than a knowledge of human ability and its everyday definition. Passing exhibits and exemplifies complex embodiment.

The usual definition of passing does not comprehend passing as disabled. Passing as disabled—or what I call masquerading—represents an alternative mode of managing disability through disguise. The masquerade depends not on the enactment of able-bodiedness but on claiming an identity marked as stigmatized, marginal, or inferior. People who masquerade display either an exaggerated image of their disability or conceal their disability with another one. These two sides of passing represent neither a frozen binary, nor do they somehow match a superior practice against an inferior one. The masquerade is not a negative version of passing. Rather, the desire to pass in all its fullness is central to how disabled people think about their identity.

Falstaff is, of course, an exquisite masquerader, and his skill explains one reason why he embodies opposition to Henry IV's murderous regime. Overstating or performing difference, when that difference is a stigma, makes one into a target, but it also exposes and resists the prejudices of society. The masquerade satisfies the desire to recount a story steeped in disability, often the very story that society does not want to hear, by refusing to embrace images of power and ability. Masquerading may stress undercompensation, when overcompensation is required, or present a coming out of disability when invisibility is mandatory. Exaggerated differences and feigned disabilities serve as small conspiracies against oppression and inequality. They subvert existing social conventions, and they contribute to the solidarity of marginal people by seizing control of stereotypes and resisting the pressure to embrace norms of behavior and appearance.

Before concluding I will provide two examples of passing by Falstaff. One shows conventional passing as a form of complex embodiment. The other shows masquerading. Please note that neither behavior could exist in absence of the longtime study of the society from which Falstaff and other disabled people are excluded. Here Falstaff gathers as recruits for the Battle of Shrewsbury a pack of ragged individuals from the bottom of society.

When Westmorland and Prince Hal ask for a defense of these recruits, Falstaff passes by imitating their idea of war, but he also exposes the attitudes of his superiors to the audience:

PRINCE HENRY: I did never see such pitiful rascals.

FALSTAFF: Tut, tut, good enough to toss; food for powder, food for powder. They'll fill a pit as well as better. Tush, man, mortal men, mortal men.

WESTMORLAND: Ay, but, Sir John, methinks they are exceeding poor and bare, too beggarly.

FALSTAFF: Faith, for their poverty I know not where they had that, and for their bareness, I am sure they never learned that of me. (4.2.61–69)

As another example of passing, Falstaff's words may seem exaggerated, but if they did not capture the beliefs of Prince Hal and Westmorland, they would immediately object to them, and they do not. Westmorland's use of the words "poor" and "bare" shows no conception of the recruits' real existence. For Westmorland, 'poor' refers to inferior military quality, not to poverty. He sees not hungry men before him but men in threadbare clothing. Falstaff's punning on "poverty" and "bareness" has comic effect, but its scope goes beyond humor to clarify that the king makes his people poor and hungry. Finally, when Falstaff calls his conscripts "food for powder," it seems unfeeling, and so it is, but his words prompt the audience to think about the cost of war to common people. If not for Falstaff, the audience might be tempted to believe that the Battle of Shrewsbury shows only Prince Hal killing Hotspur.

Later at Shrewsbury Falstaff masquerades. The use of the term "counterfeit" deserves an extended analysis, but I will focus only on Falstaff's application and defense of it. When Douglas attacks him, Falstaff falls down as if dead, and Douglas, duped, eventually leaves. Falstaff shows that he understands not only battle but also the survival techniques of the dispossessed. Falstaff is part of a disability collective. Despite his knighthood, he dwells among disabled and impoverished people, and he knows how they live and how they die, or, rather, his body knows these things, and it does what it must.

If Falstaff were to obey the ideology of ability underlying warfare, he would die in battle almost immediately. Instead, he masquerades, just as he passes as nondisabled elsewhere in the drama as a device to escape the violence around him. There is no sin in disguising oneself, Falstaff suggests, unless that disguise be in preference to death: "To die is to be a counterfeit," he reminds, "but to counterfeit dying . . . is to be no counterfeit, but the true and perfect image of life" (5.4.112–19). Falstaff embodies disability in the face of power, at once exposing and evading it. He chooses life in the counterfeit of death—at least for a little while.

Conclusion: Disability Is a Body of Knowledge

Let me conclude by showing again the proximity of the medical to the social models and demanding why we need to return the social to the social model. First, on the medical and social models, the usual methods of identifying disabled people by diagnosing a biological defect or an environmental incapacity show themselves to be not only ineffective but also discriminatory. They objectify people with disabilities and give no place to their agency, knowledge, and self-discovery. They may consider the roles of the body and the environment, but they do not theorize how they interact.

The theory of complex embodiment returns the social to the social model, but this theory does not conceal disabled subjectivity. Instead, it places a premium on the disabled subject as a knowledge producer—and to such an extent that people with disabilities are identified as such by their possession and use of the knowledge gathered and created by them as longtime inhabitants of nondisabled society. Passing as nondisabled and masquerading as more disabled, in addition to actions and statements of social critique, are practices where disabled people consistently self-identify as disabled, where they use the knowledge of society unique to them. My concluding point is that the awareness of complex embodiment reveals that disability is a body of knowledge.

WORKS CITED

Grady, Hugh. "Falstaff: Subjectivity between the Carnival and the Aesthetic." *Modern Language Review*, vol. 96, no. 3. 2001, pp. 609–23.

Shakespeare, William. *Henry IV, Part One*. Edited by Stanley Wells. Oxford UP, 1987.

Shakespeare, William. *Henry IV, Part Two*. Edited by René Weiss Jowett. Oxford UP, 1987.

Siebers, Tobin. "Disability and the Theory of Complex Embodiment: For Identity Politics in a New Register." *The Disability Studies Reader*, 4th edition, edited by Lennard Davis, Routledge, 2014, pp. 278–97.

Disability Ecology and the Rematerialization of Literary Disability Studies

Joshua Kupetz

> That I was I knew was of my body, and what I should be I knew I
> should be of my body.
> > —Walt Whitman, "Crossing Brooklyn Ferry"

Introduction: Disability as Material-Semiotic Ecology

In this essay, I offer a new conceptual model of disability and a method of doing literary disability studies called *disability ecology*. Disability ecology is part of the broader rediscovery of the body as site, critical lens, and sensuous experience already occurring throughout the social sciences and humanities. Grounded in the belief that "the material self cannot be disentangled from networks that are simultaneously economic, political, cultural, scientific, and substantial" (Alaimo, "New Materialisms, Old Humanisms" 282), this new materialist conception of disability reentwines embodiment with nonhuman actors such as biomedical practices, assistive technologies, human and nonhuman environments, and dominant beliefs and attitudes. Through such interactional relationships, these human and nonhuman actors constitute disability ecologies that shape social identities and structure the subjectivities of disabled people.

I apply this framework to literary disability studies through a reading of Richard Powers's novel *Gain* (1998) that interrogates the semantic, syntactic, and symbolic textual networks that produce literary disability and imbue it with meaning. Powers's novel serves as an exemplary site for the investigation of human-nonhuman entanglement particularly in its figurations of transnational flows of chemicals, medical practices, and capital.

Gain traces the ontological slippages between human and nonhuman subjects by linking the life stories of a human protagonist, Laura Bodey, and a corporate one, Clare International. One strand of the narrative foregrounds Laura Bodey, a successful real estate agent and single mother of two who is diagnosed with uterine cancer and dies in a matter of months. The other strand focuses on Clare International, a multinational corporation that achieves legal personhood over the course of a century and whose products—and industrial by-products—are linked to a cluster of cancer diagnoses in the fictional Lacewood, Illinois, that Laura and Clare's Agricultural Products Division call home. Laura and Clare, whose anthropomorphic and presumptively feminine corporate name emphasizes its agentic equivalence, restlessly traverse one another throughout the text. They meet under the kitchen sink when hands grasp bottles of dish soap; along the Midwestern horizon where the "black boxes" (Powers 2) of chemical plants achieve a paradoxical invisibility through their very ubiquity; and in the chemotherapy clinic where Clare's chemicals pass through PICC lines to scour Bodey's body for the tumors other Clare chemicals have urged into being.

In the sections that follow, I examine these crossing subjects—as substantive bodies, locations of meanings, and frames of reference—to reconsider how disability reveals the ontological precarity of so-called bounded humans and inert substances. First, I break the convention of writing textual analysis in the literary present by summarizing the salient points of Laura's narrative in the past tense. Laura is the principal figure that organizes the novel's examination of disability subjectivity and embodies its critique of the deleterious effects of environmental injustice produced by global capitalism particular to the end of the twentieth century. By breaking with the literary present, I acknowledge the slippage between supposed animate and inanimate materiality on which this novel and the concept of disability ecology depend. In addition, this rhetorical choice stages a common scenario in which a presumably normative audience demands, and becomes enthralled by, disability narrative. An unconventional use of the past tense, I hope, makes these conventions and expectations more available to critique in the present.

Subsequent sections situate the concept of disability ecology among other new materialist theories in contemporary critical disability studies that "rediscover" the body in ways that exceed the limitations of social construction theories. Disability ecology is a framework that can coordinate these already circulating and otherwise salient, yet differing models of disability. Disability ecology extends models such as Tobin Siebers's "complex embodiment" (22) and Alison Kafer's "political/relational model" (6) by elaborating affinities with other discourses, particularly STS (science and technology studies) and queer phenomenology. Using an STS approach, disability appears as a "boundary object," meaning a concept shared by multiple stakeholders that is loosely defined in common usage and strongly defined in specific community contexts. Sara Ahmed's work in queer phenomenology establishes a problematic that can help explain how disability ecologies orientate disabled people toward (and away from) objects, spaces, and ideas that are typically overlooked by a normative gaze. These approaches help expose types of entanglements commonly experienced by disabled people, draw new textual locations into critical focus, and provide points of access for the reimagination of disability as a material-semiotic artifact and social identity—one that is structured by systems of interactional relationships, is capable of exerting transformative pressure on those systems, and is fully embodied.

A Story of "When We Lived Wrong"

Laura Bodey was the newest member of the Million Dollar Movers Club for Next Millennium Realty in Lacewood, Illinois, when she developed ovarian cancer, underwent an unsuccessful regimen of chemotherapy, and died. She left behind a teenaged daughter, Ellen, and a twelve-year-old son, Tim. While the causes of ovarian cancer remain indeterminate, Laura belonged to an uncharacteristic "cluster" of women newly diagnosed in Lacewood. Weeks before her death in Mercy Foundation Hospital, Laura learned that she had been awarded a sizable settlement due to her participation in a class-action lawsuit against Clare International. According to Environmental Protection Agency findings, the multinational corporation's Lacewood-based Agricultural Products Division had been releasing significant yet legal amounts of carcinogenic by-products into the air and water. Additionally, several of the company's consumer products, including a common pesticide that Laura used on her flower garden, were also being studied for possible carcinogenic contaminants. Don Bodey, Laura's ex-husband, saw the settlement both as Clare's acceptance of responsibility and its tacit acknowledgment of liability, but Laura viewed the settlement in more pragmatic terms: due to the scandal surrounding the EPA findings, Clare common stock had dropped precipitously, and the settlement simply presented the most cost-effective maneuver to protect the financial positions of the corporation and its shareholders.

The object of a grave yet legal environmental injustice, Laura was expected to produce an individualistic solution to an interlocking set of systemic problems organized by their concern for profit. Upon her diagnosis
and assignment to a course of treatment, Laura was inserted into a neoliberal medical industry that expects care receivers to act as managers of
their own treatment, to make recovery their business, and to be their own
best advocates even as agents of that system determine the very pathways
toward "health" that any given person might choose. Reflecting on her
positionality as a newly diagnosed cancer patient, she recognized these
new responsibilities, claiming that "all the magazines agree: health care is
the patient's business" (Powers 80). Far from exercising agency, Laura was
shipped through medical offices as if she were a raw material being pro-
cessed through Clare's network of labs, plants, and distribution centers.
Laura moved between a general surgeon, a remote oncologist in Indianapolis, a surgical oncologist, a radiologist, and other medical professionals whose various labors attempted to shape her into the value-added
product known as a "survivor." Through her experiences of diagnosis and
treatment, Laura learned to view her specialist's office as a "giant, state-of-
the-art cancer-fixing factory that enjoys a regional monopoly" and a site
where she passes through "the medical equivalent of one of those assembly lines" (112). For this macroeconomics of cure to function, Laura—like
all patients—was expected to perform a particular form of labor, meaning
the active pursuit of cure or rehabilitation. The autonomous action demanded by the medical-industrial complex, however, merely disguised
her translation into a commodity for the use of various actors in health-
care networks. The modern medical-industrial complex had transformed
the hospital into a for-profit business similar to Clare, she believed, only
"not the kind that cares what its customers think" (82). Powers drives this
double-edged reduction home in an instance of dark irony: the narrator
divulges that many of the chemicals in her ineffective course of chemotherapy are Clare products and that Mercy Foundation Hospital, where
she undergoes treatment, owes its modern facilities to philanthropic gifts
from the company.

Her sociochemical baptism into neoliberal medical practice created an
emergent moral uncertainty regarding her own role in her cancer's development. Prior to her diagnosis, Laura had accepted the authority of clinical recommendations for healthy living—even if she often ignored them—
and believed that any occurrence of illness was a "holdover from when we
lived wrong" (Powers 13). The persuasive rhetoric of the neoliberal medical industry conditioned her to believe that cancer was her fault, her diag-

nosis appearing as a sign of a personal failure, of her somehow having "lived wrong," despite an abundance of troubling evidence pointing to toxic pollution and environmental injustice. The imposition of corporatized techniques of self-care, including the injunction to think positively—a pseudotherapeutic technique offered by medical professionals and peers alike—recalibrated Laura's sense of identity by initiating an estrangement from the social identities that had previously organized her life through their overlapping interactions. Cancer now refracted each facet of her social self—real estate agent, mother, gardener, ex-wife, lover—and roughened each edge where those disparate selves adjoined.

Laura was prescribed narrative as a therapeutic tool to shore up this rapidly disarticulating sense of self, and these rehabilitative hermeneutics demonstrate how storytelling buttresses the ideological junction of optimal health and personal responsibility. From her first postoperative consultation with Dr. Jenkins, who presided over Laura's initial cyst-removal-turned-hysterectomy, Laura was introduced to narrative as a technology of care. She was given pamphlets like *Diet and Cancer* and *Chemotherapy and You* as a technology of recovery and as a source of embodied knowledge. Although narrative has been a component of palliative care since the beginning of the hospice movement, Laura did not learn anything actionably useful from *Cheer: Your First Line of Defense.*

Instead of relying on informational pamphlets and their optimistic rhetoric of overcoming, Laura reflected on nonclinical modalities of narrative across a range of popular media as sources of lay expertise. These narratives proved equally unsatisfactory. When Laura awoke to learn that her scheduled cyst removal had become a complete hysterectomy, she initially identified with the protagonists in "amputation stories" who discover, during post-op recovery, that the surgeon had removed the wrong limb. As she convalesced, she puzzled over not having witnessed the portentous signs of impending illness common in "midnight reruns." When Hollywood films allowed young, nondisabled actors to consistently beat medical odds that she herself could not, she became aware instead of the ableist logic of filmic narratives that focus on sick or disabled characters as tropes to buttress the nondisabled. When she realized that neither clinical nor popular narratives could map onto her experiences of disabled embodiment, narrative became a form of oppression. Also oppressive: the expectation shared by friends and colleagues that she should narrate her diagnosis and treatment in an aesthetically satisfying way. She quickly learned to resent the expectation that she should craft a coherent narrative from an arbitrary event, for Laura's friends relied on her to provide a causal narrative that allowed her cancer to be bracketed, contained, and set aside. For these friends, for whom "the requests for details" elicit "vaguely excited show[s] of distress" (Powers 93), narrative rendered her cancer safe, a contained problem localized in her body.

For Laura, the disabling effects of cancer and its treatment were not simply the dialectical detritus of optimal health, nor were they merely inverse functions of failed techniques of self-care. Disability, she realized, provided a new standpoint from which she might see her life anew, a social relocation that shifted her orientation away from normative spaces, cultural practices, and interpretive methods. Although Laura had made a living by selling homeowners the greatest amount of square footage they could finance, Laura began to see the expectation of vast living space and the aesthetic division of rooms in a home as ideological forms, not inevitable givens. Likewise, when she helped Tim, her son, with an English assignment that required an explication of Walt Whitman's lyric-narrative poem "Crossing Brooklyn Ferry," she realized that she could draw on her own life as a resource for interpretation. Considering the speaker's projected speech first fifty and then one hundred years into the future, Laura concluded that Whitman could not have been ill when he wrote, "It avails not, time nor place—distance avails not." For Laura, time availed quite a bit.

Embodying Literary Disability Studies

The rhetorical gambit of introducing Laura's story as nonfiction helps foreground two issues at the center of this essay. First, I hope the framing of Laura's story as a bit of biography creates the conditions for readerly self-reflexivity, meaning that readers might find themselves complicit as eager consumers of disability narrative. Such awareness transforms Laura's increasing internal resistance to the social expectation that a disabled person "must narrate one's disability for others" (Mitchell and Snyder, *Prosthesis* xii), for her resistance to narrative itself is narrated to a reading audience hungry for stories about difference. Despite invoking issues of privacy and offering disability as a critique of mandatory causal logic, Laura's acts of denial also deny the novel its own opportunity to contest the "*undergirding authorization to interpret that disability invites*" (Mitchell and Snyder, *Prosthesis* 59).

Second, this gesture aims to reproduce the slippage between human and nonhuman subjects that preoccupies the novel and to contextualize the interventions *disability ecology* makes in disability theory and literary disability studies. Pulling back the curtain on the biographical mode in this way reveals a foundational contradiction in one of the central methods of literary disability studies: the explication of textual features that signify disability—that is to say, what makes disability textually *remarkable*—in the context of a broader political project that asserts disability's ultimate *unremarkability*. As nonfiction, the narrative sustains the naturalization of the heterogeneous ecology of actors that assail Laura's normative subjectivity, a group that includes medical professionals, private and public spaces like her home and the library, family members, chemotherapy drugs, and cultural attitudes. As fictional textualizations, however, these actors appear as contingent objects open to critique, and this critique works recursively to disrupt this naturalization in nonliterary life. Caroline Levine argues that "literary forms and social formations are equally real in their capacity to organize materials, and equally unreal in being artificial, contingent constraints" (14), and *Gain* affords an opportunity to explore the points of contact between literary disability thematics and nonliterary forms of disability subjectivity.

If disability is a material-semiotic practice, it follows that representations of disability in literary fiction can produce knowledge about disability subjectivities. Because there is no Archimedean point from which to perceive one's own disability ecology, one can turn to the limited sets of signifiers in literary texts as sources of knowledge production, self-reflection, and systemic critique of the orientating relationships that structure disabled people's lives. In *Reassembling the Social* (2005), Bruno Latour grants "the resource of fiction" the capacity to "bring . . . the solid objects of today into the fluid states where their connections with humans may make sense" (*Reassembling* 82). Here Latour echoes Herbert Marcuse, who claims that an aesthetic form, which is "the result of the transformation of a given content . . . into a self-contained whole," can be "recognized as a reality which is suppressed and distorted in the given reality" because it is "'taken out' of the constant process" of daily life (Marcuse 8, 6). Granting form to fluid experience, Marcuse argues, allows relationships between actors to become visible when they would otherwise be plowed under by the unrelenting movement of experience's furrow.

By demonstrating Clare's *personhood* as a textual effect, meaning the accumulated product of federal laws and court interpretations, the novel invites readers to consider the role of texts and other sign systems, objects, and practices in the elaboration of human subjectivities. Given that the novel establishes Clare as Laura's inverse image, its achievement of personhood runs counter to her process of disabled subjectification. Clare relies on a network of social practices and emergent technologies to power its growth from a family partnership in Boston into its final multinational form, a trajectory that takes the company from immateriality to substance through the semiotic effect of incorporation. For example, Clare benefits from early technological advances in candlemaking equipment and practices; horizontal growth into soap making; the transcontinental railroad's capacity to collapse distance and transform once-remote towns into viable markets; a boom due to shrewd government contracts during the Civil War; and deft marketing practices in order to generate ever increasing profits. An official charter of incorporation grants Clare protection from risk and constitutes the company as one "composite body" through legal language, including the Fourteenth Amendment to the US Constitution that extends due process to it (Powers 175, 179–80). Clare's lack of a conventional body does not foreclose its capacity for personhood; instead, mutable partiality is the precondition through which the narrative reveals the distributed networks of actors required to establish personhood as such.

Rematerializing Disability

Disability ecology builds on the new materialist belief that all human being is "substantially and perpetually interconnected with the flows of substances and agencies of environments" (Alaimo, "States of Suspension" 476). Disability is a material-semiotic effect of the social relationships between embodied individuals and a range of nonhuman actors, including cultural practices, institutions, and technologies. Given that disability is also relational, recursively inflecting those bodies, actors, and networks with new meanings that disability itself makes available, disability appears as a dynamic state of perpetual becoming, not a fixed condition with a stable meaning.[1] As a theory of disability and an analytic, disability ecology takes seriously David T. Mitchell and Sharon L. Snyder's call for a "definition of disability [that] must incorporate both the outer and inner reaches of culture and experience as a combination of . . . social and biological forces" (7). Presuming that "the flesh and blood givenness of the physical body is not a passive surface, but . . . in continuous interaction with textual practices" (Shildrick 178), disability ecology exposes the matrix in which any given nonnormatively embodied subject exists. Such subjects find themselves embedded in networks of co-constitutive relationships with human and nonhuman actors, such as built infrastructures, technologies, social institutions, and other discursive formations.

By connecting the material conditions of nonnormative embodiment with the cultural meanings attached to them in one model, disability ecology offers a new materialist solution to the essentialism-constructionism debate that has long attended disability studies. In this way, the study joins critical disability theorists like Tobin Siebers and Alison Kafer whose works seek to unite both positions by offering new materialist ways of thinking about disability. Siebers's concept of "complex embodiment" (22) is a theoretical framework in which identity is always both a representational and a material site of knowledge production. A "theory that describes reality as a mediation, no less real for being such, between representation and its social objects," complex embodiment offers the possibility that subjects can transform the social representation of their body or realign their social location through agential, embodied practice that achieves political ends (30, 26). While Siebers begins to map a new materialist terrain, Alison Kafer populates it with a range of intersectional bodies—texts, subjects, and social locations—that add granular specificity to Siebers's broad outlines. In *Feminist, Queer, Crip* (2013), Kafer proposes a "political/relational model" of disability that situates disability "in built environments and social patterns that exclude or stigmatize particular kinds of bodies, minds, and ways of being" (6). The political/relational model breaks from the dominant social model of disability by "pluraliz[ing] the ways we understand bodily instability" (7), particularly through a renewed attention to nonnormative embodiment and by acknowledging the value many disabled people find in medical intervention while also exposing the ableist underpinnings of many medical practices.

Moves like these that break apart the concepts of boundedness of impairment and the autonomy of an unrealistically discrete nonnormative body are vital for rendering disability legible as a material-semiotic phenomenon. Instead of affirming a Cartesian formulation of matter as inert, theories of new materialisms hold in common that "materiality is always something more than 'mere' matter: an excess, force, vitality, relationality, or difference that renders matter active, self-creative, productive, unpredictable" (Coole and Frost 9). Disability ecology locates this "something more" in the co-constituting relationships between human subjects and the material actors, human and nonhuman, that produce the effects that generate disablement and structure disability and its subjectivities. Such a view counters the essentializing assumption that disability is located in material nonnormative physical or neurochemical characteristics that determine disabled subjects, and it furthers disability's productive movement away from inert matter or disembodied sociality and toward a material-semiotic disability that structures subjectivities defined by creative interdependencies.

In order to build a model that can accommodate such a range of simultaneous usages of disability, I use the conceptual vocabulary of ecology. Three definitions of ecology impart a flexible granularity that honors the differences of individual disabled people yet addresses disability as such. Conceptual flexibility is necessary to account for the movements of individual actors and systems into positions of greater or lesser salience in the ecology—as well as into and out of it—over time and depending on context. First, this model references ecology as the study of interactional relationships between organisms and their environments; second, it references ecology as the pattern or aggregate of these relationships, or what is typically called an *ecosystem*; and third, it references ecology as human ecology, a branch of sociology that studies the spatiotemporal interrelationships between human actors and their economic, social, and political organization.

The actor-network theory (ANT) imperative to "follow the actors themselves" (Latour, *Reassembling* 12) provides a useful framework for the discovery of the actors that constitute disability ecologies. ANT is a material-semiotic method that extends agency to nonhuman actors as it maps and describes the relationships between things (material) and concepts (semiotics) in transient, heterogeneous networks. Reframing ANT as an "ecological" approach, Bruno Latour argues that all disruptions of the "collective," his term for acts of "*collecting* associations of humans and non-humans" (*Politics of Nature* 238), appear as ecological "crises" to be resolved by allowing the disruptive actors to reconfigure the collective. Within this framework, the resistance of disabled people to their own disqualification or exclusion ought to lead to the reconstitution of normalcy, not the normalization of difference on offer through contemporary forms of tepid "inclusionism," Mitchell and Snyder's term for the "embrace of some forms of difference through making them unapparent" (*Biopolitics of Disability* 4).

Disability ecology differs from Latour's approach in two ways: first, it emphasizes the human subject as the epicenter of such networks, and second, it actively intervenes in the disability ecologies it reveals through acts of interpretation. For Latour, networks *themselves*, not individual human actors, take center stage. Drawing on a sense of methodological disinterest, Latour claims that a good ANT account of a network does not critique or explain the actors and networks it perceives; instead, ANT relies upon purely descriptive writing to "*deploy* actors *as* networks" (*Reassembling* 136–40). In this light, an application of ANT to disability would *concern* disabled people, but not directly *involve* them. Scott Kirsch and Don Mitchell challenge the supposed neutrality of a typical ANT approach that does not pursue "the search for causes of, and thus accountability for, the effects of power which it traces" (692). Instead, they argue that the networked power ANT reveals may be "relational," distributed among "numerous points of contact, application[s], or effect[s]" and at the same time "'centered'—centered in institutions, in individuals, or in structured social relations" (691). Disability ecology insists on no such prohibition and actively reconstitutes the collective through acts of interpretation. Intended as a tool in the service of disability justice, disability ecology strives to intervene in, not just account for, the systems of oppression discovered through its deployment. As Gary Albrecht rightly argues, after all, "It is the *person* that has the social position and relationships with others" (71).

Gain illustrates this model of disability by embedding Laura's cancer in an ecological network of actors that runs from industrial by-products to the decision-making of Clare executives to the body's own genetic imperatives to the well-meaning-yet-ableist gestures of employers. The development of Laura's disability ecology disrupts the strong definition of disability—meaning the broad consensual understanding of disability as an individuating and embodied pathology in need of rehabilitation or cure—by narrating the development of Laura's narrow, material-semiotic usage that acknowledges disability as an embodied source of knowledge-production and creativity. In this way, disability appears as a kind of "boundary object," Susan Leigh Star and Geoffrey Bowker's term for "those objects that both inhabit several communities of practice and satisfy the informational [and work] requirements of each" (297). Such objects occur on the edges between social worlds or communities of practice—health-care providers and disabled people, for example—and act as *objects* because entities act toward or with them, not because they are necessarily composed of "prefabricated stuff" or demonstrate "'thing'-ness" (Star 603). By framing disability as a boundary object, one can prize open the monolithic, durable category of "disability" and reveal a complex and fluid network of relationships between the disabled subject and other actors, including nonhuman ones.

Powers's novel explores this material-semiotic complexity through the competing interests in cancer as well as the communicative misfirings between Laura and other stakeholders in her diagnosis and cure. Each actor who encounters Laura attempts to classify or define Laura's cancer but does so in a way that obscures it through the multiplication of local uses. Her surgeon, Dr. Jenkins, defines that cancer by stage, although the classification is indeterminate given the need for subsequent tests that in and of themselves have large margins of error. However, her radiologist, who is concerned with the likelihood of the cancer's spread to other systems, defines the cancer by grade, meaning the size and shape of the tumor's margins. Don Bodey translates each classification into a numeric variable for use in calculating Laura's five-year survival rates, and Ellen, her daughter, only wants to know if the classifications portend her mother's recovery. Laura's "specialist" in Indianapolis, an unspecified physician who is likely an oncologist given that he arranges her course of chemotherapy, seems incapable of communicating effectively with her because their individual definitions of cancer—and its meanings relevant to treatment, quality of life, and personhood—diverge so greatly. When the specialist describes her tumor as "Grade Three," Laura asks a simple follow-up question: "How can you tell it's a Grade Three[?]" (Powers 110). He misinterprets the query as a challenge to his diagnostic authority, and his immediate response, "Well, I'll grant you that the measurement is somewhat subjective" (110), suggests that cancer, for him, is an opportunity to validate his professional capabilities even as it undermines the facticity of empirical measurement itself. Later in the same conversation, he recommends a second-look surgery after she completes her course of chemotherapy, and she asks, "What will that tell?" Her query is meant to help her understand what new information such a procedure will reveal, yet he again misinterprets, replying "Well, you may be right. There's some debate about whether invasive second-look surgery is reliable enough to merit the possible complications" (110–11). Apart from being an instance of gross "mansplaining," the specialist's miscomprehension of Laura's questions suggests that their distinct social locations structure specific, divergent understandings of cancer that come into uneasy contact under the strong definition of disability and must be accounted for in any broad analysis of "cancer" as such.

Focus on Laura's diagnosis risks reasserting disability as an individuating condition of embodiment, but Powers guards against this impulse by introducing Laura into a community of people with cancer, most notably Ruthie Tapelewsky, whose chemotherapy schedule coincides with Laura's. Laura's interactions with Ruthie promote an ideology of *interdependence* while at the same time critiquing the system of overdetermined dependence on offer from the medical-industrial complex. As they undergo their monthly treatments, Ruthie and Laura create community by sharing embodied experiences and knowledge about them. They discuss wigs and hats, their children, their exasperation at current and former spouses, and the best strategies for managing the effects of chemotherapy, including what medicines produce the worst effects and what folk remedies actually help. Through such scenes, the novel establishes a disabled community, however small, without losing the particularities that belong to each individual, while Ruthie's occasional confusion about whose life relates to particular details paradoxically affirms their individuality. This experience of community reveals to Laura the extent to which self-willed autonomy is a fiction. When Ruthie declines further treatment, her absence in the chemotherapy ward registers for Laura as an act of embodied resistance against the medical industrial complex and the precedent for her own rejection of a second round of chemotherapy.

Disability Subjectivities and Nonnormative Orientations

These contingent networks of human and nonhuman actors produce *disability subjectivities*, meaning embodied experiences of "consciousness, knowing, thinking, or feeling" (Moser 377) conditioned by the interaction of nonnormative embodiments and disabling actors. Such subjectivities structure the physical standpoints and ideological points of view that appear as natural and given. If disabled and nondisabled subjects alike are "sedimentation[s] of established habits" (Braidotti 212), the contingencies that structure disability subjectivities differ in part because the shared social field—from built environments to the rights-granting institutions of biopolitical certification to aesthetics and taste—orients normative subjects as it dislocates nonnormative ones. Mitchell and Snyder refer to this phenomenon as the "life of hidden negotiations" (*Prosthesis* x) that shape disabled people's lives in ableist social locations.

Although the actors in disability ecologies *structure* disability subjectivities, they do not *determine* them, nor does the dominant ableist orientation of the public sphere consign disability to a subordinate position as normalcy's perpetually inferior remainder. Far from it: disability is also a *technique* for living differently through nonnormative embodiment.[2] The lived experience of a disability ecology appears as such a technique in that the marginalization of the disabled person creates a standpoint from which the naturalized, and therefore seemingly invisible, rules of ableist normalcy become apparent as exclusionary rather than natural, allowing the disabled person to choose whether or not to attempt their performance. Rejection of those dominant conventions leads the disabled person to create new idiosyncratic rules for living—or perhaps to live an elective absence of rules—that manifest as an embodied aesthetics or crip style that in part answers Alison Kafer's call to "begin thinking disability, and disability futures, otherwise" (7).

While disability activists have long drawn attention to the ways that the built environment directs and denies disabled people's lives through varying degrees of accessibility, disability ecology extends this awareness to the social and ideational environment, investigating how attitudes, beliefs, and practices direct disabled people toward or away from possible futures. "To be orientated," Sara Ahmed argues in *Queer Phenomenology* (2006), "is also to be turned to certain objects, those that help us find our way" (1). Of course, a turn toward one object is likely a turn away from another, perhaps many others. When social protocols direct disabled lives toward ableist objects or goals and away from objects and experiences that validate nonnormative embodiments as benign human variation, disabled people may become alienated from their own best interests as nonnormatively embodied subjects. Just as Ahmed's project involves "redirecting our attention to different objects" than those used to produce and propagate heteronormative standards (3), disability ecology emphasizes those objects that matter to disabled people and that ableist culture typically discounts or overlooks.

Gain speaks to the phenomenological power of disability subjectivity by narrating Laura's postoperative and postdiagnosis experiences of spatial defamiliarization in her own home as well as her estrangement from her own sense of embodiment. Her newly acquired embodied knowledge reveals the ways that the logic of consumption has shaped her prediagnosis sense of her home both spatially and affectively. Because she moves more slowly during her recovery from the hysterectomy than she had before, her house becomes "much bigger than it was"; sedated, she no longer remembers which rooms connect, and the house seems a tenuous, contingent assemblage of components (Powers 93). As her sense of the quantities of time and distance change, so does her sense of their affective values. She thinks that her formerly pride-inducing square footage is "massively irrelevant," that the designation of particular rooms for particular functions has less to do with their use value—"Utility room, laundry room, rec room, study, den. How many things must one person do? How many rooms does anyone need to do them in?"—and everything to do with the expectation to furnish them through acts of consumption (93). The home that had buffered her from thoughts of mortality before her diagnosis, she realizes, has "never been anything more than an obligation" to be filled with "her carefully coordinated furniture" (93). Laura's home, like the multination Clare International, operates as a composite body that disaggregates into fragments when seen through the lens of disability. Initially disorienting, this disarticulation offers a kind of freedom.

Gain represents Laura's specific disability subjectivity as a process of becoming aware of the materiality of embodiment that the figure of the liberal subject typically represses. This treatment allows disability subjectivity in general to appear as a more democratic model of human subjectivity itself. Contemporary notions of the liberal individual emphasize autonomy and self-reliance, what Ingunn Moser refers to as "centred control," meaning a subject's capacity to act from a position of "competence that implies that the person knows, has an overview of the situation, can control it, and is in a position to act" (Moser 381). As a recipe for a normative subject, "centred control" masks the network of "embodied relations and arrangements" that human subjects have with sets of "ordered relations" and other nonhuman actors such as infrastructural networks, social institutions, and technologies (Moser 382, 381). While normative characterizations underwritten by the ideology of ability typically privilege the trope of autonomy over the complex, networked relationships that shape human experience (Garland-Thomson 22), Powers's novel adopts an approach to disability that allows it to critique the idea of normative health. Disabled by her cancer and the chemotherapy drugs meant to treat it, Laura learns that so-called healthy human subjects only temporarily inhabit states of nondisability that are naturalized through cultural practices and discourse. After her first three-day chemotherapy treatment, Laura realizes that "no one really knows their real body" and that "well-being is nothing but an impostor, a beautiful girl who turns into a hag at neap tide when the spell breaks and reason at last sees through her" (Powers 129). Instead of affirming the autonomous subject on which normativity depends, Laura's experience suggests that all human subjects are permanently partial, aggregate beings who undergo ceaseless transformation through a variety of incapacitations. This awareness evokes Tobin Siebers's reframing of disability as "a form of diversity, and . . . as a critical concept for thinking about human identity in general" (3).

Subjects Unbound: "Mutable Substance Had No Final Shape"

Gain frames Laura's disability as an ecology constructed from an ever-changing network of social relationships between other human and nonhuman actors, such as the biomedical industry, the built environment, and the ideology of expressive individualism. Powers grants center-stage positions to the affective capacities of specific nonhuman actors such as medical protocols, chemotherapy drugs, corporate brand management methods, built environments, and abstract ideological structures like work, motherhood, and romantic partnership. The narrative connects each actor to Laura and explores how the interactions of their particular agentic forces structure her embodied experience of disability. Through these representations of human and nonhuman entanglements, particularly those of Laura and Clare International, *Gain* complicates conventional expectations about the experience of nonnormative embodiments by engaging issues of environmental justice; the effects of capitalist logic on disability subjectivities; the arbitrary natures of disability and ability as categories of disqualification and social inclusion, respectively; and the porosity of the no-border between human and nonhuman actors.

The contrapuntal motion of the novel foregrounds the ways in which Clare and Laura mutually constitute one another, a transportable reciprocity that becomes applicable to nonliterary contexts. The story suggests an environment where both corporate and human subjects shape and are shaped by their networked relationships to a symbolic order that is itself shaped by the spread of late capitalism. Clare, a person under law, seems to function as the antagonist, the embodiment of the malign force of late capitalism that both causes Laura's cancer and monetizes her death by offering a cash settlement as a substitute for continued life. Through this formation, the novel critiques conceptions of the post-Enlightenment subject who is an autonomous, free, and rational agent and who develops through various encounters with a nature that remains resolutely separate (Mansfield 11).

But *Gain* does not figure the new, hybrid, and distributed subject as a fall from grace in need of cure or salvation. According to the logic of the narrative world that Powers creates, any barrier between the human agent and the social world is semipermeable at most. Together, the two stories annealed within one narrative represent a contemporary human agent whose subjectivity cannot be rendered legible outside the network of mutually constituting relationships that he or she shares with other human and nonhuman actors.[3] Both the human and the corporation in *Gain* appear as material-semiotic entities, effects of physical qualities and processes as well as products of language and semiotic systems. Both Laura and Clare appear in states of perpetual becoming, two nonteleological subjects who, like the chemical by-products that Clare's chemists continuously repurpose, appear as "mutable substance" that has "no final shape" (Powers 164). Collapsing the distinctions between the human and the nonhuman at their most fundamental level, the novel interrogates the meaning of being itself and productively disaggregates the bounded liberal subject.

Powers denies any attempt to read the novel as an outright indictment of incorporation, however, through an ambivalent conclusion that ties the cure for cancer to the conditions that produced it in Laura. At the novel's conclusion, an adult Tim Bodey, Laura's son, works as a computer developer for a biotech start-up and develops a "Janus-faced" algorithm capable of working in "two directions" (Powers 405) on human proteins. While the narrative implies that a normative (single-faced?) algorithm works in only one direction, this productively disabled algorithm allows Tim's program to interact with a "score of other machines" to create a "universal chemical assembly plant at the level of the cell" capable of producing "anything the damaged cell called out for" (Powers 405). It is implied that the first use for this new network of technologies will be in search of a cure for cancer. Moreover, this use of "Janus-faced" recalls an earlier description of the initial soap-making efforts of the original Clare brothers, who perceive soap as a "Janus-face intermediary between [the] seeming incompatibles" of soluble and insoluble materials (405, 50). As the two-faced god of Roman mythology, Janus links soap—the product that guaranteed Clare's success and enabled the eventual release of the carcinogenic by-products that caused Laura's cancer—with computer code that promises cancer's imminent cure. In a similarly ambivalent sense, Tim suggests that "it might be time for the little group of them to incorporate" (405), closing the novel with a recuperation of the institution that has been linked to the unfolding tragedy of the narrative. That the money to incorporate, an act of amplification that could lead to cancer's cure, will come from Tim's inherited portion of the class-action settlement adds yet another instance of tragic irony to the novel's argument. To repurpose Mel Y. Chen's profound phrasing, *Gain* seems to argue that the toxic logic of capitalism is "already 'here,' already a truth of nearly every body" (Chen 218). Now Tim, like Laura, must embrace nonnormativity to make something meaningful and new from it.

NOTES

1. Stephanie Kerschbaum succinctly summarizes this set of interrelationships by claiming that disability is always "dynamic, relational, and emergent" (57), a phrase I

take as meaning that disability is itself an ongoing elaboration forever being shaped through embodied social practice.

2. Michel Foucault defines "techniques of the self" as "reflective and voluntary practices by which men not only set themselves rules of conduct, but seek to transform themselves, to change themselves in their singular being, and to make of their life into an *oeuvre* that carries certain aesthetic values and meets certain stylistic criteria" (10–11).

3. Many of these alternating chapters are connected by representations of Clare's marketing copy, suggesting that as one moves away from productive labor, one remains bound to economic modes of production through the practices of affective labor.

WORKS CITED

Ahmed, Sara. *Queer Phenomenology: Orientations, Objects, Others*. Duke UP, 2006.

Alaimo, Stacy. "New Materialisms, Old Humanisms, or, Following the Submersible." *NORA—Nordic Journal of Feminist and Gender Research*, vol. 19, no. 4, 2011, pp. 280–84.

Alaimo, Stacy. "States of Suspension: Trans-corporeality at Sea." *ISLE: Interdisciplinary Studies in Literature and Environment*, vol. 19, no. 3, 2012, pp. 476–93.

Albrecht, Gary L. *The Disability Business: Rehabilitation in America*. Sage, 1992.

Bowker, Geoffrey C., and Susan Leigh Star. *Sorting Things Out: Classification and Its Consequences*. MIT P, 1999.

Braidotti, Rosi. "The Politics of 'Life Itself' and New Ways of Dying." *New Materialisms: Ontology, Agency, and Politics*, edited by Diana H. Coole and Samantha Frost, Duke UP, 2010, pp. 201–20.

Chen, Mel Y. *Animacies: Biopolitics, Racial Mattering, and Queer Affect*. Duke UP, 2012.

Coole, Diana H., and Samantha Frost. "Introducing the New Materialisms." *New Materialisms: Ontology, Agency, and Politics*, edited by Diana H. Coole and Samantha Frost, Duke UP, 2010, pp. 1–46.

Foucault, Michel. *The History of Sexuality*, vol. 2: *The Use of Pleasure*. Translated by Robert Hurley. Vintage Books, 1988.

Garland-Thomson, Rosemarie. *Extraordinary Bodies: Figuring Physical Disability in American Culture and Literature*. Columbia UP, 1997.

Kafer, Alison. *Feminist, Queer, Crip*. Indiana UP, 2013.

Kerschbaum, Stephanie L. *Toward a New Rhetoric of Difference*. Conference on College Composition and Communication, National Council of Teachers of English, 2014.

Kirsch, Scott, and Don Mitchell. "The Nature of Things: Dead Labor, Nonhuman Actors, and the Persistence of Marxism." *Antipode*, vol. 36, no. 4, 2004, pp. 687–705. *CrossRef*, https://doi.org/10.1111/j.1467-8330.2004.00443.x

Latour, Bruno. "On Recalling ANT." *Actor Network Theory and After*. Edited by John Law and John Hassard, Wiley-Blackwell, 1999, pp. 15–25.

Latour, Bruno. *Politics of Nature: How to Bring the Sciences into Democracy*. Translated by Catherine Porter. Harvard UP, 2004.

Latour, Bruno. *Reassembling the Social: An Introduction to Actor-Network Theory*. Oxford UP, 2005.

Levine, Caroline. *Forms: Whole, Rhythm, Hierarchy, Network*. Princeton UP, 2015.

Mansfield, Nick. *Subjectivity: Theories of the Self from Freud to Haraway*. New York University P, 2000.

Marcuse, Herbert. *The Aesthetic Dimension: Toward A Critique of Marxist Aesthetics*. Beacon P, 1979.

Mitchell, David T., and Sharon L. Snyder. *Biopolitics of Disability: Neoliberalism, Ablenationalism, and Peripheral Embodiment*. U of Michigan P, 2015.

Mitchell, David T., and Sharon L. Snyder. *Narrative Prosthesis: Disability and the Dependencies of Discourse*. U of Michigan P, 2000.

Moser, Ingunn. "Disability and the Promises of Technology: Technology, Subjectivity and Embodiment within an Order of the Normal." *Information, Communication & Society*, vol. 9, no. 3, 2006, pp. 373–95. *CrossRef*, http://doi.org/10.1080/136911 80600751348

Powers, Richard. *Gain: A Novel*. Picador, 1999.

Shildrick, Margrit. *Leaky Bodies and Boundaries: Feminism, Postmodernism and (Bio) Ethics*. Routledge, 1997.

Siebers, Tobin. *Disability Theory*. U of Michigan P, 2008.

Snyder, Sharon L., and David T. Mitchell. *Cultural Locations of Disability*. U of Chicago P, 2006.

Star, Susan Leigh. "This Is Not a Boundary Object: Reflections on the Origin of a Concept." *Science, Technology, & Human Values*, vol. 35, no. 5, 2010, pp. 601–17.

Unique Mattering

A New Materialist Approach to William Gibson's *Pattern Recognition*

Olga Tarapata

> It is something about the footage. The feel of it. . . . it matters, matters in some unique way.
>
> —William Gibson, *Pattern Recognition*

William Gibson's fiction is fundamentally concerned with extraordinary bodies. From his early short stories to *The Peripheral* (2014) and *Archangel* (2016), Gibson portrays bodies that are damaged, deformed, and destroyed as well as sutured, restored, and healed, bodies that are technologically enhanced, or prostheticized. These overt corporeal exceptionalities elude normative classifications and instead of ossifying the characters' relations as "deviant" or "special," Gibson opens up novel ways to frame extraordinary embodiment. This chapter sets out to conceptualize the figurations of disability in Gibson's *Pattern Recognition* (2003) giving the acclaimed novel about globalization a new spin. Against the backdrop of recent debates within disability studies,[1] this essay focuses on the complex negotiation of nonnormative corporeality. In a close reading of the two protagonists, Cayce Pollard and Nora Volkova, I highlight the dynamism and unpredictability of nonnormative embodiment as expressed in the oscillating depictions of pain and pleasure. Negotiations of painful and pleasurable sensory experience in relation to disability, as found in Tobin Siebers's and Margrit Shildrick's theorizations, present a point of departure for my notion of *unique mattering*. While they diverge in focus, both ground their positions in the messy (Shildrick) or gritty (Siebers) materiality of the body. Rather than pain and pleasure as such, it is the potential for their experience that both scholars trace back to the material relationships within and without the body. To provide a potent account of the materiality of extraordinary corporeality that I find in the depictions of Cayce and Nora, I will revert to the theoretical framework of new materialism and specifically political scientist Jane Bennett's theorizations of the vibrancy of matter. While the concept of disability is not directly addressed by Bennett, this essay brings her ideas on materiality into dialogue with current negotiations of disability.

Gritty Corporeality

Within disability scholarship, it was Tobin Siebers who in 2006 reclaimed attention to the materiality of the body. Against decades of social and linguistic constructivism, largely influential within disability studies in the 1980s and 1990s, Siebers's essay invokes a "new realism of the body" (179). It is in the "gritty accounts of . . . pain and daily humiliations" that he identifies "the rhetoric of realism" (179). While Siebers articulates a concern for a particular 'rhetoric,' he is equally (if not more) interested in the ontology of disability. An embrace of "not . . . what we think it is but . . . what it really is" (180) marks his interrogation as less constructivist than essentialist. Neglected in semiotic discussions of the body, the "realism" Siebers insinuates points at the explicit physical reality and daily living conditions of people with disabilities, which, as he notes, may help to establish a "renewed acceptance of bodily reality" (179).

Siebers's criticism is directed against an overly shadowy, theoretical negotiation of pain in current body theory where "pain . . . is rarely physical" (177). Conceptualizations of suffering and disability that celebrate an "opening up [of] new possibilities of pleasure" cannot be integrated into Siebers's vision of pain as "an enemy" (177). According to his uncompromising position,

> Pain is not a friend to humanity. It is not a secret resource for political change. It is not a well of delight for the individual. Theories that encourage these interpretations are not only unrealistic about pain; they contribute to an ideology of ability that marginalizes people with disabilities and makes their stories of suffering and victimization both politically impotent and difficult to believe. (178)

This account refrains from any differentiation of pain, envisioning it as a universal corporeal condition. However, while Siebers concedes that "physical pain is highly individualistic, unpredictable" (178), he still prefers to keep it a clear and common enemy, and a unifying element for people with disabilities. When addressing the sources and triggers, Siebers emphasizes that it is not exclusively the disability in itself but the "innumerable daily actions" and "the difficulty of navigating one's environment" (177) that cause pain. People with disabilities face a "hundred daily obstacles that are not merely inconveniences but occasions for physical suffering" (177). In other words, pain is not by default an inherent quality of the disabled body but results rather from the interplay between body and environment granting them mutually constitutive power. Siebers, I argue, attempts to shed light on the transformative relationships that emerge in the enmeshment of body-material and environment-material. The "grittiness" that Siebers finds in "realistic" accounts of disability is nothing but an explicit negotiation of the body's materiality, of bodily fluids, excretions, orifices, tubes penetrating and bags attached to the body. He enumerates the material objects "that people with disabilities are forced to live with—prostheses, wheelchairs, braces, and other devices" that he considers "potential sources of pain" rather than "marvelous examples of the plasticity of the human form or . . . devices of empowerment" (177).

Therefore, pain is not viewed as an inherent quality but results from the interaction between person and environment. It is this interaction that holds the potential for sensory experiences, which are thus relational in nature. From this continuous gritty interaction within the individual network of interrelations the self emerges. With an eye on materiality, I classify this process of becoming as *unique mattering* when discussing Gibson's figurations on nonnormative corporeality. When Siebers asks "what would it mean to esteem the disabled body for what it really is" (181), my provisional answer to this ontologically driven interrogation suggests that by means of the discernment of the disabled body's unique material interrelations its appreciation can be approached.

While Siebers stresses the importance of "resisting the temptation to describe the disabled body as either power laden or as a weapon of resistance" (180) in his struggle for "a realistic conception of the disabled body," I suggest that it is equally important to resist any overdeterministic tie between disability and suffering. Siebers states,

> I am claiming that the body has its own forces and that we need to recognize them if we are to get a less one-sided picture of how bodies and their representations affect each other for good and for bad. The body is, first and foremost, a biological agent teeming with vital and chaotic forces. It is not inert matter subject to easy manipula-

tion by social representation. The body is alive, which means that it
is as capable of influencing and transforming social languages as
they are capable of influencing and transforming it. (180)

He characterizes the relationship between immaterial representation and
material body as mutually transformative and foregrounds the physicality
and capabilities of the body. Yet the physical transformations involved in
complex embodiment remain nebulous in his account. Only implicitly does
Siebers bear testimony to the material relationship between body and environment. In his attempt to carve out the vitality and capabilities of the human body, he resorts to defining it against inert and passive matter, thereby
reiterating a long-held ontological opposition between life and matter.

Particular attention to the inscription of pain in the body's materiality can
be found in the introduction of Keith Alan Blackwell, a character from Gibson's novel *Idoru* (1996). The scrutinizing look of protagonist Colin Laney dis-
cerns how the "exposed flesh [is] tracked and crossed by an atlas of scars,
baffling in their variety of shape and texture" (6). Concealing his identity during their initial encounter, Blackwell's outward appearance, characterized by
heavily scarred hands, a scarred face and head, a dental prosthesis, and a "broken nose, never repaired" (7), is all that is primarily available to Laney. However, Blackwell is not Rosemarie Garland-Thomson's freak who is simply and
passively stared at. Instead, communicative control is balanced between
"starer" and "staree" (77). Staring at the remains of Blackwell's left ear, Laney
wonders "why there had been no attempt at reconstruction" (5). The role of
the staree in such encounter is essential; and ideally, according to Garland-
Thomson's "ethics of looking" (194), both parties engage in a transitive action.
Recognizing Laney's interested look as an act of communication, Blackwell
replies, "'So I'll remember,' . . . reading Laney's eyes. 'Remember what?' 'Not to
forget'" (5). When Blackwell touches his scar tissue or squeezes his "lobe-
stump," he does it "without hesitation or embarrassment" (27). Instead of the
depiction of a disabled body in need of repair or reconstruction, Gibson foregrounds how experience, be it painful or other, informs corporeality as well as
subjectivity. This blatant display of scarred skin and nonnormative physique is
presented in a manner that recognizes realistic corporeality and in this sense
values a person's unique biography.

Dynamic Corporeality

Rather than pain, it is creativity, pleasure, and plasticity that feminist and
critical disability studies scholar Margrit Shildrick is concerned with in

her negotiation of the concept of disability. While she parts ways with
Siebers with regard to the ramifications of unstable corporeality, Shildrick,
in a similar vein, bespeaks the fundamentally messy nature of embodiment, pleading that "all corporeality is inherently leaky, uncontained, and
uncontainable" ("Beyond the Body" 7). With recourse to the works of
Jacques Derrida as well as Gilles Deleuze and Félix Guattari, Shildrick
provides a vantage point that focuses on the body's "plasticity . . . and the
capacity of disparate parts to constitute hybrid assemblages" ("Border
Crossings" 148). Her account moves far beyond an "endeavour to restore
the clean and proper body" (138). The incorporation of nonself matter
cannot restore any "originary wholeness," since the body has "never been
self-sufficient" (141) and, according to Shildrick, a "'natural' self-complete
and singular embodiment is an illusion" (140). Prostheses can thus be understood to "contest the illusion of an originary unified and singular body,
exposing instead the fluidity of categorical boundaries" (142). In search of
adequate conceptions and terminologies to describe the conditions of
what is considered "disability," Shildrick advocates "open[ing] the field to
a nexus of unexpected but constitutive assemblages that disorder the very
idea of normative corporeality" (140). Shildrick manages to capture this
"fluidity" by drawing on Deleuze and Guattari's understanding of "desire,"
according to which the "embodied self—rather than being goal-driven
and singular as it would be in a modernist model—becomes a network of
flows, energies, and capacities that are always open to transformation"
(143). Adopting this notion of the embodied self enables Shildrick—even
more forcefully—to move away from what the (disabled) body is and toward what the (disabled) body can become. She holds,

> In shifting the emphasis from the integrity and co-ordination of the
> whole body to the provisional imbrication of disparate parts, it is
> no longer appropriate to think of bodies as either whole or broken,
> able-bodied or disabled. Embodiment is simply a provisional man-
> ifestation in a process of becoming driven by the circulation of de-
> sire. For Deleuze and Guattari, such flows of energy extend em-
> bodiment beyond the merely human. (145)

In "the dynamic and always unfinished processes of assemblage [that]
point to the unlimited potential of becoming" (146), Shildrick identifies
value for contemporary discussions of the disabled body.

 I find that these productive becomings of disability in Shildrick and
Siebers work analogously to the progressive development in the depiction
of extraordinary bodies that populate the work of William Gibson. There

is a humanist undercurrent in Gibson's early fiction in that conceptualizations of the disabled body ground in a notion of a coherent, rational, autonomous self contained in the visceral tissues of the body. Yet these conceptualizations evolve toward an extended notion of embodiment notably from the Bridge trilogy onward. The days of repair as the answer to corporeal deficiency or damage are long gone, since the illusion of the norm has been exposed. In accordance with Mitchell and Snyder's argument in *Narrative Prosthesis*, one recognizes that the "prostheticized body is the rule not the exception" (7). Corporeality, rather than static or enclosed, is now considered dynamic and fluid. Moving through a field of diverse forces, the body is constituted by its possibilities of entering into relations with other bodies. Deleuze and Guattari's notion of "assemblage" aids in organizing the incessant change and reconstruction of the embodied self that exists in a condition of perpetual becoming. After all, why should we read the disabled or nonnormative body as any less dynamic than other corporeal expressions?

The Matter of Agency

In order to account for the potentiality of an ever-shifting nexus between bodies and their material environment rather than a more deterministic expression in the binary relation of pain or pleasure, this essay will turn to a theoretical approach that is devoted to the negotiation of materiality. Her endorsement of "thing-power" made Jane Bennett a prominent figure in the revival of materialism. New materialist approaches have already found their way into disability studies, for instance, in the works cited above via Siebers, Shildrick, and Mitchell and Snyder, and as the foundational organizing logic of this collection, *The Matter of Disability*.

In a recent publication *The Biopolitics of Disability* (2015), David Mitchell and Sharon Snyder turn to what they call "antinormative novels of embodiment" in which they identify narratives that "employ disability's radical potential to unseat traditional understandings of normalcy" (182) and "explore disability as revelatory of variation's potential for innovation" (181). Mitchell and Snyder refer to alternative modes of representing nonnormative corporeality in contemporary novels by, among others, Richard Powers and Stanley Elkins to develop the notion of the "capacities of incapacity." Their analyses draw on new materialist discourses and thereby embrace a vocabulary that allows for a recognition of the agency of matter. The power of alternative representation resides in the novels' foregrounding of "imperfection as a creative, biological force" (182), which echoes Siebers's emphasis on a "biological agent teeming with vital and chaotic forces" (180). While nonnormative corporeality is crucial to all three approaches, for Siebers it is mainly associated with the experience of pain. Mitchell and Snyder, by contrast, conceptualize the vital, chaotic, biological forces of the body in terms of capacities for creativity and innovation; here we can observe Siebers's impulse toward a "new realism of the body" converge with what Mitchell and Snyder call "new disability materialism" (182). By incorporating "materiality" into their analytical vocabulary, Mitchell and Snyder put renewed emphasis on the agentive and dynamic nature of the nonnormative material body and depart further from notions of passivity and deviance rooted in the medical parlance of pathology and dysfunctionality. Their process-oriented notion of biological multiplicity is read against the backdrop of neoliberalism, in particular its "unethical profiteering practices" (189) and a value system mainly based on economic productivity.

Vibrant Materiality

I will read Gibson's literary figurations against the backdrop of the field of new materialism, which updates a problematization of the life (vital, active)—matter (inert, passive) binary. In their volume *New Materialisms*, Diane Coole and Samantha Frost aim for a return to "the most fundamental questions about the nature of matter and the place of embodied humans within a material world" (3). Along similar lines, political theorist Jane Bennett's *Vibrant Matter* (2010) presents a twofold undertaking in that it is a philosophical as much as a political intervention.[2] In the philosophical strand, Bennett concentrates on "thinking beyond the life-matter binary" (20) in order to "theorize a materiality that is as much force as entity, as much energy as matter, as much intensity as extension" (20). Methodologically, by means of developing "a vocabulary and syntax for, and thus a better discernment of, the active powers issuing from nonsubjects" (ix) and "cultivat[ing] the ability to discern nonhuman vitality" (14), Bennett ultimately intends "to promote greener forms of human culture" (x)—a project that involves "the ethical aim . . . to distribute value more generously, to bodies as such" (13). How could Bennett's appeal for the revaluation of bodies in general, which seems to resonate well with the new realist demand for an explicit appreciation of the disabled body, inform the conceptualization of nonnormative corporeality?

In her new ontology of matter, she develops the concept of "thing-power" with recourse to atomists like Lucretius and Epicurus as well as natural sciences like complexity and chaos theory. In acknowledging the vitality of matter, defined as "the capacity of things—edibles, commodities, storms, metals—not only to impede or block the will and designs of humans but also to act as quasi agents or forces with trajectories, propensities, or tendencies of their own" (viii), she decidedly sides against the paradigms of social and linguistic constructivism that take matter primarily as the carrier of meaning, the passive product of discourse. Through applying Bennett to Gibson's fiction, I will argue that his figurations raise awareness of "the curious ability of inanimate things to animate, to act, to produce effects dramatic and subtle" (6). Reading Gibson against the backdrop of Bennett's vital materialist approach will allow me to discern and esteem not only "humans and their (social, legal, linguistic) constructions" as actors but also "some very active and powerful nonhumans: electrons, trees, wind, fire, electromagnetic fields" (24). From such a perspective, the interactions with prostheses, wheelchairs, braces, and other devices come into a different light; the relationship is one of symmetrical, rather than hierarchical, interrelation between human and nonhuman actors; and disability becomes one of many various forms of agential embodiment rather than the categorical other to normative embodiment.

The Power of Relations

Received as a novel about capitalism, global corporate culture, and pervasive commodification, Gibson's *Pattern Recognition* depicts a globalized world to the point of saturation, prompting critics to suggest that while the novel depicts processes and mechanisms of the present moment, this present is ultimately characterized by what science fiction scholar Veronica Hollinger calls "process-without-progress" (467). As much as Hollinger's observation applies to the general temporality of the novel, it can be equally useful in a discussion of the representation of nonnormative corporeality. In contrast, I am interested in Gibson's figurations of humans and specifically the depiction of the two heroines' extraordinary corporeality as dynamic, embedded, and semisovereign.

Against the general trend in traditional works of literature in which "disabled characters were either extolled or defeated according to their disability to adjust to or overcome their tragic situation" (Mitchell and Snyder, *Narrative Prosthesis* 19), *Pattern Recognition* neither simply fol-

lows this "kill-or-cure" formula nor merely utilizes nonnormative characters to tell a story in the sense that Mitchell and Snyder present as "narrative prosthesis." By providing readings of, for instance, Melville's Ahab and
Sophocles's Oedipus, Mitchell and Snyder expose narratives that treat disability in its own right. Their criticism is thus directed against the fact that
"while disability often marks a protagonist's difference and is the impetus
to narrate a story in the first place, a complex disability subjectivity is not
developed in the ensuing narrative" (10). In a similar vein, I will argue for
the complexity inherent in the depictions of the nonnormative corporeality and subjectivities' of the two protagonists of *Pattern Recognition*, Cayce
Pollard and Nora Volkova.

Pattern Recognition centers on Cayce Pollard, a freelance "coolhunter"
who works for international marketing companies until commissioned by
Hubertus Bigend, a marketing guru and the head of Blue Ant Agency, to
track down "the maker" (6) of a collection of film clips, enigmatically
known as "the footage," whose underground proliferation can be considered viral. Described as "a 'sensitive' of some kind, a dowser in the world
of global marketing" (2), Cayce has a talent for spotting consumer patterns and predicting trends—she anticipates markets before they surface.
However, "the truth . . . is closer to allergy, a morbid and sometimes violent reactivity to the semiotics of the marketplace" (2). The sheer density
of product information, or in Frederic Jameson's words "noisy commodities" (114), that suffuses Gibson's fiction fuels Cayce's allergy and explains
her enthusiasm for the minimalist aesthetics of "the footage." The footage,
a collection of 135 individual all black-and-white video clips without audio
or linear sequence, is anonymously distributed over the internet. Cayce
fathoms that "there is a lack of evidence, an absence of stylistic cues, that
[she] understands to be utterly masterful" (23). Bigend admires the footage as "the single most effective piece of guerilla marketing ever" (67), and
due to her private passion for the footage, "[her] talents, [her] allergies,
[her] tame pathologies" (67), Cayce becomes a valuable asset. Despite
fearing the footage becoming marketed by Bigend, she agrees to the mission out of personal curiosity for the origin of the segments.

Cayce's sensitivity produces a violent reaction that makes her "literally,
allergic to fashion" (8). What this depiction foregrounds is the interplay
between acting and suffering action between person and material environment. On the one hand, overtly and severely affected by her globalized
context and the semiotics of logos and, on the other hand, actively shaping
them in her function as coolhunter, Cayce navigates through her world in
continuous affective feedback loops. For her, catching sight of certain

trademarks has incapacitating consequences in the form of swellings, panic, nausea, and vomiting: "She's gone to Harvey Nichols and gotten sick. . . . Tommy Hilfiger does it every time. . . . When it starts, it's pure reaction, like biting down hard on a piece of foil. A glance to the right and the avalanche lets go" (17–18). Each individual interaction holds the potential for a painful allergic reaction. The unpredictability associated with the image of an avalanche mirrors Cayce's inability to predict what reaction will spring from the first sight of a new logo.

This potential of diverse experience that falls under the category of talent or allergy, knack or pathology we can consider a sort of phenotypic plasticity. This means that the quality of her reaction—as painful or joyful—and its material context emerge in mutual interdependence. The reaction therefore does not depend exclusively on the internal properties of a thing, body, or person (alone). In an insightful self-description, Cayce explains that she hunts "cool," which is not an inherent quality but instead "a group behavior pattern around a particular class of object" (88). On the watch for the "cool," Cayce thus draws on intuition rather than cognition when factoring in the various actors and their interactions. In depicting Cayce's nonnormative sensitivity to complex, singular configurations of interrelations, Gibson acknowledges the capacity of materiality to act upon and to affect the observer as well as to be acted upon and affected by those who share a cultural circumference. Cayce navigates through her environment so as to avoid her known painful triggers, since a confrontation with, for instance, figurines or drawings of the Michelin Man entail paralyzing and painful consequences. These painful reactions to brands mark "the downside of [her] ability to judge the market's response to new logo designs" (169). This extraordinary sensitivity frames Cayce less as a subject in full control of her body and environment than as an actor codependent on other actors. In the depictions of his protagonists, Gibson provides a commentary on the semisovereign status of what it means to be a full participant in a variably embodied humanity.[3] In *Pattern Recognition* nonnormative corporeality is the rule, not the exception. Bodies are vulnerable and efficacious, interdependent and dynamic as is their materiality (Mitchell and Snyder, *Narrative Prosthesis* 7).

This observation does not only apply to nonnormative corporeality in *Pattern Recognition* but the acute attention on the interdependencies between human materialities and nonhuman materialities is always already a general characteristic of Gibson's work. An exemplary scene from *Virtual Light* (1993) shows how in his negotiation of interfaces and interrelations Gibson develops a form of collective agency. Chevette Washington, the protagonist of *Virtual Light*, lives in an off-grid squatters' community on the San Francisco–Oakland Bay Bridge and works as a bicycle messenger in the city. Chevette's experience as messenger is described as follows:

> Sometimes, when she rode hard, when she could really proj, Chevette got free of everything: the city, her body, even time. That was the messenger's high, she knew, and though it felt like freedom, it was really the melding-with, the clicking-in, that did it. The bike between her legs was like some hyper-evolved alien tail she'd somehow extruded, as though over patient centuries; a sweet and intricate bone-machine, grown Lexan-armored tires, near frictionless bearings, and gas-filled shocks. She was certainly part of the city, then, one wild-ass little dot of energy and matter, and she made her thousand choices, instant to instant, according to how the traffic flowed, how rain glinted on the streetcar tracks, how a secretary's mahogany hair fell like grace itself, exhausted, to the shoulders of her loden coat. (131)

In the accelerated activity of cycling, interdependencies between the human actor that is Chevette and nonhuman actors such as the bike, the street, and the city become apparent. Their fundamentally entwined nature reveals a fluid entity, which as such makes decisions and is indivisible into either energy or matter. The performed action is collaborative and her rush, her bodily pleasure does not emerge from any false sense of autonomy or independence but instead from the action of "melding-with, the clicking-in."

Rather than defining agency in terms of a subject's free will, Bennett proposes a material and distributive agency and thereby advocates an alternative to regarding humanity as the "ultimate wellspring of agency" (*Vibrant Matter* 30). Her notion of distributive agency "does not posit a subject as the root cause of an effect" (31) and draws on a Latourian symmetry between actors. This approach not only allows accounting for Chevette's relationship with her bike outside traditional notions that strictly conceive the messenger as a subject operating on an object, but moreover sheds new light on the interdependencies of nondisabled embodiment. Coincidentally, Bennett's prime example for the relationship between "the kind of striving that may be exercised by a human within the assemblage" and distributive agency is cycling. She states, "One can throw one's weight this way or that, inflect the bike in one direction or toward one trajectory of motion. But *the rider is but one actant operative in the moving whole*" (38, emphasis added) and "an actant never really acts alone. Its efficacy or agency always depends on the collaboration, cooperation, or interactive interference of many bodies and forces" (21). Brought into the context of nonnormative corporeality Bennett's approach might effectively facilitate the dissolution of the dominant conjunction of disability with deviance, dependency, and passivity for future disability studies scholars. In turn such an emphasis could extend a common insight of the field in debunking notions of normative bodies as autonomous, coherent, and active.

The Power of the Cut

On her investigative mission, the protagonist of *Pattern Recognition* follows the actors of a complex network that take her to a contact person in Moscow by means of the watermark of a video clip. She meets Stella Volkova, who tells Cayce of her twin sister Nora, a former student filmmaker who is later unveiled as the creator of the footage. Echoing the narrative structure of Gibson's previous novels,[4] *Pattern Recognition* hinges on a character who at the novel's grand finale is revealed to have a significant physical disability. Without any material appearance or information about her identity, the maker prevails as an empty signifier until the final pages of the novel. Information about her can only be drawn from the footage itself, from the watermarking it exhibits, or at another remove from other characters' speculations, which uniformly convey that "the footage is a work of a proven genius" (69), that it is utterly masterful. Rather than merely suffusing the narrative with her absent presence, the mysterious creator of the footage appears as an actual driving force of the narrative. While Nora's introduction in the form of a surprise revelation as a paraplegic genius could be read in terms of a "narrative prosthesis," I argue that this figuration offers insight beyond a mere narrative function into the complexities of extraordinary corporeality as dynamic, extended, interrelated, and semisovereign.

Nora Volkova is the daughter of a Russian oligarch and was severely injured during a bomb attack directed at her family. As a result of a piece of shrapnel lodged between her cerebral hemispheres, Nora is paraplegic and is presented as mostly unresponsive. What dramatically changed the life of Stella's twin sister is a piece of metal whose biography is described as follows:

Something stamped out, once, in its thousands, by an automated press in some armory in America. Perhaps the workers who'd made that part, if they'd thought at all in terms of end-use, had imagined it being used to kill Russians. . . . And somehow this one specific piece of ordnance, adrift perhaps since the days of the Soviets' failed war with the new enemies, and this one small part, only slightly damaged by the explosion of the ruthlessly simple device, had been flung into the very center of Nora's brain. And from it, and from her other wounds, there now emerged, accompanied by the patient and regular clicking of her mouse, the footage. (315–16)

It is through the stark focus on the material thing that both forks and connects Nora's brain that the significance and power of materiality is foregrounded in the narrative's intricate course of events. This particular piece of metal irrevocably changes her in forms that entail paralysis and pain. At the same time, it becomes an essential part of the organism, one without which she cannot survive. Material specificity plays a crucial role since it is only due to the metallic object's conductive quality that the communication between the hemispheres is possible, which opens up entirely new pathways of connectivity. A particular material thing, therefore, plays a significant role in the emergence of the footage. The hemispheres are connected through a piece of electrically conductive material allowing for a discharge that expresses itself in the form of digital video clips.

At the end of *Pattern Recognition*, Gibson displays complex narrative modalities in his depiction of nonnormative bodies. Much in Siebers's vein, the representation of Nora's disability negotiates pain without providing any easy solution. The gritty reality becomes visible through its acknowledgment and requirement of an active negotiation, as does a nonlinear process of recovery that could be described as "process-without-progress" in my appropriation of Hollinger's words. In a scene depicting Nora's hospitalization we see the nonlinear process of her recovery:

Then she was shown her film from Cannes. That she saw, but it seemed to cause her great pain. Soon she began to use the equipment. To edit. Recut. . . . Five operations in that time, and still she worked. . . . She ceased to speak, then to react. To eat. Again they fed her with tubes. I was crazy. . . . In the end they said they could do nothing. It could not be removed. . . . The last fragment. It rests between the lobes, in some terrible way. It cannot be moved. Risk is too great. . . . But then she notices the screen. (298)

The confrontation with a former film project causes Nora great pain while at the same time prompts a process of reediting.

> The most clever of the doctors, he was from Stuttgart. He had them put a line from that camera into her editing suite. When she looked at those images, she focused. When the images were taken away, she began to die again. He taped two hours of this, and ran it on the editing deck. She began to cut it. To manipulate. . . . That was the beginning. (299)

The cut Gibson develops in the figuration of Nora operates on three levels. First, there is the cut through Nora's hemispheres. The concomitant availability of new channels of interrelation informs her desire to continuously recut video material, which in turn gives the resulting footage a quality of "cutting across boundaries, transgressing the accustomed order of things" (20). Acutely affected by this transgressive quality, Cayce can only point to "the feel of it" (78) and stresses that the footage "matters, matters in some unique way" (78). Whereas the footage uniquely matters to Cayce in symbolic terms, I would like to use the notion of *unique mattering* in a more general sense to conceptualize Gibson's figurations of nonnormative corporeality. *Unique mattering* is meant to capture the process of becoming of a singular network of interdependencies and foreground the vibrant materiality involved.

In her working process, Nora's activity and pleasure come to the fore. Drawing on Mitchell and Snyder's notion of the "capacities of incapacity" (187), we see that Nora's nonnormative corporeality effervesces with creativity. Its efficacy shows in the ways the footage is understood as utterly innovative, as "somehow entirely new" (*Pattern Recognition* 67), also deeply affecting the lives of others, and even changing international sociocultural structures. However, what simultaneously becomes clear is that she is not the epitome of a creative genius in any strong sense, but rather, intricately enmeshed in a material production network that as a whole brings forth the footage.

In the figuration of Nora Volkova, Gibson develops a complex nonnormative corporeality that both expresses pain and pleasure, stasis and transformation as contingent modalities of becoming bodies—including paraplegic corporealities. Besides the fact that the shrapnel in Nora's brain cannot be removed, and according to medical rubrics her "wholeness" cannot be restored, all other implications are much more ambiguous. Criticism regarding literary depictions of disability often focuses on the frequently depicted overcompensation of the superhuman on the one hand and the subhuman on the other. Gibson's representation addresses a problematic condition without denying its painful reality that, however, does not become the single defining criterion. In the attempt to conceptualize extraordinary bodies, Gibson circumvents unambiguous and definitive attributions of pity, tragedy, or deficit. "It is here, in the languid yet precise moves of a woman's pale hand. In the faint click of image-capture. In the eyes only truly present when focused on this screen. Only the wound, speaking wordlessly in the dark" (316). When Cayce is granted permission to watch Nora work, the description of Nora oscillates between fascination and pathologization, admiration and empathy, and eventually the recognition of potential without any conclusive deflation into common categories.

Upon their first meeting, Cayce finds Nora's gestures condensed to the movement of a single finger; the rest of her body is motionless. As Cayce watches pixel after pixel being assembled into the magical stills, she finds a first confirmation of the work-in-progress hypothesis advocated by one subgroup of self-proclaimed "footageheads." Observing how the "visual information, the grain of that imagery" (110), is manually generated confirms the entirely computer-generated nature that footageheads have already assumed exists on the basis of the identical resolution in each of the segments. What seemed to make this hypothesis unconvincing is the sheer intensity of labor it requires. Following this procedure of production, each segment needs to undergo a rendering process at so-called

> rendering farms. . . . Big room, lots of stations, Tenderers working through your footage a frame at a time. Labor intensive. . . . Rendering is expensive, human-intensive, involves a lot of people. . . . These people sit there and massage your imagery a pixel at a time. (110)

This insight into the labor-intensive demands on the production of the footage offers a first glimpse at the immense density of the network in which Nora is interwoven. Her uncle Andrei Volkov is able to contribute the facilities, the high-end technology as well as the manpower and the financial assets that enable Nora to produce the footage. In order to get Nora's clips rendered, Cayce learns, "One of Volkov's corporations decide[d] to set up a test operation, where healthy, motivated prisoners can lead healthy, motivated lives, plus receive training and career direction" (340). Thus, the inmates of an entire prison work in the service of the production of the anonymously distributed collage of film stills. The gigantic amount and diversity of actors involved in the generation of the footage becomes visible. Located at a derelict cinema that is adapted to Nora's purposes, the maker is looked after by her twin sister, who fulfills as much of a constitutive function as the computer technology that allows her uninterrupted act of editing. The subsequent rendering and final watermarking by different organizations further expand Nora's network. Her agency is radically distributed and suspended across a multiplicity of human and technological nodes. As if to highlight the hybridity of Nora's subjectivity, the email address that ultimately leads Cayce onto her tracks, stellanor@armaz.ru, fuses Nora with her sister, technology, and the internet.

The footage, as Nora's creative discharge, requires the shrapnel as well as the individual prisoner, the editing programs as well as Stella's voice. With awareness of the artist's immersion into these interrelations, "The creative process is," as Bigend prophetically proclaims, "no longer contained within an individual skull, if indeed it ever was" (*Pattern Recognition* 70). The individual skull, similar to Andy Clark's notion of "the skin-bag," is not regarded as the singular seat of subjectivity. Clark, philosopher and cognitive scientist, advocates the fundamental embeddedness of an organism within its context and holds that

> what matters are the complex feedback loops that connect action-commands, bodily motions, environmental effects, and multisensory perceptual inputs. It is the two-way flow of influence between the brain, body, and world that matters, and on the basis of which we construct (and constantly re-construct) our sense of self, potential, and presence. The biological skin-bag [alone] has no special significance here. It is the flow that counts. (114)

The flow of the network facilitates a creative process that shapes the identities of its actors as well as brings forth the footage. When Stella explains, Nora "is here, when she is working. . . . When she is not working, she is not here" (313), this foregrounds how Nora only exists in process. Without the interconnection with, for instance, the editing equipment, her subjectivity lacks all expression. In the continuous process of "mouse-click. Zoom. Into image-grain. Some quick adjustments. Clicks. Out of zoom" (314), Nora is in a state of *unique mattering*.

Moreover, disability—when understood as a fixed and unchanging state—is no longer a productive category to assess Nora's mode of non-normative embodiment. Shildrick and Price go against the general assumption that "disability is a fixed and unchanging state which pre-exists its observation" in stating that "not only is disability a fluid set of conditions but . . . the body itself is always in process" (102). The disabled body is a "material site of possibility where de-formations, 'missing' parts and prosthesis are enablers of new channels of desiring production unconstrained by predetermined—or at least normative—organization" (Shildrick, "Prosthetic Performativity" 122). In Nora's case, the shrapnel creates a universe. "A universe comes into being," mathematician and philosopher George Spencer-Brown explains in *Laws of Form*, "when a space is severed" (v). The cut, however, somewhat paradoxically, does not separate her lobes but enables novel ways of mediation between them initiating the extensive relations and facilitating the connections that become the very fabric of her subjectivity. The insertion of the T-shaped piece of metal significantly contributes to the emergence of something "entirely new." The footage creates, as Cayce explains, "that sense of . . . I don't know. Of an opening into something. Universe? Narrative?" (112).

On Productivity

If we consider Cayce's allergies as a form of nonnormative embodiment, then both main characters in *Pattern Recognition* appear as disabled figures that sometimes complement one another, and sometimes serve as counterparts. While Cayce's reactivity is congenital and proof of phenotypic plasticity, Nora's paraplegia is acquired and a condition strongly associated with stasis and passivity. Cayce travels all over the globe, constantly on the move, whereas Nora is stationed in, and never leaves, Russia. As the entire narrative is presented from Cayce's point of view, it is her subjectivity that is actively explored, meanwhile rendering Nora, who is only introduced in the final chapters, invisible. Regarding Cayce's extraordinary talent it is worth noting that it is her economic success that allows her integration into society despite her pathologies. Through the successful commodification of her disposition, she is consistently reduced to her economic function as "human litmus paper": "Cayce, with her marketable allergy, has been brought over to do in person the thing that she does best" (10). What Cayce does is pattern recognition, and whatever she spots as cool gets "produced. Turned into units. Marketed" (88) As a result, her work informs the globalized landscape to an extent similar to how far the latter affects her. Cayce's success founded on the vacillation between allergy and talent makes her "a secret legend in the world of marketing"

(67). Nora, on the other hand, herself a secret legend, is completely un-coupled from the process of commodification. Her productivity is understood as purely artistic.

While the commodification of bodies serves as the ultimate escape from or compensation for disability in Gibson's early novels and is still present in the depiction of Cayce, this pattern changes with regard to Nora. Here the turn from disability to talent is not fulfilled on the basis of economic success. If it were not for her twin sister, the world would not know about Nora's video clips: "My sister, she is the artist. I, I am what? The distributer. The one who finds an audience. It is not so great a talent, I know" (296). While Nora produces the clips, the footage would not exist without Stella.

Even more poignantly and explicitly than in any of Gibson's previous novels, disability in *Pattern Recognition* presents itself affirmatively, less than ever before in need of resolution via rehabilitation or enhancement. Corporeal wholeness is unmasked as an illusion. As if in explicit recognition of this shift Neil Easterbrook comments: "In the recent work Gibson has refused all evasive alibis and instead confronted both characters and readers with authentic, because unresolved, problematic[s]" (57). Problematized but unresolved, Gibson's nonnormative bodies disclose their dynamic and complex materiality and can be understood in a constant process of *unique mattering*.

NOTES

I would like to thank my friends and colleagues Eleana Vaja and Moritz Ingwersen for their invaluable feedback on this essay.

1. See, for instance, Mitchell and Snyder, *The Biopolitics of Disability* or Wald-schmidt, Berressem, and Ingwersen, *Culture—Theory—Disability*.

2. Bennett draws on a plethora of philosophers to develop the idea of "vibrant matter" in a politico-philosophical take on materiality. Indebted to the critical vitalists Hans Driesch and Henri Bergson, who provide a vocabulary to address the power and drive, productivity and creativity inherent to matter, Bennett develops her own, more radical, conceptualization. She explains: "While Driesch does not go as far as I do toward a materialist ontology, he does insist that the 'vital principle' has absolutely no existence independent of 'physio-chemical' matter. He makes the relationship between matter and life as close as it possibly can be while still retaining the distinction. . . . he pushes the life-matter binary to the limit, even though at the very last minute, he draws back from taking the plunge into a materiality that is *itself* vibrant or active" ("Vitalist Stopover" 49).

3. Having only partial control over one's body and surroundings can be described, in the words of Karin Harrasser, as being "semi-sovereign" (*Körper* 112). In *Körper 2.0*,

Harrasser's criticism of the neoliberal ideology of the continuous improvement of the body builds on Latour's actor-network theory. The "semisovereign body" serves as an alternative concept to the neoliberal myth that all bodies are principally equal and differentiated by individual performance depending on individual willpower. The emphasis on how bodies are embedded in an infinite meshwork of supraindividual processes and power relations is central to her argument. (117). Nobody and nothing decides self-determinately for their exact enmeshment in a particular network. It is always partially active and partially passive processes that interlock when somebody or something acts (125). See also Harrasser, "Superhumans."

4. In *Idoru* (1996), for instance, it is only at the end of the novel that by a sudden revelation protagonist Chia McKenzie learns about the identity of her virtual friend, Zona Rosa. Whereas Zona, the avatar of Mexican girl Mercedes Purissima, has all along codetermined the action, her identity through a form of narrative repression remains hidden until the sudden revelation of her deformities and reclusive life at the end of the novel.

WORKS CITED

Bennett, Jane. *Vibrant Matter: A Political Ecology of Things*. Duke UP, 2010.
Bennett, Jane. "A Vitalist Stopover on the Way to a New Materialism." *New Materialisms: Ontology, Agency, and Politics*, edited by Diana H. Coole and Samantha Frost, Duke UP, 2010, pp. 47–69.
Clark, Andy. *Natural-Born Cyborgs: Minds, Technologies, and the Future of Human Intelligence*. Oxford UP, 2004.
Coole, Diana H., and Samantha Frost, editors. *New Materialisms: Ontology, Agency, and Politics*. Duke UP, 2010.
Davis, Lennard J., editor. *The Disability Studies Reader*. Routledge, 2006.
Easterbrook, Neil. "Recognizing Patterns: Gibson's Hermeneutics from the Bridge Trilogy to 'Pattern Recognition.'" *Beyond Cyberpunk: New Critical Perspectives*, edited by Graham J. Murphy and Sherryl Vint, Routledge, 2010, pp. 46–64.
Garland-Thomson, Rosemarie. *Staring: How We Look*. Oxford UP, 2009.
Gibson, William. *Idoru*. Viking, 1996.
Gibson, William. *Pattern Recognition*. Putnam, 2003.
Gibson, William. *Virtual Light*. Bantam Books, 1993.
Harrasser, Karin. *Körper 2.0: Über die Technische Erweiterbarkeit des Menschen*. Transcript, 2013.
Harrasser, Karin. "Superhumans—Parahumans: Disability and Hightech in Competitive Sports." *Culture—Theory—Disability: Encounters between Disability Studies and Cultural Studies*, edited by Anne Waldschmidt, Hanjo Berressem, and Moritz Ingwersen, Transcript, 2017, pp. 171–84.
Hollinger, Veronica. "Stories about the Future: From Patterns of Expectation to Pattern Recognition." *Science Fiction Studies*, vol. 33, no. 3, 2006, pp. 452–72.
Jameson, Fredric. "Fear and Loathing in Globalization." *New Left Review*, vol. 23, Sept.–Oct. 2003, pp. 105–14.
Mitchell, David T., and Sharon L. Snyder. *Narrative Prosthesis: Disability and the Dependencies of Discourse*. U of Michigan P, 2001.

Mitchell, David T., and Sharon L. Snyder. *The Biopolitics of Disability: Neoliberalism, Ablenationalism, and Peripheral Embodiment*. U of Michigan P, 2015.

Nigianni, Chrysanthi, and Merl Storr. *Deleuze and Queer Theory*. Edinburgh UP, 2009.

Shildrick, Margrit. "Beyond the Body of Bioethics." *Ethics of the Body: Postconventional Challenges*, edited by Margrit Shildrick and Roxanne Mykitiuk. MIT P, 2005, pp. 1–28.

Shildrick, Margrit. "Border Crossings: The Technologies of Disability and Desire." *Culture—Theory—Disability: Encounters between Disability Studies and Cultural Studies*, edited by Anne Waldschmidt, Hanjo Berressem, and Moritz Ingwersen, Transcript, 2017, pp. 137–51.

Shildrick, Margrit. "Prosthetic Performativity: Deleuzian Connections and Queer Corporealities." *Deleuze and Queer Theory*, edited by Chrysanthi Nigianni and Merl Storr, Edinburgh UP, 2005, pp. 115–33.

Shildrick, Margrit, and Janet Price. "Breaking the Boundaries of the Broken Body." *Body & Society*, vol. 2, no. 4, 1996, pp. 93–113.

Siebers, Tobin. "Disability in Theory: From Social Constructivism to the New Realism of the Body." *The Disability Studies Reader*, edited by Lennard Davis, Routledge, 2006, pp. 173–84.

Spencer-Brown, George. *Laws of Form*. Allen & Unwin, 1969.

Waldschmidt, Anne, Hanjo Berressem, and Moritz Ingwersen, editors. *Culture—Theory—Disability: Encounters between Disability Studies and Cultural Studies*. Transcript, 2017.

Part II
The Matter of Meaning

Hannah Weiner's Transversal Poetics

Collaboration, Disability, and Clairvoyance

Patrick Durgin

> I wanted to create the feeling that people all over the world were
> doing a related thing at a related time, although they would be doing
> it individually, without an audience and without knowledge of what
> others were doing. It is an act of faith. We have unknown
> collaborators.
>
> —Hannah Weiner, "World Works" (1970)

Hannah Weiner (1928–1997) was an artist and poet whose best-known work
was conditioned by and often directly about her experience of schizophrenia, or, as she put it, "clairvoyance," which manifests mainly as hallucinated
or "seen words." This essay is about her collaborations, which I read as "encounters." Gilles Deleuze developed a theory of such encounters as "a technique of contriving, and yet improvising each detail. The opposite of a pla-
giarist, but also the opposite of a master." He claimed that a collaborator
could be virtual or actual: "Having a bag into which I put everything I encounter, provided that I am also put in a bag" (Deleuze and Parnet 6–8). As
a historian of philosophy whose most important articulations of his own
philosophy were written in collaboration, he had experience with both. As
did Weiner. In reading these encounters, I shall make claims about ways in
which disability studies can gain from new materialism, and develop an understanding of new materialism informed by the concept of transversality.
However, in pairing the Deleuze-Guattarian backstory of new materialist
theory with Weiner's practice of experimental collaborative writing, I shall
not claim a transparent correspondence. I rather wish to elucidate the ob-
scurities involved, as essential features of Weiner's self-diagnosis. We cannot

expect to see Deleuze and Guattari's version of the experience of schizophrenia in her claims to clairvoyance because schizophrenia is for them a product of the systemic concealment of experience itself, by a normative "order of reasons" lodged like a command within subjectivity. We will see how Weiner's efforts to reveal and share her experience illustrate the dilemmas to which "schizoanalysis" responds.

Neurodiversity is increasingly, if often elliptically, evoked in both critical surveys and specific arguments currently defining posthumanist neomaterialism. Steven Shaviro and Erin Manning point to autistic phenomenality, Manning to theorize Deleuze and Guattari's theory of minority-becoming as an aesthetic practice, and Shaviro to argue that only the aesthetic can operate in a milieu "unfit for cognition" (Shaviro 131–33). For these writers, neurodiversity exemplifies the becomings of the body as the sort of pure immanence first explored in schizoanalysis, a critique built on a theory of transversality. Object-oriented ontologists like Graham Harman critique such "relational metaphysics" by treating "relations adequately as new compound objects," Harman's objection to transversal theories of matter being that "pure immanence cannot account for change, and therefore lead[ing] to the notion that what is currently expressed in the world is all the world has to offer" (17, 33). In "Systems and Things," Jane Bennett shows how Harman still relies on a theory of relationality, "locat[ing] activity in the relationships themselves" (230). Warren Neidich, meanwhile, develops a notion of "neuropower" to extend the critique of biopower as a detrimental imbalance between "machine intelligence" and sites of "decisions . . . made for an active body projected into the future" through emancipatory contingencies of avant-garde artistic practice (136). I wish to inform and extend these debates by reading Weiner's clairvoyant collaborations as a nonnormative, positive form of sociality, though in all of her work she focused on the social mechanisms influencing the distinctions made between looking and reading, and for this and other reasons long associated with Language poets, her work was removed from the *Norton Anthology of Postmodern American Poetry* when the second edition appeared. Just as the consistency and richness of such a project is vouchsafed to posterity, her purposiveness and continuity must qualify the single best-known "fact" about her: that she was schizophrenic. This I will do to render that social fact a "critical concept that reveals the structure of dependence inherent to all human societies" (Siebers, unpaginated). In an inventory of the New York poetry and "happenings" scene of the 1960s, Fluxus composer Philip Corner suggests that Weiner's primarily linguistic relationship to her body provided the groundwork for Yvonne Rainer's early work (Bergé). Yet her goal, in her own words, was to "show the mind" by securing "a detail watch over [her] body" (*The Fast* 36). Weiner presents clairvoyance as an impairment as much as a mode of access. Disruptive neuroactive forces bear upon dexterity and mobility, while triggering heightened sensitivity to otherwise materially withheld aspects of life, and experience is the nexus of these mutually ramifying series of events. That clairvoyance is an exclusive, though not individual, capacity allows her to portray it as a kind of visuality without perpetuating ocularcentric assumptions, for instance, that what you mean should be *apparent* to me. This does not preclude our successful interdependence, however. Instead, it affirms it in and as difference. Insofar as her methods evoke the recently revived problem of the status of embodied experience in speculative realist strains such as new materialism and object-oriented ontology, as well as critiques of "biopower" and neurotypicality in disability studies, I want to recall the Deleuzian backstory in this regard.

I.

Although notorious, the Deleuze-Guattari method of schizoanalysis, developed in *Anti-Oedipus* (1972), is poorly understood without the conceptual term "transversality," developed in the clinical practice Guattari undertook in the field of institutional psychotherapy. And without some understanding of transversality, the relevance of Deleuze and Guattari's work to disability studies remains obscure. Schizoanalysis is the term Deleuze and Guattari gave to a critical method aimed at the obscure yet effective collusion of psychoanalysis with capitalism. They described it as a quality of attention to the mechanics of society rather than interpretative dynamics of an individual, famously claiming that if you want to know how a system works, look at where it breaks down.

As Guattari scholar Gary Genosko puts it, transversality entails "intersubjectivity" insofar as it is "engaged by non-subjective arrangements, extra-human and non-organic components not necessarily available for interpretation" (48). Guattari realized that psychiatric institutions (and psychiatry itself) *required* the *persistence* of psychological illness, and this reinforced the hierarchy descending from doctors to staff to patients, even at La Borde, the rural clinic and residence Guattari and Jean Oury directed for most of their careers. This hierarchy, reinforced at the climax of the talking cure by the moment of "transference," systematized and rehearsed the relation of punishment to a lack that Freud described as the Oedipus complex. So Guattari worked out a "grid" to reattribute and constantly shift the tasks of everyone at the clinic, from the janitor to the executive director, to the patients themselves.

These aren't reversals, but *trans*versals in that the shifts don't turn things on their heads, merely playing the same hierarchy upside down. Transversal relations have the benefit of disclosing habits as symptoms of a larger, malignant order, a "group fantasy," as Guattari called it, that was historically determined rather than led by the economy of desires structuring denizens' lives. The concept contrasts against the articulatory practice of diagnosis, a minimal obligation of Guattari's profession. Diagnosis affects "incorporeal transformations," those permutations of bodies by civic discourse, by the "order word," marking the body as lawfully wedded to another, as criminal, as educated, and so on. When a language is absorbed, a whole "order of reasons" is inherited and is forever redundantly announced in the disguise of thought or expression (*A Thousand Plateaus* 86–88, 170). The grid is meant to open the psyche to its outside and make power responsible to multiple subjective configurations, forces, and objects (the institution itself, ultimately). Neither an act of metaphoric substitution nor a performative reversal—much less a transgressive appropriation—transversality is a conceptual alternative to oppositions of all kinds. Deleuze and Guattari even say transversality is a new "image of thought" (*What Is Philosophy?* 37).

Contemporary writer and artist Emily Roysdon makes the point that "those of us who [do] identity politics . . . [want] them to be unstable and intersectional categories. But they're not used that way against us" (272). Deleuze would say, "We said the same thing about becomings: it is not one term that encounters the other, but each encounters the other, a single becoming [is] something between the two, outside the two, and which flows in another direction" (Deleuze and Parnet 6–7). A direction that is neither nor both is transversal. The opening lines of *A Thousand Plateaus* put it another way: "The two of us wrote *Anti-Oedipus* together. Since each of us was several, there was already quite a crowd. . . . We are no longer ourselves. Each will know his own. We have been aided, inspired, multiplied" (3). The connective tissue between these two volumes of their *Capitalism and Schizophrenia* series thus extends their notion of schizoanalysis, but it is also the point at which the "schizo" trope is dropped (the term being used only a small handful of times in the second book) in favor of less controversial tropes. Yet part of the problem in deriving useful models from Deleuze and Guattari remains the way specific disciplinary differences between their contributions are obscured when projected onto a more capacious tropic of "rhizomatic" difference. Another part of the same problem is simply the perpetuation of these tropics.

Which brings me to another problem: the love/hate relationship that disability studies seems to have with Deleuze-Guattarian thought.[1] One of the best-known critiques of schizoanalysis in disability studies is Catherine Prendergast's participant-observer-style work "The Unexceptional Schizophrenic," wherein she entertains a comparative reading of Deleuze and Guattari's *A Thousand Plateaus* and a passage from Avital Ronell's *The Telephone Book*, then with a passage in a letter from Barbara, "a friend who'd been diagnosed and institutionalized as schizophrenic" (56). I say *entertains* because Barbara and Catherine together decided not to offer the comparison for the risk of reifying medical and legal dictates, that is to avoid "selective appropriation" (56). The upshot, according to Prendergast, is that "to be disabled mentally is to be disabled rhetorically. [Barbara's] definition of disability she has phrased at times as 'a life denied significance'" (57). Prendergast marks the closing of a rhetorical "distance" posited by minority "identity work" with "an increasingly public citizenry of schizophrenics who . . . claim the right to unexceptional instability, which is not something postmodern theory has readily granted them" by "metaphorizing schizophrenia" and thus taking "rhetorical ownership" of it, rendering their own figures of liberation from the cogito a cliché (57). Yet for Deleuze and Guattari, the "schizo" is by no means visible, cut off from reality, or "subsumed by the rhizome." All of Prendergast's assumptions regarding their work are uninformed in this regard.

First, she misreads Deleuze and Guattari's line, "We have never seen [a schizophrenic]" (*Anti-Oedipus* 380). Guattari, whom she barely acknowledges lived with and cared for schizophrenic patients daily, elsewhere clarified the matter: "Within the framework of repressive hospitalization, you don't have access to schizophrenia. You have access to mental patients locked in a system that prevents them from expressing the very essence of madness. They express only a reaction to the repression to which they are subjected, which they are forced to endure" (Deleuze and Guattari, "Capitalism and Schizophrenia" 234). Deleuze adds that under this systemic duress, one is "without any epistemological guarantee, [and so] sticks closely to reality and this reality causes him to move . . . [so if] people in the human sciences and in politics should, in a sense, go a little schizo," this would not mean "embrac[ing] that illusory image which the schizophrenic gives us when he is trapped in repression" (236). He is describing the illusory image Prendergast traces, inexplicably, back to Deleuze and

Guattari, rather than the system they were fighting from within. "I hear the objection," Deleuze writes elsewhere,

> with your puny sympathy you make use of lunatics, you sing the praises of madness, then you drop them, you only go so far. . . . This is not true. We are trying to extract from love all possession, all identification to become capable of loving. We are trying to extract from madness the life which it contains, while hating the lunatics who constantly kill life. (Deleuze and Parnet 53, 66)

So far from rhetorical ownership, in fact the schizoanalytic project is an attack on ableists, eugenicists, and lobotomists—not to mention bourgeois psychotherapists. "No one has the right," said Deleuze, "to deride or treat with flippancy the fact that the tearing open, the breach [or schism, schiz] slips into or coincides with a kind of collapse. This danger," he warns, "must be considered fundamental" (Deleuze and Guattari, "Capitalism and Schizophrenia" 240). Because it comes "at what price? The price of a collapse that must be qualified as schizophrenic. The breakthrough and the breakdown are two different moments. It would be irresponsible to turn a blind eye to the danger" (240).[2] And although Deleuze suggests that despite the unknown cost, the risk is "worth it," Guattari responds by calling the potential gain a sort of articulation normally denied to madness. "The practice of institutional psychotherapy" aim[s] to place "the schizophrenic . . . in a 'clairvoyant' situation with respect to those individuals who, crystallized in their logic, in their syntax, in their own interests, are absolutely blind" (241).

There is neither claim to ownership nor romanticization here. And though Deleuze will quip that "real and pretend schizophrenics are giving me such a hard time that I'm starting to see the attractions of paranoia" (*Negotiations* 3), the important thing here is acknowledging that transversality of the "real and [the] pretend" is an a priori condition of rhetorical power, rather than an abuse of it. "Transversal relations . . . ensure that any effects produced in some particular way . . . can always be produced by other means. . . . Who's to say I can't talk about medicine unless I'm a doctor, if I talk about it like a dog? . . . why shouldn't I invent some way, however fantastic and contrived, of talking about something, without someone having to ask whether I'm qualified to talk like that? . . . Arguments from one's own privileged experience are bad and reactionary arguments. My favorite sentence in *Anti-Oedipus* is: 'No, we've never seen a schizophrenic'" *Negotiations* 11–12).[3]

Guattari wrote the first drafts of what became *Anti-Oedipus* while first working on alternatives to the "bi-univocalizing psychic causality" of psychoanalysis:

> If you immerse schizos full time in the police-like environment produced by nurses and hospital institutions, you end up, obviously, with the kind of description of schizophrenia that we are very accustomed to. . . . At La Borde . . . you have the production of some group drive—group Eros. But for a singular—transversalized—group. . . . The point is not to put the schizo candidate back into his body, but to produce an other subjectivity. (*Anti-Œdipus Papers* 145)

Deleuze scholar Aidan Tynan points out that, for his part, "Deleuze regretted" the perception that they had "idealize[d] the schizophrenic," "insisting that he and Guattari 'never stopped opposing the schizophrenic process to the repressive hospital type'" when what they set out to do was to "distinguish schizophrenia as a pathological product from schizophrenia as a nonpathological process" (51). Tynan emphasizes how reversible the terms really are, hence the need for an alternate logic, when the going routines "end up being unable to present the history of desire except as the reproduction of the social or else as a pathology that refers us back to infantile revolts against socialization" (55). Every dichotomy devolves upon and restricts "the schizo candidate," who can't win because, basically, they are not a subject at all, but an ideal object. In Angela Woods's mercifully even-handed reading of *Anti-Oedipus*, she calls the "hospital type . . . product" of psychoanalysis "the interruption of schizophrenia-as-process; the outcome of trying and failing to break through social and psychic repression" (149). Woods elucidates the distinction Deleuze and Guattari develop between categories of paranoia, schizophrenia, and "schizo." The last of these is the equivalent of self-determination, creative becoming, and the "immediate" connection to "the political" that they will later claim to characterize minority identity (*Kafka*). In Woods's account, "'the schizophrenic' is 'the schizo' who has been re-absorbed or trapped in the capitalist system" (149). At the same time, she questions whether their extreme "micro-politics" doesn't necessarily hinder "collective and individual political action," since it is left to the singularity of unmediated and ultimately inscrutable madness to "reconstitute social, psychic, and organizational boundaries" (149).[4]

Like Woods, Ronald Bogue questions Deleuze-Guattari models of intersubjectivity for their ability to foster "collective political action" (98). But unlike Woods, Bogue surveys the philosophical precedents of these tropes (102–3). Among the most important elucidations Bogue offers concerns the trope of "molecular" politics, typically opposed to the "molar" movement of a majority language, science, or geographical organization (the "nomadic war-machine" versus the "sedentary state"). Bogue explains that the distinction is not "about actual physical scale but about qualitatively different processes that take place at all levels of social interaction," and that the term "molecular" modifies political becomings as "decentered, multivalent" (103). This is a remnant of Georges Canguilhem's oft-cited theory of the *Normal and the Pathological*: "There is no such thing as abnormal, if by the term we mean merely the absence of a previous positive condition or state" (110). Every pathological state "has its norms," and so, as molar politics represent and reinforce these by definition and demonstration, the normal state of affairs is as "pathological" as the biological object is elastic, degenerative, creative, always in "sympathy . . . with" others (110, 109).

Deleuze and Guattari, then, not only critique psychoanalytic institutions on the level of precepts and methods, but critique capitalism for its complicity with the outer reaches of psychiatric practice, its most "sublime" (to use Woods's term) objects. But they don't stop there. One necessary result of transversality is a way to approach seemingly inscrutable aesthetic procedures, poetics or ways of making that are relatively imperceptible because they follow a milieu logic that won't respond to our habits of attribution: attribution of skill, craft, invention, and style. In their chapter "The Transversality of New Materialism," Rick Dolphijn and Iris van der Tuin make some headway in this direction by showing how "new materialism is itself . . . a device or tool for opening up theory formation" (100–101). Dolphijn and Tuin argue that new materialism is properly transversal only when it "emerges *from* a discipline" (101).

An exemplary effort of this kind is linguist Mel Y. Chen's book *Animacies*, which draws from disability studies and queer-of-color criticism, but emerges *from* linguistics. Chen develops transversal concepts: "transobjectivity" and "transcorporeality" in the context of toxins and by analogy with invisible disabilities like madness (200–206). Chen writes an ontology of "proximal relations" mediated by "how holistically you are interpreted and how dynamic you are perceived to be" (210). Yet she also worries that Deleuze and Guattari's precedent is likely to devolve into "mere metaphors" that obscure "a certain concrete reality" (206). Still, her project remains to complicate such certainty. This is why and how "animacy" means grammatical agency, critically, "purposefully suspend[ing]" the materiality of "verbal particles" (7–9, 206).[5] When disability theory works on issues of prosthesis, for example, it anticipates Chen's recourse to iterability in a mode that signals nonnormative positivism. Here we might consider Vivian Sobchack's critique of the "metaphorical (and, dare I say, ethical) displacement of the prosthetic through a return to its premises in live-body experience" (18). A harsh critic of new materialism, Graham Harman offers, as a figure for the displacement of disease onto diagnostic regimes, "synecdoche," a whole-part relation of metonymic substitution that expresses "symbiosis" rather than immanence (43, 50). For Sobchack, in her account of using a prosthetic leg, there is both an "oppositional tension and a dynamic connection," "a material but also a phenomenologically lived . . . pragmatics" that governs these discursive practices. The milieu, or "ensemble" logic of lived experience, she describes as "like the turns and effects of language in use," in other words contingent upon "the nature of my engagements with others," producing a "dynamic and situated but also ambiguous and graded" relationality (26–27). A nonnormative positivism of madness would have to square iterative and positive modes by, as Bradley Lewis has convincingly argued, "connect[ing] a rhetorical discussion of [the institution] with the literature on 'models of madness,'" something I have attempted elsewhere and will extend here (107).[6] Pathologies are treated as a site of "enhancement" rather than being subjected to dualisms like "normality and pathology," in a biopolitical economy constantly buying and selling personhood on the marketplace (Lewis 90). It is this reduction to the physical in tandem with psychochemical alteration that demands a thoroughgoing aesthetics to offset the phenomenological givens such market laws entail.

This is why seeking Weiner's voice as an authoritative narrator of the experience of schizophrenia would be a bit like disinterring Barbara's voice from Catherine Prendergast's critique of metaphor—both would rely on metaphoric substitution. The theory of transversality lends conceptual nuance to the act of substitution and allows us to reexamine appropriation and transgressive appropriation alike, body/mind, relation/object, the very binaries that the revival of materialism is now negotiating. Countercultural reverse paradigms promise to overwhelm, overthrow, and overcome. But, overturning's turn was over by 1972—the year of *Anti-Oedipus* and *Unnatural Acts*—the first of the Weiner texts I will discuss below—so it is not enough to "deconstruct" these features of minoritarian, critical theory formation. As early as 1964, Guattari presented "transversality" as a question of appellation and rhetorical authority for a "political group condemned by history" (16), which unfolds as a fraught, dramatic collaboration with the material conditions of nominalization, every act defying the nature of self-expression, the nature of the medium, by finally doing no more than staking a claim on the definition of the word.[7] This act of definition is not an act of substitution of signifiers nor a materialization of the signified. And so we will not see Weiner's minority experience emerge in a Deleuze-Guattarian fashion. Minority is that which cannot take a state form, according to Deleuze and Guattari[8]—just as we never hear from Barbara, though in this case for a very different reason. Transversality is less a bulwark against misidentification than it is an acknowledgment of the generative potential of disidentification. Rather than "cripping" poetics, these unnatural acts are, naturally enough, material transversals.

II.

Elsewhere (Durgin 2006, 2009) I have argued that psychosocial disability is the decisive factor when we talk about the body, an aboutness whose fissures are lodged in questions of intentionality made only more obvious by the case of Weiner's clairvoyance. Clairvoyance is a trope with deep roots in the myth of the mad genius of letters, yet with a singularly original and influential potential to address questions of poetics. Clairvoyance is either an extraordinary power gained through a struggle to overcome mental illness, or it is a poetic form, "clair style" writing (Durgin 2004, 2014). Either way one tropes the phenomenon begs the question of language's materiality. Like the burden and privilege of seeing words, clairvoyance mitigates how one chooses to exert one's will; it matters. Its conceptual purchase on self-determination is most vivid when obstructions present or capacities withhold themselves. In Weiner's case, this acute materiality of the signifier appealed to and complicated Language poetry's materialist project; Weiner was long remembered primarily as a Language poet, but lately the neglected affectivity of clairvoyance is being increasingly addressed. This shift is in small part due to the renewed attention to her work caused by the publication of *Hannah Weiner's Open House*. Maria Damon's review of that book claims Weiner as "a spiritual ancestor—a 'page mother'—of many writers and aspiring creative women now, myself included, but there has persisted a stigma or stain of craziness surrounding single women who are creatively unorthodox, and in some ways underneath the admiration is a kind of fear, as if she were a cautionary tale about disoriented-because-unattached female vision-creators" (unpaginated).

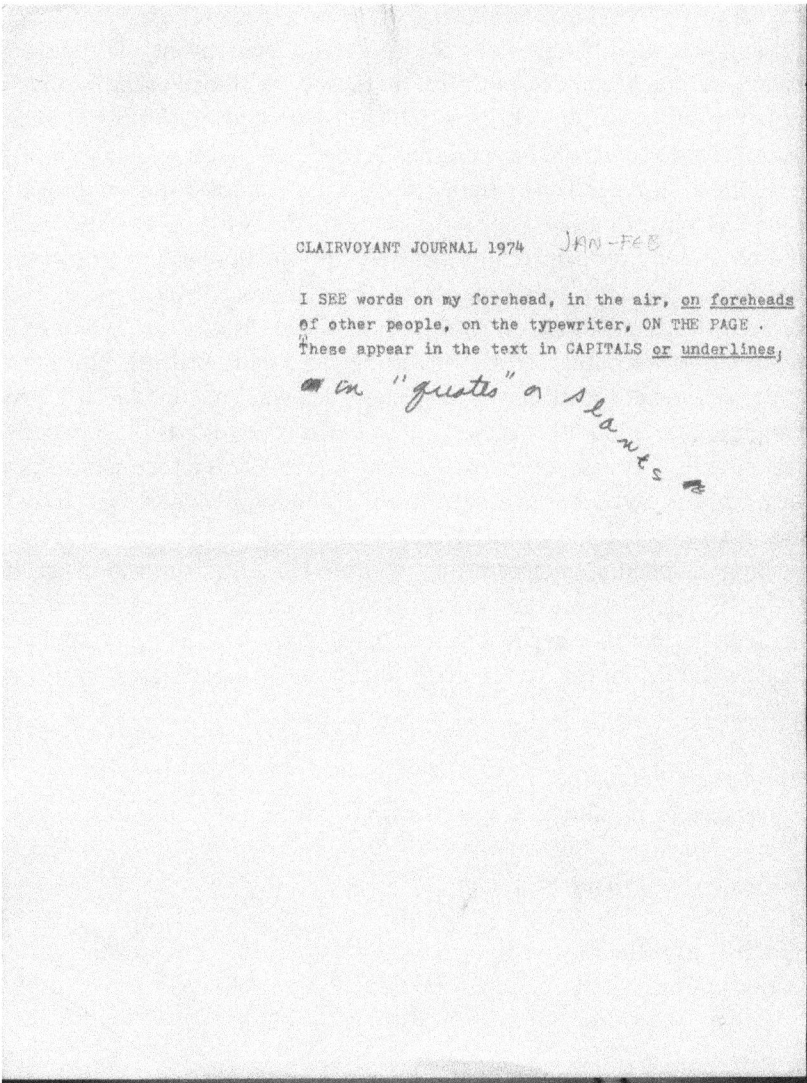

CLAIRVOYANT JOURNAL 1974   JAN-FEB

I SEE words on my forehead, in the air, on foreheads
of other people, on the typewriter, ON THE PAGE .
These appear in the text in CAPITALS or underlines,
or in "quotes" or slants

Fig. 1. *Clairvoyant Journal*, 1974. Image courtesy of the Archive for New Poetry, University of California, San Diego.

After spending the greater part of the 1960s involved with experiments in concrete, proprioceptive, and conceptualist writing, performance, and intermedia art, Weiner became a regular at the St. Mark's Church in the Bowery, programmed by the new Poetry Project, meeting and impressing important poets like John Ashbery, Ted Berrigan, Jackson Mac Low, and Bernadette Mayer. From the mid-1970s onward, Weiner referred to herself as "clairvoyant" because she claimed to see words;[9] and she is best known for semiautobiographical works she also called "clairvoyant," written in a "clair-style" that would capture the many voices (mostly seen but also heard) in her mind or field of vision. Her best-known work is entitled *Clairvoyant Journal*, and it is prefaced as shown in figure 1.

In creating typescripts from her original notebooks, she would continue to see words and attempt to capture them on the page—type them into place—and developed a format based on the options her typewriter offered her: regular roman type for her "own," nonseen voice, ALL CAPS for seen words, and *italics*/<u>underlines</u> for the words of a third voice that mediated between the other two during the typing process. The third voice hectors her sometimes. Sometimes it is a voice of conscience. Often it attempts to fill in for the gaps produced as new words arrived so rapidly that a thought, phrase, or even a word had to be left as a fragment before the next took over, as we will see shortly. Weiner understood by clairvoyance as much an impairing disadvantage as a skill to be mastered. In transforming the phenomenon of seeing words to her advantage, the advice of Robert Creeley—whom she met and heard speak at the Berkeley Poetry Conference in 1965—appears pivotal. She relays in a letter to Michael Heller several "quotes" which are probably more paraphrases, from his lecture there:

> language as activity
> engaged by the situation of your own needs
> . . .
> create your own environment
> . . .
> words have their own reality
> everything is literal
> activity as writing, not as writing can tell about it.
> . . .
> how shall we have that possibility of what we are (not a description)

The list can be read syllogistically, but then it ends with a paradox in that the self and the "environment" are mutually referential and even mutually constitutive of the "real" in the "literal" fact of "language." Language offers itself as material in two ways: iterative and positive. "Writing that can tell about" things reiterates them in *its* capacity to possess *its* "own" thingness, its objective fact, which is none other than "activity." Language might *de*scribe. But then it could *in*scribe everything; Creeley's example suggests it must.

The logic Creeley is using and the work he was already doing goes like this: activity *posits* as it *transposes* itself in what we do with language: "writing." The inevitable motion and the motivating consciousness are taken together to be the sole material "reality"—in the virtual sense of intension and the actual sense of extension. Here is transversality *avant la lettre*: a new materialism of relationality that would present itself as so many exceptions to collusion (hence the emphasis on "your own"), and therefore as collaboration (hence the "possibility of what we are"). There is a sense in which the polyvocality of clairvoyant writing depicts collaboration among "levels" of the mind, each with its "own" authorial "environment," yet all under the sign of one proper name, "Hannah Weiner." The positive epistemological value implied by Weiner's claim that these ecstatic, hallucinatory textual conditions were a "power" of "awareness and communication" ("Awareness and Communication") permits her to affirm the value of another lifeworld beyond the normate. For Weiner, artistic collaboration was a non-normative, positive form of sociality, but an immanent position of discrepancy and difference rather than a pageant of congruency. This is what Deleuze would call the "logic of sensation," according to which "sight discovers in itself a specific function of touch that is uniquely its own, distinct from its optical function" (Bacon 125). I will critically contrast two such collaborations for the remainder of this section.

Unnatural Acts was a short-lived mimeograph magazine of collaborative writing edited and published by Bernadette Mayer and Ed Friedman between 1972 and 1973. Each issue gathered together poets involved with the Poetry Project and students from Mayer's ongoing workshops held there. The second issue was written on November 11, 1972, by Joe Ceravalo, Rosemary Ceravalo, Peggy de Coursey, Friedman, Yancy Gerber, John Giorno, Kevin Kerr, Mayer, Ann Powell, Anne Waldman, and Hannah Weiner. Friedman recalled that *Unnatural Acts* was intended "to compress the collaboration process" and designed as "a present-time document of the writer's mind while writing"; the eleven writers present for the second issue wrote "in the same place for an extended time period [logged in one-, two-, five-, or ten-minute increments in the magazine, as a running tally between the texts]" (Kane 199). The process was narrated as taking place in this manner by Friedman:

> Everyone anonymously contributed a piece of writing, which someone else in the group used as the basis for composing a new work. The "originals" were then discarded and the afternoon proceeded

> with everyone continuing to write works inspired by the rework-
> ings of reworkings of reworkings. (Kane 199)

Friedman's scare quotes around *originals* signal the ambition to challenge "the conventional view of writing as expression naturally unique to a solitary individual," and to "undermine normative and essentialist assumptions about what made a writer a writer and about what it meant to 'own' one's own writing" (200). These are literary historian Daniel Kane's words—and it should be appreciated that in assessing the results, Kane also has recourse to scare quotes, not only because he concurs, nor necessarily because the endeavor succeeds, but because the procedure sets up a hall-of-mirrors effect whose cause is harder to specify. The editors' logic in staging the experiment and presenting its results is clarified by statements on the cover of certain copies of the magazine. A "process" statement explains that each participant was to bring one "solid" piece of finished writing; these were placed in a stack and others would randomly pick one up and rework or respond to it; these originals, the putatively "natural" originals, were then discarded; the responses then were responded to in like fashion, saving only these proliferated, secondary documents, which were compiled chronologically into the magazine. Another way they put it is offered thus: "Whoever *you* are, that pushes me into the chaos of your own invention."

However, some copies of the magazine replaced these process statements with photos of World War II soldiers trudging back from the front across a barren battlefield, tanks in the distance, a clutch of captured enemy soldiers with their hands upon their heads looking off at their captors out of frame. And on the back cover is a wraparound shot of ecstatic civilians waving from a roped-off sidewalk, presumably to a parade, with the caption, "The liberation of Paris was the most unforgettable day in the world." The images of defeat, desolation, liberation, and euphoria link *Unnatural Acts* to a lineage of high-modernist, avant-garde collaboration, especially the technique of "exquisite corpse," reading the substitution of the images for an editorial statement as the New York school's liberation of surrealism from the dustbin of history. Unlike in a collaboration whose authors are clearly attributed,[10] *Unnatural Acts'* deliberately organized version of partial anonymity grants participants semi-omniscience. In an exquisite corpse, *no one* knows what *everyone* is in on. The work is paradoxically overdetermined and undermined, like the writing in *Unnatural Acts*.

Recently I had the opportunity to ask Mayer about *Unnatural Acts*. I posited that, since the voices in Weiner's visual field had very recently arrived to complicate her compositional methods, she was *already* negotiating the terrain of the "writer's mind" naturally enough before coming to the church to write that day. I asked if that wouldn't complicate Mayer's editorial procedure somehow. And Mayer replied that Weiner was unusually receptive to it among her cohort, that collaboration was "still a very unpopular idea," although "Hannah liked it." You asked her along, I responded. Isn't she collaborating already, whether or not she's with others when she does it? Mayer replied, "Things for Hannah were so complicated already, that could never have complicated things further." In September of that year, she began writing *Pictures and Early Words*, a journal chronicling her attempt to understand, control, and record in a literary form what she called her "unfriendly spirits." Rhys Chatham, a close friend in these years, says he found the presence of these spirits "perfectly natural" given the experimentation with hallucinogenic drugs, intermedia, improvisation, and other new art forms in their milieu. "Being with Hannah," he says, "was to be with these words."

Unnatural Acts number 2 ends up a mess of threads. Some of the conversations are contentiously gendered—vague accusations of phallic overreach and claims of superior perspectives due to "an estrogen effect" suffuse the text. The ostensible "impoverishment" of the project is personified by "the detached and distracted beautiful woman" who is then pitted against a "true metaphysical bridge" that is righteously owned by an "I" with a "personal vision," conditioned by the claim, "I've always felt distracted, always felt detached / from the true devil, the true child, the true vision" (unpaginated, timestamp 235). This cannot then be, in the logic of this passage, "a mistake, not / an unnatural act." Crawling across the previous five minutes are several mentions of "colors cover[ing] the surface, spreading in widening," very much like the phenomena recounted in Weiner's "own" coterminous writing project (230). And this astonishing passage, written in faux-Girono "repetition style" (Kane 200):

People
are allowed
People are allowed
to break
down
to break down
People are allowed to break down;
        they're not
        allowed

they're not allowed

to put

themselves

to put themselves

back

together

back together

they're not allowed

to put themselves back together

(234)

At 315, a thread begins that becomes characteristic of the whole by re-sisting absorption into it. Anonymity, narcissism, the opacity of the me-dium to accurately record the mind's wanderings, the failure to wander and will to focus—as though, as will happen at a party, several private conversations in tandem make up a generalized murmur—identity in the sense Gertrude Stein gave it (she is quoted twice near the end of the mag-azine), as what others can know about you, that is, what a dog acknowl-edges in its master. In short, *Unnatural Acts* 2 rejects the rational correla-tive of subjectivity that is authorship, but it reclaims it in the name of self-determination rather than relinquishing it in a quest for radical com-munity.

> Does it bother you
> yes you
> that to be late like Anne
> is not a transformation of reality
> at all . . .
> and Narcissus has nothing on any of us
> when it comes to transformations of reality

Twelve minutes later: "Yes, it bothers me,"

> Narcissus binds us
> to our complete footprint.
> And that soon
> in the form of different spaces
> I will not be able
> to record a single thing

So why do I insist on searching for Weiner here? Because it seems that at this pivotal moment in the development of clair-style writing, her contributions should stand out as the most appropriate and that, as such, they should also fade indiscernibly into the group mind who is that putative "act[or]." Perhaps she is in the above passage expressing doubt in her ability to replicate an unnatural act on her own. Perhaps I've found her here, describing the flashes of light, the words, the bed she replaced in *Pictures and Early Words* (the bedding, too, needed refreshing):

The moment
I was freed by light
I remember
the moment I was freed by light
Many words are moving around
in my bed
I remember many words in my bed
Many words were freed by light
Many lights are moving
in my bed (340)

The repetition is not atypical, but the coincidence of the imagery could be merely that, if it is indeed a part of the game being played. As someone (else?) writes five minutes later, picking up on the aforementioned "metaphysical bridge," "Temperament seeks confirmation, not bridges or stories and where does that leave us. . . . Whether you identify this or not is the measure of visions, which are never personal." There is a consensus in dissensus here, which is the balance required to effectuate an internal dialogue among eleven subjects, that any "objective occurrence in the field" will result from "the predetermined plan" (346). Or is that Weiner holding out hope, at 430, when we read

the measure of a vision is never personal

. . .

please don't stop or give up
the powers are still before us

and we can speak them[?]

And again at 630, insisting that "if we can continue to struggle with the absence of any order but our many, the own," that "the secret poetry" they "discover" will short-circuit "the fascists" among us? And does the whole change *qualitatively* when it changes in *quantity*? Otherwise, would it be necessary to implore the others, even oneself, to adhere to the "plan"? It must be both necessary to try and immaterial whether you succeed, if the plan is "predetermined" and nothing else is. The very last text, written at 645, is a self-contained lyric in a blues metric, the only section with its own title, whose generic and prosodic formality makes it an oddity here. It also seems to signal the lesson learned and the experiment, in a negative sort of way, successful.

The Airport Blues

don't go to the airport if you don't want the airport blues
oh don't go to the airport babe if you don't want them airport blues
they'll take you high up in the sky and feed you lotsa terrible foods

but before you get on they'll search you high & low
yeah honey before you get on they'll search you high and low
they'll take away your camera and run their fingers through your
    clothes

i think i'll go take a train the next time i want to take a ride
i think i'll take a train the next time the next time i want to take a ride
and leave my identity in the baggage car instead of way up in the sky

This lyric seems to depict the *enforced* milieu logic as not unnatural *enough* but all too human. Transcending the ego is a private journey, a less ephemeral ambition, something best undertaken not by accretion and uplift but by asceticism and tradition, traction rather than distraction. Or, put another way, by knowing yourself by yourself, through the otherness that introspection inevitably provides. Elaboration was all that was possible—"lotsa" invasive "search[ing]"—by collaborating, as we say, in person.

Yet the sky is simple; there is only one. So when Ron Silliman uses the plural "Skies" (1980–81) as a proper name, and Weiner subsequently titles her "reworkings" of this poem "Skies," she renders literal what Silliman presents as a figure, a grammatical figure. His title refers. Her title quotes. Treating sky as a bounded expanse makes sense only by paying it intermittent attention, the sky being a partitive object, and "sky" a mass noun.

What there is at any given moment is *some* sky. Demarcating its moments is purely artificial, which is precisely the point. This is what Silliman's chapter of his epic poem *The Alphabet* does. "Every day for one year I looked at the sky & noted what I saw," he explains (1060). The result is a long prose poem of "new sentence[s]"[11] in four parts, one for each season.

As a topic fit for the juxtapositional, paratactic form of the new sentence, "Skies" is suitably impersonal and indistinct. Part 1 begins, "The sky is a grey plane tending toward white, without depth, without detail, barely with light" (457). Surely not to be confused with just any sky, that particular sky is yet not at all a part. It is rather momentous, and it announces the aesthetic logic of the whole, the spectral quality of skies. The sky and its observer make do with the same paradox Weiner announced on the cover of *Code Poems*: "When does it or you begin?" Sky is properly that which keeps its distance, an uncertain critical distance.

Weiner published a sort of homage, response, or writing-through of "Skies" part 3 in the Ron Silliman issue of *The Difficulties* (1985) and a revised version found in her archive appears in *Hannah Weiner's Open House*. I trust Weiner would appreciate the pun when I say that Silliman's title *elevated* the status of the common, mass noun "sky" to an improper count noun "skies," and then of course even higher, transforming it into a proper noun. In reply, she elevated the status of collaboration by bringing Silliman's gaze down to earth, laying emphasis on the observer rather than the "objective occurrence in the field." *This* sky appears first under the auspices of "Ron Silliman" (the man's title and the magazine's subtitle), and second in revising the first, which removes any such attribute and is just, finally, a poem by "Hannah Weiner."

Comparing all three versions of "Skies" should begin with the framework set out in *The Difficulties*' version's subtitle, which is written in clairstyle's third voice, the one playing a supervisory role. There is the proper name in full and bibliographic reference to the proper name, *THIS* 11, the magazine where Silliman's poem first appeared. And then there is the directive to "*quote the page*," a phrase that could stand in for page numbers upon which Silliman's poem appears (i.e., cross-reference) *or* as a signal to the reader-cum-writer to *report* the text in whole or part, to carry it across, *translate* it. Silliman's poem is evidently appealing to Weiner for its own emphasis on visuality. Like part 1, part 3 begins already involved with partial transparence, and in a suitably pastoral mode.

> Blood & glass: the sky is invisible (rain streaks windows already distorted with age), only certain streets on the next hill can be seen

HANNAH WEINER

Ron Silliman   SKIES III from THIS 11 and quote the page

```
one line per winter day assaid quote and said  mybythesee   Plurals
by donttype I see my words except carrots quotes thats the seen orthodox
plurals describe multis not describing circumstances and period.   Plus
avoided the quarrel avoidthecharleswhowasworking   he can imagine this
line and quote "the carrots" dontunderline were eaten by the children
who avoid the circumstances thas a line youre stuck    some line    duscribe
show his errors    even myname know the concrete walks    made two
comments whistfully OPEN  i a m s  t e a c h i n g  at suds the
clear often duscribe the life of the city    MYME THATS A VERY REAL
COMMENTnot obliged speaking on quote the page thethis    Hannah any
carrots "Babytears & carrots"    why duscribe the events we know wearethe
children eating thecarrots for vitamin    the children are b e r n a
d e t t e beginning to open    and the next line
altruist    put the words down a taste of following the report
instructions paper    all sentences begin and end    that was hard    we
believe    and we laugh didn't we forget    somewhere we are here    the
carrots    the children    we the centure    hannah hehurts us a little
by the farmers opinion    anyone else would continue by not quote    sis
its mostly prose that we do anyway    thinnest    did you cost measure
buy the    all the figures disguise    wearque    someone is overigged
skip the farmers some quote on the page    but the line deepen use a
period.    and mother forgets    Iron he forgives you    some farmers
skip line    you're answering his questions    remember the quote    famous
he has winter possessions on his babytears mind and you dont unless we
plural are working in the field why buy atall the eating and carrots
his word sometime ecstasy plural carrots sometime    like in the spring
this season farmer ground soft will grow upstate farmers choice    and
then its a return to the page myname its ok with us just describing
quit and answer
mother would just believe in it herself and let everything else go last
line forgive iamspell andcorrect
```

Fig. 2. Poem by Hannah Weiner ("Skies"). Image courtesy of the Poetry Collection of the University Libraries, University of Buffalo, the State University of New York.

> (partly, barely, without color), I want to describe description, what is always already there (sound, light, weather), an umbrella opens the way some flowers bloom (metonymy is the problem of choice), rain is also a sound. (468–69)

The *Open House* version of the poem begins, "plurals describe multisquar-relavoided brothertwo time he can / imagine this describes show his mis-takes ᵉᵛᵉⁿ smyname know" (97). In *Difficulties*, "mistakes" reads "errors," so Weiner softens the connotation from one of strictly fallacious logic to one of miscreant views or, in a cinematic sense, different *takes*. This is one way of teaching: interpolating comments and corrections. Both feature the line, "made two comments whistfully OPEN I a m s / t e a c h i n g." The run-together phrase concretely and lexically insists on familiarity in nonidentity; "multisquarrelavoided brothertwo" effectively pacifies the differences between competing versions, "plurals," the teacher assuming the role of sis to ("two") a "brother." "The problem of choice" Silliman contemplates by way of describing description, that is, of getting what he "want[s]" from his viewpoint. This is necessarily complicated by what for Silliman is a product of the imagination but for Weiner is an image repro- duced: "mybythesee . . . I see my words" (*Difficulties*).

There are just two moments of seen words beyond the page, two all capitals, "OPEN" and most significantly "MYME THATS A VERY REAL COMMENT." Note the pun on "mime" and on "mimesis" (my me "sis"). Fidelity to said page of *THIS* 11 means "not obliged speaking on quote the page thethis Hannah, any carrots 'Babytears & carrots'" (*Difficulties*). In reported speech, direct quotes, the reporter is not obliged to mean what he says, only to say it exactly as someone else meant it to be heard. That's a real obligation fulfilled, an actually cited passage that, in Silliman's poem, indicates where one day ends and another begins. The structure is a hinge between skies. "Blood & glass:" and next "Muscle & Blood" and then "Root & muscle," and so on, the colon suggesting that each day is defini- tive but also consequential. Another system or metric Silliman uses is the parenthesis. For Silliman, these are spaces apt for clarification and com- mentary or directives, a space Weiner's underlines occupy. We've already seen that desire—"want" and "choice"—are under surveillance there. And as the days go by, the plot thickens: "(the definition of light)"; "(I prefer the prepositional form of possession's discreteness, adjectives are not aspects (but projections))"; "(half-blinded by my own breath which blows back into my face), no such thing as eyes' perfection (placement in the sky will differ)"; "(I am not interested in description, but detail, transition, all the nameless, half-known tones reducible to blue)"; "(restricted vocabulary, limitless world)"; "skies is eyes (words are)"; "under grey cloud (dimen- sionless smear)" (469, 474, 475, 477).

There are many others, but these illustrate the motivation behind the poem developing by the technique of embedding, grafting, and coinci- dence, all of which are key to Weiner's fixation on it. Weiner's desire rela- tive to vision ("eyes (words") is reactive until clair-style is mastered. SEEN WORDS impose hermeneutic difficulties that depend on the "dimension- less smear" between image and imagination: "projections." Is it me? Or the spirit? Are the words replying or implying? And what are they supplying, useful information? The difficulty is reducible to telling the difference and then representing that difference on the page, exactly, between interiority and exteriority, subject and object. Introspection and extroversion must be fused without becoming confused. And when this is taken up through collaboration, the problem is lent a specifically psychosocial dimension. Can collaboration occur without collaborators being entirely aware that they are "teaching" each other, revising what each beholds in the other? Can they operate with one being out of frame?

One technique Weiner uses to address these questions is to render names for "all the nameless, half-known tones" that are "already there" in the field of vision, whether these are categorical (weather), sensible (visual, audible), or intelligible ("vocabulary"). Silliman's interest in relationships, prepositions over qualifiers, gives a signal of permission to revise. Where Weiner sees her own words as "mistakes" of quotable obligation, Silliman is half-blinded by the immediate report of his speech (blowback); the "perfection" imputed by possession, the authorial propriety here, is relative to "placement in the skull" (the eyes, of course, but also the discerning mind and buried brain). If the problem of "Skies" is participatory at the outset—alignment of the faculties of vision—Weiner's further participation precipitates from the positive difference of revision: "placement in the skull will differ." The problem remains "reducible to blue" (adjectival) on one level—across the sentences or between them—hinging one day to the next in common. But it is proper to the distinction, if there is one, between introspection and extroversion. In Silliman's poem, the problem can be expressed by the hinges alone—what William Carlos Williams called "cleavage" and Ezra Pound called "ply o'er ply"—say, "Conceived & sought . . . Considered & conceived . . . Caught & considered . . . Overturned & caught" (472). A dialectical listing, where every consequence makes a precedent, every textual condition more circumstantial evidence, "(restricted vocabulary [leads to] limitless world)." But it can also be contained in any one sentence.

> Caught & considered: for 15 seconds the candles' flames in the (otherwise) dark room flicker as I dropped my flannel shirt (how low is the sky), outside newspapers in the rain dissolve into mush (in the morning the canary shrills pleasure to the cleansed world), the roses in their vase so slowly open. (472)

What constitutes "sky" in this interior "take" is strategically confused with various strata of the mind's eye, topped with an image of ink washed right off the reflective surface of the page.

Weiner's variations of Silliman's poem constitute multiples. She neither erases nor compounds material. It is not a dialectical effulgence.

How could it be? Silliman's poem *is* her field of vision. To quote is already to taste one's own breath as though it were another's; one is obliged to reiterate. But it is always in excess of that obligation insofar as the first iteration (the "original" in *Unnatural Acts* 2 and Weiner's namesake in *THIS* 11) is deemed insufficient. It was thought necessary to revisit the statement: "one line per winter day assaid quote and said," she says in *The Difficulties*. Look again at the subtitle. It is not one unless we read the proper name "HANNAH WEINER" as the title. Hence "multis"; Weiner's prose always exhibits her tendency to pluralize the copula rather than its atomized elements, as in "I ams psychic." There is nothing redundant in that move, placing a letter *s* on the end of "multi. "I see my words except carrots quotes thats the seen orthodox / plurals describe multis not describing circumstances and period." When she later writes another "SKIES," she alters it to say "describe variable description . . . Hannah . . . you notice the differences because you are entirely conscious" (*Open House* 97).

Yet Weiner's reworkings are not exegetical. As a "silent teacher," she prefers encouragement to didacticism, silhouetting, limning, or outlining to defining by "complete abstinence." Consider this, from Silliman's poem:

> Carrots & crips: gull sweeps low over the damp grass, under gusts of a winter fog (headlights on a schoolbus shine thru), jays in the plum tree, hummingbirds in the bush, fog feels like rain. Babytears & carrots: the next hill shimmers in the sudden heat, the buzz of flies fills the yard, cats stretch sleepily on the porch (steam coils from a coffee cup). Bougainvillea & babytears: fogdrifts limit distance (microscopic rain), the greens deepen (predawn clouds backlit by the moon), skies is eyes (words are). (475)

In this densely layered landscape, childlike wonder at obscured vision is catalyzed curiosity, stoked by diminished views contained by definite shapes. Young people can't resist looking through a peephole and figuring out the whole of what lies behind, summing it all up. An effective teacher knows this. So Weiner marks the difference between the words on the page she's reading (a magazine, *THIS* 11) and the scenario she writes to describe. One is seen in the mind's eye—"describe the events we know wearethe children eating thecarrots for vitamin"—but it takes two, "multi" diacritical marks, quotes and underlines together, to mark seeing what one reads. Reading normally occludes the sight of a word; noticing the visual properties of letterforms only obstructs the activity of reading.[12] Of course, skies are transparencies blown into proportion by such project(ion)s.

I have suggested that the relation between Weiner and Silliman is one of collaborator, sibling, or headmaster to schoolmistress, rather than to say one poem inspired the next. I have also been suggesting that the similarity of each version mirrors the slippage between authority that inheres in the lexical values of language per se (connotation, denotation, pun), "plural are working in the field." But this relation is not ultimately a duality, nor a dialectical triplet. We have a trio of poems, yes, but the relation is transversal insofar as, in Weiner's second reworking, "the sheet is clear / but isn't two words . . . baby carrots and unend like me separate" (98). The unending likeness ("limitless world") is equivalent to the interchangeability of the proper name when approached with the milieu logic of the "quote." The "secret poetry" *Unnatural Acts* 2 meant to discover was foiled by the discrepancy between enforced intimacy and voluntary physical proximity. The solution with the "Skies" series is to collaborate remotely and just beneath the actual awareness of the author(s). If in 1972 Weiner's collaborators felt trapped, a decade on it became impossible to cheat and unnecessary to work the trap. The logic of reversal becomes a milieu logic instead. This is apparent when we analogize two transformations. There is first an elevation of count noun to mass noun, then an elevation to proper name that retains the bounded extent of a count noun: "Skies." The second transformation is inherent in the use of collaborating authors' proper names, themselves juxtaposed with the title(s) "Skies." The latter is the result of the lesson in nominal transversality learned from the failure of *Unnatural Acts*.

Pairing a critique of the discourses around transversality with an examination of radical poetic collaboration suggests that disability, as a critical category, might function less as a set of stable centers—less by recognition and inclusion—than like a wandering line that revises what matters by metastablizing identity and its investments, what I have earlier called the generative potential of disidentification. This challenges some givens of disability theory and disability aesthetics that rely on the assumption of independent, individual agency—especially conceptual agency or intention. We saw this challenge in *Unnatural Acts* versus the "Skies" poems. We saw this in the airplane that contains versus the diffuse environs of unaccountable skies. But we also saw this in Prendergast's attempt to recode Deleuze and Guattari's tropics as metaphor, as a known quantity, a single tenor for a diverse set of vehicles under the rubric of rhetorical authority. We also saw this in new materialism's imputing of objecthood to the master set of all subject matters you can name, on one hand, or the "vibrant" or animating act of naming that which will not conform to any signifier. What we saw, in short, is that collaboration is between but on neither side of collaborators. It is not a matter of distinct and stable centers of creativity coming to a consensus, no matter how surprising the result. It is rather a question of the contingent force of categorization itself—the way matter and ideal impart to one another a contour that never resolves itself into allegiance, celebration, or the backdoor patriotism of certain poetics of witness, in Neil Marcus's term, a "Disabled Country." Deleuze and Guattari's famous Heraclitan image of the river picking up and sending its banks flowing, incessantly setting the map's legend wandering with it, is an image of transversal poetics. And it is also an image of disability.

I have claimed that what Weiner called clairvoyance challenged self-determination because it challenged the construction of the self, and in ways that resonate with the turn to objects and matter in critical theory as well as the turn to interdependence and psychosocial elasticity in disability studies. But collaboration takes this challenge a step further and discloses what is perhaps ultimately at stake for critical theory that takes up disability as an operative concept. As an artist with a disability, Weiner's efforts to fuse experience with formal innovation illustrate the dilemmas to which transversality responds, which I hope to have shown are the very dilemmas to which new materialist thought has responded, but in ways disability studies might specifically inflect, to the benefit of all concerned.

NOTES

1. Performativity and iterability have been the most frequent theoretical platforms for disability theory's transdisciplinary efforts. Drawing from a strain that runs from Jacques Derrida through Judith Butler and others, scholars such as Robert McRuer and Ellen Samuels have explored intersections between disability, gender, and queer theory. For Butler, matter itself is transformed through "repetition" and "resignification" such that performances of gender offer a way "to work the trap that one is inevitably in" (83). Deleuzian feminists like Claire Colebrook have questioned the limits of iterative materialism by theorizing a non-normative positivism; "we need to look at the positivity of each encounter. How do bodies establish relations in each case, and what powers are opened (or closed) to further encounters and modifications?" (21). Deleuze and Guattari were wary of working the trap; the encounter is designed as a way out—"The point is to get out" (*A Thousand Plateaus* 207). See also Kuppers and Overboe.

2. Ableist idioms are not uncommon in Deleuze and Guattari's writing, yet this and the following instance equating ignorance with being "absolutely blind" can be strategically paired with Weiner's sense that visuality is immanent to "the mind." So I deliberately leave these idioms in play to preface the close readings below.

3. Deleuze and Guattari would claim that a successful collaboration makes the respective collaborators "imperceptible" from moment to moment, so that they may thieve from one another and thus take their concepts further than they would go if they had individual ego investments in them, enjoying the impunity and solidarity of "bandit[s]" (Deleuze and Parnet 67). Moreover, biographer Francois Dosse depicts the duo as in some respects disabled. Guattari suffered from what might be diagnosed as chronic major depression, where Deleuze suffered from addiction to alcohol and a degenerative lung disease. The former impairment he at times used to exemplify transversal processes of "evaluation" (see *A Thousand Plateaus* 438–39 as well as the "B for Boire" chapter in *Gilles Deleuze from A to Z*).

4. Indeed, in his interviews with Claire Parnet, Deleuze was almost arrogantly dismissive of party politics and denied that revolutions concern outcomes, insisting that we can only bring about a pragmatic attention to pure events, a kind of "jurisprudence" ("G for Gauche," *Gilles Deleuze from A to Z*). He calls proponents of "rights" and "justice" "weak intellectuals." The "professors" and "chiefs"—those who police the disciplines and the citizens—are "organs" of a body politic that expressly—following Antonin Artaud's phrase—seeks to become a body without organs.

5. Timothy Morton, by contrast, has argued that the animacy, relationality of things is merely a "statistical performance"—"there are no particles as such, no Matter as such, only discretely quantized objects" at the scale of electrons through to the hyperobjects of ecological thought (183–84).

6. Lewis proposes and performs a history and close reading of the *Diagnostic and Statistical Manual*. In a previous essay on Weiner and psychosocial disability, I offer a reading of the *DSM* (see Durgin 2008), but here I take him to mean the mandates and other structures of the institution of psychiatry, and psychosocial models at large.

7. Peter Osborne's recent and important *Anywhere or Not at All* posits that nominalization of this kind is precisely the goal of "contemporary art" insofar as it is inherently, historically, and necessarily "post-conceptual art."

8. See Sibertin-Blanc 222–66, but also Deleuze's claim, in his preface to *Dialogues II*, that all subjects are like "states of affairs" rather than like citizens of a state.

9. The first scholarly article devoted to Weiner's work rightfully focused on the challenge put to readers in negotiating this incredible claim, and it remains an important introduction to her work (see Goldman).

10. Weiner's undated collaborative poem "Narrative," written with Abigail Child (probably in the early 1990s), was written one stanza at a time, the poets handing the page back and forth, building downward, and published without attribution of the respective stanzas. When editing her selected works, I discovered in Weiner's papers a typescript version with the authors' initials beside the respective stanzas, indicating some ambivalence on Weiner's part about the issue of authorial identification. See *Hannah Weiner's Open House*.

11. Silliman's 1977 essay "The New Sentence" describes features of prose poetry he had noticed in contemporary experimental writing, including an especially paratactic relationship between sentences that shifted the logical balance of the writing to the internal grammar of each sentence, mirrored in the nonnormative sum of its parts, which may be otherwise systematically cohesive.

12. This is the premise of Silliman's influential essay of 1976, "Disappearance of the Word, Appearance of the World," collected in *The New Sentence*.

WORKS CITED

Asch, Adrienne. "Critical Race Theory, Feminism, and Disability: Reflections on Social Justice and Personal Identity." *Ohio State Law Journal* vol. 62, no. 1, 2000, pp. 391–423.

Bennett, Jane. "Systems and Things." *The Nonhuman Turn*, edited by Richard A. Grusin, U of Minnesota P, 2015, pp. 223–39.

Bergé, Carol, editor. *Light Years: An Anthology on Sociocultural Happenings (Multimedia in the East Village, 1960–1966)*. Spuyten Duyvil, 2010.

Bogue, Ronald. "Nature, Law and Chaosmopolitanism." *Revisiting Normativity with Deleuze*, edited by Rosi Braidotti and Patricia Pisters, Bloomsbury, 2012, pp. 98–112.

Butler, Judith. "The Body You Want: Liz Kotz Interviews Judith Butler." Interview by Liz Kotz. *Artforum*, Nov. 1992, pp. 82–89.

Chatham, Rhys. Interview. Feb. 1, 2016.

Chen, Mel Y. *Animacies: Biopolitics, Racial Mattering, and Queer Affect*. Duke UP, 2012.

Colebrook, Claire. "On the Very Possibility of Queer Theory." *Deleuze and Queer Theory*, edited by Chrysanthi Nigianni and Merl Storr, Edinburgh UP, 2009, pp. 11–23.

Damon, Maria. Review of *Hannah Weiner's Open House*. *Karub*, 2008. http://www.kaurab.com/english/books/open-house.html

Deleuze, Gilles. *Francis Bacon: The Logic of Sensation*. Translated by Daniel W. Smith. U of Minnesota P, 2003.

Deleuze, Gilles. *Negotiations, 1972–1990*. Translated by Martin Joughin. Columbia UP, 1995.

Deleuze, Gilles, and Félix Guattari. *Anti-Oedipus: Capitalism and Schizophrenia*. Translated by Robert Hurley, Mark Seem, and Helen R. Lane. U of Minnesota P, 1983.

Deleuze, Gilles, and Félix Guattari. "Capitalism and Schizophrenia." *Desert Islands and Other Texts, 1953–1974*, edited by David Lapoujade and translated by Michael Taormina, Semiotext(e), 2004, pp. 232–41.

Deleuze, Gilles, and Félix Guattari. *Kafka: Toward a Minor Literature*. Translated by Dana Polan. U of Minnesota P, 1986.

Deleuze, Gilles, and Félix Guattari. *A Thousand Plateaus: Capitalism and Schizophrenia*. Translated by Brian Massumi. U of Minnesota P, 1987.

Deleuze, Gilles, and Félix Guattari. *What Is Philosophy?* Translated by Hugh Tomlinson and Graham Burchell. Columbia UP, 1994.

Deleuze, Gilles, and Claire Parnet. *Dialogues II*. Translated by Hugh Tomlinson and Barbara Habberjam. Columbia UP, 2002.

Dolphijn, Rick, and Iris Tuin. *New Materialism: Interviews and Cartographies*. Open Humanities P, 2012.

Dosse, François. *Gilles Deleuze & Félix Guattari: Intersecting Lives*. Columbia UP, 2010.

Durgin, Patrick. "Avant-Garde Journalism: Hannah Weiner's Early and Clairvoyant Journals." *Early and Clairvoyant Journals*. Archive for New Poetry, University of California, San Diego, Special Collections, 2004. orpheus.ucsd.edu/speccoll/m504/index.html

Durgin, Patrick. "Big Sensible: Introductory Remarks on *Clairvoyant Journal*." *Jacket2* and f-u-t-u-r-e.org, 2014. http://f-u-t-u-r-e.org/r/34_Patrick-Durgin_BIG-SENSIBLE_Introductory-Remarks-on-Clairvoyant-Journal_EN.md

Durgin, Patrick. "New Life Writing." *Jacket2*, 2012. https://jacket2.org/article/new-life-writing

Durgin, Patrick. "Post-language Poetries as Post-ableist Poetics." *Journal of Modern Literature*, vol. 32, no. 2, 2009, pp. 159–84.

Durgin, Patrick. "Psycho-Social Disability and Post-ableist Poetics: The 'Case' of Hannah Weiner's Clairvoyant Journals." *Contemporary Women's Writing*, vol. 2, no. 2, 2008, pp. 131–54.

Fox, Ann M., and Joan Lipkin. "Res(crip)ting Feminist Theater through Disability Theater: Selections from the DisAbility Project." *NWSA Journal*, vol. 14, no. 3, 2002, pp. 77–98.

Garland-Thomson, Rosemarie. "Integrating Disability, Transforming Feminist Theory." *NWSA Journal*, vol. 14, no. 3, 2002, pp. 1–32.

Genosko, Gary. *Félix Guattari: A Critical Introduction*. Pluto P, 2009.

Goldman, Judith. "Hannah=hannah: Politics, Ethics, and Clairvoyance in the Work of Hannah Weiner." *Differences: A Journal of Feminist Cultural Studies*, vol. 12, no. 2, 2001, pp. 121–68.

Guattari, Félix. *The Anti-Œdipus Papers*. Translated by Stéphane Nadaud. Semiotext(e), 2006.

Harman, Graham. *Immaterialism: Objects and Social Theory*. Polity P, 2016.

Kane, Daniel. *All Poets Welcome: The Lower East Side Poetry Scene in the 1960s*. U of California P, 2003.

Kudlick, Catherine J. "Disability History: Why We Need Another 'Other.'" *American Historical Review*, vol. 108, no. 3, 2003. Historycooperative.org/journals/ahr/108.3/kudlick.html

Kuppers, Petra, and James Overboe. "Introduction: Deleuze, Disability, and Difference." *Journal of Literary & Cultural Disability Studies*, vol. 3, no. 3, 2009, pp. 217–20.

Lewis, Bradley. *Moving beyond Prozac, DSM, & the New Psychiatry: The Birth of Postpsychiatry*. U of Michigan P, 2006.

Manning, Erin. *The Minor Gesture*. Duke UP, 2016.

Mayer, Bernadette. Interview. April 21, 2016.

McRuer, Robert. *Crip Theory: Cultural Signs of Queerness and Disability*. New York University P, 2006.

Morton, Timothy. "Here Comes Everything: The Promise of Object-Oriented Ontology." *Qui Parle*, vol. 19, no. 2, 2011, pp. 163–90.

Neidich, Warren. "Neuropower: Is Resistance Fertile?" *Foucault, Biopolitics, and Governmentality*, edited by Nilsson, Jakob, and Sven-Olov Wallenstein, Södertörns högskola, 2013, pp. 133–44.

Osborne, Peter. *Anywhere or Not at All: Philosophy of Contemporary Art*. Verso, 2013.

Parnet, Claire, Gilles Deleuze, and Pierre-André Boutang. *Gilles Deleuze from A to Z*. Semiotext(e), 2011.

Prendergast, Catherine. "The Unexceptional Schizophrenic: A Post-postmodern Introduction." *Journal of Literary & Cultural Disability Studies*, vol. 2, no. 1, 2008, pp. 55–62.

Roysdon, Emily, Dipesh Chakrabarty, David Joselit, Kara Keeling, Kobena Mercer, Michelle Kuo, and Huey Copeland. "Collective Consciousness: A Roundtable." *Artforum*, vol. 54, no. 10, 2016, pp. 266–76.

Samuels, Ellen. "Critical Divides: Judith Butler's Body Theory and the Question of Disability." *NWSA Journal* vol. 14, no. 3, 2002, pp. 58–76.

Shaviro, Steven. *The Universe of Things: On Speculative Realism*. U of Minnesota P, 2013.

Sibertin-Blanc, Guillaume, and Ames Hodges. *State and Politics: Deleuze and Guattari on Marx*. Semiotext(e), 2016.

Siebers, Tobin. "Disability and the Right to Have Rights." *Disability Studies Quarterly*, vol. 27, nos. 1–2, 2007. http://dsq-sds.org/article/view/13/13

Silliman, Ron. *The New Sentence*. Roof Books, 1987.

Silliman, Ron. "Skies." *The Alphabet*. U of Alabama P, 2008, pp. 457–80.

Sobchack, Vivian. "A Leg to Stand On." *The Prosthetic Impulse: From a Posthuman Present to a Biocultural Future*, edited by Marquard Smith and Joanne Morra, MIT P, 2006, pp. 17–41.

Tynan, Aidan. "Reading *Anti-Oedipus*: Literature, Schizophrenia, and Universal History." *Understanding Deleuze, Understanding Modernism*, Edited by Paul Ardoin, S. E. Gontarski, and Laci Mattison, Bloomsbury, 2014, pp. 48–60.

Unnatural Acts. Edited by Ed Friedman and Bernadette Mayer. St. Marks Poetry Project, 1972.

Weiner, Hannah. "Awareness and Communication." MSS 504, Box 15, Folder 23, Mandeville University of California, San Diego, Special Collections.

Weiner, Hannah. *Clairvoyant Journal*. Angel Hair, 1978.

Weiner, Hannah. *Code Poems: From the International Code of Signals for the Use of All Nations*. Open Book Publications, 1982.

Weiner, Hannah. *The Fast*. United Artists Books, 1992.

Weiner, Hannah. *Hannah Weiner's Open House*. Kenning Editions, 2006.

Weiner, Hannah. Letter to Michael Heller. August 1965. Box 13, Folder 15, Stanford University Special Collections.

Weiner, Hannah. *Pictures and Early Words: Early and Clairvoyant Journals*. Edited by Patrick Durgin. Archive for New Poetry, University of California, San Diego, Special Collections, 2004. orpheus.ucsd.edu/speccoll/m504/index.html

Weiner, Hannah. "Skies." *The Difficulties*, vol. 2, no. 2, 1985, p. 48. *Eclipse Archive*. http://eclipsearchive.org/projects/DIFFICULTIES/D2-2/pictures/027.html

Weiner, Hannah. "Skies" (second version). *Hannah Weiner's Open House*, Kenning Editions, 2006, pp. 97–99.

Woods, Angela. *The Sublime Object of Psychiatry: Schizophrenia in Clinical and Cultural Theory*. Oxford UP, 2011.

Dis-affection

Disability Effects and Disabled Moves at the Movies

Angela M. Smith

In the fall 2012 TV season, several pop-culture sites declared a surprising "Hottest Trend": amputation. *Tvline, Vulture*, and the *Hollywood Reporter* noted bodily appendages "flying off the screen" in shows such as *American Horror Story, The Walking Dead, Grey's Anatomy*, and *Criminal Minds*.[1] In foregrounding flying limbs, the articles and shows sensationalize disability, using the shocking spectacle of amputation to generate horrified thrills. But *American Horror Story* and *The Walking Dead* also offer viewers extended encounters with recurring amputee characters, as do other recent televisual texts such as *Nikita, Arrested Development, Sons of Anarchy, Game of Thrones*, and *Once Upon a Time*. Amputee figures have also garnered significant movie-screen time lately, in films such as *The Man with the Iron Fists* and sequel *Snowpiercer, Men in Black 3, Iron Man 3, The Amazing Spider-Man, Battleship, Dolphin Tale 2, The Fault in Our Stars, Mad Max: Fury Road*, and *Kingsman: The Secret Service*.

In describing this phenomenon as a "trend"—a turning, bending, or drifting in a certain direction—these articles suggest we turn toward and are moved by amputee bodies. Consider responses to the story of six-year-old Alex Pring, born without most of his right arm. In July 2014, Alex received a prosthetic arm designed and built from 3D-printed parts. The *Huffington Post* ran an emotional article: "6-Year-Old Boy Hugs His Mom for the First Time Ever, Thanks to a 3D-Printed Arm." Commented prosthesis engineer Albert Manero, "[Alex] said it was their first real hug. There wasn't a dry eye in the room" (Bologna). In March 2015, Alex was back in a viral video where actor Robert Downey Jr. presented him with an Iron Man–themed prosthetic arm. Canadian website *The Loop* averred that the video "melts everyone's heart" (Miranda) and the *Pedestrian Daily* advised, "You might want to grab the tissues and get ready to *feel*, because this [video] has got ugly happy crying embedded in its code" ("Watch Robert Downey Jr").

The popularity of Alex's story and video suggests we have an *affection* for disability, in the sense of being emotionally drawn to it. To experience certain affects, we repeatedly produce, disseminate, and consume images or stories featuring disabled figures, whose nonnormative forms or functions seem to explicitly register human vulnerability or *affectability*. (The "we" used here indicates the primarily nondisabled audience presumed and constructed by these representations; as I suggest below, disabled viewers are likely to read these representations more critically.) "Affection" can also mean a bodily condition or abnormality, so that visibly impaired bodies seem *especially* to connote a state of affectedness and in turn powerfully affect their viewers.[2] Thus, the arrival of disability images on our newsfeed subliminally instructs us: "Get ready to *feel*." But Alex's video also suggests mainstream visual texts use disability in carefully coded and delimited ways, to produce only certain kinds of feelings.

Focusing particularly on amputee representations, this chapter explores the idea that disability images generate potent affective experiences. They often do so through acts of "disability drag" and special-effects simulations that support ableist assumptions about disabled bodies' inferiority. But the omnipresence of disabled figures also reveals a persistent desire and affection for disability, an attraction toward disability encounters that also opens unexpected spaces for disabled performers and their nonnormative moves.

Ableist Affect / Disability Drag

Perhaps nothing so literally conjures for us the concept of embodied suspension and material intractability as the cinematic spectacle of amputation: it depicts bodies profoundly affected, shows characters immersed in physical and psychological transformation, and produces an intense, visceral viewer response. Brian Massumi describes "affect" as "a prepersonal intensity corresponding to the passage from one experiential state of the body to another and implying an augmentation or diminution in that body's capacity to act" ("Notes on the Translation" viii). Massumi notes that "body" should be "taken in its broadest possible sense to include 'mental' or ideal bodies" (viii). But a key example in his book *Parables of the Virtual* suggests the suspensive experience of affect is most viscerally grasped via the material experience of bodily injury or disabling. Massumi cites the moment in the 1942 film *King's Row* when Ronald Reagan's character, Drake, wakes to find both his legs have been amputated and cries out in anguish, "Where's the rest of me?" Writing about this moment in his autobiography, Reagan recalled, "In some weird way, I felt something horrible had happened to my body. . . . I opened my eyes dazedly, looked around, slowly let my gaze travel downward. I can't describe even now my feeling as I tried to reach for where my legs should be. . . . I asked the question—the words that had been haunting me for so many weeks—'Where's the rest of me?'" (quoted in Massumi 52–53).

Massumi suggests Reagan convincingly emotes a traumatized response to impairment because he had experienced a series of actual blockages, frustrations, and disablings: exhausting and unsatisfying rehearsals of his line, inconclusive research into amputee experience, and subjection to a rigged hospital bed that made Reagan feel his body really ended at his torso (53–55). Massumi contends that Reagan's performance thus enters a space of intense affect and dislocation: "He is in an in-between space composed of accumulated movements bled into one another and folding in upon the body. . . . He is in the space of the duration of an ungraspable event" (57). But while Reagan briefly loses himself in this abject becoming, he later plots the instant of amputee affect as merely motivation toward self-completion. As suggested by Reagan's title for his autobiography—*The Rest of Me*—this momentary undoing propels him into politics, where he recovers a whole and capable self (55).

Massumi's narrative of Reagan's simulated amputation illustrates how enacted moments of disabling can generate intensely felt affect that coalesces into despairing emotions; these can only be offset by a narrative of eventual uplift and overcoming. The choreographing of disabled bodies thus draws together the affective and the corporeal to impart certain "felt truths" about disability embodiment. Samantha Frost and Diana Coole draw on Althusser to explain a "new materialist" conception of the ways ideology emerges in everyday bodily practices:

[Althusser] . . . draws attention to the way "ideas" are inscribed in actions whose repetitive, ritualized performances are borne by concrete individuals who are thereby practically constituted as compliant or agentic subjects. While such performances are institutionalized in rituals and ceremonies, they also become sedimented at a corporeal level, where they are repeated as habits or taken for granted know-how. . . . It is indeed this nonreflexive habituality and the way it imbues objects with familiarity that makes artifacts, commodities, and practices seem so natural that they are not questioned. (34)

The simulated disabled figure on-screen constitutes one such familiar object, whose moves are constrained so as to generate seemingly "natural" depressive viewer responses and confirm the "obviously" degraded nature of the disability experience.

Accordingly, fiction films usually choreograph the traumatic aftermath of amputation as the beginning of an inevitable decline: they explicitly construe the amputee body in terms of abjection and horror and confine amputee expression to despairing (e)motions perceived as degraded or incompetent, such as falling, dragging, and crawling. A salient example appears in the 1994 film *Forrest Gump*, where digital special effects turn nonamputee Gary Sinise into bilateral lower-limb amputee Lieutenant Dan. The film confirms amputation as a degrading experience: after his injury, Dan plunges into misery, castigating Forrest for saving his life and disgustedly declaring himself "a helpless cripple, a legless freak!" The movie intuits the recent amputee's suspended state, as Dan asks Forrest wildly, "What am I going to do now? What am I going to do now?" But it maps Dan's trajectory thereafter as an inevitable and unwilled descent. When Forrest reencounters Dan years later, the latter's diminishment is signaled by bodily changes conventionally read in terms of failure or loss: his ragged and unshaven appearance, his alcohol dependence, his wheelchair use. Dan loses control of his chair and goes careening down an icy ramp, a comic manifestation of the incapable, angry cripple, affirming that disabled bodies have trouble acting in purposive or accomplished ways.

In a scene confirming the amputee experience as inevitable decline, Dan rages at two sex workers who have mocked Forrest as "stupid." Yelling at them to get out of his room, Dan gesticulates fiercely and accidentally falls from his wheelchair. The women laugh and insult Dan, leaving him lying, panting, on the floor. As Forrest moves to help, Dan resentfully waves him off and slowly hauls himself back up into his chair. Disability registers as incapacity to extend intense affect into normative emotional expression: Dan's effort to express righteous anger leads only to his humiliating toppling from and painful reascent into a chair already depicted as the inadequate and uncontrolled extension of a damaged body.

This production of amputee affect through despairing emotion, clumsy falls, and dragging moves was more recently elaborated in the 2012 French movie *Rust and Bone*, in which whale-trainer Stéphanie, played by Marion Cotillard, wakes to discover her lower legs have been amputated. A long shot shows Stéphanie slowly regaining consciousness in her hospital bed, in an antiseptic and coldly lit room. Pushing herself up on her hands, she moves her leg and, confused, pulls aside the sheet to reveal amputated and bandaged limbs. Panicking, she flails her arms and tries to get out of bed. Steph's friend Louise hurries down the hall and enters the room to find Stéph crawling across the floor, trailing tubes and IV bags. Cradled by Louise, Stéph wails, repeatedly, "What have you done with my legs?" her upper body arcing with grief, her mouth open and gasping, tears on her face, until she falls asleep, exhausted. Here we see the understandable shock of utter and unwilled transformation, but such intense affective suspension swiftly morphs into prescribed disabled moves of falling, dragging, and despairing: failed efforts at sovereign action.

The dragging element of these affective moves is closely related to the phenomenon of nondisabled actors playing disabled characters that Tobin Siebers labels "disability drag." When nondisabled actors take on such roles, Siebers argues, "disability appears as a façade overlaying able-bodiedness." Accordingly, disability drag "renders disability invisible because able-bodied people substitute for people with disabilities similar to white performers who put on blackface at minstrel shows or to straight actors who play 'fag' to bad comic effect."[3] Such caricatured performance of marginalized identities serves to affirm the dominant group's superiority, since disability drag signifies first and foremost "the acting abilities of the [nondisabled] performer." Further, as actors cast off their disability costumes, they receive plaudits for brave descents into stigmatized forms; as they move on to disabled roles, disability appears to be overcome (116).[4]

I argue the term "disability drag" is also apt for these performances because "to drag" means "to draw with force, effort, or difficulty; pull heavily or slowly along; haul."[5] Some etymological investigations of "drag" as a term for men donning women's clothes suggest it originates in this material and physical experience, specifically "the unfamiliar sensation to men of long skirts dragging on the ground" (Quinion 103). Disability drag, then, requires able-bodied actors to carry out unfamiliar motions in ways that caricature and confirm disability embodiment as a drag and only a drag: a depressing, oppressive emotional and physical experience. The ubiquity of disability drag excludes disabled actors from the scene of their own representation and forecloses on alternative performances and readings of disabled moves: as functional, purposive, ordinary, pleasurable, or even beautiful.

Disability drag thus simulates disabled bodies to affirm the pleasures of normal embodiment. This dynamic also describes the affective trajectory of many films featuring amputee characters. First plunging viewers into despair at these ostensibly diminished and descending bodies, these movies then counter their depressive affect by uplifting their amputee characters, making them more "normal" in form and movement. Late in *Forrest Gump*, as Dan arrives at Forrest's wedding, the groom is delighted to see his old friend has cleaned up, appearing in a neat pressed suit; cheered up, beaming as he approaches Forrest and Jenny; hooked up, proudly introducing his shyly smiling fiancée; and stood up, thanks to new legs of titanium alloy. In *Rust and Bone*, Stéphanie, too, cheers up, hooks up, and stands up on prosthetic legs. Both films swiftly channel the affective suspension of disabling into pain and sadness, before elevating both their characters' bodies and viewers' emotions by enhancing and/or "curing" the amputees, correlating happiness with upright stature and conventional walking motion. In carefully managing their affective outcomes, these movies, like the Alex Pring video, have "ugly happy crying embedded in [their] code."

Dis-FX

Movies relying on disability drag often also depend on disability special-effects—or what I am calling "dis-FX"—to convincingly pass off able actors as disabled characters. The amputee body has long been a figure through which cinema parades its technical capacity. Before digital special effects, amputee characters were still presented in disability drag: the illusion of an amputee body was produced through costume, prostheses, props, in-camera effects, and the amputative act of cutting film. When Siebers writes, "The more disabled the character, the greater the ability of the actor," we might also add "and of the special-effects technician" (116).

Take, for instance, a 1904 French short film titled *The Automobile Accident*, described by F. A. Talbot in his 1912 book *Moving Pictures: How They Are Made and Worked*. A drunken man falls asleep in the street. A passing cab runs over and severs his legs, and the man awakens in shock. But a doctor in the cab miraculously reattaches the legs, and the man walks away. The film offers a condensed version of disability drag: it shows the shockingly amputated body, immobilized on the ground, and the magical cure that restores happiness via an upright body that moves "normally." To uncover the trick, Talbot presents a behind-the-scenes photo from the film as his book's frontispiece.

TRICK CINEMATOGRAPHY--THE AUTOMOBILE ACCIDENT.

The producer giving instructions to the principal actor and his double, the legless cripple. The dummy legs in the foreground. - *See page* 211.

Fig. 1. The frontispiece to *Moving Pictures: How They Are Made and Worked* (1912), showing the actor and the amputee stunt performer.

An able-bodied actor and a stunt amputee actor, identically costumed, sit on the ground next to each other, legs outstretched, while a man leans over them from behind, instructing their performance. The men's parallel positions contrast the able-bodied actor's legs with those of the amputee, whose upper legs are separated by a gap from a prop set of lower legs. The photo indicates how filming stopped to switch out the original actor for the amputee actor and prop legs, giving the illusion that the man's limbs had been severed. Another image in Talbot's book shows the amputee actor lying on the ground as the able-bodied actor stands over him; its caption reads, "The actor being replaced by the legless cripple with the dummy legs" (210–11). Filming was then stopped again to reverse the switch, producing the apparent cure.

Talbot views this deception as a wonder of trick cinematography, proof of the new film medium's superiority over theater. Theatrical disappearances involved clumsy trap doors, while filmic "stop and substitution," he marvels, reveals "not the slightest trace of movement" (213, 215). This trickery erases the disabled performer, since, the amputee body *did* move, in and out of its allocated position: Talbot writes, "At this juncture, the producer stepped forward with the legless cripple mounted on his self-propelled wheeled truck" (212). By stopping recording, the film avoids showing the amputee actor's self-propulsion, a "trace of movement" that might undermine views of disability as something that only drags down and immobilizes. The disabled body instead becomes a vehicle for exhibiting film's newfound capacity to cut up reality, to amputate and reassemble bodies, to prostheticize reality. *The Automobile Accident* nonetheless *needs* the amputee body, even as it is concealed and controlled: Talbot states, "The legless cripple is, of course, key to the whole situation" (212).

Contemporary films instead rely on digital wizardry for their dis-FX. *Forrest Gump*, one of the first mainstream films to use extensive digital effects, has its trickery explicated on the movie's 2006 DVD, in a featured interview with visual effects supervisor Ken Ralston. Just as Talbot applauds film's transcendence of awkward theatrical illusions, Ralston explains how digital effects surpass older devices like costumes, props, stunt actors, and editing. Digital cinema can produce an even more seamless illusion of an amputee body without needing a real amputee at all. As Ralston explains:

The Lieutenant Dan leg scenes—we had to take off Gary Sinise's legs. The one thing that I wanted to do, because it would add so much to the audience believing this had occurred, was to have him passing

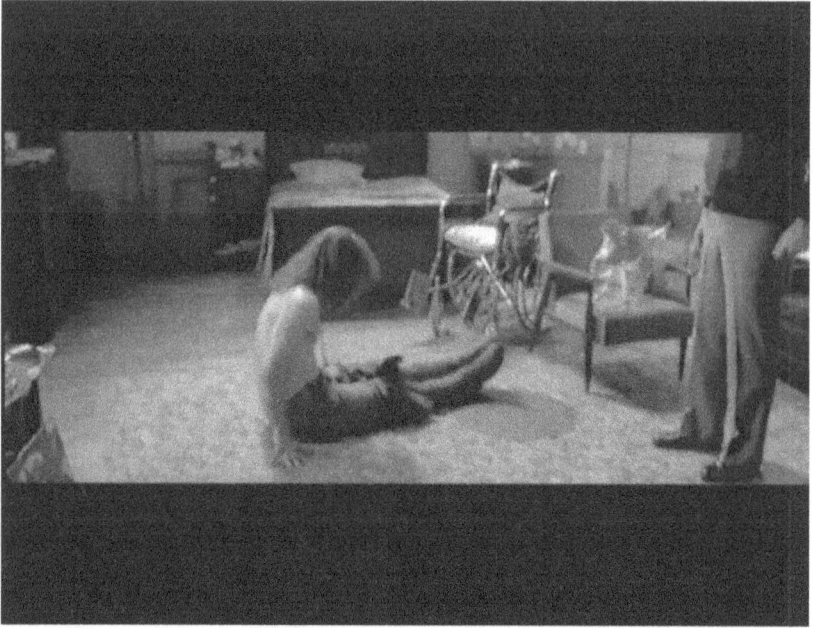

Fig. 2. Scene from *Forrest Gump*. (*Top*) Gary Sinise's lower legs, wrapped in blue, cross the space where the table will be composited into the image; (*bottom*), the final shot, with Sinise's legs erased.

through the physical space of tables or whatever it is, with the stumps of his legs, where if it was a fake, and you had your legs sticking straight out, like he really did in a lot of these shots, he would hit the table, he wouldn't be able to pass through it. . . . Now if we didn't do that, you could have almost believed that he had his legs tucked under. . . . You told the audience you weren't hiding anything.

Ralston dwells on the moment after Lieutenant Dan falls from his chair when he swings his residual legs close to a small table, positioning himself to push back up into the chair. The DVD feature shows Sinise's lower legs wrapped in blue tape, moving through empty space, and then displays a computer screen on which the shot is digitally composited with another shot that displays the table but no actors.

Comments Ralston:

I think the more successful shots there which telegraphs [*sic*] the idea that his legs are cut off, is when he falls out of the wheelchair in that desperate scene in that crummy apartment. . . . We took the table out of the scene, and then he swings with his real legs going right through where that table is and comes forward to the audience, right before he forces himself back up into the wheelchair. And once we got that shot, we put the table back into the scene. We shot what's called a blank plate, basically, no actors are in it, and then that table and that area is put back into the scene with Gary, digitally, basically composited in there. So, then, the legs are painted out, and it just takes a little bit more away from the artificial quality of it. He could never have done that with real legs anywhere.

Ralston locates the success of the disability effect in its exploitation of apparent spatial and temporal continuity, enabled by the digital "amputation" of Sinise's lower legs.

The convincing spectacle of an able-bodied actor apparently missing his lower legs thus exemplifies and anticipates a world of exceptional human and technological effectiveness. A feature on the *Rust and Bone* DVD similarly flaunts digital mastery, alternating between a series of pre-production shots, with Cotillard's lower legs in green stockings, and post-production shots, in which her lower legs have vanished. In repeatedly conjuring and erasing Cotillard's legs, the feature positions the effects artist as a magician and the amputee body as a vehicle for potent digital wizardry.

William Brown has argued that such digitally manipulated continuity may be called "posthuman," because it provides credible visions of things yet to be realized and propels us into a future where we've overcome current human limitations (71). Interviews with filmmakers about digital cinema in the documentary *Side by Side* explicitly associate digital FX with extending potency and control. Director Lana Wachowski states: "We're free of the old technology of capturing those images . . . [Digital] gives you more control, more choice, more ways to access what you're imagining in your head." Jonathan Fawkner, video effects supervisor, concurs: "Computers will only get better. We'll be able to produce anything you want, realistically." And Jim Jannard, founder of Red Digital Company, comments, "To me, everything in the world can and will be made better, and the only question is when and by whom."

DVD extras explaining digital amputation thus aggrandize filmmakers' accomplishments in and through constructed disabled bodies. These illusions erase amputee bodies and performers from the cinematic scene, for disability drag requires the absence of "actually" nonnormative bodies and their disabled moves, which might interfere with the choreography of disability drag. Further, with no legs to delete, there would be no impressive trickery, and it is the fact that these *are* tricks that helps offset depressive disability affect, delighting and uplifting audiences with proof of human and technological capacities. As Kenny Fries comments in the documentary *Vital Signs*, the Dan effect construes disability as "a trick," "an illusion," unreal. Visual effects render disability insubstantial, overwriting disabled realities with spectacles of technology's increasing capacity to improve human bodies.[6]

The effect of such effects is exclusionary: disabled actors struggle to get hired, while audition spaces and studio sets remain difficult for many disabled actors to access.[7] More broadly, these illusions effectively erase disability from the world and our imagined futures, assuming disability as undesirable and pursuing technological fixes for amputee bodies. Alison Kafer identifies such representations as part of a "curative imaginary" (27), one that perhaps explains today's cultural admiration for amputee stars: athletes, models, pop singers whose prostheticized bodies appear as emblems of beauty and ever-greater ability for future humans.[8]

And yet disability simulations always risk error or failure. For instance, astute viewers note that after Dan falls from his chair, Sinise uses his apparently nonexistent lower legs to push—rather than haul—himself back up; this lack of realism means the digital trick falls short of its stated pur-

Fig. 3. Scene from *Rust and Bone*. Dis-FX error: the shadow of Marion Cotillard's erased legs is visible on the sand beneath the wheelchair.

pose.[9] Similarly, the IMDB "Goofs" page for *Rust and Bone* notes, "When Ali first carries Stéphanie to swim in the sea, as he lifts her . . . the actress's real legs cast a shadow" (*"Rust and Bone*: Goofs").[10]

Such mistakes call into question the presumed capacity of "able" bodies: both the capacity of able-bodied actors to conceive and perform appropriate actions and the capacity of FX practitioners to control the mechanics of disability illusion. They also call into question the presumed *in*capacity of disabled bodies, since an actor with bilateral leg amputations could have performed the maneuver more aptly than Sinise. As Sharon L. Snyder and David Mitchell note, the action is somewhat unrealistic, since "the capacity to move one's body from the floor to a wheelchair solely with one's arms involves the execution of a substantial feat of strength" (180). Thus, Dan's maneuver fails to correspond to the realities of disabled embodiment, instead projecting both hyperbolic disability drag/falling and supercrip accomplishment/ascent. If an amputee actor had been used, and had required personal assistance or conducted more complex maneuvering, those disabled moves may have interfered with the scene's generation of ableist affect.

These dis-FX errors interrupt the vision of ever-increasing human capacity, pointing to nondisabled filmmakers' *incapacity* to imagine or produce an array of nonnormative moves. New materialist theories, Coole and Frost note, contest visions of human-directed progression toward complete control, instead foregrounding dynamics of emergence, improvisation, and contingency. New materialists visualize human agency as enmeshed in a network of forces generated by agential entities not usually seen as such, including machines, animals, and animate and inanimate matter. Within this schema, bodily encounters remain irreducible to social scripts, and "History emerges . . . as the continuous transformation of provisional forms by new, indecipherable and unanticipated events" (35). In the encounter among Sinise's legs, wheelchair, gravity, floor, the movie camera, and digital effects, the unanticipated reemergence of deleted limbs fractures filmmakers' claims to absolute control, and redirects the affective and material responses usually dictated by the encounter with simulated disability.

Dis-affection

If these errors of amputee representation uncover the compromised agency of the filmmakers and nondisabled actors, they also glimpse as agential the movements of disabled bodies within their environment. Coole and Frost identify a key aspect of "the new biomaterialism" as "the role played by the body as a visceral protagonist within political encounters" (19); they suggest we should perceive "bodies exhibiting agentic capacities in the way they structure or stylize their perceptual milieu, where they discover, organize, and respond to patterns that are corporeally significant" (20). As a result of these errors in disability drag, such disabled agency may become visible: viewers may contemplate how disabled moves would differ, would demonstrate the disabled individual's capacity to negotiate matter and gravity in a nonnormative body.

For the viewer, then, the able-bodied mistakes in disability drag and dis-FX produce "dis-affection," a term I use to encompass an affection for and desire to be affected by disability, a disorienting distancing from ableist affects, and an opening toward alternative disability affects. It is somewhat akin to the literary affect Ato Quayson has called "aesthetic nervousness," which arises from encounters between disabled and nondisabled characters, moments inflected with "the embarrassment, fear, and confusion that attend the disabled in their everyday reality." In such moments, Quayson argues, a text's reductive uses of disability may falter, as "the disability representation is seen predominantly from the perspective of the disabled rather than from the normative position of the nondisabled." At this instant, the text's and reader's ableist views of disability fracture (19).

Dis-affection thus encompasses attraction, affection, and unsettling affective reorientation: viewers are drawn to and affected by disability simulation, but when they apprehend an error and can no longer suspend disbelief, they experience fragmentation or blockage. This blockage compares to that experienced by Reagan in performing disability: it is an instant of affective suspension and disorientation that may morph into Reagan's defensive reclaiming of normalcy but may also open up nonableist affective experiences. Quayson's emphasis on the perspective of the disabled person reminds us that disabled viewers must *often* inhabit a state of dis-affection, of distance and disbelief, as they watch ableist misrepresentation of bodies supposedly like their own.[11] But such blockages, especially if recognized as encounters with or affectedness by "actually" disabled bodies, might also reorient nondisabled viewers and their affective relations to disabled people. As Elizabeth Christie and Geraldine Bloustien suggest, quoting Anna Hickey-Moody, "Media representations 'have the potential to 'reimagine . . . disabled bodies' . . . in the respect that: 'they can be used to fold a viewer into the embodied subjectivity of a disabled person and create [a] new relationship between disabled and non disabled people. New affects are made this way'" (493).

An encounter with disabled performers, then, opens toward new affects, allowing viewers to glimpse disabled moves as agential adaptations, alternative ways of being and affecting. Such conceptions resonate with disability scholars' insistence that "it is easy to tell disabled people what they are missing; much more difficult to listen to, and understand, what they have" (Joseph Grigely); or that "movement is a product of physiology . . . : there is no 'normal' body and concomitant movement, but rather an array of differences that reflect themselves in different movements" (Grigely); or that "DISABILITY IS AN ART. It is an ingenious way to live" (Neil Marcus, quoted in Christie and Bloustien 494).

For an example of how dis-affection might occur in encounters between disabled performers, nondisabled filmmakers/viewers, and special effects, consider the 1972 sci-fi film *Silent Running*, directed by Douglas Trumbull, an appropriate choice both because of Trumbull's status as an FX wizard and because of the film's imagining of a futuristic world. In *Silent Running*, Bruce Dern plays Freeman Lowell, a crewman on a space freighter who depends on three robotic drones he names Huey, Dewey, and Louie. The drones were played by four bilateral leg amputees in robot costume: Larry Whisenhunt, Mark Persons, Steve Brown, and Cheryl Sparks. Trumbull explained the casting by recalling his impressions of Johnny Eck in the 1932 film *Freaks*:

> Well, there's one little fellow; he's very handsome, and neat—he's dressed in a tuxedo and a bow tie. Only, from the waist down, he isn't there. So, here's this remarkable, beautiful guy, with this amazing agility, leaping and running on his hands through the room, jumping up on chairs, etc. And not once did you feel horrified. You're amazed and respectful at his adjustment. That impression stayed with me when it came time to cast the drones. I knew what I wanted. (Trumbull)[12]

Trumbull's encounter with Eck derails the expected affective response of horror, producing instead amazement and aesthetic pleasure: Trumbull decides that disability is something he *wants* for his film.

While *Silent Running's* costuming hides the amputee actors, making it difficult for viewers to recognize their encounter with disability, it also suggests disabled moves—unpredictable and self-generated motions by impaired bodies—as desirable, capable, and appealing. For instance, in one moment, a drone impatiently taps his foot, and in another, one drone draws another's attention by touching it on the arm. In interviews, Trumbull has explained that these gestures were unscripted. In the case of the arm-touching, the motion emerged as an adaptation to the bulky costumes encasing the actors. Writes Mark Kermode,

> The actors would apparently "speak" to each other through a combination of clattering gestures, of which the tap on the shoulder was but one. Picking up on the organic interaction between the performers, Trumbull opted to put this unscripted gesture into his shot, framing Lowell's arrival from a low POV which places the audience in a position of conspiratorial intimacy with the Drones— observing the world from *their* perspective, rather than that of the human lead. (54)

The foot-tapping, too, appears to mark a disabled performer's agency. Stated Trumbull, "A lot of the behavioral things emerged as we were shooting. . . . I didn't necessarily preconceive everything. I just created a situation where things could evolve and emerge. Like that moment you're talking about. . . . [T]he Drone just stands there very gently tapping his foot. Well, that was Mark—that was what he was doing! . . . I think it's the director's job to embrace serendipitous moments of performance" (Kermode 55–56).

Even as Trumbull "embraced" these unanticipated motions, they worked against his own intended representation of the drones. Responding to a statement that the drones contribute "warmth" to the film, Trumbull disagrees: "If you were to see the film again, you'd see that most of the humanity of those machines is a result of your own projection. . . . They're simply tools" (Trumbull). But as Kermode notes, the drone's patting another on the arm "is often cited as one of the most touching elements of *Silent Running*" (55). A fan writes, "The performers added a human dimension to the robots, infusing human-like mannerisms, such as an impatiently tapping foot, into inanimate hunks of plastic and metal" and adds, "I have a lot of affection for this film" (Barry P). Thus, although the amputee actors remain hidden, their disabled moves move audiences in ways Trumbull cannot dictate. Their actions assert disabled bodies' distinctive affective capacities, exceeding Trumbull's use of the amputees as "simply tools."

Disabled moves also emerge in more contemporary movies featuring digital effects. For instance, 2007's *Spider-Man 3* presents a conventionally digitally amputated character, as nonamputee Dylan Baker plays right-arm amputee Curt Connors. However, shadowing this disability drag/dis-FX is the moment elsewhere in the movie that relies on an "actual" amputee to prop up a nonamputee body. As Spider-Man (Tobey Maguire) battles the Sandman (Thomas Haden Church), the former's arm penetrates his adversary's torso and emerges out the other side. The appearance of Spider-Man's arm plunging through the Sandman's chest is enabled by the body and movement of stunt actor and kick-boxer Baxter Humby, whose right arm ends just below his elbow.

This effect produces a moment of dis-affection for attentive viewers. A writer for a pop-culture website comments, "Given the notoriously high levels of SFX inherent to the rest of *Spider-Man 3*, this moment just seems sort of insane" (Barnard), registering the apparent eccentricity of using a real amputee body when computer-generated imagery would have done as well. Indeed, the scene in question *also* uses CGI, to fabricate a hand protruding out of the Sandman's body. Perhaps accustomed to movies that employ digital effects to simulate disability, this viewer balks at the use of a "real" disabled body to simulate (super)human potency: he even employs a disability term—insanity—to convey his unease.[13] We can explain the odd inclusion of Humby, however, if we consider that digital movies are unwilling or unable to fully surrender or erase the disabled body and its unexpected effects/affects. The movie *wants* this disabled body, not because it embodies loss or trauma, but because it can more effectively convey material collision than digital effects. The emphasis on *capacity* transforms disability drag, suggesting disabled moves as sources of creative potential.

Attending to the presence of disabled bodies on-screen works against eugenic visions of the future. Rosemarie Garland-Thomson argues we should not aim to erase disability from our futures but conserve it as a vital part of human existence. Thomson cites Michael Sandel's critique of medical enhancements as a "drive to mastery" and "a kind of hyperagency—a Promethean aspiration to remake nature, including human nature, to serve our purposes and satisfy our desires." Instead of assuming the erasure of disability as a good thing, Thomson insists we acknowledge the narrative, epistemological, and ethical benefits that disability brings, especially as it generates "flexibility and openness to forces outside of our will as a form of creative and flexible dialectical engagement with the world" (348). It is worth noting that the *Spider-Man 3* effect does not simply fetishize the amputee figure as an icon of posthuman potency but combines powerful action with an unexpected material collision.

It is this openness to the unexpected and unpredictable that disabled bodies can help preserve. Michael J. Fox, discussing how his Parkinson's disease has altered his acting, observes:

> I used to be really nervous and sit in my dressing room and fret about a scene that was coming up and sweat it out and say, "What am I going to do? You say 'Action,' and I have to do something. What am I going to do? . . . And now it's just like, 'OK, what's happening?' And if something happens, I react to it and if nothing happens, I don't react. I don't worry about that bit I was going to do or the look I was gonna give because when I get there I may not be *able* to give that look or do that thing or move that glass." (Hiatt)

Fox's impairment introduces unpredictability into predetermined scripts, while his statement affirms a capacity to improvise according to the ways his body now works. The *Spider-Man 3* effect similarly calls on a disabled body to register the exciting persistence, even in our imagined futures, of embodied vulnerability in our encounters with the world. In this "insane" effect, we glimpse a future that cannot imagine itself without disability.

To conserve the flexibility and unexpectedness of disability, then, we must challenge the dominant representation of disability as charade or digital simulation. We must trouble renditions of disabled bodies merely as affect-generating machines that give vicarious depressive experiences, emotional catharsis, and uplift. This is not to require that all amputee roles be played by amputees, nor that all disabled characters be played by someone similarly disabled, nor that we eschew prostheses: such strategies cling to impossible and unproductive essentialisms. But it is to suggest that greater media inclusion of diversely disabled people can conserve and convey a wide range of disabled embodiment, motion, and emotion. Only such inclusion can widely disseminate the unexpected dis-affections of disability encounter, show the ways in which disability matters, and expand viewers' conceptions of what is possible and desirable.

Making on-screen bodies more diverse and less predictable not only changes what we can imagine and desire for our futures but also contests nondisabled assumptions about how disability *feels*. For instance, the 2013 documentary film *Fixed: The Science/Fiction of Human Enhancement* features an interview with Gregor Wolbring, a biochemist, disability advocate, and congenital amputee. Wolbring, whom we see moving down from a wheeled chair and across the floor of his apartment, notes that many see crawling as "the ultimate of undignified living." However, he asserts, he loves to crawl and does so whenever possible: "Crawling is in. Walking is out." Wolbring refuses the logic of disability drag, resignifying crawling as purposive, pleasurable movement.

Wolbring's description of his own moves proffers dis-affection, rerouting viewers' expectations about how crawling feels and what it means. A recent *New York Times* blog post does similar work, especially when juxtaposed with the "feels" produced by the Alex Pring stories. The post is by Catherine Campbell, mother of eight-year-old Thaddeus, who was born without a right hand. Campbell had been researching a 3D-printed prosthetic hand for Thaddeus when friends flooded her with excited email messages about the Alex Pring *Iron-Man* video. Campbell describes showing the video to Thaddeus.

> "Isn't this great?" I said, smiling. "That's going to be you very soon!"
> We were sitting on the couch and he turned toward me. "I've been thinking about it," he said. "And I don't want a new hand."

Campbell writes, "I was devastated." Thaddeus explains to her that, first, he does not want to lose his sense of touch, of "how things feel"; second, he asserts he can quite happily "figure out how to do stuff [his] own way," because his brain "works different"; and, third, he does not want friends to like him only for his "robot hand." Campbell concludes, "For eight years, I had focused only on what was lost with my son. . . . And during that time, he had seen what was there to stay for his lifetime—an arm that simply ended at the wrist—and the possibilities that could grow from that" (Campbell). The event is an affective interruption: the *Iron-Man* video uplifts Catherine, holding out hope for the shining completion of the amputee body. But Thaddeus doesn't feel the same way about his body and its moves. He reroutes the expected interaction, momentarily devastating his mother, by asserting the pleasure and value of his nonnormative embodiment and the affective inadequacies of prosthetic technology.

The exchange concludes in affection, in a tight mother-son hug. This hug is no more or less "real" than Alex Pring's prostheticized or unprostheticized hugs; each embrace brings into contact different bodies that together effectively produce and convey affect. The disabled body exerts an affective agency here that exceeds ableist scripts: Thaddeus's words and actions challenge his mother's assumptions about how disability feels and ask her to contemplate how disabled moves might generate new and unanticipated affects, effects, and ways of moving (in) the world.

NOTES

1. See "Is Amputation TV's Hot Trend?," *TVline.com*; Margaret Lyons, "This Season's Hottest TV Trend: Stumps," *Vulture.com*; Lesley Goldberg, "Cut! Amputation Is Having a Hollywood Moment," *Hollywood Reporter*; and Matt Webb Mitovich, "Jessica Capshaw Talks 'Creepy' Grey's Anatomy Twist, Weighs In on TV's Amputation Craze," *Tvline.com*.

2. Definitions of "affection" include "a moderate feeling or emotion," "a tender attachment," "a bodily condition" or "disease, malady," "the feeling aspect of consciousness," and "the action of affecting; the state of being affected." *Merriam-Webster Dictionary*, "affection," accessed April 25, 2015, http://www.merriamwebster.com/dictionary/affection

3. While cross-racial, cross-gender, or cross-sexual performances are not neatly analogous to disability drag, the comparison does usefully raise questions about why some identity or bodily differences are seen as more fungible than others.

4. For analysis of the complexities of fakery, reality, and masquerade in disability performance, see Ellen Samuels, *Fantasies of Identification*, especially Part I.

5. *Dictionary.com Unabridged*, Random House, accessed April 25, 2016, http://www.dictionary.com/browse/drag

6. Such technological erasures of disability thus work in tandem with the narrative expulsion or extermination of disabled characters that, as Paul K. Longmore pointed out in one of the earliest studies of on-screen disability, "relieves both the individual viewer and society" of the need to grapple with "antidiscrimination and accessibility laws" permitting them to "escape the dilemma of . . . social accommodation and integration" (5–7).

7. See Danny Woodburn and Kristina Kopić, whose survey of employment of disabled actors covers a number of the factors that obstruct disabled actors' efforts to find employment.

8. Examples include actress/model/athlete Aimee Mullins, athlete/model Alex Minsky, and pop star Viktoria Modesta.

9. This error is noted in a number of locations, including the "*Forrest Gump*: Goofs" page of the *Internet Movie Database*; the *Forrest Gump Wiki*; and a thread entitled "Forrest Gump Bloopers" on *vhlinks.com*.

10. The full statement reads: "When Ali first carries Stephanie to swim in the sea, as he lifts her off the sun lounger, the actress's real legs cast a shadow" ("*Rust and Bone*: Goofs"). This statement reminds us of the variability and unreliability of film experience, since the writer misremembers the fact that Ali lifts Stéphanie from her wheelchair. For a disability critique of *Rust and Bone*'s failure to realistically represent rehabilitation and adjustment to prostheses, see Lawrence Shapiro. His criticism recalls the many denunciations of *Million Dollar Baby* for its failure to realistically depict Maggie's postinjury situation and leg amputation. See, for example, Steve Drake and Scott Richard Lyons.

11. For example, discussing Jessica Capshaw's performance on *Grey's Anatomy*, one self-identified above-the-knee (AK) amputee comments, "She has no clue what it is to walk with an AK prosthesis" (Mark Farrell). Amputee blogger Jason Sturm writes, also of Capshaw, "In the show, after learning to walk on her prosthetic, Arizona goes from barely walking and coping to walking in high heels, without a limp and absolutely no visual queues [*sic*][.] [S]he is an amputee [for] what seems like 2–3 episodes. It's a miracle!" Sturm's experience conflicts with this depiction: "It's difficult for an above knee amputee to walk and move without a noticeable limp" (Sturm).

12. The film *Freaks* features several amputee performers, along with a range of other unusually embodied actors; their presence, as Trumbull intuits, destabilizes the film's horror elements and unsettles easy interpretations of the film as an ableist or exploitative text.

13. The use of "insane" to describe something odd, surprising, or strange has been critiqued by disability activists and scholars, who see it as an ableist term akin to "lame" or "retarded." See, for instance, Liat Ben-Moshe.

WORKS CITED

Barnard, T. J. "10 Insane Ways Iconic Movie Special Effects Were Achieved." *What Culture*, May 30, 2013. whatculture.com/film/10-insane-ways-iconic-movie-special-effects-were-achieved.php/6

Barry, P. "Classics Revisited: *Silent Running*." *Cinematic Catharsis*, Sept. 2, 2015. http://cinematiccatharsis.blogspot.com/2015/09/classics-revisited-silent-running.html

Ben-Moshe, Liat. "'Lame Idea': Disabling Language in the Classroom." *Building Peda- gogical Curb Cuts: Incorporating Disability in the University Classroom and Curricu- lum*, edited by Liat Ben-Moshe, Rebecca C. Cory, Mia Feldbaum, and Ken Sagen- dorf, Graduate School, Syracuse University, 2005, pp. 107–15. thechp.syr.edu/ wp-content/uploads/2014/11/buildingpedagogicalcurbcuts.pdf

Bologna, Caroline. "6-Year-Old Boy Hugs His Mom for the First Time Ever, Thanks to a 3D-Printed Arm." *Huffington Post*, July 28, 2014. www.huffingtonpost. com/2014/07/28/3d-printed-arm-for-child_n_5627098.html

Brown, William. "Man without a Movie Camera—Movies without Men." *Film Theory and Contemporary Hollywood Movies*, edited by Warren Buckland, Routledge, 2009, pp. 66–85.

Campbell, Catherine. "Giving Up a 3-D Printed Prosthetic for a Different Vision of Per- fect." *New York Times*, May 17 2015. parenting.blogs.nytimes.com/2015/05/17/giv ing-up-a-3-d-printed-prosthetic-for-a-different-vision-of-perfect/

Christie, Elizabeth, and Geraldine Bloustien. "I-cyborg: Disability, Affect, and Public Pedagogy." *Discourse: Studies in the Cultural Politics of Education*, vol. 31, no. 4, 2010, pp. 483–98.

Coole, Diana, and Samantha Frost. "Introducing the New Materialisms." *New Material- isms: Ontology, Agency, and Politics*, edited by Diana Coole and Samantha Frost, Duke UP, 2010, pp. 1–43.

Drake, Steve. "Dangerous Times." *Ragged Edge Online*, Jan. 11 2005. www.ragged edgemagazine.com/reviews/drakemillionbaby.html

Farrell, Mark. Comment on *Grey's Anatomy's* Jessica Capshaw on Arizona's Loss." *Tv- line.com*, Mar. 13, 2014. tvline.com/2012/09/28/greys-anatomy-arizona-leg-ampu tated-spoilers/

"Forrest Gump Bloopers." *Van Halen Links*. www.vhlinks.com/vbforums/archive/index. php/t-19850.html

"*Forrest Gump*: Goofs." *Internet Movie Database*. www.imdb.com/title/tt0109830/ goofs?item=gf0933601

Forrest Gump Wiki. en.wikipedia.org/wiki/Forrest_Gump#Production

Garland-Thomson, Rosemarie. "The Case for Conserving Disability." *Journal of Bioethi- cal Inquiry* vol. 9, no. 3, 2012, pp. 339–55.

Goldberg, Lesley. "Cut! Amputation Is Having a Hollywood Moment." *Hollywood Re- porter*, Nov. 7, 2012. www.hollywoodreporter.com/live-feed/amputation-tv-walking- dead-greys-american-horror-story-387435

Grigely, Joseph. "Postcards to Sophie Calle." *Michigan Quarterly Review*, vol. 37, no. 2, 1998, hdl.handle.net/2027/spo.act2080.0037.203

Hiatt, Brian. "Michael J. Fox: The Toughest Man on TV." *Rolling Stone*, Sept. 26, 2013. www.rollingstone.com/movies/news/michael-j-fox-the-toughest-man-on- tv-20130926

"Is Amputation TV's Hot Trend?" *TVline.com*, Oct. 26, 2012. tvline.com/2012/10/26/ popular-tv-shows-2012-revenge-good-wife-sons-anarchy

Kafer, Alison. *Feminist, Queer, Crip*. Indiana UP, 2013.

Kermode, Mark. *Silent Running*. Palgrave Macmillan, 2014.

Longmore, Paul K. "Screening Stereotypes: Images of Disabled People." *Screening Dis- ability: Essays on Cinema and Disability*, edited by Christopher R. Smit and Anthony Enns, UP of America, 2001, pp. 1–17.

Lyons, Margaret. "This Season's Hottest TV Trend: Stumps." *Vulture.com*, Nov. 7, 2012. www.vulture.com/2012/11/tv-stumps-greys-anatomy-walking-dead-american-horror-story.html

Lyons, Scott Richard. "Million Dollar Bigotry." *Counterpunch*, Mar. 1, 2005. www.counterpunch.org/2005/03/01/million-dollar-bigotry/

Massumi, Brian. "Notes on the Translation and Acknowledgments." *A Thousand Plateaus: Capitalism and Schizophrenia*. Gilles Deleuze and Felix Guattari. U of Minnesota P, 1987, pp. viii–xix.

Massumi, Brian. *Parables for the Virtual: Movement, Affect, Sensation*. Duke UP, 2002.

Miranda, Matilda. "Iron Man Presents Bionic Arm to Boy, Melts Everyone's Heart." *The Loop*, Mar. 17, 2015. www.theloop.ca/iron-man-presents-bionic-arm-to-boy-melts-everyones-hearts.

Mitovich, Matt Webb. "Jessica Capshaw Talks 'Creepy' Grey's Anatomy Twist, Weighs In on TV's Amputation Craze." *Tvline.com*, Jan. 23, 2013. tv.yahoo.com/news/jessica-capshaw-talks-creepy-greys-anatomy-twist-weighs-031934992.html

Norden, Martin F. *The Cinema of Isolation: A History of Physical Disability in the Movies*. Rutgers UP, 1994.

Quayson, Ato. *Aesthetic Nervousness: Disability and the Crisis of Representation*. Columbia UP, 2007.

Quinion, Michael. *Port Out, Starboard Home: The Fascinating Stories We Tell about the Words We Use*. Penguin, 2005.

"*Rust and Bone*: Goofs." *Internet Movie Database*. www.imdb.com/title/tt2053425/trivia?tab=gf&ref_=tt_trv_gf

Samuels, Ellen. *Fantasies of Identification: Disability, Gender, Race*. New York University P, 2014.

Seigworth, Gregory J., and Melissa Gregg. "An Inventory of Shimmers." *The Affect Theory Reader*, edited by Melissa Gregg and Gregory J. Seigworth, Duke UP, 2010, pp. 1–25.

Shapiro, Lawrence. "Cinematic Impressions of the Female Amputee." *Disability Studies Quarterly*, vol. 33, no. 2, 2013. dsq-sds.org/article/view/3595/3241

Siebers, Tobin. *Disability Theory*. U of Michigan P, 2008.

Snyder, Sharon L., and David T. Mitchell. "Body Genres: An Anatomy of Disability in Film." *The Problem Body: Projecting Disability on Film*, edited by Sally Chivers and Nicole Markotic, Ohio UP, 2010, pp. 179–206.

Sturm, Jason. "Hey Hollywood, You Got Some Splainin to Do!" Jason Sturm blog, Oct. 16, 2013. jasonisturm.blogspot.com/2013/10/hey-hollywood-you-got-some-splainin-to.html

Talbot, F. A. *Moving Pictures: How They Are Made and Worked*. J. P. Lippincott Company, 1912. *Internet Archive*. archive.org/details/movingpicturesh00talbgoog

Trumbull, Douglas. "A *Silent Running*: Interview with Director Douglas Trumbull." *Castle of Frankenstein* 19 (1972). *Cybernetic Zoo*. cyberneticzoo.com/not-quite-robots/1971-silent-running-drones-doug-trumbull-don-trumbull-paul-kraus-james-dow-american/

"Watch Robert Downey Jr Present a 7 Year-Old with an Iron Man Robotic Arm." *Pedestrian*, Mar. 13, 2015. www.pedestrian.tv/news/entertainment/watch-robert-downey-jr-present-a-7-year-old-with-a/94eadafb-4dc2-4d3b-9576-852aaa18bf63.htm

FILMS

Fixed: The Science/Fiction of Human Enhancement. Dir. Regan Brashear. New Day Films, 2013. dma.iriseducation.org

Forrest Gump. Dir. Robert Zemeckis. Paramount, 1994. Paramount, 2006. DVD.

Rust and Bone [*De rouille et d'os*]. Dir. Jacques Audiard. Why Not Productions, 2012. Sony Pictures Home Entertainment, 2013. DVD.

Side by Side. Dir. Christopher Kenneally. Prod. Justin Szlasa and Keanu Reeves. 2012. Tribeca, 2013. DVD.

Silent Running. Dir. Douglas Trumbull. Universal Pictures, 1972. Universal Studios, 2002. DVD.

Spider-Man 3. Dir. Sam Raimi. Columbia Pictures, 2007. Sony Pictures Home Entertainment, 2007. DVD.

Vital Signs: Crip Culture Talks Back. Dir. Sharon L. Snyder and David T. Mitchell. Fanlight Productions, 1995.

Part III

The Matter of Mortality

Spider-Man's Designer Genes

Hypercapacity and Transhumanism in a "DIY World"

Samuel Yates

In the 2010 Broadway production *Spider-Man: Turn Off the Dark* Peter Parker and Norman Osborn are transformed into hypercapable subjects—Spider-Man and the Green Goblin, respectively—through a series of accidents in the genetics laboratories at Oscorp Industries. When Stan Lee beckoned Marvel Comics readers in *Amazing Fantasy*, volume 1, issue 15, writing, "Like costumed heroes? Confidentially, we in the comic mag business refer to them as 'Long Underwear Characters'! And, as you know, they're a dime a dozen! But, we think you may find our Spiderman just a bit . . . different," little did he realize he was setting the stage for one of the most popular icons of the twentieth and twenty-first centuries (Duncan and Smith 180).[1] Lee's promise of something "different" in the introduction of Peter Parker and his alter ego Spider-Man intimately shaped the production aesthetics structuring the Broadway performance of the mutant hero. Presentations of the Spider-Man universe are tightly controlled by Marvel Comics, with the aim of standardizing and protecting depictions of the material. While the onstage treatment of the comic's canon in the Julie Taymor–led *Turn Off the Dark* is rather traditional in its approach to mutation and desirability, the musical offers novel depictions of the Green Goblin—Spider-Man's infamous nemesis—and rhetorics of mutation.[2]

Despite genetic enhancement's centrality to the Spider-Man mythology, serious meditations on its material and ethical impact are missing in the multiple performance-oriented film franchises. This chapter complicates the Broadway musical's characterization of mutation by proposing its transhumanist performance as a step toward the posthuman, as a way of apprehending the genetically engineered subject—those peripheral embodiments that fall between delineated social categories of ability and disability, and therefore cannot be suitably registered within liberalism's diversity model. The musical's explicit rejection of a "normal" human body as an inadequate framework for existing in the modern world begs inquiry into the alternatives suggested by the characters onstage, particularly scientist-turned-villain Norman Osborn. Singing that "DNA is the way, now that evolution's had its day," Osborn argues that we now are in a "DIY world" in which humans must take control of their own genetic development to avoid extinction (Bono and The Edge 7). For these reasons, the effort of this chapter is to work through how *Turn Off the Dark* frames the mutant body as an imperative next step for the human race.

Norman Osborn's project of engineering human bodies to stave off hurt, disease, and death in *Turn Off the Dark* demonstrates how a transhuman logic for evolutionary "progress" is faulty. Transhumanism's central argument is for a human-directed escape from the miscoding errors in our genetic material, reifying man as both the baseline and the benchmark in our search for the next stage in man's progress. In other words, transhumanism aims to move the body beyond its biology in search of an "ideal" materiality. Posthumanism, by contrast, helps us oppose the premise of erroneous materialities by appreciating the ways different embodiments flourish: "Many invocations of posthumanism," Alexander Weheliye contends, "whether in antihumanist post-structuralist theorizing or in current considerations of technology and animality, reinscribe the humanist subject (Man) as the personification of the human by insisting that this is the category to be overcome, rarely considering cultural and political formations outside the world of Man that might offer alternative visions of humanity" (9–10).

Following Weheliye, I understand genetic enhancements of the ostensibly healthy neoliberal subject as producing the very "exceptional" nonhuman populations used as the impetus for enhancement itself. Thus, we cannot use posthumanism as the analytic tool to understand the representations of disability and cultures of ableism in *Turn Off the Dark* because a posthumanism attempting to "overcome" man is actually engaged in a transhumanist discourse. To become posthuman is to dwell in a mode of humanity that does not rely on social contracts; it is a way of being that revels in corporeal difference rather than denying or erasing biological divergences. Posthumanism dwells in abject, risky, and vulnerable states without presumptions of change or sociopolitical valuation. Posthumanism signals the death of the humanist subject by understanding the limits of human as a conceptual category instead of a designation or destination.

Osborn imagines himself capable of shaping natural selection, "the process by which life-forms change to suit the myriad opportunities afforded by the physical environment and by other life-forms," but evolution is a creative adaptation between the material body and biospheres that either preserve or end life—a process of chance, not design (Ridley 24). If progress as such does not exist, then humanity's attempts to control our own evolution are necessarily futile. Accordingly, Osborn's fantasy of scripting regulatory control over the human gene pool is a transhumanist response to failed eugenic fantasies of eliminating illness, disability, and death itself as conditions of life. Through genetic manipulation, precarious humanist subjects in *Turn Off the Dark* can be recuperated into late capitalist popular culture as one of what David Mitchell and Sharon Snyder call the "'able-disabled'—those who exceed their disability limitations through forms of administrative 'creaming' or hyper-prostheticization but leave the vast majority of disabled people behind" (12).

Although the musical generated frequent media coverage, relatively little critical work has been written about *Turn Off the Dark*—which is surprising not only because of the combined star power of its creative team and the capital behind the Spider-Man franchise, but also because of the musical's brazen intersection of eugenics, freak discourse, and disability. I will first contextualize the musical's introduction of eugenic logic through Norman Osborn's seemingly benign humanitarian project, which I understand to be a guise for a more insidious commodification of the human genome by Oscorp Industries, notwithstanding its displacement of the normate body. Then I examine Norman Osborn's transformation into the Green Goblin, and the forced mutation of his lab workers into the Sinister Six, to theorize *Turn Off the Dark*'s genetic manipulation as a transhumanist project. I argue that despite the lyric's rhetorical invocation of a posthuman condition, genetic mutation is still deeply invested in the human body; this inability to decenter the human necessitates that we view the musical's mutants as transhuman rather than posthuman. Having established this context, my third section considers *Turn Off the Dark* as an addition to the freak show canon. Here I examine the song "A Freak Like Me" to unpack the musical's bid to connote every body in the theater as a "freak" through the shared performance. This is crucial for understanding the material impact of *Turn Off the Dark*'s ideological work on the production itself; the pursuit of performing a fictional hypercapacity that, ironically, disabled multiple actors during the production's run.

Engineering a "DIY World"

There are multiple layers to *Turn Off the Dark*'s engineering of hypercapable bodies in performance. With twenty-seven aerial flight sequences and an additional four aerial combat sequences—to say nothing of the immense set changes—it was, as Patrick Healy writes, "the most technically complex show ever on Broadway" (2010). Actors performing the roles of Spider-Man, the Green Goblin, and Arachne used an intricate harness system to "fly" across the stage and into the theater's house, providing a spectacle not unlike the stage magic of Mary Martin flying off to Neverland in the 1954 Broadway production of *Peter Pan*. The language of the music and lyrics, which script eugenic fantasies of better bodies, compounds these flying effects. Just as the unsavory strings attached to eugenics were frequently erased by the blinding promise of biological perfection, so too were the harness wires forgiven to aid the biological narrative of *Turn Off the Dark*. What do audiences make of this site at which hypercapacity not only proliferates, but is the new normal? *Turn Off the Dark* opened for previews in November 2010 and concluded its run on January 4, 2014; despite whatever troubles the production encountered, a three-year run indicates a viable commercial interest in the transhuman subject. If the show's "legs" are any indicator, audiences were keen to experience a staging of what Roy Ascott calls "the post-biological era"—"the site of bionic transformation at which we can recreate ourselves and redefine what it is to be human" (376). The expansion of bodily ability afforded by the musical's intricate rigging system and the narrative of genetic enhancement encoded in the book and lyrics recreate the human onstage in order to playact recreations of the human species.

Norman Osborn first introduces genetic enhancement in the musical during Peter Parker's school trip to Oscorp Industries. The science magnate uses experimental technologies to advance cross-species integration. In various comic and film series Norman Osborn is presented as a hardened amoral industrialist, but the musical rewrites his character as a humanitarian scientist. Instead of making money, Osborn is interested in harnessing animal capabilities for humans (such as devising a way for humans to replicate their own limbs as a starfish would). Although this shift is, in part, due to the introduction of his oft-absent wife, Emily, Osborn's good intentions reveal the moral framework structuring the script's approach to genetic manipulation. As geneticists Norman and Emily Osborn sing to a group of high school students visiting at Oscorp in "DIY World," their work centers on shoring up the sustainability of the human race: "The human race can take a hit / We're gonna sink but you can swim / If you don't mind a little change of skin / Designer genes are a better fit" (Bono and The Edge 7). Their good-natured goal of saving the human race is consumed by capitalism in one quick stanza, moving from species sustainability to consumable designer models in two sung lines. This "DIY World" echoes plainly what Garland-Thomson calls "Eugenic World Building," or the "ideology and practice of controlling who reproduces, how they reproduce, and what they reproduce in the interest of shaping the composition of a particular population" (2015). The Osborns' bleak projection that humanity is "gonna sink" is countered by their estimation that humans have only one alternative for survival—changing their "skin," or bodily capacities.

Oscorp is experimenting on augmenting the human genome in an attempt to create the next iteration of human: hypercapacitated, or "supered," bodies. Norman Osborn creates a new hierarchical structure that is reflective of a biopolitical economy within neoliberalism: affluent humans unsatisfied with swimming in the public gene pool can opt for "designer" genetic modifications, reinscribing linkages between class divisions and natural order. Neoliberalism, as described by Mitchell and Snyder, "involves strategies of the seizure of the very materiality of life at the level of the individual" (8). If so, then Oscorp Corporation is invested in the biopolitical project of norming alternative corporealities; the engineered bodies onstage represent hyperprostheticized bodies as productive difference in order to reveal ways to approach transhuman peripheral embodiment. Taken collectively, the repertoire of augmented bodies displaces hegemonic able-bodied norms, emerging as a "fetishized product of 'bare life' while referencing disability as the dissonant expression of a distant kinship" (Mitchell and Snyder 181). Singing, "'Cause we can be what we gotta be / And we need to be what we gotta be," Osborn's simultaneously eugenic and agentic worldview reifies the anthropocentrism situated at the heart of genetic research, in which human-animals become the standard unit of measurement against all other life.

Proclaiming, "DNA is the way, now that evolution's had its day," Osborn attempts to establish mutation as an adaptation necessary for survival, instead of aberrant. This is complicated, however, by his change of vocabulary after his transformation into the Green Goblin. When Osborn was conceptually *homo sapient*, he imagined a "DIY World" that links humans and animals together in a coalition of bodies benefiting from each other's capacities; after mutating into a monstrous goblin, he changes his tune, singing, "A freak like me needs company" (Bono and The Edge 11).

Through his transition from a global humanity to a solitary "freak," we see the Green Goblin fall on his own imagined animacy scale: Osborn rejects his human name and takes up the monstrous moniker "Goblin" in its stead. This plunge moves counter to Spider-Man's ascent. Parker's "productive" mutation gifts spider-like abilities while still allowing him to maintain his status as "man." As Spider-Man, Parker is the superhuman of Osborn's imagination made manifest, the body beyond (but not post-) human. And perhaps it is this tempered change that makes Parker's mutation desirable, while the Goblin is rendered freakish.

When the Green Goblin calls himself a freak, he actively acknowledges his own hand in the process—as Norman Osborn he purposefully manipulated his genetic makeup to effect change and, in doing so, engaged in a process of enfreakment. "Enfreakment," as Ellen Samuels describes, is the "process by which individual difference becomes stylized as cultural otherness" ("Examining Millie and Christine McKoy" 56). A keyword to Samuels's enfreakment is "stylized," which opens up the choices of production, of making, of *styling*—a purposeful fashioning of a subject into a "freak" identity, as Garland-Thomson argues in *Freakery*. To *style* takes an explicit performative action, a narrative spiel, a doing. In theatrical contexts, stylizations include scripted remarks, scene blocking and choreography, and costume changes. Although Samuels cites Garland-Thomson's "array of corporeal wonders," like the morbidly obese midgets and Siamese twins, this process array often requires an aesthetic of normate able-bodiedness to constitute its center (56). Spider-Man, having been transformed and still appearing "normal" (if not ostensibly better, by conventional standards of male beauty), escapes the title "freak," while Norman Osborn's skin is transfigured into a green, misshapen approximation of his previous flesh.

The Green Goblin uses genetic mutations to make a case for victimization of "freaks" and coalition-building with the audience—creating a conflict of interest for audiences who may well empathize with Patrick Page's campy Green Goblin more than Reeve Carney's angsty Spider-Man. There's more to be said here about the link between morality and aesthetics of the hypercapable subject—specifically regarding physical deformity. Across town, another green-skinned mutant flies above the Gershwin Theatre eight performances a week—*Wicked*'s protagonist Elphaba is cast as a "Wicked" witch and colored a sickly green. *Turn Off the Dark* enacts a similar aesthetic coding for Norman Osborn / Green Goblin, linking greenness to sickly pallor, wickedness, evil. Meanwhile, Peter Parker's need to wear a masked costume while exploring the full potential of his alternative embodiment demonstrates one way in which the mutant body is tyrannized by ideological constructs of the "normal" body, as Lennard Davis theorizes in *Enforcing Normalcy*: "In fact, the very concept of normalcy by which most people (by definition) shape their existence is in fact tied inexorably to the concept of disability, or rather, the concept of disability is a function of the concept of normalcy" (2). If disability is brought into being as the necessary opposition of "normal" (or, tautologically, able-bodied/minded), as Davis suggests, then mutants are forced into a subordinate biological status despite their remarkable capabilities.[3] Further, since existence within a normed society is shaped by a supposition that mutants do not exist or are the subjects of fantasy, the genetic differences yielding hypercapacity are doubly erased from consideration or concern: once by a disbelieving public, and again by a policing of able-bodied/mindedness by the mutant him- or herself. The mutant, then, is analogous to Haraway's cyborg in that she operates from multiple positions simultaneously, with every perspective "reveal[ing] both dominations and possibilities unimaginable from the other vantage point" (154).

Stacy Alaimo refigures the boundaries of human as such in *Bodily Natures* by arguing that the "'outside' is already within, inhabiting and transforming that which may or may not be 'human' through continual intra-actions" (154). In thinking through how transhumanism functions alongside (or as a product) of Alaimo's philosophy of transcorporeality, *Turn Off the Dark* positions these intra-actions as dependent on the surrounding environment, but precoded within the genome: bodily responses, adaptation, or mutations are catalyzed by environmental interactions, but the blueprint for such change is always already within the human-animal. We can see this most clearly in the Green Goblin's plan to genetically alter other humans as he did himself in the number "A Freak Like Me Needs Company." Through his experiments on former employees, the Green Goblin manages to create six different villains from the same experiment; the Sinister Six—Carnage, Electro, Kraven the Hunter, Lizard, Swarm, and Swiss Miss—exemplify how different genetic coding yields a variety of reactions to the same catalyst.[4] What Elizabeth Grosz says of Darwin's concept of variation might also be said of the mutations in *Spider-Man*: "The continuity of life through time . . . is *not* the transmission of invariable or clearly defined characteristics over regular, measured periods of time (as various essentialisms imply), but the generation of endless variation, endless openness to the accidental, the random, the unexpected" (7). This precondition for mutation troubles our ability to fully render mutation as a posthuman condition, but it productively points to the interrelation of human change and technology in modern culture. The generative affordances of the serum's toxicity refigure the forms of being and relation in common with the human and the (im)material. Moreover, Mel Y. Chen advocates for "the queer productivity of toxins and toxicity, a productivity that extends beyond an enumerable set of addictive or pleasure-inducing substances," provocatively suggesting that toxins induce pleasure, love, rehabilitation, affectations, and assets (*Animacies* 211). In other words, while the scientific leaps Osborn suggests may sound far-fetched, the more-than-human trajectory humorously cushioned in Bono's high-energy pop score are on-trend with discourses in contemporary transhumanism.

The publication *h+* magazine indexes the broader growth of transhumanism in popular culture. Read as "h-plus," where letter *h* signifies human, the magazine defines the bodily modifications that promise and threaten to radically alter human life as including longevity, self-modification and performance enhancement, virtual reality, and NBIC (nano-bio-info-cog). In "Nano-Bio-Info-Cogno: Paradigm for the Future," *h+* writer Surfdaddy Orca argues:

> Just as we battle over the right to life today, it's almost a given that we will battle in the future over the right to personal enhancement. New and radical choices will be available to parents who want certain characteristics for their unborn children—for example, augmentation of intelligence or corrective genetic procedures. Improvement and human performance enhancing drugs and neurotechnological devices are already entering the global marketplace. (Surfdaddy Orca 2010)

Transhumanism seeks improvement upon man's natural human abilities; Oscorp, being committed to augmenting the human race, positions itself to sell these enhancements as "designer genes" on the global marketplace. Designer genetics hinges on the eradication of disability, illness, and aesthetic "imperfections"—biological preconditions that inhibit a full flourishing of life. Because the genome is both the baseline and the benchmark against which change is measured, Osborn's project should not be described as posthumanist; his investment in preserving human life and positioning genetic augmentation as a marketplace choice directly contradicts the conceptual posthumanisms of Lyotard and Habermas. The genetic augmentation in *Turn Off the Dark* is, if anything, an aggrandize-

ment of anthropocentrism given that its predicated entirely on hyperca-
pacitating the human body.

In the song "Pull the Trigger," Osborn knows his secrets to enhanced
genetics, superhuman kinetics, and muscle augmentation are the key to
financial success: "And look at that, web bio-generation. / Your secrets.
Getting Sold. Getting bought. / . . . Get Funded! Or your baby won't live!"
(Bono and The Edge 7). Osborn's ascription of "life" to his technological
project animates transhuman technologies as a living force capable of
growth. Yet transhumanism in philosophical practice and theatrical performance is counterproductive when it limits the perspective of human
ability and denies the very precariousness that links humans with other
animals. Concerned with the "human race [taking] a hit," Osborn resists
pain, aging, and death in his promise that "we could live a thousand years"
(Bono and The Edge 9). Oscorp, then, presents technology as the answer
to the natural "disability" shared by all humans: mortality. Moreover, there
is also a less universal eradication of disability at stake here, in that mortality's erasure covers over disability as a shorthand for truncated life.

Performers' bodies are technologically transformed through an intricate theatrical design and, indeed, it is the blatant transparency of spectacle that enables the hero's story to be acted onstage at all. The seemingly
superhuman ability of the actor playing Spider-Man is characterized by
his acrobatic ability to appear and disappear across the stage in mere sec-
onds and "web-sling" through the theater, traveling by a visible harness
system. Instead of a single, virtuosic performer navigating the aerial choreography, audiences see multiple ensemble actors switching off the role
of Spider-Man in order to create the superhero's omnipresence within the
theater. This company of ten Spider-Men visually indexes a creative anxiety about the commoditization of the superhero, as well as broader concerns about the collapse of unique identity into consumption and transhuman self-interest.

As audiences watch the musical unfold, they temporarily become hypercapacitated themselves; the spectators' investment in the premium
ticket prices at the Foxwoods Theatre gives them a designer "change of
skin" by augmenting their capacity for sight. In the performance venue,
the spectator's perception is morphed to supered specificity: the production design isolates the audience's capacity for sight through focused lighting and a harness system that exaggerates the onstage actor's physical
movement. By creating tight fields of vision with ever-moving points of
interest, the direction emulates a cinematic effect through a pointedly

guided optical experience that stifles the eye's ability to wander freely within the world of the play. In this way, the audience eye is aesthetically standardized, much like a movie guiding audiences through scenic editing and focus shots, even as it is supered to a greater capacity for attention to detail. The precarious politic is all the more perilous through its innocuous presentation: audiences enjoy their heightened sight and tap their fingers along to the pop stylizations of Bono and The Edge, applauding the message of DNA modification as the "Solution" to human death at the end of a rousing musical chorus. *Turn Off the Dark*'s success relies on the explicit performance and tacit acceptance of the transhuman body's changing materiality upon interaction with new technologies.

Toward a Transhuman "Freak Show"

Turn Off the Dark's fetishization of corporeal and ontological difference situates the production beyond the Great White Way; the transhuman bodies populating the theater and the mutant-freak rhetoric scripting their participation asks that we imaginatively place this musical in the tradition of the freak show. By recapitulating the Peter Parker origin story already told in comic books, television cartoons, and three popular film franchises, Taymor's blockbuster musical typifies a cultural implosion born from an artistic commoditization and also creates a "freak discourse" that interconnects these disparate media forms and resists critique. Rosemarie Garland-Thomson describes the freak discourse as a specific narrative form that entwines a spiel (show advertisement), the freak's extraordinary identity, a specific staging, and ancillary media that confirms the staged freakishness (film representations) ("Introduction" 6–7). It also cultivates identification with the mutant Spider-Man through the audiences' experiencing the narrative from Spider-Man's point of view. This perspective accelerates a desire for futurity as the audiences experience the fantasy of productive, nonharmful, genetic mutation that refigures the limits of the human without violating the aesthetic normate. Thus, audience interaction and contemporary media extend the performance beyond the stage, becoming co-constitutive aesthetic elements that generate a larger commercial success. Such an expansion, however, necessitates that we more carefully attend to positive rendering and circulation of genetic modification in pop culture. Unlike freak shows of the late nineteenth century, *Spider-Man: Turn Off the Dark* is able to promulgate its narrative through a worldwide web, if you will, of media forms.

Freak shows, Robin Blyn argues, are theaters of mass entertainment that feature "a complex orchestration of conflicting ideologies, libidinal displacements, and anxious flirtations with an otherness from which the viewer can always safely retreat" (xviii). Parker, Osborne, and the audience begin the show in a *normal*, or perhaps more appropriately *neutral*, state. Portrayed by actors without spectacle or extra theatrics, each character is ostensibly like any audience member—average in bodily ability. Much like the enacted transformations into Spider-Man and the Green Goblin, the musical maps freakishness onto the audiences' otherwise unremarkable bodies through their spectatorship:

> I said goodbye to my straight life cuz I love a freak
> (A freak like me needs company)
> All the weirdos in the world are right here now in New York City
> All the brazen boys and girls (Bono and The Edge 11)

The "brazen" freakishness the Green Goblin sings about opens itself to multiple readings of otherness: the embrace of queerness by abandoning one's "straight life"; the coalition politic and transhuman utopia of identifying other self-described freaks; the abject weirdness of life in the musical's version of a technologically saturated New York City; the brazenness of returning to or achieving perpetual childhood youth through mutation. Unlike the traditional freak show Blyn maps, however, there is no safe retreat from the transhuman otherness in *Turn Off the Dark*. Every body in the Foxwoods Theatre is physically augmented for the duration of the musical, and mentally altered afterward through the consideration and experience of the augmented bodies.

Watching Spider-Man proclaim, "And you can rise above (Free your soul) / Open your eyes up (Rise above yourself and take control)," the public buys into self-actualization of the "DIY World" Osborn articulates (Bono and The Edge 12). In this way, *Spider-Man the Musical* positions the human body at what David Savran describes as a "site of struggle between economic and symbolic capital on the one hand, and cultural capital, on the other" (277–78).[5] Although C. B. Macpherson and Blyn remind us that self-ownership and escaping death in a capitalist market are an illusion, the ideology of the self-determined freak subject enables the chimera of freedom onstage and elides contradictions between precarious life and capitalism (Blyn xxix).

Actor Implications

Broadway is metonymic with the commercial theater industry and it has long served as a litmus test for the political passions and social appetites of American culture. Accordingly, we must pay attention to bodily configurations on the Broadway stage to better understand how disability is leveraged against the American imaginary's normate body. Given that *Turn Off the Dark* is also a superhero myth, the musical provides a particularly worthwhile site for exploration. Superhero genres, as José Alaniz writes, provide "a rich 'mirror universe' of American society" (8). This production provides the dire warning that the space between our reality and the "mirror universe" Alainz invokes is rapidly collapsing. At this point, it is worth considering the material impact of the eugenic logic and the resulting fantasy of hypercapacity at play in *Turn Off the Dark*. Although there are several directions this exploration could take, I address two effects here: the preclusion of disability and the simultaneous disablement of actors.

Disability inclusion is already forgone in *Turn Off the Dark*—the normate body, for all its constructedness, is taken as the body in need of rehabilitation. It follows, then, that in performances of crip and queer bodies we are not only *entertained by* the everyday management of peripheral embodiments (while still maintaining distance enough for a "safe retreat," as Blyn describes), we *entertain* these same events as an operative mode for present or future action. In *Turn Off the Dark* Norman Osborn preys on a fear of disability by refiguring the normate body as the body already in decline. The musical never quite delves into the disability terms of its argument in that disability subjectivity is always intertwined with performance. *Turn Off the Dark* requires additional capacities, accommodations, and modes of embodiment to render its hypercapable subject significant. In this way, disability and hypercapacity become counterpoints to each other as strategic executions against the normate body. Rather than partaking in a "disability masquerade" in order to look "disabled enough" to require help, as Ellen Samuels writes, the production's hypercapacity demands the failure of a "normalcy masquerade" to reveal itself to the spectator (*Fantasies of Identification* 137). The hypercapable body waits in the wings, ready to facilitate and liberate the imagination of the paying spectator.

Turn Off the Dark's erasure of disabled bodies is complicated by the musical's production history, in which eight highly publicized accidents highlight the precarity of able-bodiedness.[6] Between 1997 and 2007, the

US Department of Labor's Occupational Safety and Health Hazard Administration (OSHA) investigated thirty-five incidents in live shows, twenty-five of which involved stagehands and technicians, ten involving performers. After in-theater rehearsals (the show had no out-of-town try-outs due to the intricacy of the production's fly system) and the first full month of previews, OSHA had investigated violations of workplace safety standards regarding four separate incidents (Hosier). This means that *Turn Off the Dark*'s initial stages of production (rehearsals and first month of previews) alone prompted nearly half as many performer-related investigations into violations of workplace safety standards as the past decade of *all* Broadway productions. In a March 2011 press release OSHA reported issuing 8 Legged Productions three "serious citations,"[7] due to the "substantial probability that death or serious physical harm could result from a hazard about which the employer knew or should have known" (Fitzgerald). Two weeks after OSHA issued its citations, T. V. Carpio, the actress playing Arachne, sustained a neck injury; three more serious injuries followed during the production. Neither OSHA nor the New York State Department of Labor (NYDOL) cited *Turn Off the Dark* beyond the first three injuries, but the effect is clear: the show's aim of performing hyper-capacity comes at the expense of able-bodiedness.[8]

Actors Equity Association (AEA) president Nick Wyman, responding to mounting calls for accountability following Christopher Tierney's serious injuries, stated: "I have been very disturbed and distraught by the serious injuries sustained by our member Chris Tierney at the December 20th performance of SPIDER-MAN: TURN OFF THE DARK" ("Spider-Man and Equity"). But "Part of the joy of live theatre—for both the audience and the performers," Wyman argued, "is its immediacy and its vitality." This advocacy for "immediacy" and "vitality" hinges on the able-bodiedness assumed of triple-threat Broadway performers, whose multiple skills in singing, acting, and dancing approximate a different kind of hypercapacity. "A 'boy in the bubble' strategy of taking everything down to half speed, of wrapping everyone and everything in cotton wool, obviously will not work. Live theatre, exciting theatre involves risk," Wyman emphasized. Wyman not only uses the disabled condition of severe combined immunodeficiency as a metaphorical straw man, but also succinctly argues against any notion of crip time on the Broadway stage. Although Wyman speaks of a commitment to safety and minimizing risk in the theater, the way in which he articulates actor performance echoes the neoliberal desires to become *more* that we see throughout the script of *Turn Off the Dark*. A desire for safety ensconces the normate actor in a protective bubble or cotton wool, rhetorically suggesting ailment and deficiency. My argument is not that the narrative's expendable treatment of the normate body directly caused the lax regulations and responses guaranteeing actor safety, but rather that the musical's precarious framing of the human body clearly did *not* facilitate greater care structures ensuring the actors' well-being in the production.

Conclusion

In this chapter, I have demonstrated how *Spider-Man: Turn Off the Dark* uses a hybridized theatrical design and pseudoscientific plots to create hypercapacitated bodies, and that this production situates these extracapable performers and spectators as transhuman. The transhuman subjects in *Turn Off the Dark* explicitly reject humankind's vulnerable embodiments; Spider-Man's altered, amazing body is a prophylactic narrative against the specters of disease, disability, and death. As the first superhero musical since *It's a Bird, It's a Plane, It's Superman* (1966) to appear on Broadway, it signals a reemergence of the superhero in the American imaginary, in an important departure into the realm of possibility for the generation and purchase of extrahuman capabilities. The stagecraft and public fetishization of mutation engendered by this production has allowed the musical to reenter the twenty-first century as a more accessible, flexible form in popular culture. While the democratization of superhero materials and the accompanying expansions of bodily capacity ultimately bring a diversity of backgrounds into the theater, *Turn Off the Dark* is unable to critically assess and structure a moral value system around the establishment of a transhuman body through theatrical production. The musical was slated to undergo a creative overhaul before relaunching as an "arena spectacular" designed to tour across the United States by winter 2016, but as of this writing, such a tour has not opened (Cohen). Regardless of *Turn Off the Dark*'s future, its Broadway production ushered in a new moment for the commercial theater industry—one requiring new questions concerning the limits of bodily capacity, the representation of ability and disability, and our valuation of the boundary between the actor as a sensate human body and as an objectified material means of production. *Spider-Man: Turn Off the Dark* is caught in a web of adaptation as it makes a case for its own scientific relevance, even though it is unable to unharness itself from its theatrical trappings. Suspended somewhere between science and spectacle, the musical itself enacts the lines of the aptly named opening ballad,

"Boy Falls from the Sky": "I'd be myself, if I knew who I'd become" (Bono and The Edge 2).

NOTES

1. This direct address is discussed in Randy Duncan and Matthew J. Smith's *The Power of Comics: History, Form and Culture* (2009); the original issue is Marvel Comics' "Amazing Fantasy #15," by Stan Lee (w), Steve Ditko (i), and Jack Kirby (i), published August 10, 1962.

2. The extensive legal battle following writer-director Julie Taymor's ousting from the production in March 2011, and the subsequent direction by Philip William McKinley that culminated in the "Version Two" performed for the official Broadway opening on June 14, 2011, make creative and authorship credits to *Spider-Man: Turn Off the Dark* difficult to parse. In this chapter, all music and lyrics are credited to Bono and The Edge. The book was written by Julie Taymor, Glen Berger, and Roberto Aguirre-Sacasa.

3. Sadly, *Turn Off the Dark* misses an even greater opportunity here to play with the fantastic. Each mutation in the show is represented as a bipedal humanoid, demonstrating how a compulsory able-bodiedness is embedded even in the biologically nonnormative space.

4. *Turn Off the Dark*'s version of the Sinister Six is a marked departure from the mythology of Spider-Man universe. In the theatrical version the Sinister Six have mutation thrust upon them by the Green Goblin as punishment for abandoning Osborn and Oscorp industries. The original Sinister Six included Doctor Octopus, Electro, Kraven the Hunter, Mysterio, Sandman, and Vulture; they first appeared in *The Amazing Spider-Man Annual* 1, 1964, with art by Steve Ditko. The character Swiss Miss is wholly original to *Turn Off the Dark*.

5. When using terms associated with *Spider-Man: Turn Off the Dark* in the Google search engine, the common misnomer "Spider-Man the Musical" is the first suggested search item, an aggregate result based on popular searches of all Google users and purchased search terms. This is partially because the production's website does not market itself by its proper name as most musicals do. Instead, its web domain is http://spidermanonbroadway.com

6. I am only tracing a brief history of the significant legal response to the dubious workplace safety standards during the run of *Turn Off the Dark*. For a more thorough inquiry and legal recommendations see Brooke Day.

7. 8 Legged Productions is a subcompany of Foresight Theatrical, a general management company for big-budget Broadway musicals. Other Foresight productions include *Les Misérables, Miss Saigon, The Phantom of the Opera, Side Show,* and *Kinky Boots*.

8. Regarding actual expense, OSHA cited 8 Legged Productions a proposed $12,600 in proposed fines for "serious citations." The inspection detail released after the case closed in January 2012 reported that the penalty paid was $10,630. The smaller amount is accounted for by a reduction of two violations from "Serious" to "Other." Interestingly, OSHA has a "repeat" category for safety violations, but this does not appear to have been invoked at any point after the initial citations. *See* United States Department of Labor, OSHA, Inspection: 314883919-8 LEGGED PRODUCTIONS, LLC, available at http://www.osha.gov/pls/imis/establishment.inspection_detail?id=314883919. NYDOL is-

sued nonmonetary citations that subjected the production to unannounced safety inspections to ensure compliance. See Healy, "New York Issues."

WORKS CITED

Alaimo, Stacy. *Bodily Natures: Science, Environment, and the Material Self.* Indiana UP, 2010.

Alaniz, José. *Death, Disability, and the Superhero: The Silver Age and Beyond.* UP of Mississippi, 2014.

Ascott, Roy. *Telematic Embrace: Visionary Theories of Art, Technology, and Consciousness.* Edited by Edward A. Shanken. U of California P, 2003.

Blyn, Robin. *The Freak-Garde: Extraordinary Bodies and Revolutionary Art in America.* Minneapolis: U of Minnesota P, 2013.

Bono and The Edge. "Music from *Spider-Man Turn Off the Dark.*" 2011. Digital Album Booklet. Mercury Records Limited, 2011.

Brooke Day, Lori. "Turn Off the Danger: The Lack of Adequate Safety Incentives in the Theatre Industry." *NYU Law Review*, vol. 88, no. 4, 2013, pp. 1308–47.

Chen, Mel Y. *Animacies: Biopolitics, Racial Mattering, Queer Affect.* Duke UP, 2012.

Cohen, Stefani. "'Alvin and the Chipmunks,' 'Rio' to Be Adapted for the Stage." Speakeasy Blog. *Wall Street Journal*, July 25, 2014. blogs.wsj.com/speakeasy/2014/07/25/alvin-and-the-chipmunks-rio-to-be-adapted-for-the-stage/

Davis, Lennard. *Enforcing Normalcy: Disability, Deafness, and the Body.* Verso, 1995.

Duncan, Randy, and Matthew J. Smith. *The Power of Comics: History, Form and Culture.* Continuum, 2009.

Garland-Thomson, Rosemarie. "Eugenic World-Building and Disability: The Strange World of Kazuo Ishiguro's *Never Let Me Go.*" *Journal of Medical Humanities*, Dec. 2, 2015. doi.org/10.1007/s10912-015-9368-y

Garland-Thomson, Rosemarie. "Introduction: From Wonder to Error—a Genealogy of Freak Discourse in Modernity." *Freakery: Cultural Spectacles of the Extraordinary Body*, Edited by Rosemarie Garland-Thomson, New York University P, 1996, pp. 1–19.

Grosz, Elizabeth. *The Nick of Time: Politics, Evolution, and the Untimely.* Duke UP, 2004.

Haraway, Donna J. "A Cyborg Manifesto: Science, Technology, and Socialist-Feminism in the Late Twentieth Century." *Simians, Cyborgs, and Women: The Reinvention of Nature.* Routledge, 1991, pp. 149–81. First published as "A Manifesto for Cyborgs: Science, Technology, and Socialist Feminism in the 1980s," *Socialist Review*, no. 8, 1985, 65–108.

Healy, Patrick. "Concussion Sidelines 'Spider-Man' Actress." ArtsBeat, *New York Times*, Dec. 3, 2010. artsbeat.blogs.nytimes.com/2010/12/03/concussion-sidelines-spider-man-actress/

Healy, Patrick. "New York Issues 2 Safety Violations for 'Spider-Man' Accidents in 2010." *New York Time*, Feb. 13, 2011, A6.

Hosier, Fred. "Spiderman Is No Match for OSHA." *Safety Alert News*, Dec. 30, 2010. safetynewsalert.com/spiderman-is-no-match-for-osha/

Mitchell David T., with Sharon L. Snyder. *The Biopolitics of Disability: Neoliberalism, Ablenationalism, and Peripheral Embodiment.* U of Michigan P, 2015.

Ridley, Matt. *Genome: The Autobiography of a Species in 23 Chapters.* Harper Perennial, 1999.

Samuels, Ellen. "Examining Millie and Christine McKoy: Where Enslavement and En-freakment Meet." *Signs: Journal of Women in Culture and Society*, vol. 37, no. 1, 2011, pp. 53–81.

Samuels, Ellen. *Fantasies of Identification: Disability, Gender, Race.* New York University P, 2014.

Savran, David. "Shadows of Brecht." *Critical Theory and Performance: Revised and Enlarged*, edited by Janelle Reinelt and Joseph Roach, U of Michigan P, 2007, pp. 268–83.

Surfdaddy Orca. "Nano-Bio-Info-Cogno: Paradigm for the Future." *H+ Magazine*, Feb. 12, 2010. http://hplusmagazine.com/2010/02/12/nano-bio-info-cogno-paradigm-future/

US Department of Labor, Occupational Safety and Health Administration. "US Department of Labor's OSHA Cites Spider-Man Broadway Musical Production Company Following Injuries to Cast Member." *Occupational Safety and Health Administration*, Mar. 4, 2011, osha.gov/news/newsreleases/region2/03042011

Weheliye, Alexander G. *Habeas Viscus: Racializing Assemblages, Biopolitics, and Black Feminist Theories of the Human.* Duke UP, 2014.

Wyman, Nick. "Spider-Man and Equity." *Actors Equity Association*, Jan. 2, 2016. actors equity.org/NewsMedia/news2011/jan2.spiderman.asp

An Arm Up or a Leg Down?

Grounding the Prosthesis and Other Instabilities

Chris Ewart

> There are cases where a prosthesis is *still* a prosthesis.
> —Michael Davidson, *Concerto for the Left Hand* 176

Sarah S. Jain's "The Prosthetic Imagination: Enabling and Disabling the Prosthesis Trope" (1999) critiques applications of prosthesis that seldom consider the bodies and people who use them. Among other "problems emerging from overgeneralizations of the prosthesis trope" (38), Jain discusses Mark Seltzer's influential "double logic of prosthesis," which arrives from Henry Ford's appropriation of disabled labor. Within such logic, a cancellation of self (and agency) occurs with the violent loss of body—from what Seltzer calls a "natural body" (157)—extended (and regained to an extent) with the incorporation of a prosthesis. In the architectural domain, Jain notes Mark Wigley's idea that the prosthesis "becomes a side-effect [that] reconstruct[s] the body, transforming its limits, at once extending and convoluting its borders. The body itself becomes artifice" (qtd. in Jain 38).

Given how "the prosthesis [i]s a tempting theoretical gadget [to] examine the porous places of bodies and tools" (49), Jain helps establish a critical discourse of prosthetic theory and embodiment. She considers the prosthesis a multivalent object that, for some, seldom leaves the medical domain, operating as a metaphor and as a manufactured desire for products. She notes, for example, the proliferation of and cultural reliance upon the automobile as a quintessential, problematic (North) American prosthesis and that Ford's automobiles were inaccessible for many disabled workers who built them or who were disabled in the process. Such assembled, biopolitical exclusion reminds us that we do not all experience or afford prostheses in the same ways—either during the machine age or under neoliberalism.

Jain's argument also draws attention to an "overwrit[ing]" of embodiment via "assumptions of a physically disabled body and the liberal premise of the choice of the perfect body" (49). This chapter similarly seeks to intervene in key instances of the kind of "overwriting" signaled by Jain. I explore aspects of the prosthesis's roles in narrative and in lived experience as a way to situate its conceptual diversity and materiality "that imprints itself upon human bodies" (Godden 1278). I then examine representations of disability and prosthetics in two sensationalist, revenge-themed films—Robert Rodriguez's *Planet Terror* (2007) and Noboru Iguchi's *Machine Girl* (*Kataude Mashin Gâru*) (2008)—that comment on particular national and social contexts. *Machine Girl* reflects a trajectory of post-atomic Japan's national emasculation and the cultural phenomenon of yakuza while *Planet Terror* satirizes material realities of those who cross the border from Mexico into Texas, calling out inequity and othering around border experiences. In addition, each film's brutality and over-the-top plot fulfill a pattern of cultural representations that use the prosthesis as narrative enabler, moral barometer and spectacle of excess. Though these films generate agency for their recently disabled female protagonists, empowerment accompanies militaristic and gangster-style violence where prostheses—and disabled bodies—become contemporary fetishizations of violence as power.

Proselytizing the Prosthetic: Not So Smooth After All

> *Advertise* your leg in the largest way possible.
> —Henry W. Bellows (1862; qtd. in Herschbach 26)

> He's going to become a whole man, paradoxically, without that leg.
> —Dr. Russell Reid (2000; qtd. in Evans 309)

The allure of prosthetic theory invites a "grounding" of the prosthesis as a way to mark the space between lived experiences of disability and the at-times excessive narrative freight and metonymic spectacle of fictional prosthetics (i.e., it's a leg *and* a gun). Creative renderings of disability and prostheses in narrative that objectify the disabled subject in ways that—to borrow from Jain, "overwrite" disability—whether through

compulsory able-bodiedness or fetishized, embodied weaponization—
tend towards ableist idealizations of disability. These spaces and rewrit-
ings reveal what I call sociotextual inequity. A disability theory of sociotextual inequity illuminates moments in which disability's employment
and representation (as metaphor or aesthetic signifier) in texts is dispro-
portionate to histories, contemporary experiences, and real exclusions
of people with disabilities. That such representations often distance
themselves from the matter of ordinary experience reveals how prosthetic ideology can appropriate bodies—while simultaneously shaping
them. To this end, the prosthesis, as Richard Godden suggests, is "a reminder of the immanent vulnerability of all bodies" (1274) allowing us to
"consider more closely the role that objects play in constituting the subject, that is, how the body is just one entity among others in a prosthetic
ecology that forms the self" (1275).

In "Interrogating the Founding Gestures of the New Materialism"
Dennis Bruining suggests that "the turn to agentic (non-human) matter as
well as the expressed desire to avoid representationalism is linked to the
idea that there has been an excessive focus on discourse and language to
the detriment of materiality" (24). Noting the connections between body,
disability, and the agency of pain, for example, Mariah Crilley argues for a
"dynamic materiality" (306) that is "never so simple, so static, or reductive
in its representations in medicine and literature [and] is always
inseparab[le], a congealing of sometimes competing agencies [that]
challeng[e] static definitions of 'normal' and 'natural'" (307). Similar to
disability theory's undoing of normative constraints, a (new) materialist
perspective devalues "Enlightenment"-inspired anthropocentrism and its
consolidation of power over centuries in part via representations, text, and
language. The "success" of post-Enlightenment empiricism and eugenics
(that continue to privilege some bodies more than others) is a perpetual
reminder for the disabled community and its allies to recognize the importance of language and text as material within and without metaphor
while also recognizing the importance of objects (from allergens to curb
cuts) and their often inseparable influence upon many of us. Emphasizing
material over the representational a new materialist approach within disability studies can help provide more equitable understandings of disability in narrative and the larger social world from which they emerge—to
challenge "enlightened" oppression and consumption of the disabled subject and to recognize the self-shaping agency—for better and for worse—of
prosthetic technologies.

On the importance of matter in our lives and our thinking, Diana

Coole and Samantha Frost remind us of its "restlessness and intransigence even as we reconfigure and consume it" (1). As they ask: "How could we ignore the power of matter and the way it materializes in our ordinary experiences or fail to acknowledge the primacy of matter in our theories?" (1). In "A Leg to Stand On," Vivian Sobchack explores the vexed problem of how material discussions of prostheses contend with many difficult figurative and theoretical applications of the term. She writes that, "with the exception of disability studies,"

> the literal and material ground of the metaphor has largely been forgotten, if not disavowed. . . . [T]he experience and agency of those who, like myself, actually use prostheses without feeling "posthuman" and who, moreover, are often startled to read about all the hidden powers that their prostheses apparently exercise both in the world and in the imaginations of cultural theorists [as] a rhetoric . . . that is always located *elsewhere*[,] displac[e] and generaliz[e] the prosthetic before exploring it first on its own quite extraordinary complex, literal (and logical) ground. (20)

While Sobchack's focus on material prostheses and the experiences of those who use them is significant to disability studies, part of the complexity of the term arrives in its cultural appropriation for use as a theoretical master key outside of embodiment, even while it persists as a significant component of embodiment itself.

Davidson's suggestion that sometimes a prosthesis is just a prosthesis reminds us to consider the materiality of the body in theoretical discussions. It is important to stop short of declaring the prosthetic as universal—insofar as *everything* is a prosthetic (from my computer to your glass eye) and *we* all use them. From a disability perspective, I share in Simi Linton's critique of the neoliberal idea that "everyone is disabled in some way" ("What Is Disability Studies?" 520). Dianne Price Herndl suggests, "If we are all disabled in some way, then we cannot possibly discriminate against the disabled and there can be no legal protections and no serious attempts at making venues accessible" (594). Her observations reveal the importance of spatial, material considerations to existence and how inequity plays out in very real ways—including through the stereotype of a disabled person who requires access or assistive technologies in the workplace or other social spaces as an incessant complainer or drain on capital resources.

The idea that *we are not all disabled* requires particular emphasis in relation to people who use prosthetics—for access, mobility, work, security, and so on—as a part of themselves. Loree Erickson, disabled artist and porn star, who describes her own practice as a productive "Femmegimp" politics (Campbell 42) is "adamant [in that] she 'moves through the world in a wheelchair,' which she considers part of her." Bringing attention to people's relationship to assistive technologies as extensions of themselves reveals how technology can "unif[y] and transmogrif[y] the corporeal and psychic life of the person with disability" (54). Ruthee, a person who also uses a wheelchair, shares her/"our" collective unease when people

> kick our chair, move our chair while we're in it, or touch our chair without necessarily touching our body, there's no difference. . . . The chair is a part of me! People don't understand that this is not a place to sit, it is not a piece of furniture, it is who we are, it's an extension of ourselves. (qtd. in Campbell 54)

Here a prosthetic shapes identity and materializes the often abstract notion of distance and space beyond the objects and signs that signify them. As Crilley suggests, for Ruthee, the body and matter are "inseparable" (307). By resisting normative oppressions or overwriting of disabled experience, Ruthee's chair also becomes a site for the body beyond the body, or, in a sense a "postbody." Distinguishing this term from the "posthuman" shifts discussion of prostheses from one of general cultural theory to a focus upon physical materiality. Without diminishing concerns about the prosthetic as reduced to a "fetishized and 'unfleshed-out' catchword" (Sobchack 21), the interconnective, interdependent relationships between prostheses and users challenge theoretical meanings of the term and expose the agential inequities that play out upon disabled bodies within and outside the text.

What's the Difference Between a Limb and a Machine Gun?

> He's right. I am a murderer. But until six months ago I was just an ordinary high-school girl who could hold her little brother with her left arm.
> —Ami, from *Machine Girl*

> Humanity's last hope rests on a high-powered machine gun.
> (Tagline from a promotional poster for *Planet Terror*)

V. A. Musetto's *New York Post* review of Noboru Iguchi's *The Machine Girl* from May 23, 2008, begins as follows:

> DID you hear the one about the schoolgirl who loses her left arm in a fight with mobsters and has it replaced by an eight-barrel machine gun (shades of Rose McGowan in [*Planet Terror*]), which she uses to exact vengeance on the bullies who killed her brother and his best pal?

Musetto's rhetoric asks us to agree that Iguchi's *Machine Girl* is a joke—and be *in* on it, even as did-you-hear-the-one-about jokes often invoke stereotypes of race, gender, and disability that result in inequities for targets of the joke. The film's many excesses (such as a yakuza boss who feeds his blood to his son and makes their sushi chef eat sushi made of the chef's own fingers) and uneasy humor—like Ami having her arm battered and fried into tempura—reflect a stylized grindhouse genre in a literal grinding-of-the-body sense, replete with sexualized prosthetic gadgets, including a drill-bra. The grinding that propels this film via fleshy movie props and misogynistic objects of fetishization, like Rodriguez's *Planet Terror*, critiques a vapid entertainment industry as a biopolitical meatgrinder while simultaneously maintaining a spectacle of violence and torture upon disabled and female characters.

Each film's troubling narrative inclination to fetishize militarization and violence through disabled bodies reflects, in some ways, Alexander Weheliye's idea of "pornotroping." Discussing texts that represent the visceral and visual unease of slavery, Weheliye situates victims' often inexpressible experiences within the limits of film. Though *Machine Girl* and *Planet Terror* occur in different contexts without slavery as a reference, misogynistic violence (carried out by yakuza and zombies) creates and perpetuates disabled, female, prosthesized characters' hyperbolic responses to (fictional) injustices. Such responses maintain normative, ableist cultural imaginaries within each film's cultural context (from post-atomic Japan and the contemporary analogy of yakuza to US-Mexican border tensions referenced in Rodriguez's film). Each film relies on the objectification of women's bodies and portrays the overcoming of disability through extreme violence that (akin to slavery's motivations) promotes national survival through human exploitation. Weheliye writes, "Since cinema cannot give a first-person account of the horror of torture, its testimony remains suspended between the cinematic apparatus and the tortured body, which in turn, when it encounters slavery, produces a sexual surplus: pornotroping" (69). This ideological and representational surplus then exists in film as a "politico-sexual form of life" whose excesses "cannot be contained by the legal order [and are] disseminated in the visual realm" (69). For Ami and Cherry, the torturous removal of their limbs (an arm and a leg, respectively), their subsequent mandatory prosthetic enablement, and their violent, avenging narratives occur without recourse to the law. All the while each character wears an outfit of objectification (Ami as Japanese schoolgirl and Cherry as go-go dancer), and each expels her sexual excess through violent, weaponized hyperability.

Machine Girl's and *Planet Terror's* use of prosthesized characters in disabled-avenger narratives promotes violence as a troubling normative response to fictional injustices whereby a disabled character's achievements are measured in violent acts enabled by prostheses. Clearly we are not all disabled, nor do we experience injustice in the same ways. Such inequity reveals how, and perhaps why, narratives "overcome" or "avenge" bodily violence (the loss of a limb) with the material of prosthesis, however fantastical. The trailer for *Machine Girl*, for example, evokes a universal ableism/revengism with image and text. Scenes of an able-bodied Ami playing basketball, walking to school, and joking with her brother ("A Normal High School Girl, Living a Normal Life, From a Normal Family") precede scenes of a yakuza ceremony, a young, well-dressed yakuza gang and flashes of physical struggle ("Until a Ninja Yakuza Family, Took away Everything"). The latter phrase accompanies the amputation of Ami's arm by sword and subsequent omnipresent spray of blood. Blunt and imperative, the film's advertisement equates the loss of a limb with "everything." Neoliberalizing disability with binaric, totalizing logic also implies that those of us missing a limb have "nothing." Such extreme ableism invokes an extreme version of Paul Longmore's disability avenger plot: In "Screening Stereotypes: Images of Disabled People," he cites three well-worn tropes of disability in film: "Disability is a punishment for evil; disabled people are embittered by their 'fate' [and] disabled people resent the nondisabled and would, if they could, destroy them" (4). Though more vengeful than embittered, Ami defies yakuza power and avenges her brother's murder by "destroying" those responsible.

A tradition of recuperation exists in modern Japanese narratives that feature amputations and prosthetics. Amanda Landa's "Mechanized Bodies of Adolescence: Weaponized Children, National Allegory and Japanese Anime" discusses the futuristic *Akira* (1988) as an example of how narratives "write over national historical trauma [and] rise above the psychic wounds within the body politic" (21). *Akira*, also the name of a child telepath responsible for Tokyo's destruction and eventual World War III, takes place in a dystopian Neo-Tokyo. The film's main antagonist, Tetsuo Shima, who shares powers similar to Akira's, is targeted by a satellite-based government weapon and loses his arm. He then fashions a prosthetic limb out of found material. Later, when Tetsuo smashes a container of Akira's government-safeguarded biomatter, the limb morphs—billowing flesh, organs and cable-like tendons—into a giant inside-out, bodily mass that subsumes Tetsuo. Following a period of Japanese global economic and technological dominance, the film foretells Japan's economic crash of the 1980s. Landa writes, "*Akira* likens Tetsuo's bodily metamorphosis and eventual self-destruction to the rupture of Japan's economic inflation. In fact, the unbound excess of Tetsuo's physical growth, alongside the mechanical pieces and multi-colored wiring[,] can be read as an allegory of the bloated success of the Japanese electronics industry; a cautionary tale for those who desire too much power but cannot control it" (21). Tetsuo's boundless matter marks Japan's economic collapse and its electronic dependence through bodily trauma. While Tetsuo's new body brings power on an individual level—as a teen seeking acceptance with the biker gang—it also reflects a desire to avenge post-atomic Japan's "castrating loss of power by the U.S. imposition of democracy and the de-militarization of the country" (Landa 31). Figuring the nation as an emasculated body subject to violence, amputation, *and* excess through a fictional character who uses a prosthetic limb illustrates the metaphorical, sociohistorical, and material power of the prosthetic to "imprin[t] itself upon human bodies" (Godden 1278), along with the heteronormative overwriting that takes place through a disabled body in order to "overcome" a range of wounds—psychic, physical, or national.

The yakuza's cultural presence, including a popular film genre, in Japan reveals how amputation and use of the body as artistic medium—as in Ami's transformation in *Machine Girl*—compel revenge or signify atonement. As Katherine Mangu-Ward notes: "Members of the yakuza have long favored tattoos covering the entire upper body to signal their mafia status. They also amputate all or part of a pinky finger. One study estimated that between 40 percent and 70 percent of the yakuza had sacrificed a digit, generally making the cut themselves." She continues, "Even with tattoos and auto-amputations, this traditional mafia once operated almost completely in the open" (64). While invoking a brief sense of social panic caused by nonnormative bodies, Mangu-Ward observes a recent past where, to borrow from Weheliye, yakuza bodies and their excesses—in part due to amputation—are a politicized, sexual life-form outside the legal order. As self-punishment for significant crimes, pinky amputation, ironically, becomes a means to signify and regulate yakuza order internally and externally. If "by 1974 the Japanese B-movie industry was producing 100 yakuza movies a year" (Mangu-Ward 64), then many audiences would be able to "read" yakuza bodies and their scarification on-screen and off while understanding amputation or bodily violence as a reciprocal act of retaliation or punishment. Gambetta considers such scarification generative, unifying and agential, calling it "the joint production of a signal of courage—I slash your face, you slash mine" (144).

Further historical context adds to Iguchi's characterizations of Ami. After receiving a weaponized prosthetic that enables her revenge, she operates primarily as a killing machine. Ami's partial machine body then erases her biological and reproductive possibilities on film (something Rodriguez's film counters with Cherry Darling). Hirabayashi Hatsunosuke's machine-age short story "Robot" (1928) evokes anxieties of emergent technology and eugenics by mechanizing the female body's reproductive abilities. Mimi Nakamura notes that the story "reveals both desire and fear towards the mechanization of human bodies and explores the bodily boundaries and responsibilities of female bodies" to reflect "certain eugenic dreams (the mechanization of biological reproduction)" (171, 182). Like Ford's assembly line and other *Brave New World*–esque, mechanized "dreams" of the modernist era, they often arrive with systemic exclusion, sterilization, and the privileging of some biological or physical traits over others to offer a "utopian" future that erases female (reproductive) agency. Nakamura notes David Skal's discussion of a "mad science genre" (182) where the female body and biological reproduction are rejected in favor of mechanical intervention. Taken further, "The female body in the mad lab, as in the larger culture, simply can't be left alone; it must [be] surgically retooled and transformed, rearranged, replaced, or replicated" (Skal, qtd. in Nakamura 183). In other words, the technologically altered female body becomes something else. For Ami, a history of technology subsuming female reproduction limits her narrative possibilities in sociotextually inequitable ways with no alternatives other than disabled character as vengeful killer.

The amputation of Ami's arm by the yakuza who kill her little brother, Yu, and his friend Takeshi helps establish her short-lived friendship with Takeshi's mom, fellow protagonist, training partner, and mechanic, Miki (Asami Sugiura). The narrative expedites its prosthetic dependence following some brief preprosthetic medical care. Ami's wounded arm is expertly stitched by Miki's husband (also the son of a doctor, we are told), who—just before ninjas attack and slice him like a jelly mold—completes Ami's machine-gun prosthetic and throws it to her. As onscreen characters watch it float overhead in slow motion, attaching seamlessly and ready to fire from her stump, Ami's high-powered arm/gun becomes the vehicle for the film's graphic movement and resolution.

Fritz Lang's *Metropolis* (1927) and its scientist-inventor character Rotwang—who has a prosthetic lower arm clad in black—offer additional biopolitical history concerning the *reach* of prosthetics and how narratives rely on the loss of a limb and its prosthetic replacement.[1] After he successfully animates the now-iconic, sexless "machine-man" (who resembles a woman), to the city/factory boss Fredersen's amazement, the film invites the possibility of replacing workers with (theoretically prosthetic) machines. While gazing emphatically at his prosthesis, Rotwang exclaims, "Isn't it worth the loss of a hand to have created the man of the future, the machine-man?" As Carole Poore notes, Lang's film helps establish and maintain "the social trend toward functionalizing the bodies of workers in the service of industry and capitalist profits rather than transforming alienated working conditions so that workers would be treated like human beings rather than machines" (75). Though *Machine Girl* is not as worker-focused as its title might imply, the loss of Ami's arm leads to the creation of a weaponized body, whose purpose is to kill. Even as her acts are couched in an established genre of revenge, she is unable to control or stop her actions at times. Such excess echoes Poore's concerns, insofar as Ami's newly functioning body "alienates" her in a pseudo-Marxist fashion from her previous "working" conditions. Her materially oppressive prosthetic marks a precarious shift from a Foucauldian biopolitics to a contemporary necropolitics, or, as Marina Gržinić notes of Achille Mbembe's concept, "the violent execution of bio-power, but with the logic of war and the military machine" (15).

The importance of a prosthetic limb to films like *Machine Girl* and *Planet Terror* illustrates that a prosthesis is *not* just a prosthesis.[2] Read against the grain of Davidson's literalization of prosthesis as a loss of the disability real, film and digitization enable an artistic possible of future bodies. Yet such excessive violence located upon and carried out by the disabled body becomes troubling—even for the main subjects of grindhouse-like films. Here, the often culturally devalued disability real, or, the "missing" in prosthetic logic (a short-lived state for the films' heroines) is replaced with physically impossible weapons and destruction, thereby charging disability experience with fictional spectacle and dangerous implications.

In an interview, Iguchi reveals his intentions and inspirations for *Machine Girl*, stating:

> It was originally "One Armed Big Busty Girl." It was [a] simple idea such as a girl in bikini got her arm chopped off then takes revenge. . . . [W]hen I started to think of plot, the idea of putting [a] machine gun on the arm was added. It was based on my passion to make a woman-fighting-action movie. . . . I was influenced by the ghost houses or freak shows at Japanese play lands. I was easily scared but [have] loved those facilities since I was a little child. I always think a movie should [be] an entertaining tool. (qtd. in Brown)

How do Iguchi's tools and influences suggest *Machine Girl* is merely a joke or merely entertainment? Using the body and technology to attribute violent potential to disabled experience—especially drawn from the oppressions of the freak show—harms disabled people who struggle to live in an ableist world.

Machine Girl's and *Planet Terror*'s sensationalized femininity intersect with popular spectacle and deepen militarized culture in ways that disabled people rarely do. From an American perspective, Ami's and Cherry's bodies are fetishized on behalf of the Second Amendment—as a bodily imperative to literally bear arms—that few people with disabilities cite as crucial to their daily existence. *Machine Girl* draws almost exclusively on violent spectacle and shock value to disrupt bodies. Beyond its gore, however, the film presents an at-times supportive, empowering onscreen female relationship between Ami and Miki—through their shared grief in losing family members—from training together (like much of the film, a send-up of serious martial arts films) to an extensive final battle that features Miki wielding a chainsaw. In avenger-narrative fashion, hyperbolic characterizations of bullying and organized crime are met or exceeded by the protagonists' violent response—as a more extreme marking of a "joint production of a signal of courage" (Gambetta 144).

At the end of the film, after a few rescued schoolboys who were used as human shields by the teen-yakuza boss bully—sliced up by Ami's brief use of a chainsaw prosthetic—thank Ami, Yu appears to her as a smiling, clapping, sunlit apparition. Picking up a nearby sword and pressing it to her neck, Ami declines suicide as atonement for her violent revenge and failure to protect her brother. Her parents, we are told early on, committed suicide after being framed for murder, which left Ami to look after her brother. At the beginning of the film a flash-forward frames a male student in the midst of a William Tell routine in an abandoned concrete building. In a tame visual metaphor for the scenes to follow, he holds an apple—pierced by a bully's knife—atop his head. While the other high-school heavies await their turns, Ami shouts an off-screen imperative for them to "cut it out." When confronted, she comes into view with her left arm tucked conspicuously behind her back. Flashing a picture of her brother, she holds them all responsible for his death. Her intimidating behavior is met with a misogynistic, murderous comment: "Crazy bitch. I'm gonna kill you." Ami's swift response brings a slow-motion leap, dissonant sounds, and, using a scythe, a quick slicing off of the commenter's hand. Excessive screams and fake blood abound as Ami reframes ideas of male-dominance on her hyperpowered terms of disablement. She yells, "Oh, stop screaming. You're a man aren't you? You're not gonna die just because you got your hand chopped off. You see?" And with a whooshing sound (like Foley from a kung fu move), Ami thrusts her CGI'd stump into view and shouts, "I only have one arm too!" As narrative often works against its own declarations, Ami's interlocutor dies, though not from his now-absent arm but from the weaponized prosthetic she subsequently attaches and uses. Importantly, however briefly, Iguchi empowers Ami (albeit via a CGI'd stump) *without* her prosthetic. Ami's comment and bold foregrounding of her amputation challenges—artistically and narratively—Seltzer's notion of the double logic of prosthesis. Here, agency does not disappear with a missing limb even as normative ideology equates bodily wholeness with power.

Prior to one of the final climactic scenes in Robert Rodriguez's film, former go-go dancer Cherry Darling (Rose McGowan) blasts herself over the wall of a military compound that houses a deliberately leaked, zombie-causing toxic agent, "Planet Terror." Her actions allow fellow survivors of the zombie apocalypse to get to nearby helicopters. Before she clears the wall with the help of her high-powered prosthetic leg / machine gun / grenade launcher, her love interest, co-hero of the film, Wray / El Wray (Freddy Rodríguez) says, "Cherry Darling, it's all you." And, for the purposes of the film's narrative and prosthesis's role in its closure—Wray's inspirational comment works on several levels. Though he dies on the tarmac after being shot by a zombie who was about to shoot Cherry, he, as a sharpshooter who "never miss[es]," pats her belly. This gesture contextualizes their earlier sex scene in reproductive terms. The film closes with Cherry on a white horse leading "the lost and the weary" to an idyllic Mexico—a beautiful beach-laden shoreline and a Mesoamerican pyramid.

Fig. 1. *Top to bottom:* screenshots of heroines Ami Hyuga (Minase Yashiro) from *The Machine Girl* (DVD) and Cherry Darling (Rose McGowan) from *Planet Terror* (DVD) and the starring role of weaponized prosthetics as part of sexualized characters. The films were released in North America within a year of each other and marked a brief resurgence of the grindhouse genre—with disabled twists that are difficult to miss.

True to sexual innuendo and viewer imagination, she has a baby girl on her back and a multibarreled machine gun for a prosthesis protecting the way to a new, zombie-free utopia.

Christopher González notes how Rodriguez's inclusion of Tulum (an ancient Mayan settlement on the southeast coast of Mexico) to close out the film "dynamically alters [its] sense" (121) in a symbolic fashion. Moving from a perpetually dark, foggy atmosphere to a sunny, historical seascape shifts the film's mood and reinforces its motivation of survival. Situating Mexico as the "promised land" outside the scope of the zombie plague also enables Rodriguez's use of "the zombie genre to comment satirically upon real life-or-death situations and material realities that compel people to cross human-made borders" (González 122). Reading the film in this way "allows the audience to simulate crossing a border in order to activate a survival plan" (131), and, more importantly, the elaborate front-loading of the film's narrative to achieve a salient contemporary critique—along with the illogical means of escape from the military complex that the film's main characters endure (along with many other absurdities within the film)—illustrates González's apt observation that "the absurd scale of escape is a stringent commentary on the nature of being Latino in the United States" (131). Although *Planet Terror* is a US-made zombie film, it is also a Latino film that satirizes border-crossing experiences and comments upon the "other" who is both foreign national and zombie. Like Iguchi's *Machine Girl*, Rodriguez's film utilizes the prosthetic for (trans)national purposes where the militarized, disabled female body reflects and avenges historical and present losses and anxieties in order to perpetuate normative, stable, national, and cultural imaginaries.

As Javier Martinez avers, "Cherry's body dominates the film" (333). *Planet Terror* features and exploits many performative aspects of bodies, dancing, fighting, turning into—or being torn apart by—zombies. From Cherry's routine at the local go-go bar, to an increasingly chaotic local hospital, the film features the visceral, and viscera, of the body (much like *Machine Girl*, in a less-camp way with more fleshed-out characters and a bigger budget), as its narrative material. Rodriguez's film often privileges a heterosexual male gaze and audience by focusing upon Cherry's legs during her onstage routine or while she washes blood from a cut on her leg after avoiding an oncoming car. The camera's objectification of Cherry's legs as beautiful and ideal foreshadows their wholeness as precarious. The violent cannibalization of one of them aligns able-bodiedness with heteronormativity, and generates space for the revenge narrative to follow.

Cherry's body dominates in ways that fetishize (like Ami's continuous wearing of a school uniform) her embodiment as both an able-bodied dancer and recent amputee. After initially injuring her leg, she walks away with a limp and offers a "Do I look okay to you?" comment to an inquiring passerby. She eventually makes it to "The Bone Shack," a neon-signed bar-beque joint that later acts as the film's gathering spot, to strategize about cars and guns and how to deal with the zombies. Here she meets Wray, with whom she shares a romantic past. Though they aren't entirely clear about their professions, Cherry does reveal, dryly, that she wants to be a stand-up comedian—a comment that becomes an able-bodied joke throughout. Their meeting precipitates their car accident—where Cherry loses her leg—not from the crash, but from zombies who pull her out of the car (into the perpetual greenish haze that lights the outdoor scenes in the film) and consume her. Wray fends off the zombies to reveal Cherry's new physical state. In the next scene, Cherry lies in a hospital bed. She pulls back the sheet to reveal her swaddled stump with a small square metal peg attached to the end. After sounds of her holding back vomit, she starts to cry. Her tears very deliberately etch the layers of makeup on her face, as a sort of double reveal of a new vulnerability with her alternative physicality. In terms of narrative time, she reconciles with her phantom limb and new, disabled ontology rather quickly.[3] This inequitable "mira-cle" reinforces an immediate normative-narrative requirement for a pros-thesis so that the film can continue.

After battling his way into the hospital, Wray notices a single boot of Cherry's in the hall, signifying her location and her recently disabled body. He removes the sheet that now covers her head—presumably to hide from the danger outside the door—and the following dialogue ensues:

WRAY: Get up. We're leaving.
CHERRY: I can't walk.
WRAY: So what? Get up. Get up!
CHERRY: Motherfucker. Look at me. Look at me! I was gonna be a stand-up comedian, but who's gonna laugh now?
WRAY: Some of the best jokes are about cripples. Let's go—
CHERRY: It's not funny. It's pathetic.
WRAY: Would you stop crying over fucking . . . spilt milk?
CHERRY: I have no leg! [Wray breaks off a nearby table leg and jams it into the base of her stump, she grunts slightly]
WRAY: Now you do. What do you think?

[Now they are walking briskly down the hospital corridor, arm in arm]

CHERRY: You could carry me, Wray?
WRAY: You never wanted that before. Why start now?

Their obtuse exchange—including Wray's predictably uneasy double take at Cherry's swaddling—suits the narrative's pressures of immediate danger and normative outcome, while simultaneously suspending our disbelief. From this point on, however (as in *Machine Girl*), Cherry's prostheses (which endure a rapid, militaristic shift from table leg to Gatling gun / rocket launcher) motivate the entire film. In terms of on-screen physicality and narrative perspective, the story and its multivalent prostheses refuse her convalescence—a point their dialogue plays up with a mix of comical understatement and urgency. Having one's leg stolen by zombies is certainly more than crying over spilt milk; however, without physically moving from the under-siege hospital, we are inclined to believe Cherry and Wray will become zombies themselves. The prosthesis is a compulsory enabler—a bootstrap prosthesis—that supports the narrative and privileges workability.

As unrealistic as Cherry's experiences are, the prosthesis occupies the often-negative physical, social, and medical spaces of disability in contemporary society. Paradoxically, a prosthesis provides her as an (ultra)disabled character with empowering experiences along with excesses of stylized spectacle for presumably normative audiences. Though problematic, and aware of itself (Cherry as the physical material of the best joke material, for example), the above scene refuses sympathy and pity even while forcing its narrative of compulsory able-bodiedness on-screen.

The bolt at the base of Cherry's stump, which Martinez calls (via prosthetic extension) a "rod," allows for a more sexualized prosthetic discourse to "support" the film. Somewhat obviously, given how prostheses motivate the narrative, he notes:

This device seems necessary to advance the plot. How else will the machine gun attach? But why include this plot device that will rationalise one absurdity among so many others? The stump with the protruding rod becomes Cherry's main interface to the world around her, especially in her relationship with Wray, who on two occasions thrusts onto her stump a prosthetic device: first a chair leg and later a modified machine gun he has made especially for her. Cherry's reaction as the prostheses attach is on both occasions sexualized—her expressions and sounds mark a kind of intercourse. It can be argued that the two lovers make their deepest

> physical and psychic connection only when there is a prosthetic
> involved. (333)

Martinez's observations, following from problems of prosthesis theories that do not consider people's material experiences of prostheses, reveal a couple of convenient assumptions—even as fictional representations. As a fetishized relationship of curiosity, the stump/prosthesis becomes a focal if illogical detail given what else we are supposed to believe in the film. From an entertainment-value perspective, however, Cherry is the star of the show, and viewers are cued to be most interested in her status—especially given the film's earlier focus on her legs. Martinez's thinking through the small peg/bolt as a more sexually and visually protruding "rod" does enable his intercourse theory. Recalling that Cherry and Wray actually *do* have nonprosthetic sex during the film's nondiagetic narrative, we might ask why Martinez's theory also chooses to "rationalize one absurdity among so many others" when many people who use prosthetic legs beyond the screen have a pin or peg interface? Wray's earlier disavowal of disability's dominance in the visual field—with his I-can't-look-but-I'll-look behavior—also reinscribes Cherry's stump as spectacle, as a space that once again must be filled in normative-narrative ways. As Garland-Thomson suggests, "Fitting and misfitting are aspects of materialization" (595), and the resulting disability aesthetic helps the film succeed by playing up ideas of what a prosthesis should look like and achieve. Cherry's "protruding rod" also acts as an interface helping her to walk, escape zombies, and so on, beyond an overdetermined "main interface to the world around her" that generates sociotextual inequity by limiting her existence or communication without it. Martinez also observes: "If at first Cherry is portrayed as a hypersexualized object, her sexuality becomes increasingly muted even as the film focuses on her augmented form" (334). Assistive technology (however spectacular) becomes desexualized *because* the film focuses on her prosthesis and its accumulative metaphorical weight.

Planet Terror's threading of compulsory ability in the form of "standing up" manifests as a physical requirement for Cherry's comedic aspirations, which the film cleverly (if discreetly) spools into its able-disabled resolution. While escaping from the military compound, Wray gives Cherry a machine gun prosthetic that he's (somehow) been working on (like Miki's husband on Ami's prosthetic in *Machine Girl*) for her. As he attaches it to her, he says (as ominous tones mix with Spanish guitar), in near evangelical fashion, "I need you to become who you're meant to be. Stand!" Not surprisingly, Cherry is a quick study and is able to decimate, in a kind of burlesque barrage, any zombie or enemy in her path—though it is unclear, as with Ami's device, how she actually *fires* it.

Such representation certainly resists the intent of medical prosthetics insofar as they "help and imitate nature" (Paré, qtd. in Wills 243). However, *Planet Terror* (and its companion *Death Proof*) digitally destabilizes and degrades the stability of the film (via scratchy, melting frames and slipping soundtracks), as if natural elements and time have conspired to create a worn-down, nostalgic aesthetic. Taking this idea further, Knowles discusses the agency of matter amid a contemporary artistic lament for the loss of celluloid through "cameraless film practice, where physical engagements emphasize time as material and embodied." She suggests a "prevalent tendency is the act of burying or submerging the film stock in earth or water or exposing it to various weather conditions [to] give rise to visible (and, in certain cases, audible) biochemical degradations" (148). Rodriguez's manipulation of film's materiality coincides with its use of prosthetics and other props. Cameron notes that *Planet Terror* "constantly foregrounds the materiality of traditional cinema as cinema and connects it with the deterioration of zombie flesh" (84). The film, its biopolitical content, and commentary act as digital prosthetics. Effects imitate analog film to generate nostalgia for a "lost" era that reinstates people's interactions with old technology as normative. Similarly, during the course of the film, CGI works in multivalent prosthetic fashion to transform Cherry's character into a technologically enhanced body.

Conclusion: Empowering the Prosthesis to Enable Lines of Contemporary Constraint

> Isn't it worth the loss of a hand to have created the man of the future, the machine-man?
> —Rotwang, from Fritz Lang's *Metropolis*

The multivalent prosthetic becomes important in a larger sociocultural, economic, and biopolitical discourse of ability and narrative as it governs the body. These films, and most notably Cherry Darling's character, hinge their success on overt representations of disability that magnetize the body/prosthetic relationship via spectacle—where bodily loss also brings material agency—and textual element (joke) to sustain their narratives. While such embodiments and writerly choices might seem innocuous, the biopolitical and necropolitical roots of these artistic and playful moves stem from similar "stand up" imperatives of near-religious fervor. As Herschbach outlines, it became a national (American) cultural and economic project, following the Civil War—contemporary with the rise of eugenics and constructions of normalcy—to convince people (mostly soldiers) who had lost a leg, for example, to achieve, contribute economically and normalize socially and physically via a prosthesis.[4] She writes that the burgeoning industry "drew on evangelical idioms that had proved so effective in getting volunteers to serve, casting their sacrifice as heroic and indispensable to the moral, political and military triumph of the Union," noting that "limb manufacturers participated wholeheartedly in this spectacle" (28). Invoking ideas of valid citizenry via able-nationalism, Davis suggests such companies were motivated to "restor[e] the limbs of soldiers who had given part of their bodies so that their country's body would remain whole and undivided" (93). As an imperative postwar rehabilitative process takes hold as normalcy and results in a massive prosthetic limb industry, sensationalizing prosthetics in militarized ways via a contemporary film titled *Planet Terror* is no coincidence and shares new materialism's interest in "controversial political issues which involve the politics of matter" (Cudworth and Hobden 135). Given the film's border (and broader) implications—where militarization becomes geopolitically specific to the contentious space of the US-Mexican border—and that a militarized prosthetic enables characters' escape *to* Mexico adds to the complexity of prosthetics, film, and materiality in contemporary culture.

Both Iguchi's *Machine Girl* and Rodriguez's *Planet Terror* are so overwrought with prosthetics that they offer ableist projections upon prostheticized individuals. Thus, the films' protagonists' revenge is not focused on the loss of normative ability, but rather on an overheated symbolic mechanism that their prostheticized bodies create and maintain. Reading their bodies involves more than social satire. Each film's satirization of a given culture (yakuza and bullying in *Machine Girl*, militarization and borders in *Planet Terror*) links disability with violence. Although disabled, weaponized bodies share a lineage with post-atomic Japanese fantasy (like *Akira*) to ward off widespread terror and destruction, the overt objectification and sexualization of disabled female characters such as Ami and Cherry seeks titillation through bodies that a posthuman culture overoutfits on behalf of fears of vulnerability to random violence. Given recent attacks in France, the UK, Bangladesh, San Bernadino, Newtown, Orlando, and Munich, violent acts carried out by female, disabled characters become additionally troubling. Significantly, in *Machine Girl* and *Planet*

Terror, vulnerable bodies (disabled, female) become the most militarized and "protective" in their revenge narratives. Hence the disabled body continues to signify something else beyond itself—sexualized, militarized, compulsory violence. In other words, disability in these films becomes emblematic—and enables—violence within current contexts of global panic while also ensuring "stable and happy" endings.

NOTES

1. In *Disability in Twentieth Century German Culture* Poore mentions an "ironic short prose piece" written "Shortly after the Kapp Putsch in 1920 [by] the dadaist Raoul Hausmann" suggesting that, as Poore notes, "Germany needs workers with prostheses because artificial limbs never tire and the proletarians could then work twenty-five hours per day." An "officer's solution for rebuilding Germany [after World War I and a failed revolution] is 'a prosthetic economy instead of a Soviet dictatorship.'" She suggests that the "article was not mere dadaist silliness but rather a concrete satire that referred to the peppy discourse in rehabilitation circles about getting disabled veterans back to work as soon as possible" (33).

2. A recent viral video features amputee Christina Stephens, who builds and attempts to use a lower-leg prosthesis made of Legos.

3. Oliver Sacks's *A Leg to Stand On* shares several "case studies" of phantom limb experiences.

4. In *Claiming Disability* Simi Linton shares some "oral history conducted with disabled Canadian World War II veterans and other disabled people" and their "transition from hospital-style wicker wheelchairs used to transport patients to self-propelled, lighter-weight, folding chairs" (27). One person recalls, "There were a few cerebral palsy chaps there. . . . If they transgressed any rule . . . they'd take their wheelchairs away from them and leave them in bed for two weeks." A vet described how the medical staff's efforts were geared toward getting veterans to walk with crutches, but when the vets discovered the self-propelled chairs, they realized "it didn't make much sense spending all that energy covering a short distance [on crutches] . . . when you could do it quickly and easily with a wheelchair. . . . It didn't take long for people to get over the idea that walking was that essential" (Tremblay, qtd. on 27). "As *Appleton's Journal* noted in 1875, 'Some connoisseurs have collections of legs—week-day legs, Sunday-legs, dancing-legs, each expressly made for a distinct purpose'" (Herschbach 28)—arguably, to sell more legs.

WORKS CITED

Brown, Todd. "When *Machine Girl* Director Noboru Iguchi Speaks You'd Best Listen or This Girl Will Smack You Hard!" *twitchfilm.com*

Bruining, Dennis. "Interrogating the Founding Gestures of the New Materialism." *Cultural Studies Review*, vol. 22, no. 2, 2016, pp. 21–40.

Cameron, Allan. "Zombie Media: Transmission. Reproduction, and the Digital Dead." *Cinema Journal*, vol. 52, no. 1, 2012, pp. 66–89.

Campbell, Fiona K. *Contours of Ableism: The Production of Disability and Abledness.* Palgrave Macmillan, 2009.

Coole, Diana H., and Samantha Frost. "Introducing the New Materialisms." *New Materialisms: Ontology, Agency, and Politics*, edited by Diana H. Coole and Samantha Frost, Duke UP, 2010, pp. 1–46.

Crilley, Mariah. "Material Disability: Creating New Paths for Disability Studies." *CEA Critic*, vol. 78, no. 3, 2016, pp. 306–11.

Cudworth, Erika, and Stephen Hobden. "Liberation for Straw Dogs? Old Materialism, New Materialism, and the Challenge of an Emancipatory Posthumanism." *Globalizations*, vol. 12, no. 1, 2015, pp. 134–48.

Davidson, Michael. *Concerto for the Left Hand: Disability and the Defamiliar Body.* U of Michigan P, 2008.

Davis, Lennard J. "Stumped by Genes: *Lingua Gattica*, DNA and, Prosthesis." *The Prosthetic Impulse: From a Posthuman Present to a Biocultural Future*, edited by Marquard Smith and Joanne Morra, MIT P, 2006, pp. 91–106.

Evans, David H. "CUT! . . . Flannery O'Connor's Apotemnophiliac Allegories." *American Literature*, vol. 81, no. 2, 2009, pp. 305–31.

Gambetta, Diego. *Codes of the Underworld: How Criminals Communicate.* Princeton UP, 2009.

Garland-Thomson, Rosemarie. "Misfits: A Feminist Materialist Disability Concept." *Hypatia*, vol. 26, no. 3, 2011, pp. 591–609.

Godden, Richard H. "Prosthetic Ecologies: Vulnerable Bodies and the Dismodern Subject in Sir Gawain and the Green Knight." *Textual Practice*, vol. 30, no. 7, 2016, pp. 1273–90.

González, Christopher. "Intertextploitation and Post-Post-Latinidad in *Planet Terror*." *Critical Approaches to the Films of Robert Rodriguez*, edited by Frederick L. Aldama, U of Texas P, 2015, pp. 121–39.

Gržinić, Marina. "We Need Not a New but an Indecent Materialism: Transmigrant, Transfeminist and Transgender Struggles." *AM Journal of Art and Media Studies*, no. 8, 2015, pp. 13–20.

Herndl, Diane Price. "Disease versus Disability: The Medical Humanities and Disability Studies." *PMLA*, vol. 120, no. 2, 2005, pp. 593–98.

Herschbach, Lisa. "Prosthetic Reconstructions: Making the Industry, Re-making the Body, Modelling the Nation." *History Workshop Journal*, no. 44, 1997, pp. 22–57.

Jain, Sarah, S. "The Prosthetic Imagination: Enabling and Disabling the Prosthesis Trope." *Technology and Human Values*, vol. 24, no. 1, 1999, pp. 31–54.

Knowles, Kim. "Slow, Methodical, and Mulled Over: Analog Film Practice in the Age of the Digital." *Cinema Journal*, vol. 55, no. 2, 2016, pp. 146–51.

Landa, Amanda. "Mechanized Bodies of Adolescence: Weaponized Children, National Allegory and Japanese Anime." *Red Feather Journal*, vol. 3, no. 2, 2012, pp. 16–33.

Linton, Simi. *Claiming Disability: Knowledge and Identity.* New York University P, 1998.

Linton, Simi. "What Is Disability Studies?" *PMLA*, vol. 120, no. 2, 2005, pp. 518–22.

Longmore, Paul. "Screening Stereotypes: Images of Disabled People." *Screening Disability: Essays on Cinema and Disability*, edited by C. R. Smit and A. W. Enns, UP of America, 2001, pp. 1–17.

Mangu-Ward, Katherine. "Reading People's Faces: Tattoos, Dueling Scars, and Other Rational Acquisitions." *Reason Magazine*, vol. 41, no. 7, 2009, p. 64.

Martinez, Javier. "*Planet Terror* (Review)." *Science Fiction Film and Television*, vol. 3, no. 2, 2010, pp. 331–35.

Musetto, V. A. "Gunning for Outrage." *nypost.com*

Nakamura, Miri. "Marking Bodily Differences: Mechanized Bodies in Hirabayashi Hatsunosuke's 'Robot' and Early Showa Robot Literature." *Japan Forum*, vol. 19, no. 2, 2007, pp. 169–90.

Poore, Carol. *Disability in Twentieth-Century German Culture*. U of Michigan P, 2007.

Sacks, Oliver W. *A Leg to Stand on*. Summit Books, 1984.

"Screenshot from *Planet Terror*." Directed by Robert Rodriguez, performance by Rose McGowan, StarPics, 2012.

"Screenshot from *The Machine Girl*." Directed by Noboru Iguchi, performance by Minase Yashiro, Media Blasters, 2008.

Seltzer, Mark. *Bodies and Machines*. Taylor and Francis, 2014.

Sobchack, Vivian. "A Leg to Stand On: Prosthetics, Metaphor and Materiality." *The Prosthetic Impulse: From a Posthuman Present to a Biocultural Future*, edited by Marquard Smith and Joanne Morra, MIT P, 2006, pp. 17–41.

Stephens, Christina. "My Legoleg." *YouTube*.

Weheliye, Alexander G. *Habeas Viscus: Racializing Assemblages, Biopolitics, and Black Feminist Theories of the Human*. Duke UP, 2014.

Wills, David. *Prosthesis*. Stanford UP, 1995.

FILMS

Akira. Dir. Katsuhiro Otomo, Pan Vision, 2005.

The Machine Girl. Dir. Noboru Iguchi. Performances by Minase Yashiro, Asami, Kentarō Shimazu, Honoka, Tarō Suwa, and Ryôsuke Kawamura. Media Blasters, 2008.

Metropolis. Dir. Performances by Brigitte Helm, Alfred Abel and Rudolf Klein-Rogge. Kino, 2002.

Planet Terror. Dir. Robert Rodriguez. Performances by Rose McGowan and Freddy Rodríguez. StarPics, 2012.

Breeding Aliens, Breeding AIDS

Male Pregnancy, Disability, and Viral Materialism in "Bloodchild"

Matt Franks

Narratives of male pregnancy breach traditional conceptions of reproductive materiality. Pregnant men simultaneously embody material excess and lack, bodily enhancement and deformity, and a capacity for empathy as well as an enforced reliance on others. They take on nonmasculine traits of maternal interdependence and challenge traditional ideals about male self-sufficiency. The pregnant man can neither socially nor biologically sustain the fiction of masculine selfhood as an individualistic, able-bodied endeavor, since his material body is no longer his own. As Michael Davidson has argued, representations of male pregnancy can be read as disability narratives, since they defamiliarize bodily normativity, on the one hand, yet often use disabled life to amplify the horrors of a genetically altered future, on the other (208).[1] I would add that male pregnancy disrupts the material production of normative bodies by violating the boundaries between subject and object, between human and nonhuman life, and between bodily matter and corporeal experience. For example, while media coverage has framed pregnant trans men like Thomas Beattie as freakish and mentally unsound in his violation of material bodily norms of pregnancy—such as having top surgery and using hormone therapy—such stories also force mainstream viewers to split the materiality of reproductive organs from the experience of being a gendered body.[2] As such, male pregnancy offers a unique model for theorizing the gendered, racialized matter of disability.

Nowhere is the trope of male pregnancy more famously depicted than in the 1979 film *Alien*. In the film a parasitic extraterrestrial species impregnates a human male, and a phallic alien baby subsequently bursts through the host's ribcage, birthing itself in a gush of blood. *Alien* reverses traditional sexual and reproductive roles within bodily matter itself, since the male host is orally penetrated, made passively unconscious, and forced to sacrifice his all-too-material body for the birth of another. The alien ruptures norms of masculine capacity and mobility by literally breaking through human skin and bone. *Alien*'s portrayal of male pregnancy relies on narrative prosthesis, however, since material bodily disfigurement comes to stand in for the consequences of violating both social and bio-logical norms of gender.[3] The monstrous birth represents gender and spe-cies difference as nightmarishly repulsive, and the disfigured body of the host father links disability with death. *Alien* uses the specter of deformity to play into its audience's fears about the instability of the body's gendered matter as well as its socialization. In the film's logic, in other words, violat-ing social and material boundaries results in deformities that kill.

In her 1984 short story "Bloodchild," Octavia E. Butler reimagines the interspecies reproduction of *Alien*—complete with a similar bloody birth scene—by portraying male pregnancy as a disability, but one that produces dependent life rather than death. The story is about an alien species, the Tlic, who impregnate human males in order to reproduce. With the care of a Tlic parent in the story, however, the brown-skinned human host in the birth scene is kept alive after the alien grubs eat their way out of his abdomen. Unlike *Alien*'s portrayal of disability as a deathly metaphor for violating gendered materiality, "Bloodchild" portrays alien insemination as an act of state-sponsored disabling that manages popu-lations in ways akin to chattel slavery.[4] I use the story to explore how the US state materially exposes bodies of color to HIV/AIDS as a technique of control in the afterlife of slavery. Although one could read "Blood-child" as trafficking in the same kind of narrative prosthesis as *Alien*—since Butler likewise portrays male pregnancy as horrifying, violent, and bloody—I insist that the story moves beyond positioning disability as a placeholder for other kinds of difference such as gender and race. Therí Pickens makes this argument about Butler's texts in general, demon-strating that she "does not rely on disability solely to begin her texts. Rather, disability suffuses [them] and becomes the scaffolding that aids in understanding the text qua text" (175). While, like *Alien*, "Bloodchild" depicts bodily difference as monstrous, I take up Pickens's approach to reading disability beyond positive and negative representations and in-stead examine Butler's textual engagement with interspecies reproduc-tion as a way to depict the material production of HIV/AIDS-related disabilities. Further, Sami Schalk demonstrates that Butler's work is an example of how "disability metaphors often provide cogent allusions to the historical and contemporary intersectionality and mutually constitutive nature of blackness and disability" (148). Following Schalk, I refuse the split between disability metaphors and disability structures, and I read alien insemination in "Bloodchild" as a metaphor that does not obscure disability, but instead draws attention to how disability biopolitics are racialized in material ways.

In this spirit of reading racialized disability as a material element in "Bloodchild," I argue that the story demonstrates how disability, and HIV/AIDS in particular, has been made to work in the service of producing racialized state-dependent life as well as death. Critically, the aliens in the story ensure their own survival by continually reproducing the materially dependent bodies of their human reproductive hosts. They are not concerned for the lives of the humans except as reproducers, and I extend this reading to account for how people with HIV/AIDS-related disabilities are not the primary beneficiaries of state care. Instead the state serves its own interests by continually reproducing certain people with HIV/AIDS as passive health-care consumers, while preventing others—largely people of color—from access to care, and disallowing any alternative forms of interdependence or care outside of its own network. Such a reading demonstrates how state biopolitics have harnessed HIV/AIDS-related disabilities as part of what Foucault calls "campaigns to teach hygiene and to medicalize the population" (*Society* 244). Butler allows us to see that the state no longer eliminates all people with disabilities, but instead produces material bodily difference along racial lines to reproduce some as docile medicalized populations and others as disposable. Timothy Lyle calls this the domestication of HIV, which entails the rehabilitation of HIV-positive subjects into normative embodiment and thus "depends on the abjection of other queerer black bodies and their supposed values and behaviors" (154). While the reproduction of certain disabilities like HIV/AIDS is no longer a death sentence, instead it has become a tactic for the state to continually produce dependent populations by manipulating the matter—viral and pharmaceutical—that goes into and out of its subjects' bodies. And "Bloodchild" demonstrates that for black people in the United States, who are the highest-risk group for contracting HIV and who have been largely barred access to treatment and prevention, the material production of disability on and in the black body is a part of the biopolitical afterlife of slavery.

HIV/AIDS Biopolitics

"Bloodchild" traces how state biopolitics exposes bodies to viral matter at unequal rates, and I use the story to account for how the state implants some who contract HIV with life-prolonging antiretrovirals while leaving others to die. I use biopolitics to describe coercive state practices of population management, and I apply a new materialist lens to disability biopolitics in order to account for this viral manipulation of dependent and disabled bodies. My approach responds to Diana Coole and Samantha Frost's call for a materialist understanding of "the biopolitical interest the modern state has taken in managing the life, health, and death of its populations" by taking into consideration "the unprecedented micropowers that biotechnology is engendering" on and within the body (22–23). I read Butler's portrayal of interspecies breeding as a way to grasp how the state uses viral infection and the micropowers of pharmaceutical consumerism to manage life and death for those with HIV/AIDS. I thus engage with new materialism by reading male pregnancy in "Bloodchild" as a representation of the dislocation of human by nonhuman viral bodily matter. Sophia Magnone argues that "Bloodchild" is a story about the domestication of nonhuman animals and the animalization of humans, challenging "humankind's altogether violent, repressive, and deadening treatment of livestock, pets, and other domesticated creatures" (109).[5] Analogous to this reading, and in the spirit of Lyle's account of domesticating HIV, I focus on how the manipulation of viral matter domesticates some animalized humans with HIV/AIDS while exposing others to death. My reading is also in line with the work of Mel Chen, who chronicles the racialization of nonhuman matter in the human body. Her account of the racialized toxicity of lead, for example, parallels my reading of virality, since both examples demonstrate how the state manages the "potential threat to valued human integrities" posed by toxic and viral substances in order to preserve racialized "animacy hierarchies" (159).

My reading of "Bloodchild" demonstrates that HIV infection and care is one subset of the state's hierarchical biopolitical management of crip/queer/black bodies.[6] This supports David Mitchell and Sharon Snyder's recent argument, in *The Biopolitics of Disability*, that the state increasingly incorporates disabled bodies into national life—or domesticates them—in profoundly discriminatory ways. Previously consigned to death, privileged individuals with HIV and AIDS are now rehabilitated and enlisted into life. They are subject to forms of self-disciplinary care that manage their viral load in order to make them productive, pliant citizens. In other words, they are the targets of what Jasbir Puar characterizes as a "recapacitation of a debilitated body" ("Coda" 152). In Puar's terms, attending to rehabilitation means theorizing how biopolitical aggregates of capacity and debility work in tandem to manage populations. For populations with or at risk of contracting HIV/AIDS, those who have access to prevention and treatment are either kept on the side of capacity or recapacitated through pharmaceutical regimens, while those who do not—often people of color—are exposed to debility or premature death through neglect.

In his book *Unlimited Intimacy*, Tim Dean demonstrates how some men have rejected these forms of population management by practicing barebacking: intentionally passing and contracting the HIV virus by having sex without condoms. Tim Dean describes barebacking as a radical practice of rejecting risk management by becoming pregnant with and reproducing a virus. He argues that barebackers revalue having HIV as a positive form of embodiment rather than a stigmatized one, and that they form radically new kinship networks through sharing the virus. Dean sees intentional HIV infection as radical in its rejection of able-bodied norms of health, aligning it with a disability studies critique of able-bodied standards of health. Despite the radical potential of barebacking as a model for "desiring disability," however, I explore how the biopolitical state has increasingly neutralized such forms of resistance by developing ways to regulate HIV/AIDS transmission without condoms and restigmatize the virus. In other words, biopolitical intervention has transformed a crip/queer barebacking subculture into a self-disciplining, condomless, able-bodied gay mainstream. My reading of "Bloodchild" traces how transgressive crip/queer bodies, while potentially resistant to or unincorporable within biopolitics, have been brought into the service of producing state-dependent life.

The effect of such a reincorporation into state-managed life is that HIV/AIDS, and disability in general, is once again produced as something to fear and avoid at all costs. Additionally, people with HIV/AIDS, and especially those who are people of color, are blamed for having failed to protect and care for themselves. By blaming the individual, the state masks the profound lack of access to prevention and treatment for those without white economic privilege. Butler's treatment of slavery in "Bloodchild" illustrates the way that the state has long used disability to enforce the disposability of black bodies, and continues to do so through the racialized biopolitics of HIV/AIDS in the afterlife of slavery. The story modulates this history of biopolitical racism through speculative fiction, tracing how the aliens implant the story's protagonist Gan with nonhuman matter, debilitate him under the illusion of free choice, and then compel him to recapacitation through state care. Such care legitimates direct intervention into the material composition of the normatively disabled bodies to ensure their prolonged state-dependent life or death as the state sees fit: as the head Tlic ominously pronounces to Gan after impregnating him at the end of the story, "You will live now" (29).

"Bloodchild" was first published in 1984, only a few years into the AIDS crisis. Even though this was an early and chaotic moment in the epidemic, well before bareback subcultures emerged, I want to suggest that the story offers a way to think through how HIV/AIDS would later be incorporated into state biopolitics. Marty Fink briefly points toward a reading of "Bloodchild" as an HIV/AIDS narrative in its viral portrayal of how "the Tlic co-opt humans as incubators for the creation of their own spawn" (418). In the story male pregnancy is a risky, torturous, and bloody process, he states, "that nevertheless inspires inseparable closeness and the physical intimacy of sex" (418). Butler alludes to early reactions to the AIDS epidemic by evoking the intense pleasure and pain associated with queer sex, as well as portraying it as risky in its reproduction of nonhuman biological matter. For example, Gan assists in the bloody birth scene, and he describes it in sexual and sadomasochistic terms: "She opened him. His body convulsed . . . I felt as though I were helping her torture him, helping her consume him . . . I couldn't possibly last until she was finished" (15). His feelings of sickness are inseparable from his sexual pleasure, and his orgasmic experience of pleasure/pain connote homophobic reactions to "alien" desires and viral presences in the queer body in the 1980s. Moving such discourses of gay sex as death that "consumes" life, though, Butler also anticipates how biopolitics would incorporate normative HIV/AIDS patients into life as dependent crip/queer consumers of life-prolonging medical goods and services. "Bloodchild" speculates about the future of HIV/AIDS biopolitics by imagining what might happen to interspecies forms of reproduction like barebacking once they become manageable within systems of racialized, gendered, and economic life.

In order to engage with these HIV/AIDS politics, Butler uses male pregnancy as a metaphor for bodily dependence. Carrie Sandahl points out that the material process of HIV/AIDS transmission has long been conceptualized in terms of procreation: "The AIDS virus, after all, tricks the body's cells into surrogate parenthood by forcing them to replicate bad copies of themselves, renegade robot copies that eventually take over and destroy the originals" (51). Further, Dean illustrates how barebacking communities have taken up the language of pregnancy to describe passing sperm and reproducing the virus from person to person, most notably in the use of the term "breeding." "With the virus coded as a gift, seroconversion can be understood as successful insemination," he writes (86). Since protection was never needed to prevent pregnancy in sex between men, he argues, men who bareback "represent their deliberate abandonment of condoms as an attempt to conceive" (86). Far from mimicking heteronormative reproduction, however, according to Dean reproducing the virus breaks up traditional lines of inheritance by dislocating human life in favor of virality. Thus barebacking moves along the precarious lines of sexual encounters and creates new hierarchies of family based on shared vulnerability rather than protection.[7] Connecting this analysis with disability, Octavio Gonzalez argues that for bugchasers—those who seek seroconversion through bareback sex—"their HIV/AIDS-*philia* suggests one means of crafting a radical 'critically disabled/critically queer' sensibility" (103). Bugchasers reject the stigma and disability-phobia inherent in discourses of safe sex by intentionally reproducing the virus, removing the latex barrier that prevents exchange of bodily matter and become "pregnant" with each other's viral "seed." This material bodily openness to alien matter and to disability refuses disciplinary regulations that would recapacitate the debilitated queer body into hygiene and able-bodiedness.

Despite this crip potential, in the years since Dean's influential analysis, material practices and representations of barebacking have swung back toward risk management. While I do not wish to ignore the ongoing, creative models for refusing risk management and forging alternative forms of kinship that continue to exist in and outside of barebacking communities, nonetheless disciplinary self-care has begun to contain such disruptive practices through newer techniques of pharmaceutical prophylaxis, and particularly as barebacking has spread to the gay mainstream. The vast majority of mainstream gay porn has converted to bareback sex in the past six years, and typical mainstream gay porn videos begin with a warning screen encouraging viewers to reduce risk and assuring them that all performers have been meticulously tested for HIV/AIDS, many even specifying the method and type of test used. More fundamentally, bareback sex has become much less risky with the introduction of HIV enzyme blockers like PrEP and antiretroviral treatment-as-prevention (TasP) drugs.[8] These drugs minimize risk and protect the health of its able-bodied, normatively gendered stars, removing disability from the realm of possible outcomes of "risky" sex and reinforcing ableist definitions of HIV as undesirable and "dirty." Rather than actual risk, PrEP offers safe barebacking and fetishizes the illusion of risk. For example, bareback porn privileges the moment of insemination by fetishizing the thrill and danger of inserting viral semen into the anus. But now that insemination can happen without passing on HIV, thanks to pharmaceutical intervention, the risk has become hollowly symbolic rather than real. In place of the crip/queer bonds and risks of male pregnancy, biomedical care now redirects barebacking back toward the paradigm of safe sex, which restigmatizes HIV/AIDS and disabled embodiment.

By tracing the stigmatizing effects of PrEP and TasP, I do not wish to detract from the important recent advancements in HIV/AIDS treatment. However, I also insist that the widespread usage of biomedical prevention must not restigmatize HIV/AIDS, must not become coercive in its attempt to eradicate disability, and must not cover over the continued lack of access to care experienced by many, and in particular disabled people and people of color. I am not arguing against using PrEP and TasP, particularly since, as with condoms earlier in the epidemic, there are many homophobic barriers toward education, accessibility, and the implementation of protective measures against the spread of HIV/AIDS that desperately need to be overcome. I also insist on the importance of maintaining opposition to the many homonormative naysayers like Larry Kramer who condemn PrEP because they fear it will lead to unbridled promiscuity, and whose position ironically demonizes gay sex by employing the same respectability rhetoric initially used against condoms.[9] Instead, I attend to how using pharmaceuticals as a form of risk management itself risks stigmatizing and controlling crip/queer/black lives, and I argue that adopting treatment need not mean sacrificing resistance to state biopolitics.

For the remainder of this chapter, I use "Bloodchild" to intervene into some of the risks of HIV/AIDS biopolitics for crip/queer/black subjects. Foremost among such dangers is the stratification of care not only between but also within queer, crip, and black communities, whose lives are seen as more or less valuable in the state's animacy hierarchy. As Mitchell and Snyder argue, "The price of recent attempts to fold disability into the life of the nation might prove quite steep—for those disabled subjects who aspire to find themselves comfortably ensconced among the normatively disabled while further distancing themselves from those who decline such membership" (62). In other words, those who have access to state medical care reproduce norms of bodily health while they simultaneously stigmatize those who refuse such care, are ineligible, or seek alternative modes of community-based support. I also recognize the seemingly contradictory nature of my argument, since it lies at the center of what Puar has recently identified as a tension between maintaining disability pride and condemning the violent deployment of disability by the state. Extrapolating from work by Nirmala Erevelles and Helen Meekosha, Puar argues that affirming disability culture and halting the state's production of disability are projects that must be seen as "relational supplements" rather than conflicting agendas (*Right to Maim* 88). Following this imperative, I argue that HIV/AIDS must be destigmatized and also that we must stop the uneven production of HIV/AIDS on racialized bodies. I turn to "Bloodchild" not to resolve the tension between these positions, but to insist that, for both, HIV/AIDS care must be wrenched away from state biopolitics.

Producing Dependence

Butler traces how potentially transformative crip/queer/black practices of kinship and support are seduced back into the biopolitical state through enforced dependence on—and exclusion from—medical consumerism. The Tlic character T'Gatoi represents the intertwining of state and kinship in the story, since she is not only the head of Gan's family but also the "government official in charge of the Preserve" where all the humans are kept (3). T'Gatoi assumes the state's role in administering biopolitical care, and she institutes kinship networks that are dependent on the state by breaking up human family ties. The Tlic keep their human families passive by feeding them "sterile eggs," which are nonreproductive but bring pleasure, prolong life, and increase vigor (3). The eggs are a kind of drug, and T'Gatoi encourages Gan to eat them so he can "enjoy not being sober" (5). The Tlic also sting humans with their tails in a way that is not painful, but draws blood, dulls pain, and induces sleepiness. The sterile eggs and painless injections are techniques of risk management in the story, since they insulate against the natural and pregnancy-related deterioration of human health. The eggs and injections also coerce the human reproducers into passivity by drugging them, producing their consent to being held captive and impregnated. In other words, the Tlic use biopolitical techniques that manipulate the bodily matter of the humans to extend and optimize life, thereby reducing them to passive reproductive hosts.

The story's treatment of male pregnancy differs from HIV infection in distinct ways, since in reality the state does not directly implant the virus directly in its subjects as the Tlic do in "Bloodchild." However, the state does expose many crip/queer/black subjects to the virus by limiting access to prevention and then claiming the right to intervene in their material bodies. Robert McRuer argues, for example, that "global capitalism (and specifically the multinational pharmaceutical companies most invested in the traffic in protease inhibitors) reins in or constrains justice for people with HIV/AIDS, short-circuiting their capacity to exercise choice in relation to the collective future" (230). Just as the human hosts do not have the ability to choose whether to receive the "benefits" of the sterile eggs and injections, people with HIV/AIDS and other disabilities often do not have the ability to choose alternative options for treatment or to refuse care in the first place. This is symptomatic of what McRuer calls a "rehabilitative logic" that "governs contemporary understandings of and responses to what we should still call the AIDS crisis" (108). The imperative of rehabilitation is coercive because it lulls and "drugs" people with HIV/AIDS into accepting forms of state and medical care that are predicated on the undesirability of disability.[10]

Butler refutes the pretense that such biomedical intervention serves the interests of people with HIV/AIDS, and instead demonstrates that "care" primarily serves the interests of the state in reproducing compliant health-care consumers. In the birth scene, for example, T'Gatoi administers stings like anesthetics to the pregnant man, saying, "I've stung you as much as I dare for now. . . . When this is over, I'll sting you to sleep and you won't hurt anymore" (14). She also tells him that when the Tlic who impregnated him arrives, "she'll give you eggs to help you heal" (14). While T'Gatoi assures him that it is for his own good that she administers such care, it is clear that her real concern is not for his life but for the survival of her own species. "A good family," she declares as she pulls six healthy grubs from him, explaining that if the Tlic used other species besides humans to reproduce, she would be "happy to find one or two alive" (17). In other words, the Tlic administer such thorough care only because humans serve as optimal reproducers compared with other animals. The care administered by the Tlic certainly has a desirable effect by saving the lives of their reproductive hosts, but this care would not be needed if the Tlic did not impregnate humans in the first place. It is also clear that such care is motivated by the desire to extend human life only in order to produce passive host bodies within the Tlic baby industry. When T'Gatoi cuts into the pregnant human host, for example, the man screams and convulses, but she "seemed to pay no attention as she lengthened and deepened the cut, now and then pausing to lick away blood" (15). Her lack of attention to his pain demonstrates that she only cares about the future generations he will eventually carry if he lives. Licking his wounds is a form of both consumption and care, since, as Gan explains, "His blood vessels contracted, reacting to the chemistry of her saliva, and the bleeding slowed" (15). The ambiguity between consuming and caring for the host demonstrates that T'Gatoi is not concerned with saving his life in itself, but for the purposes of prolonging his material existence as a host body that she and her grubs will continually consume and replenish.

T'Gatoi's consumptive care is analogous to HIV/AIDS pharmaceutical markets. HIV/AIDS medicine is a part of what Mitchell and Snyder call a disability consumption market, and what Merri Lisa Johnson and Robert McRuer have termed a "crip economy." "Disability identity is now part of capitalism's array of target markets," Johnson and McRuer argue, constituting an emergent "'crip economy' akin to the globalized queer pink economy" (128). By prolonging the life of those with and at risk of getting HIV/AIDS who can afford health care, the medical industry maintains an endless stream of pharmaceutical consumers at the intersection of crip and pink economies, rather than losing them to death. Quite literally, as "Bloodchild" demonstrates, "licking the blood away" is a more sustainable form of "consuming" and replenishing HIV/AIDS patients, since it continually produces them as consumers dependent on biomedical care. While the economy in the story is fundamentally different from HIV/AIDS biomedicine, in that the story portrays a scenario more akin to reproductive slavery than medical consumerism, by linking the two I demonstrate how "Bloodchild" exposes that biomedical capitalism is a part of the afterlife of slavery. For example, certain resistant, unruly characters, like Gan's mother and brother, are unincorporable within the Tlic state, and this demonstrates how transgressive crip/queer/black subjects are implanted with disability and left to die outside of state care, even while upstanding subjects like Gan are incorporated into the state. This aggregation of populations demonstrates that, while HIV/AIDS biopolitics is not a form of slavery, it nonetheless works along and within racialized lines forged in slavery to ensure the dependence and disposability of black bodies.[11]

Mitchell and Snyder articulate such forms of dependence on a larger scale, noting that "neoliberalism tends to produce all bodies as languishing . . . in order to exploit new treatment markets" (40). The voracious appetite of such markets is evident in "Bloodchild," when Gan wonders about T'Gatoi, "Did she like the taste? Did childhood habits die hard—or not die at all?" (17). Once a grub herself, eating her way out of her human host for her own sustenance, she now continues to consume human blood with techniques that ensure an indefinite supply. This mirrors how pharmaceutical companies perfect techniques of prolonging dependent life so that they will continually consume and replenish their patients, ensuring a continual flow of profit. As Nishant Shahani argues, "the biopoliticization of AIDS" is expanding such markets "through continued pharmaceutical profiteering, a regime of intellectual 'rights' that mediates drug affordability, and patent exclusivity that is implicated in a form of necropolitics" (27). Such trends suggest that the bloodlust of pharmaceutical profit is what drives the crip economy of HIV/AIDS consumerism, rather than a concern for patients themselves.

Perhaps the most viable model for resistance to biopolitical consumerism in the story comes from Gan's mother, Lien. In the first pages of the story, while Gan is comfortably cradled within T'Gatoi's limbs and drinks greedily from the drugged eggs, his mother refuses to drink. Gan wonders why she "denied herself such a harmless pleasure," since "Less of her hair would be gray if she indulged now and then. The eggs prolonged life, prolonged vigor. . . . But my mother seemed content to age before she had to" (3). Clearly, though, Lien is aware that the eggs are not "harmless," since although they prolong life, they also induce consent. When Lien reluctantly takes a small sip from an egg, Gan describes her as "unwillingly obedient" (4). Lien's failed attempts to refuse care mirror Kane Race's discussion of the increasing pressure of HIV/AIDS biomedicine: "The persistent appeal to an AIDS-free generation effectively overrides any in-depth consideration or balanced discussion of the material needs of actually existing adults, not least those living with HIV infection" (11). In the story the Tlic similarly override Lien's material needs: T'Gatoi coerces her into an arranged marriage and forces her to surrender her children into reproductive slavery. As a result Lien winds up branded with the stigma of one who would rather be disabled than continue to rely on biomedical care, and nonetheless forced into rehabilitation.

The imperative of eradicating risk in the story, and in HIV/AIDS prevention itself, reproduces disability stigma in that it assumes that a world without impairment is universally desirable. Disability studies critics have consistently pushed back against such rhetoric, insisting that, as Rosemarie Garland-Thomson writes, "the ostensibly progressive socio-medical project of eradicating disability all too often is enacted as a program to eliminate people with disabilities" (15). Butler, though, draws our attention to how such projects of eradicating disability have developed processes of extending life for certain people with disabilities in addition to eliminating others. The Tlic eradicate the risk of birthing "bloodchildren" but simultaneously perpetuate dependence on state care. Race outlines a similar process in terms of HIV/AIDS, arguing that "the possibility of queer resistance to [ending HIV] is rendered unthinkable . . . strategic optimism is practically compulsory" (11). The "optimism" of ending HIV/AIDS and disability makes it impossible to refuse care and wishes disabled people out of existence through killing as well as biopolitical life-making.

The Biopolitical Afterlife of Slavery

"Bloodchild" showcases how HIV/AIDS is fundamentally racialized, as the humans in the story are described as having "brown flesh" (14). The story mirrors Alexander Weheliye's argument that "the politicization of the biological always already represents a racializing assemblage" (12). More specifically, Julie Minich stresses that disability is "highly racialized— both in the sense that disability is disproportionately concentrated within communities of color, which receive unequal health care and experience elevated risk of experiencing workplace injuries, environmental contamination, and state violence, and in the sense that disability is often used rhetorically to reinforce white supremacy" (para. 7). HIV/AIDS is a prominent manifestation of how disability is racialized in material ways: as Nirmala Erevelles demonstrates, just as black women's bodies were used in the reproduction of slaves, the "construction of African American women's sexuality and reproductive capacity continues to manifest itself in policies representing African American women with HIV/AIDS as both dependent and diseased and, thus, ineligible for resources needed for survival" ("Color of Violence" 122). The state allows the virus to disproportionately infect and kill people of color, who are excluded from treatment and prevention efforts that rely on racist notions of black bodies as already diseased and disabled.

To read "Bloodchild" as an HIV/AIDS narrative entails seeing virality as a metaphoric and material mode of bodily difference that is interwoven with historical practices of racism. Neel Ahuja argues that, in the expansion of the US empire over the long twentieth century, "the purported universality of imperial public health was betrayed by its circulation of racial fears of disease. This made the microscopic bodies of viruses and bacteria into the very matter of racial differentiation, the lively conduits of debility and death that threatened a dangerous intimacy between species and social groups in a globalizing world of empire" (5). Such dangers called for biomedical management techniques that would insulate against the risk of racial and species mixing on a material level, to ensure prolonged life in a racially stratified order. "Bloodchild" represents this order in an enslaved human population who are trained to participate in their own enslavement, as Elys Weinbaum argues. Gan and his family are forcefully "implanted" with alien DNA and then subject to the imperatives of "care" and disposability dictated by their alien overlords. In terms of HIV/AIDS, the story illuminates that, as Shahani argues, "the attempts to manage 'risk' only place queer communities of color in greater proximity to death and disposability" (26). In other words, Butler demonstrates how the modes of biological control over black bodies that were developed in slavery have adapted to the racialized micropowers of HIV/AIDS biopolitics.

As an allegory about slavery coded in terms of male pregnancy, "Bloodchild" makes apparent how disability is materially produced on the flesh to institute racial control. As Pickens argues about the protagonist Dana in Butler's novel *Kindred*, "Her disability remains tethered to historical black experiences of enslavement in America. So, disability moves beyond metaphor or narrative prosthesis to foreground Dana's embodiment as testimony about the reality of having social and political ideology emblazoned on one's flesh" (170). In other words, slave owners mutilated black bodies, producing physical and social disabilities as a technique of controlled dependence. And, like the Tlic, slave owners forcibly impregnated female slaves, raping them in order to ensure a steady supply of future slave generations. Erevelles argues that "slave women were utilized not only to meet the Master's sexual needs, but also in a very concrete way to reproduce the labor force in the slave economy" (*Disability and Difference* 57). Erevelles and Pickens demonstrate the materiality of disability as it was inscribed on black flesh under slavery, tracing how masters enforced ownership over slaves by physical disabling them as a way of administering their dependence and obliterating black kinship structures. In "Bloodchild," the Tlic similarly produce disability on and in the bodies of their human reproductive hosts. They implant material dependence into the "brown flesh" of their slaves, since the pregnant humans will die if unattended by Tlic care. As Elyce Helford argues, "T'Gatoi, like slavemasters of the antebellum South, attempts to win cooperation through coercion and contentment through narcotics" (267). "Bloodchild" makes apparent the thread that connects the narcotic, sexual, physical, and mental control over black slaves with the current exposure of black populations to HIV/AIDS.

Butler highlights the sinister nature of this system of dependence by describing how the Tlic eggs are "anchored" into the human host's blood vessels with "hooks," suggesting not only the parasitic nature of the alien brood but also the fact that killing or removing them would also kill the host (18). While disability theorists insist that dependence is a common feature to all human life, disabled people and people of color are particularly vulnerable to the manipulation of dependence when the biopolitical state hooks them to its own institutional lifelines. As Mitchell and Snyder demonstrate, for example, "Contemporary bodies find themselves increasingly colonized by 'big pharma' through a process that segments body parts into insufficiencies, ailments, and shortcomings in need of chemical and surgical interventions" (40). Such economies of dependence are also part of the afterlife of slavery: as Christina Sharpe argues, slavery "simultaneously exhausted the lungs and bodies of the enslaved even as it was imagined and operationalized as that which kept breath in and vitalized the Black body," and we are now "living in the wake" of such managed forms of "aspiration" (112–13). The state reduces the autonomy of people with disabilities and people of color by enforcing dependence on state institutions in ways that prevent alternate forms of community support. Within its context of slavery, "Bloodchild" demonstrates how the management of disability was, and continues to be, central to the management of black bodies—not only because slaves were literally disabled via amputation, torture, and forced physical and reproductive labor, but also because disability was inscribed on black flesh to ensure dependence on white masters and on the state.[12]

Resistance to such forms of enforced dependency has often tended to reassert black able-bodiedness. But, as "Bloodchild" crucially demonstrates, such recourse to rehabilitation is destined to fail. Resistance, Butler's text insists, can only be achieved by forging new relations of dependence through crip/queer/black practices of taking ownership over one's communal and individual risk, precarity, and dependence rather than attempting to purge disability from blackness. As Ellen Samuels argues, from the slave era to today, critics have been "deeply invested in the recuperation of the black body from a pathologizing and dehumanizing racism that often justified enslavement with arguments that people of African descent were inherently unable to take care of themselves—in other words, disabled" (30). The tight bind between disability and blackness in the time and afterlife of slavery means that in attempting to fight to regain bodily and symbolic freedom, resistance has often denigrated disability and attempted to assert the able-bodied, able-minded independence of black individuals, communities, and populations.[13] In "Bloodchild" Gan's brother, Qui, represents how such strategies of recuperating the debilitated black body to resist enslavement are destined to fail. Qui's strategy is to run—an able-bodied activity that represents his determination to escape from being enslaved by using his individual, capable body to flee his Tlic masters. But in an enclosed, prison- and plantation-like compound on an alien planet, there is literally nowhere to run. The very ground and infrastructure is set up to deny him mobility: "He began running away—until he realized there was no 'away'" (19). By attempting to recuperate his individual, able-bodied, masculine independence, Qui only further entrenches his enslavement.

In contrast to Qui's running, Butler insists that unofficial, non-state-sponsored forms of crip community care, like Lien's, are the only potentially empowering ones for crip/queer/black people, because individual rehabilitation and institutional state care are always disciplinary and many crip/queer/black subjects are barred access to them. "Bloodchild" is rife with imagery of cages that represent the enfolding protection offered by the state, but also the entrapment that they learn not to see, or to see as a comfort rather than an institutional structure of enslavement and incarceration. The insect-like limbs of the Tlic represent this comforting imprisonment. Gan, who was "first caged within T'Gatoi's many limbs only three minutes after [his] birth," finds it comfortable and secure to be enclosed in them (8). But the other members of his family, who did not experience this "embrace" until they were older, "said it made them feel caged" (6). The Tlic cage humans to foster passivity and make them adapt to and even grow to love their imprisonment.[14] In the afterlife of slavery, moreover, this aspect of the story demonstrates how the mass incarceration of black people in prisons continues to materially segregate racialized populations.

The caging is also a way to monitor the bodily fitness of the humans as reproductive vessels. In a sly reference to "Hansel and Gretel," Butler suggests that T'Gatoi is trying to fatten Gan up—not for her, but for her babies to eat. "It was impossible to be formal with her while lying against her and hearing her complain as usual that I was too skinny," thinks Gan (4). "You're better . . . You're gaining weight finally. Thinness is dangerous," says T'Gatoi, as Gan describes her "probing me with six or seven of her limbs" (4). T'Gatoi cultivates a sense of comfort and care in Gan by caging him, which prevents him from resisting (by, say, throwing her into a fire). Butler pointedly highlights how such consent is produced when Gan notices that T'Gatoi's "probing changed suddenly, became a series of caresses" (4). The Tlic optimize the health of the humans under the illusion of care, blurring the line between a cold probe and a warm caress. Such care encourages privileged black subjects to accept state-sponsored, institutional forms of treatment that perpetuate their biopolitical dependence rather than to forge crip/queer/black forms of support on their own terms. In the afterlife of slavery, the cages are not as literal and visible as they are in "Bloodchild" or in the era of slavery—although mass incarceration certainly comes close.

Black people continue to be, by far, the racial/ethnic population in the United States that is most vulnerable to HIV/AIDS, and it is in part this active exposure to risk that legitimates state discipline and biopolitical intervention into black lives ("HIV"). For Gan, being skinny is dangerous only because of the risk that is imposed upon him by implanting him with the parasitic Tlic grubs. And the only recourse he has to managing that risk is to accept the "loving" care of T'Gatoi as a state official and family member who will protect him. As a story about enslavement and virality, then, "Bloodchild" exemplifies how exposure to the risk of living with or dying from HIV/AIDS enables state intervention into black lives as part of the afterlife of slavery. Weheliye articulates these biopolitical valences of Saidiya Hartman's concept of the afterlife of slavery, arguing that "racial slavery and its afterlives in the form of hieroglyphics of the flesh intimately bind blackness to queering and ungendering" (97). While black bodies are no longer physically enslaved, in other words, they are still disabled and queered, and as such painfully feel the phantom limbs of slavery. And Gan quite literally carries such queer disability on and in his flesh as a pregnant black boy.

Care or Coercion?

Like *Alien*, "Bloodchild" reverses traditionally gendered reproductive materiality. Beyond the fact that the Tlic exclusively impregnate male humans to reproduce their young—as Gan explains, they calculatingly save women "to provide the next generation of host animals"—it is the female Tlic who penetrates the host with her phallic ovipositor to deposit the alien eggs inside of him (21).[15] Yet when T'Gatoi insists on implanting him with her eggs at the end of the story, Gan takes up a shotgun to resist her and protect himself. This is a reversal of his reverse gendering, since brandishing such a phallic weapon is a way for him to reassert his lost masculinity. While Gan eventually gives in, he insists on keeping the gun and tells T'Gatoi to "accept the risk" that it presents (26). On the surface it seems that T'Gatoi is vulnerable here, and that she indeed is sharing some of Gan's risk in a kind of biopolitical partnership that mitigates his own powerlessness. The gun does not represent a fundamental risk to the state's biopolitical system, however, since the humans' captivity on the preserve would render any attempt at armed resistance futile, even if Gan were to kill T'Gatoi. In fact, in a more sinister way, the gun provides Gan with an illusion of his own power and the risk to the Tlic, and this makes him yet more passive and manageable. I argue that Gan's illusion of power corresponds to how barebacking on PrEP, for those who can afford it, reduces unprotected sex to the fetishized illusion of risk and produces barebackers as passive consumers of pharmaceutical and state care. As with the loaded gun, an item that has often been compared to an HIV-positive erect penis, the risk is not real.[16] As Gonzalez argues, such "ambient fantasies rehearse attitudes toward the monstrosity of gay desire and gay desire for the monster—our collective fascination with and titillating fear of the HIV-infected body as queerly enabled *because* queerly disabled" (104). But it is now merely the fetishized fantasy of risk as resistance that is titillating—while real resistance to the state biopolitical management of HIV/AIDS is rendered unthinkable.

In the history of HIV/AIDS, there are countless examples of crip/queer/black resistance to the state-sponsored management of the virus. Many of these examples, in seeking to dislodge the stigma around HIV/AIDS, are based in grassroots kinship networks of dependence and pride rather than either relying on the state or attempting to eradicate disability. Dean's analysis of barebacking is one model—but there are many others, from the AIDS quilt to ACT UP.[17] But once the state enforces the promise of a world free from HIV/AIDS and its related disabilities, the ability to craft bottom-up forms of care or to refuse risk management dwindles. For example, when Gan thinks about his mother's refusal to accept the Tlic sterile eggs and drugging stings, he thinks, "I wondered when she had stopped, and why" (6). Race ends his analysis similarly wondering "what to make of such refusals of prevention and care . . . there are broader questions about the reluctance of marginalized subjects to access care that acquire particular significance in the biomedical prevention context" (25). While Butler and Race do not give us a solution, "Bloodchild" does illustrate the coercive nature of state biopolitics as it envelops anti-biopolitical practices like barebacking, and the importance of keeping open alternative, community-based networks of resistance and care. Forgoing resistance runs the risk of (re)stigmatizing disability and HIV/AIDS, locking crip/queer/black subjects out, and playing into the interests of the state by perpetuating pharmaceutical economies of dependent care. The final lines of "Bloodchild" eerily encapsulate how the imperative of biomedical care manufactures consent by passing itself off as an inevitable public good:

after T'Gatoi states her caring command to the newly pregnant Gan, "You will live now," she assures him, "I'll take care of you" (29). In "Bloodchild," such "care" for male pregnancy, as a metaphor for HIV/AIDS, signifies not only the promise of protection but also the threat of retaliation for any act of resistance.

NOTES

1. Davidson argues that scenes of male pregnancy "lay bare the artifice of bodily normalcy by imagining biological reproduction as an unnatural act performed through an unnatural body" (214).

2. For example, Lisa Jean Moore and Mary Kosut articulate how Beattie "defied the long-standing cultural belief that anatomy always dictates a person's gender" (5).

3. In their articulation of narrative prosthesis, Mitchell and Snyder point out how in such metaphoric uses of disability, "the 'real' stigma of a disability deforms the otherwise evident value of gender and race as cultural differences" (*Narrative Prosthesis* 33).

4. Elys Weinbaum's important reading of "Bloodchild" eschews Butler's insistence that it is not a story about slavery, arguing that Gan is "a slave who nurtures his desire for unfreedom" (64).

5. I cannot, however, agree with Magnone's reading of the story as offering a "viable mode of collaborative partnership rather than a necessarily parasitic exploitation" (120). Butler does not offer a model for HIV/AIDS community care outside of pharmaceutical consumerism and state dependence, particularly since forms of resistance by minor characters are proscribed and because partnerships outside of the state are prohibited.

6. Mitchell and Snyder use the term "crip/queer" to mark how "all bodies identified as excessively deviant are queer in the sense that they represent discordant functionalities and outlaw sexualities" (3). My use of "crip/queer/black" throughout this essay is an attempt to push such an analysis to account for the triangulation of race within such an analysis by drawing attention to how black bodies are materially produced as sexually, physically, and cognitively deviant.

7. Dean, however, fails to interrogate how barebacking subcultures and representations produce racist stereotypes, confirm able-bodied norms, and exclude women and trans people. See Shaka McGlotten for an analysis of racism in porn and hookup sites.

8. According to Jeffrey Escoffier, "Since 2003 bareback videos have been among the fastest-growing segments of the gay porn market" (136). A casual glance over titles on gay porn websites or video stores demonstrates that this is a gross understatement. As of 2017, bareback videos have almost completely eclipsed condom-only titles in visibility and popularity.

9. As Kane Race argues, resistance to PrEP has come from all sides, from homophobic conservatives to HIV/AIDS activists like Kramer who worry about the loss of a moral high ground through "reckless hedonism" (12).

10. See, for example, Henri-Jacques Stiker's critique of how rehabilitation frames disability as a lack that must be overcome idealizes the sameness of the able body, and asserts immanent control over disabled people in the name of cure and reintegration.

11. Saidiya Hartman, for example, traces "the coerced and cultivated production of race" through subjection, spectacle, and even enjoyment and humanization (57).

12. Like Erevelles, Cassandra Jackson demonstrates that, in the context of slavery, "the meaning of disability . . . is indelibly entangled in the meaning of blackness, both its ideological meaning and the ways in which it manifests materially as a violated body" (33).

13. See Jennifer James for a disability studies reading of black rehabilitation politics.

14. This love of imprisonment evokes the figure of the dying child in the Mettray penal colony, whom Foucault quotes famously as lamenting, "What a pity I left the colony so soon" (*Discipline* 293).

15. In her reading of "Bloodchild," Kristin Lillvis argues that Gan must come to understand his own "femaleness" as a penetratable body.

16. For example, see the title screen in *The Gift*, Louise Hogarth's 2003 documentary film about barebacking (178).

17. See McRuer's analysis of the AIDS quilt as a disability artifact, for example, and his reading of ACT UP as embodying crip activism.

WORKS CITED

Ahuja, Neel. *Bioinsecurities: Disease Interventions, Empire, and the Government of Species*. Duke UP, 2016.

Butler, Octavia E. *Bloodchild and Other Stories*. Seven Stories P, 2005.

Chen, Mel Y. *Animacies: Biopolitics, Racial Mattering, and Queer Affect*. Duke UP, 2012.

Coole, Diana H., and Samantha Frost. "Introducing New Materialisms." *New Materialisms: Ontology, Agency, and Politics*, edited by Diana H. Coole and Samantha Frost, Duke UP, 2010, pp. 1–46.

Davidson, Michael. "Pregnant Men: Modernism, Disability, and Biofuturity in Djuna Barnes." *Novel*, vol. 43, no. 2, 2010, pp. 207–26.

Dean, Tim. *Unlimited Intimacy: Reflections on the Subculture of Barebacking*. U of Chicago P, 2009.

Erevelles, Nirmala. "The Color of Violence: Reflecting on Gender, Race, and Disability in Wartime." *Feminist Disability Studies*, edited by Kim Q. Hall, Indiana UP, 2011, pp. 117–35.

Erevelles, Nirmala. *Disability and Difference in Global Contexts: Enabling a Transformative Body Politic*. Palgrave Macmillan, 2011.

Escoffier, Jeffrey. "Sex, Safety, and the Trauma of AIDS." *Women's Studies Quarterly*, vol. 39, nos. 1–2, 2011, pp. 129–38.

Fink, Marty. "AIDS Vampires: Reimagining Illness in Octavia Butler's *Fledgling*." *Science Fiction Studies*, vol. 37, 2010, pp. 416–32.

Foucault, Michel. *Discipline and Punish: The Birth of the Prison*. Translated by Alan Sheridan. Vintage, 1995.

Foucault, Michel. *Society Must Be Defended: Lectures at the Collège de France, 1975–76*. Edited by Mauro Bertani and Alessandro Fontana. Translated by David Macey. Picador, 2003.

Garland-Thomson, Rosemarie. "Integrating Disability, Transforming Feminist Theory." *NWSA Journal*, vol. 14, no. 3, 2002, pp. 1–32.

Gonzalez, Octavio. "Tracking the Bugchaster: Giving *The Gift* of HIV/AIDS." *Cultural Critique*, no. 75, Spring 2010, pp. 82–113.

Hartman, Saidiya. *Scenes of Subjection: Terror, Slavery, and Self-Making in Nineteenth-Century America.* Oxford UP, 1997.

Helford, Elyce Rae. "'Would You Really Rather Die Than Bear My Young?': The Construction of Gender, Race, and Species in Octavia E. Butler's 'Bloodchild.'" *African American Review*, vol. 28, no. 2, 1994, pp. 259–71.

"HIV among African Americans." *HIV/AIDS*, Center for Disease Control and Prevention, Feb. 4 2016. http://www.cdc.gov/hiv/group/racialethnic/africanamericans

Jackson, Cassandra. *Violence, Visual Culture, and the Black Male Body.* Routledge, 2011.

James, Jennifer C. "Gwendolyn Brooks, World War II, and the Politics of Rehabilitation." *Feminist Disability Studies*, edited by Kim Q. Hall, Indiana UP, 2011, pp. 136–58.

Johnson, Merri Lisa, and Robert McRuer. "Cripistemologies: Introduction." *Journal of Literary and Cultural Disability Studies*, vol. 8, no. 2, 2013, pp. 127–47.

Lillvis, Kristen. "Mama's Baby, Papa's Slavery? The Problem and Promise of Mothering in Octavia E. Butler's 'Bloodchild.'" *MELUS*, vol. 39, no. 4, 2014, pp. 7–22.

Lyle, Timothy. "'Tryin' to Scrub That 'Death Pussy' Clean Again: The Pleasures of Domesticating HIV/AIDS in Pearl Cleage's Fiction." *African American Review*, vol. 50, no. 2, 2017, pp. 153–68.

Magnone, Sophia Booth. "How to Love Your Livestock: Negotiating Domestic Partnership in the Multispecies World of 'Bloodchild.'" *Palimpsest*, vol. 6, no. 2, 2017, pp. 106–28.

McGlotten, Shaka. *Virtual Intimacies: Media, Affect, and Queer Sociality.* State U of New York P, 2013.

McRuer, Robert. *Crip Theory: Cultural Signs of Queerness and Disability.* New York University P, 2006.

Minich, Julie Avril. "Enabling Whom? Critical Disability Studies Now." *Lateral: Journal of the Cultural Studies Association*, vol. 5, no. 1, 2016. http://csalateral.org/wp/issue/5-1/forum-alt-humanities-critical-disability-studies-now-minich

Mitchell, David T., with Sharon L. Snyder. *The Biopolitics of Disability.* U of Michigan P, 2015.

Mitchell, David T., and Sharon L. Snyder. *Narrative Prosthesis: Disability and the Dependencies of Discourse.* U of Michigan P, 2001.

Moore, Lisa Jean, and Mary Kosut. "Introduction: Not Just the Reflexive Reflex: Flesh and Bone in the Social Sciences." *The Body Reader: Essential Social and Cultural Readings*, edited by Lisa Jean Moore and Mary Kosut, New York University P, 2010, pp. 1–30.

Pickens, Therí. "Octavia Butler and the Aesthetics of the Novel." *Hypatia*, vol. 30, no. 1, 2015, pp. 167–80.

Puar, Jasbir. "Coda: The Cost of Getting Better: Suicide, Sensation, Switchpoints." *GLQ*, vol. 18, no. 1, 2012, pp. 149–58.

Puar, Jasbir. *The Right to Maim: Debility, Capacity, Disability.* Duke UP, 2017.

Race, Kane. "Reluctant Objects: Sexual Pleasure as a Problem for HIV Biomedical Prevention." *GLQ*, vol. 22, no. 1, 2016, pp. 1–31.

Samuels, Ellen. *Fantasies of Identification: Disability, Gender, Race.* New York University P, 2014.

Sandahl, Carrie. "Performing Metaphors: AIDS, Disability, and Technology." *Contemporary Theatre Review*, vol. 2, nos. 3–4, 2001, pp. 49–60.

Sharpe, Christina. *In the Wake: On Blackness and Being.* Duke UP, 2016.

Schalk, Sami. "Interpreting Disability Metaphor and Race in Octavia Butler's 'The Evening and the Morning and the Night.'" *African American Review*, vol. 50, no. 2, 2017, pp. 139–51.

Shahani, Nishant. "How to Survive the Whitewashing of AIDS: Global Pasts, Transnational Futures." *QED: A Journal in GLBTQ Worldmaking*, vol. 3, no. 1, 2016, pp. 1–33.

Stiker, Henri-Jacques. *A History of Disability*. Translated by William Sayers. U of Michigan P, 1999.

Weheliye, Alexander G. *Habeas Viscus: Racializing Assemblages, Biopolitics, and Black Feminist Theories of the Human*. Duke UP, 2014.

Weinbaum, Alys Eve. "The Afterlife of Slavery and the Problem of Reproductive Freedom." *Social Text*, vol. 31, no. 2, 2013, pp. 49–68.

Why Lennie Can Teach Us New Tricks

Reading for Idiocy, Caninity, and Tropological Confusion in *Of Mice and Men*

David Oswald

On July 5, 1941, one of the final *Merrie Melodies* shorts directed by Tex Avery, legendary animator and cocreator of the carrot-munching icon Bugs Bunny, was released. Entitled *The Heckling Hare*, it follows that rascally rabbit as he is pursued by Willoughby the Dog, one of Avery's lesser-known characters. The cartoon is noteworthy, argues Robert Morsberger, because this "dim-witted dog" mocks a popular—and keenly melancholic—literary idiot: namely, Lennie Small from John Steinbeck's 1937 classic *Of Mice and Men* (112).[1]

In a telling scene, Willoughby avows that he *is* Lennie, a mentally disabled human incarnated in a dog's body. The scene begins with Bugs hiding behind a hollow tree. When Willoughby plunges his paw through its trunk in hot pursuit, Bugs tricks him by plopping a tomato into his outstretched paw instead. Then, as Morsberger explains, the dog speaks in an unmistakable idiom:

> Willoughby promptly squashe[s] the tomato and withdr[aws] his hand, to find it covered with red pulp and juice, which he mist[akes] for blood. "I crushed him," wail[s] Willoughby. "I done a bad thing. I didn't mean to crush him. I done a real bad thing." . . . [T]he refrain "I done a bad thing" comes verbatim from Steinbeck. (112)

No doubt Willoughby is a thinly disguised Lennie Small. However, I disagree with Morsberger that this confusion of idiot and canine tropes bears little consequence, that it "does not signify anything more profound than

Steinbeck's being adopted by popular culture" (112). On the contrary, the meanings and feelings that accrue to Lennie *as canine* are far from silly, benign, or simple. Unstable matters of dis/ability, sex/gender, and race are complexly interwoven with unstable matters of species in Steinbeck's aesthetics, and it is no hyperbole to propose that the interpretive stakes are life and death.

Writ large, this essay examines how Steinbeck's novella impinges on the physical world, and why this relates to stereotypes—even ontological fictions—about historical bodies. At the same time, it considers ways intimate embodiments—albeit ones reconceptualized according to Mel Y. Chen's argument that bodies are not singular and discrete, but always mixed in greater-than-human relations—might catalyze a hermeneutics that addresses the "co-substantiating contingencies" between nonhuman and human animals (193). My close readings do not prioritize bodies over tropes (or vice versa), but affirm their constitutive interimplication. Playing with this tension, I turn Lennie, an idiot/dog figure, against *Of Mice and Men*'s alleged privileging of the normative human subject, an approach that requires bringing the fields of disability studies and animal studies into closer discussion.

Willoughby the Dog clearly capitulates to Steinbeck's animalization of Lennie as canine. As is well known, besides his mental disability and powerful strength, Lennie's murderous capabilities and mortality hang over *Of Mice and Men*. After unintentionally crushing his boss's daughter-in-law to death, he is executed by George Milton, his only friend. It's also well known that George's heart-wrenching decision to personally "put down" Lennie comes informed by the prior mercy killing of an old, physically impaired dog. The dog's owner, Candy, confides that he regrets letting Carlson, another ranch hand, kill his companion: "I ought to of shot that dog myself, George. I shouldn't ought to of let no stranger shoot my dog" (Steinbeck 108). In the end, Candy's dog and Lennie are shot in the same spot—the back of skull—with the very same gun—Carlson's Luger. Critics have noted the "heavy-handedness" of this analogy, which implies Lennie is George's pet (Cardullo 19). Usually, however, this depiction of idiocy as tantamount to caninity gets written off in favor of plucking out a sentimental theme about the value of behaving humanely, a moral lesson "suitable for children" (Halliwell 142).

However, dogs are key to enciphering mental disability as degraded biology—as "not quite human" (Goffman 14)—along lines contiguous with the "received racist image of the black [American] as simianlike" (Gates 52). In fact, Lennie's animalization epitomizes a more sweeping confusion of mental disability and caninity across twentieth-century US culture, which is undergirded by the rise and inextricably entwined practices of the eugenics movement and the dog-breeding industry.[2] It is neither arbitrarily conceived nor purely discursive, but historically material. From this angle, Steinbeck's conflation of idiocy and caninity intersects with polygenetic theories and racist proscriptions against miscegenation—a term broadly connoting a mix of incompatible kinds (Peterson 34). Louis Owens cannily pinpoints this subtext in the idiot/dog parallel: "Steinbeck was clearly aware of the widespread eugenics movement. . . . And based on his awkward repetition of the word 'Luger,' . . . it would seem that he wanted his reader to associate the supposed 'mercy killings' of the novel with the rise of Fascism in Germany" (331). The rise of dog breeding and eugenic practices also finessed ableist and racist notions about biological inheritance and selective reproduction in the United States, as well as fears of bodily contamination, inferior offspring, and impure populations; this spawned violent acts of segregation and euthanasia under the guise of medical and scientific techniques.[3] As Donna Haraway argues, literal *and* figurative dogs are directly linked to the biopolitical emergence of population management and regularization techniques:

> Dogs return us to crucial nineteenth-century economic and cultural innovations rooted in the biosocial body. . . . The breeding system that evolved with the data-keeping system was called scientific breeding, and in myriad ways this paper-plus-flesh system is behind the histories of eugenics and genetics, as well as other sciences (and politics) of animal and human reproduction. (53)

Historically, then, idiot/dog conflations suggest profound political, ethical, and corporeal consequences that are not yet adequately recognized.

To this end, reading for idiocy and caninity in Steinbeck's novella uncovers another layer of meaning: not only that certain privileged lives and bodies are thought to matter more than others in the United States, but that mentally disabled humans and canines have both been made—that is, forced *and* produced—to bear an inordinate affective burden when it comes to shaping what counts as an unremarkable or "normal" human life. Moreover, it suggests that they have been made to do so in figurative and literal registers at once. I call this conflation of idiot and dog tropes, as well as the ambiguity that it activates for readers, tropological confusion.

Can Lennie be approached as a harmful representation of mental disability and, simultaneously, as an opportunity to contest the denigration of animality and embodiment that preconditions the derogatory meanings that accrue to critical terms like "animalization" and "dehumanization"? To answer, I will first outline specifics regarding Lennie's life-and-death stakes, discussing his deployment from 2004 until 2017 in Texas law to foist capital punishment onto prisoners who claimed to be constitutionally exempt from an imposed death. Next, turning to depictions of Lennie's body, I locate and unpack tropological confusion in the text. At this point, Lennie comes into view as an idiot/dog figure. By refusing to submit that disability or animality automatically signifies inferiority, I draw out how idiot/dog confusion opens untapped hermeneutic and epistemological possibilities. Hewing closely to biopolitical theories regarding social affection, I then address how *Of Mice and Men* reinforces a fictive discourse of normative US subjectivity that was wrought within the primary eugenics period: Steinbeck's aesthetics finesse *a sentimental moral pedagogy* reliant on animal figures and aimed at young readers, which promulgates loving social attachments as the proper way to learn "our humanity" (Boggs 116). As pathetic identification with Lennie the idiot/dog is cultivated, this supports readers' fantasies of their own subjectivization, namely, by "extrapolat[ing] a human subject circularly from the phenomenon of emotion" (Terada 11). Readers' orientations toward dogs, idiots, and even idiot/dog confusions prove key to this "humanization" training. Lastly, the conclusion revisits my close readings vis-à-vis Lennie's material effects within the historical terrain of US biopower.

Lennie *Matters*

Punning on the word "matter," Sara Ahmed argues that physical substances and discursive conventions, including figures, are always affectively inter-implicated (235). Following Ahmed's lead, I contend that the life-and-death stakes of Steinbeck's figures are nowhere more glaring than in the legal context of *Moore v. Texas*.

Bobby James Moore, an African American male convicted of capital murder in 1980, petitioned the Supreme Court to intervene in a prior ruling handed down by Texas's Court of Criminal Appeals (CCA). Despite ample clinical evidence that Moore is mentally disabled, the CCA rejected his claim; this, in turn, barred him from constitutional protection under the Eighth Amendment and *Atkins v. Virginia*, which forbids capital punishment for mentally disabled defendants. The CCA maintained, however, that Moore did not satisfy Texas's definition of mental disability, which was set out in 2004 with *Ex parte Briseño*. More popularly known as the "Briseño factors," this precedential ruling authored by Judge Cathy Cochran became a de facto law, providing guidelines for defining mental disability, with Steinbeck's Lennie as the benchmark. In short, if the CCA found that a defendant was *less* disabled than Lennie, then—absurdly enough—a capital sentence would stand (Long 868).

On March 28, 2017, the Supreme Court ruled in favor of Moore (Liptak). A key component of his petition was that a literary character was an excessively arbitrary and flexible legal standard compared to current medical diagnostic frameworks. The Supreme Court unanimously agreed, ruling the "Briseño factors" were an "unacceptable method" for enforcing *Atkins* (Liptak). Other factors were arguably implicated in Moore's case too. His racial identity was not a superfluous detail, evincing the CCA's history of rampant racial bias in deciding constitutional protections.[4] Though less salient, the complicated meanings accruing to Lennie's animalization were also implicated in the state's pursuit of Moore's capital sentence.

Moore v. Texas helps me to reveal a key paradox of idiot/dog tropological confusion: it's *because of* Lennie's tacit caninity—not in spite of it—that he served as Texas's juridical exception to capital punishment. To date, disability scholars have mainly interpreted Lennie through a hermeneutic of euthanasia, claiming his animalization justifies his execution. In turn, they have condemned the resolution of Steinbeck's plot for typifying a degrading "'cure or kill' approach to disability" (Jensen-Moulton 150). Some have also tried to restore desirability to Lennie with assertions about his "human stature" (152). Though well intentioned, this rehumanizing approach risks reinscribing the cultural script that human life is ontologically superior to animal life. Granted, at the level of Steinbeck's plot, being treated like Candy's dog is hazardous: the convergence of disability and animality seems to reduce a vulnerable human to the status of "bare life"—a mere biological existence outside of the law (Agamben 2). And yet, in a more nuanced reading, the pet dog tropes accruing to Lennie pathetically rouse readerly concern for him; this affectively domesticates his "threatening" aspects—physical, sexual, and reproductive—and renders his death unfortunate, thereby preserving and protecting his moral worth. The complicated affects and manifold meanings attached to this figure suggest that tropological confusion always subtended the CCA's ambiguous definition of mental disability. On the one hand, idiot/dog confusion is a stigmatizing exclusion of disability that costs Lennie his subjectivity and life; on the other, it fosters pathos, which absolves him from accountability within a system of human law.

Also, *Moore v. Texas* helps me show that anthropocentrism is not the sole condition of possibility for stigma. Put another way, animalization *alone* is not "what makes the abjection of human others possible" (Peterson 2). Ableism and racism are equally at play. Rather than reducing distinct forms of abjection to a common disavowal of human "animal" bodies, my close readings of Lennie follow Ellen Samuels's recent argument: to evoke the body as both the referent and sign of a corresponding identity—one based on an absolutist notion of biology—is, ipso facto, to dovetail with preexisting "fantasies of identification" (13). These fantasies are suffused with desires "to definitively identify bodies, to place them in categories delineated by race, gender, or ability status, and then to validate that placement through a verifiable, biological mark of identity" (2). I agree there are constitutive intersections between disability, sex/gender, and race, but add that species is enmeshed with these taxonomies. The myriad histories and meanings of disability, sex/gender, race, *and* species converge, especially under regimes of management and regularization, since each can purportedly be bio-certified. Moreover, these fantasies are historically embedded in eugenics-inflected cultural scripts (161). Thus, they perform a linked tropological function that sustains the cultural fantasy that nature is constant and stable—an empirical kernel of ontological truth. Extending Samuels's insights to Steinbeck's aesthetics, I propose that critical efforts to rehumanize Lennie—to make appeals to his species as proof of his desirable identity—are exercises no less riven with this kind of fantasy.

Reading for tropological confusion destabilizes fantasies of identification. To the extent that Steinbeck's idiot/dog figure moves or "directs" readers in significant ways, and inasmuch as "matter [itself] is affected by orientations, by the ways in which bodies are directed toward things, it follows that matter is dynamic, unstable, and contingent"—not some immutable truth (Ahmed 234). Intimate relations, including cross-species relations, indelibly shape the physical world. The presuppositions informing one's interpretations are also integral to that shaping. As *Moore v. Texas* attests, matter's relative dynamism, instability, and contingency comes with steep risks: words—and, by extension, literary figures—can produce ontological fictions about historical bodies, sometimes with lethal effects (Chen 2–3). Although the CCA's definition of mental disability was ruled to be in violation of the Eighth Amendment and *Atkins*, this does not undo the thirteen-year span during which it was repeatedly used to enforce capital sentences. Potentially impeding future harmful effects, tropological confusion offers readers an alternative hermeneutic for *Of*

Mice and Men and suggests why interpretations of this novella still *matter*—in both senses of the term.

Tropological Confusion: Reintroducing Lennie

Besides Willoughby the Dog, Lennie has reappeared in numerous television, film, radio, ballet, opera, and theater adaptations, as well as in contemporary burlesques on *Saturday Night Live* and *Key & Peele*. Additionally, Steinbeck's novella remains "one of the most commonly taught texts in secondary literacy classrooms" (Borsheim 125). Critically perceived as a sympathetic and naturalist literary document of the harsh social reality faced by migrant workers following the stock market crash of 1929 (Halliwell 138–39), the text is more popularly insinuated into the US cultural imagination as a dramatic revamp of the Cartesian subject/object dyad. George and Lennie are presumed to figure, respectively, the mind/body division (Levant 135). From this angle, it is shot through with a tropology that capitulates to the most enduring cliché of humanist doctrine: a strict ontological division between the fully rational human subject and (all other) animality.[5] Yet the tropological confusion of Lennie the idiot/dog evinces disruptive aesthetic effects, which arguably impede anthropocentrism—the very discourse his animalization seems to secure.

Lennie's idiocy is never clinically diagnosed, but his difference from George is contrastively pronounced. George is introduced first as "small and quick, dark of face, with restless eyes and sharp, strong features" (Steinbeck 9). Lennie emerges from his shadow as "a huge man, shapeless of face, with large, pale eyes, with wide, sloping shoulders" (9). Although both are white males, the order of their appearance affirms George's priority, which the narrator marks by labeling Lennie his "opposite" (9). This term establishes the two figures as polar physiological exemplars. For Martin Halliwell, it "fixes them" with distinct images to suggest they are also psychologically mismatched (1). This characterization plays out in the introductory scene: the duo enters the scopic field of the text alongside the Salinas River, and when George comes to an abrupt stop his "follower nearly [runs] over him" (Steinbeck 10). Labeling Lennie a "follower" undermines his agency, especially since his large body seems out of control, prefiguring a possible threat (Owens 325).

Slowly, it is revealed that the duo, drifting through California in search of work, has arrived in Soledad after evading a lynch mob in Weed, where

Lennie did "bad things" (Steinbeck 16). Later on, readers learn what this means: he stands accused of rape (75). Defending Lennie to Slim, their "God-like" ranch foreman (72), George explains away the charge: "[Lennie] wants to touch ever'thing he likes. Just wants to feel it. So he reaches out to feel this red dress an' the girl lets out a squawk, and that gets Lennie all mixed up, and he hold on 'cause that's the only thing he can think to do" (74–75). The accusation of sexual violence conjures the novella's miscegenation subtext: the menace that Lennie connotes has less to do with this particular woman's safety than with his reproductive potential to pollute the national stock.[6]

According to George, Lennie is simply a "poor bastard": confused, impoverished, worthy of pity, and in need of brotherly caritas (19). George's epithet cultivates readerly pathos for Lennie, but it suggests more about George's self-conception as a moral agent than it confirms his friend's innocence. His construal of Lennie as "nuts" and the charitable rationalization that he provides is, at bottom, an ontological fiction (168). The central irony, driving home the partiality of George's discourse, is that he is no less dependent on Lennie for social affection. After Lennie accidentally kills Curley's wife—an act that is similarly overdetermined as sexualized violence, another mob is organized to hunt him down. George appears "hopelessly" resigned to the impossibility of taming Lennie's physical strength and mental disability (163). So he sets out to euthanize him.

When he discovers his friend back at the Salinas River clearing, Lennie confesses his crime: "I done another bad thing" (178). But he does not perceive the precariousness of their situation, and he does not foresee that his life hangs in the balance. Thus, mental disability serves as a hermeneutic device woven into the fabric of Steinbeck's narrative: "Intellectual disability provides the structure for the narrative irony, and the narrative irony defines the novel. Lennie knows not what he does, and we know he knows not what he does" (Bérubé 14). Whereas readers are implicitly distinguished by the text as having interpretative insight and knowledge, implying hermeneutic and epistemic mastery, Lennie seems to be primarily an irrational body within it.

George approaches his companion armed both with Carlson's Luger and Candy's confession of regret over letting a stranger kill his dog. He instructs Lennie to gaze off into the distance, and recites their shared dream of living off "the fatta the lan'"—but he augments this version with an ideal of perpetual peace: "Ever'body gonna be nice to you. Ain't gonna be no more trouble. Nobody gonna hurt nobody or steal from 'em" (Steinbeck 183). And then,

> George raised the gun and steadied it, and he brought the muzzle of it close to the back of Lennie's head. The hand shook violently, but his face set and his hand steadied. He pulled the trigger. The crash of the shot rolled up the hills and rolled down again. Lennie jarred, and then settled slowly forward to the sand, and he lay without quivering. (184)

The image of Lennie's serene corpse contrasts with the "violently" shaking hand that pulls the trigger, implying that suffering now belongs to George. Lennie's death might be anticipated, but the plot's resolution remains notoriously distressing for its melancholic ambivalence.

Lennie's death has been widely accepted as George's humanitarian "gesture of sacrifice and responsibility" primarily because it is prefigured by the execution of Candy's dog, another "intensely lachrymose" scene (Owens 321–22). When this dog is first introduced, he is likewise described as a follower: "The old man came slowly into the room. . . . And at his heels there walked a dragfooted sheepdog, gray of muzzle, and with pale blind old eyes" (Steinbeck 45). As with George and Lennie, this order affirms Candy's priority. Later, when Carlson complains that the dog is stinking up their bunkhouse, he appeals to Candy on compassionate grounds: "'This ol' dog jus' suffers hisself all the time. If you was to take him out and shoot him right in the back of the head—' he leaned over and pointed, '—right there, why he'd never know what hit him'" (80). Candy replies that he cannot kill his beloved companion: "'I'm so used to him,' he said softly. 'I had him from a pup'" (81). But Carlson appears unmoved, arguing that the dog is too physically impaired and old:

> "If you want me to, I'll put the old devil out of his misery right now and get it over with. Ain't nothing left for him. Can't eat, can't see, can't even walk without hurtin.'"
>
> Candy said hopefully, "You ain't got no gun."
>
> "The hell I ain't. Got a Luger. It won't hurt him none at all." (84–85)

Carlson relentlessly appeals to Candy by invoking the dog's sensory and physical disabilities as forms of embodied suffering that justify euthanastic violence, and he promises his Luger will kill the dog with merciful swiftness. He declares the dog will not "quiver" (82). Though Candy resists, he ultimately cedes his companion to Carlson, and the dog is immediately led away to its death.

"Quiver"—the term that Carlson uses to convince Candy to relinquish his canine companion—resurfaces in the end with the narrator's report that Lennie's dead body "lay without quivering" (184). This repetition ballasts the disability/pet analogy, while ostensibly confirming Carlson's promise: the dog and Lennie appear to perish without suffering. Nevertheless, by positing disability as the rationale for both mercy killings, having both characters "put down" in an identical manner, and then marking this parallel with a phraseological echo, Steinbeck stacks the deck to ensure that Lennie's tacit caninity is identifiable, yet seemingly presented to rouse readers' desires for narrative order. To put it bluntly, this is reader-bait. It exemplifies "that which makes a plot 'move forward,' and makes us read forward, seeking in the unfolding of the narrative a line of intention and a portent of design that hold the promise of progress toward meaning" (Brooks xiii). Yet, on a tropological level, the idiot/dog association seems to be of secondary significance—something that isn't missed, but that doesn't warrant much scrutiny. If one reads exclusively for the plot, then George's possible avenues of action appear very slim and Lennie's death seems inevitable; this is emblematized—appropriately enough—by Slim's authorization: "You hadda, George. I swear you hadda" (186). Slim's approval echoes the ableist sentiment in his prior approval for killing Candy's dog: "Carl's right, Candy. That dog ain't no good to himself. I wisht somebody'd shoot me if I get old an' a cripple" (81). By touting disability as moral justification for euthanasia in both cases, the novella's meanings of idiocy and caninity begin to bleed together.

But are the mercy killings as necessary as Slim suggests? Or are they vexed supplications to the normative order of the ranch? Lennie and the dog are arguably killed because their disabilities impede profitability and productivity. For Louis Owens, Steinbeck's narrative is more a dramatization of "Social Darwinism" (326) than "a coldly objective rendering" that documents naturalist violence (331). Published on the brink of World War II, this novella captures Steinbeck grappling with the implications of the eugenic era—"the profound human crisis of his times" (331). Though I agree with Owens, I veer from his characterization of the crisis as exclusively human. Informed by Chen and Haraway, I contend instead that Steinbeck's canine figures help to show that the scope of this crisis was always greater than human.

Considering how routinely Lennie is associated with dog figures, it is surprising that Steinbeck's critics have not addressed the nuances of his animalization. In the introductory scene, Lennie is contrasted with George for behaving "like a terrier who doesn't want to bring a ball to its master"

(20). Later, Crooks explains that, without George as a caregiver, Lennie would be institutionalized and fitted with "a collar, like a dog" (126). George also slanders Lennie by calling him a "son-of-a-bitch" (24). After inadvertently killing a puppy he intends to adopt, Lennie then mimics George and calls it a "son-of-a-bitch" (149). This ironically literalizes the analogy upon which George's expletive was based.

When Lennie displays the pup's limp body to Curley's wife, she tries to console him: "Don't you worry none. He was jus' a mutt. You can get another one easy. The whole country is fulla mutts" (151). Her appeal abstractly invokes a human/animal binary, suggesting no trespass has occurred. More specifically, however, the term "mutt" raises the subtext of miscegenation once again, suggesting an omnipresent threat that haunts canine pedigree and US identity alike. The irony, of course, is that Lennie is associated with caninity throughout, implying that he is likewise a threat—one that can be killed with impunity. This remarkable dialogue manifests the submerged scripts of breeding and miscegenation, which implies dis/ability, race, and species mixing. Meanwhile, the association of Lennie with the "mutt" seems to reinscribe ableist, racist, and anthropocentric norms regarding the recalcitrant deviancy of mental disability and animality—a link justifying the two mercy killings as permissible violence.

However, the signifying functions of Steinbeck's tropes are trickier than such a reading permits. This idiot/dog comparison coexists with less-salient idiot/dog confusion. After Lennie kills Curley's wife and attempts to bury her corpse in the barn, he is framed as both human and canine *at once*: "He pawed up the hay until it partly covered her" (159). By suggestively appending paws to Lennie, the text organizes this idiot figure's lack of self-reflexivity so that he is no longer doglike; instead, his species identity itself appears fungible and uncertain. Whereas the idiot/dog analogy hinted at an underlying likeness, while maintaining distance between the terms "idiot" and "dog" and their referents, this homology dissolves that gap into a catachrestic equation of biological identity—a hitherto unrealized intersection of "idiot" and "dog." Now, idiocy is tropologically confused with caninity—or *idiocy is caninity*.

Tropological confusion points readers toward this representational gap, a material-semiotic muddle—indeed, a textual aporia—where it is possible to discern both anxious demarcations of the human and the animal even as Lennie is, paradoxically, denied such distinctions. Framing Lennie's body in this way serves as a synecdoche for the narrator's inability to capture and masterfully represent a desired division between subjects and objects. This aporia signals a pivotal inscrutability: the narration flaunts its own semantic limits through taxonomic confusion, signaling a moment of indeterminacy—of trembling and infidelity—wherein the narration appears to recoil from mimetic readings and to expose its own ontological fiction as partial. A fundamental undecidability exists within the narrative order regarding how its tropes function, which rouses aesthetic effects that at once undermine interpretative mastery and subvert the autonomy of the subject of interpretation by exposing humans and other animals as discursively and materially entwined. On one level, tropological confusion renders hermeneutical logics that would perpetuate the human/animal order and confirm subjectivity over and against the objective world inoperative; this excessive representational turn delivers a destabilizing epistemic jolt. On another, it precipitates a crisis of interpretation that suggests readerly incertitude is morally significant.

Steinbeck's aesthetics can thus be used to unlock otherwise hidden meanings: a hermeneutic of tropological confusion allows for biological identities—ontological fictions themselves—to be critically seized upon and troubled from within. This concept is closely aligned with Ato Quayson's "aesthetic nervousness" and, specifically, its "short-circuiting of the hitherto dominant protocols of representation" within a text in relation to disability (26). Whereas Quayson's guiding metaphor of the "short-circuit" can be critically applied to this text to describe an internal disabling "function" that disrupts readers' extratextual comprehension vis-à-vis disability representations (Bérubé 58), the hermeneutic of tropological confusion is more capacious, extending beyond Quayson's tight focus on disability figures. Rather, it is an invocation, mix-up, and destabilization of manifold *tropes*, which, in turn, serve to mix up and destabilize readers' expectations and presuppositions regarding conventional meaning. As my next section elaborates, though Lennie's love bond with George can be read to reinforce an extratextual illusion about his readers' own self-possessed *humane* subjectivity, the critically overlooked effects of tropological confusion remain a potent counterpoint.

Learning to *Feel* Superior

From Sally Chivers's disability studies perspective, Lennie's animalization is an insult that only "disappoints" disability scholars; this explains why his "dehumanization" is rarely analyzed at length. In her reading, Steinbeck's plot and its "simple moral lesson leaves little room for complex analysis," ensuring there is little to be redeemed by a field that largely seeks to redress the dispossession of disabled people (Chivers). Granted, Steinbeck's plot is symptomatic of the era in which it was wrought—an era when mental disability was pervasively feared as degraded biology and, without the implementation of historically legalized restraints like institutionalization and sterilization, was supposed to lead to "crime, indiscriminate sexual activity, and careless reproduction" (Keely 207). However, Lennie's association with dogs appears to be exclusively—and irredeemably—negative for Chivers. Stephanie Jensen-Moulton concurs, arguing Lennie symbolizes a threat because he seems monstrously nonhuman: "[He] perpetuates the stereotype of the intellectually disabled as animalistic or subhuman" (140); this is why he "deserves to die" (145). Approaching Steinbeck's plot exclusively through the hermeneutic of euthanasia, Lennie emerges as a prima facie case of abjection: "[He] is cruelly executed in exactly the same manner as Candy's old dog," so he comes off "as a pernicious and unpredictable member of society, no better than an unruly pit-bull" (152). From this angle, caninity is merely a figurative substitute for idiocy, producing a stylistic resemblance; in other words, idiocy is perceived to be the literal term. Meanwhile, animality's so-called unruliness extends fears of retrogression and "caus[es] a general apprehension about intellectually disabled people [as dangerous]" to flourish in the US cultural imaginary (140).

Both of these disability studies readings appeal to an abstract human/animal binary, and neither addresses the tropological nuances of Lennie's animalization. Instead, they arguably assume the luminous value of humanity, while evincing a metonymic slide between "animality" and "embodiment"—a slide that is also problematically evident in a number of influential biopolitical theories. Giorgio Agamben's concept of "bare life" is one paradigmatic example. For Agamben, "Animality functions predominantly as a metaphor for that corporeal part of 'man' that becomes subject to biopolitical calculation" (Shukin 10). Agamben understands "bare life" as a biopolitical body that can be sovereignly killed with impunity, a *merely* "animal" biology "included in politics in the form of the exception, that is, as something that is included solely through an exclusion" (8, 11). The plot-oriented readings of Chivers and Jensen-Moulton accord with Agamben's biopolitical framework: *Of Mice and Men* merely dramatizes how the animal(ized) body of an idiot figure is rendered exceptional, cordoned off from the human collective, and killed with impunity. But Steinbeck's novella is more biopolitically complex than a reading for "bare life" permits.

Described by its author as "a tricky little thing" (Steinbeck and Wallsten 132, qtd. in Owens 320), *Of Mice and Men*—and, more specifically, its idiot/dog tropological confusion—fosters lines of cross-species feeling and intimacy, even of interdependent contingency, between human and nonhuman animals. The trope of idiocy marks exclusion, but it simultaneously functions as a "symbolic repository for that which defies categorization" (Halliwell 5). The trope of caninity marks exclusion too, but it also evokes the excess and ambivalence of figurative and literal canines. Since dogs are primarily viewed as pets in the United States, they figure the remarkable opposite of the unremarkable human in the human/animal binary, and also produce interspecies intimacies as "mediators" straddling the interval in the binary (Boggs 19). Steinbeck's mixing of idiot and dog tropes constitutes a flexible *aesthetic* resource for abjection, affection, or—confusingly—both at once, thereby uncovering the complicated, contradictory significations and affects accruing to mental disability in US culture. Since Lennie's disability is associated with caninity, and because caninity tropologically encodes a domestic, loyal, sentimentalized, or even "humanized" animality, the meaning behind his animalization is not only degradation. Rather, it emerges as ambiguous and paradoxical: being doglike is a vicarious experience of being human, as something humans can and do sympathetically and anthropomorphically possess; meanwhile, being doglike translates as being less than human and prone to being "humanely" killed (Fudge 108).[7]

I turn now to consider textual evidence cited by Chivers that Lennie's animalization is only negative. Crooks—the novella's "crippled" African American figure—teases that, without George, Lennie would be institutionalized by the state:

Crooks bored in on him. "Want me ta tell ya what'll happen? They'll take ya to the booby hatch. They'll tie ya up with a collar, like a dog."

Suddenly Lennie's eyes centered and grew quiet, and mad. He stood up and walked dangerously toward Crooks. "Who hurt George?" he demanded.

Crooks saw the danger as it approached him. He edged back on his bunk to get out of the way. "I was just supposin'," he said. "George ain't hurt." (126)

Crooks's "like a dog" simile implies Lennie's precarious position, suggesting he does not qualify for the full rights and freedoms of legal citizenship. Crooks is also an authority on disenfranchisement: this is not only marked by signs of race and physical disability, but also emblematized by one of his few "personal possessions"—"a mauled copy of the California civil code for 1905" (117)—a text responsible for enacting eugenic fears of miscegenation into law (Moran 31–32). As well, prior to teasing Lennie, he confesses he is terribly lonesome: "There ain't a colored man on this ranch an' there's jus' one family in Soledad" (Steinbeck 123). Deprived of intimacy, Crooks has internalized his marginalization. In Chivers's reading, this scene problematically juxtaposes and homogenizes "a number of [distinct] forms of marginalization" in order to launch a lament about oppression in general—one without much bite.

However, whereas Chivers appears to take for granted that Crooks's canine simile confirms Lennie's abjection, I propose that dogs are also ciphers for idiocy because they are signs of loving fidelity and obedience. Although the dog trope is no doubt suggestive that animalization justifies abuse, Lennie also appears to be a sympathetic, likable character in this scene because he remains unconditionally faithful to George. It is precisely when he is rendered canine that he appears prepared to serve and protect the person he loves most against all possibility of threat: he experiences a defensive rage when Crooks suggests George might be hurt, and this overwhelms whatever has been said about him. This unconditional love bond is evoked alongside Lennie's tacit caninity, which sympathetically incites readers' vicarious identification with him.

As Mel Y. Chen highlights, to be treated like a dog is widely assumed to be synonymous with dehumanization; however, "the statement that someone 'treated me like a dog' is one of liberal humanism's fictions"—fictive because "some dogs are treated quite well, and many humans suffer in conditions of profound indignity" (89). On top of that, Chen points out that "dehumanizing" representations of "humans as abjected matter or less than human . . . cannily assert human status as a requisite condition for securing nonhuman comparators, thereby rendering the idea of 'dehumanization' paradoxical" (13–14). As an emotionally affective figure, Lennie's paradoxical animalization seems designed to cultivate pathos, predisposing readers to feel loving sympathy, but also fear, toward people living with mental disability. These emotional responses—or "gut feelings"—are subsequently accepted as a measure of truth, rather than being recognized as the ontological fictions they are.

Whereas affects tend to be associated with physiological bodies, the superior power to experience and express personal emotion is most often reserved for human subjects (Terada 2). What is "at stake in" reserving emotion for individual humans, according to Colleen Glenney Boggs, "is

the production of a particular notion of subjectivity marked by an individuality independent of others and clearly demarcated by the separation
of reasoning from embodiment" (134). Against this notion, she traces an
alternative genealogy of US liberal biopolitical subject formation, charting
how the nation's pedagogical models and institutions bear the influence of
the British empiricist John Locke. Locke maintained that individuals are
not born in full possession of human subjectivity, but *learn* to become human (Boggs 138). Humanity, then, becomes a *status* achieved by and
through embodied practices of feeling in relation to others (138). Boggs
suggests that a Lockean education in humane attachments is pivotal to the
emergence of this more affirmative ontological fiction of human subjectivity and that it, in turn, supplements disciplinary techniques of sovereign biopower that are the focus of Agamben's biopolitical theory. The illusion of a distinctively human subjectivity thus gets reinforced through
claims to sovereign reason *as well as* the "bonds of sympathy that underlie
civic society" (Boggs 140).

Of Mice and Men's intimate companionships, whether inter- or intraspecies, and its mercy killings come into focus here as sentimental scaffolding for the compassionate treatment of both human *and* nonhuman
others—a humanitarian sentimentalism that is a regulatory resource for
biopower. Young readers' relationships with literal and figurative nonhuman animals are key to inculcating these bonds since "humanity is the
product of an educational process that relies on the relationship to animals to elicit and direct emotions" (141). This sympathetic education cultivates "appropriate" cross-species intimacies, especially with pets, through
sentimental aesthetic depictions of human and nonhuman others (141). In
this way, *Of Mice and Men* can be—indeed, it has been—put to use as
"humanization" training.

Insofar as this Lockean pedagogy implies that readers' emotional responses offer "proof" of liberal human subjectivity, Steinbeck's classic reinforces what Rei Terada calls an "*ideology of emotion*": that is, emotions
can be construed to perform the extratextual and normalizing function of
positioning readers as naturally free subjects (3). For example, when I
weep after reading Steinbeck's scenes of euthanasia, this emotional response permits me to claim that I am a humane subject who is capable of
vicariously sympathizing with fiction. Put another way, readerly emotion
gets interpreted and repackaged as autoaffective evidence for subjectivity's
self-possessed power to interpret and respond to the objective world: "The
beholder—the Cartesian would-be subject—feels [emotions] when it represents itself to itself, when it reads its self-representation" (21). Yet when

emotion is understood as that which hermeneutically fills in and connects the subjective and objective realms with meaning, the underlying logic appears positively circular: the fully human subject is assumed to be not only rationally superior to a figure like Lennie; it is now also "naturally" equipped with the power to *feel* the truth of itself (3,14).

Accordingly, it is not only idiot/dog figures that are fashioned to various effects by Steinbeck's aesthetics, but the affective production of a human reader whose superiority rests not only on the possession of reason, but on freely given humane feeling. This pedagogy suggests why *Of Mice and Men* is a staple in the US high school canon: it remains institutionally disseminated because it reinforces a fiction of biopolitical subject formation through the consensus-building ideology of emotion. Steinbeck's idiot and canine tropes are crucial to an understanding of how this novella inculcates humane feeling. Both seem to stabilize the human subject by figuring its binary opposite. What singles dogs out from other species is how flexible a resource they have proven to be for reinforcing the notion that subjectivity is a natural identity that corresponds to *Homo sapiens*. Against this naturalization, tropological confusion exposes subjectivity as one trope in relation to manifold intersecting tropes, one that fundamentally "relies on *affective relationships* that cross the species line" and that "strategically get worked out by biopower" (Boggs 6).

Indeterminate Conclusions

Far from simple, Steinbeck's aesthetics are complex, contradictory, and indeterminate. As my analysis shows, for instance, unstable biological markers of identity accrue to Lennie, including dis/ability, race, sex/gender, and species, and these routinely overlap and converge. The animalization of his disability can be approached as mere denigration, serving hazardous cultural scripts of miscegenation and eugenics—ones that rationalized historical cases of segregation and euthanization; at the same time, his love bond with George can be read to serve the extratextual production and biopolitical regularization of a "superior" humane subjectivity that hinges on humans' feeling ability. Yet, more complexly, Steinbeck's tropological confusion of idiocy and caninity offers readers an alternative hermeneutic, one that is decidedly text-based even as it is aporetic. A critically overlooked paradox in the novella, tropological confusion destabilizes anthropocentric notions that the human subject is ontologically discrete and self-sufficient. Also, it provides readers with an extratextual opportunity to modestly reconsider the corporeal contingencies underlying everyday bonds of greater-than-human intimacy. My close reading of this idiot/dog confusion vis-à-vis disability studies and animal studies never assumes that the meaning or moral value of human being is a self-evident priority: humanness is not a biological identity or norm, but a fantasy that must be anxiously reproduced by means of a number of intersecting tropes at once.

I also acknowledge that prior interpretations of *Of Mice and Men* cannot be disarticulated from the thanatological workings of US biopower. As Chen suggests, ontological orders might not be fixed, stable, or essential, but they still constitute limiting frames for fleshy bodies. These provisional orders can be resisted as fictive stereotypes, but they remain affectively powerful scaffolding for biopolitics, for "the governmentality of animate hierarchies, . . . how acts seem to operate with, or against, the order of things" (12). Historically, as the "Briseño factors" attest, Steinbeck's novella has been interpreted in reductive ways that have conceptually coerced and indelibly shaped historical bodies.

Michael Bérubé was the first to bring my attention to the potential dangers—and even lethal effects—of Lennie, referring me to *Ex parte Briseño* and the 2012 execution of Marvin Wilson, a mentally disabled African American male (192). On January 30, 2015, Robert Ladd, another African American male, was executed despite likewise meeting clinical definitions of mental disability. He was administered a lethal dose of pentobarbital in the same Huntsville County facility where Wilson was killed (Pilkington). Recalling my earlier suggestion regarding *Moore v. Texas*, however, it is a mistake to suggest that Steinbeck or Lennie is to blame for these deleterious material effects; rather, readers' interpretations are what *matter* most here.

The legacy of the "Briseño factors" serves as a case in point. On February 11, 2004, Judge Cochran "disregarded the standardized results of an adaptive behavior assessment" of the defendant, Jose Garcia Briseño, who was seeking exemption from the death penalty under *Atkins v. Virginia* (Long 869). That assessment, which was to be considered alongside Briseño's clinical IQ score, was developed over years of specialized psychological research; nevertheless, Cochran ruled that its results were "exceedingly subjective" (869). In an absurd twist, she installed Lennie instead as the state-sanctioned benchmark for determining the legitimacy of a defendant's claim to mental disability. The "Briseño factors" were designed by Cochran to be used on a case-by-case basis (869). Comprising seven questions, they included the following:

Has the person formulated plans and carried them through or is his conduct impulsive?

Does his conduct show leadership or does it show that he is led around by others?

Is his conduct in response to external stimuli rational and appropriate, regardless of whether it is socially acceptable?

Can the person hide facts or lie effectively in his own or others' interests? (868)[8]

Though Lennie was not explicitly mentioned in these guidelines, he informs them as the implied negative case. Judge Cochran's rationale for inscribing a fictional character into legal procedures was linked to his popularity: she reasoned that he was so well-known and well-loved that "most Texas citizens might agree that Steinbeck's Lennie should, by virtue of his lack of reasoning ability and adaptive skills, be exempt" from the death penalty (869). In other words, this judge assumed that the majority of Texans would agree with *her own humane interpretation*. As well, her direct invocation of Lennie in this ruling laid claim to the CCA's own sympathetic feeling—a display of its superior humane subjectivity. Ironically, however, it did so while establishing the grounds for enacting sovereign violence on bodies constructed as criminal. In this light, then, Cochran's interpretative act enshrined a sympathetic approach to *Of Mice and Men* as a deciding factor in whether Texas could pursue capital punishment of defendants who claimed to be exempt under *Atkins*—at least until *Moore v. Texas*.

I conclude my analysis by citing the specific historical cases of Wilson, Ladd, and Moore, not to morbidly sensationalize or conflate them, but to stress that Steinbeck's aesthetics have had indisputable physical effects in the terrain of US biopower. In lieu of the life and death stakes of the "Briseño factors," this claim is practically inarguable. Judge Cochran's Lennie-inspired guidelines proved far too flexible in practice, allowing Texas to carry out the executions of "several intellectually disabled individuals"—people who would have been legally protected in other states (865). Like Wilson and Ladd, the majority of those executed were people of color; this indicates—once again—that neither anthropocentrism nor ableism is the sole condition of possibility for stigma, bigotry, and disqualification in US culture. To the extent that the executed were predominantly marked as African American and male, this evinces the overdetermined and entwined biological meanings that attend tropes of race, gender/sex, dis/ability, as well as species. I emphasize the racialized identities of Wilson, Ladd, and Moore to highlight how Lennie's excess as an idiot/dog figure can be radically reduced and instrumentalized. Rather than uncovering complex layers of meaning in Steinbeck's novella, the likes of which I have steadfastly pursued, the CCA deployed this character as a mere stereotype to justify the state's lethal imposition on the bodies of particular citizens—mortal bodies that had already been made to bear the burden of supporting a fantasy of an unremarkably "normal" human subject in US civic and economic life (i.e. white, adult, middle class, able-bodied, rational, and male subjectivity). It's difficult to imagine a more flagrant or contemptible example of literary fiction being used by a state power—and in such a reductive way no less—to frame bodies as criminal and inferior.

For thirteen years, Lennie Small was used to kill in the name of biopolitically protecting a population. This is an odious historical legacy. In the wake of *Moore v. Texas*, I initially drew tentative hope from the Supreme Court's ruling. After all, the CCA would be required to revise Texas law to ensure that the determination of mental disability comports with current medical professional standards, not a judge's reductive reading of *Of Mice and Men*. At the time of writing this conclusion, those glimmers of hope—though not dashed—have been sharply tempered. In June 2018, the CCA once again denied Moore's application for habeas relief under *Atkins* in a majority ruling of 5–3. As Judge Alcala writes in the dissenting opinion, the CCA majority arguably pursued a faulty interpretation and application of the DSM-5 that led to its determination that Moore is not mentally disabled, a clear "outlier" position at odds with the consensus reached by the state prosecution, the habeas court, the Supreme Court, and six experts (qtd. in McCullough). Evidently, constitutional protections continue to be decided in an uneven, biased manner in Texas. It is horribly unjust that Bobby Moore remains on death row. Still, I reiterate that expurgating the "Briseño factors" from the state's criminal justice system is, unequivocally, a "good thing." Regarding Steinbeck's classic more specifically, I insist that it can—and should—be interpreted otherwise. To this end, Lennie can teach us new tricks.

NOTES

1. I use the term "idiot" to denote a historically defined disability and trope. Following Waggoner, I also use "mental disability" even though many "scholars and activists have adopted the term *intellectual disability* to distance cognitive disability from the stigma of 'mental retardation,' which 'mental disability' risks echoing. However, this

term's focus on 'intellect,' defined as the capacity to reason, risks recentering liberal humanist rationality, a dangerous category for disabled and racialized people alike" in the context of contemporary US civic and economic life (91). I acknowledge all terms' discursive instability.

2. For another canonical example of idiot/dog confusion, see my essay "Otherwise Undisclosed: Blood, Species, and Benjy Compson's Idiocy."

3. Snyder and Mitchell chart how, in the nineteenth and twentieth centuries, US eugenicists pathologized disabled bodies, framing them as reproductive threats to the national population (69–99). This biologization of disability, Snyder and Mitchell argue, is entwined with questions of race and sex and, thus, has an international scope, culminating in the Nazi Holocaust (100–129).

4. See Perlin for how "ethnic adjustments" are used in Texas to make some defendants "who would otherwise have been protected under Atkins . . . eligible for the death penalty" (1439).

5. See Derrida's *The Animal That Therefore I Am* for the now-classic deconstruction of the priority of human response over animal reaction.

6. See Jensen-Moulton for how "California's eugenics laws allowed for the sterilization of more than 21,000 people between 1907 and 1939 in order to prevent the passing of 'feeble-mindedness' from generation to generation. . . . This obsession with sterilization or even eugenic elimination . . . represented a particularly U.S. approach to dealing with disability" (130).

7. See Fudge for statistics about euthanasia in the US pet industry: "For every four healthy companion animals one is destined . . . [to be] humanely killed" (109).

8. See Long for all seven "Briseño Factors" (868).

WORKS CITED

Agamben, Giorgio. *Homo Sacer: Sovereign Power and Bare Life*. Translated by Daniel Heller-Roazen. Stanford UP, 1998.

Ahmed, Sara. "Orientations Matter." *New Materialisms*, edited by Diana H. Coole and Samantha Frost, Duke UP, 2010, pp. 234–57.

Bérubé, Michael. *The Secret Life of Stories*. New York UP, 2016.

Boggs, Colleen Glenney. *Animalia Americana: Animal Representations and Biopolitical Subjectivity*. Columbia UP, 2013.

Borsheim-Black, Carlin, Michael Macaluso, and Robert Petrone. "Critical Literature Pedagogy: Teaching Canonical Literature for Critical Literacy." *Journal of Adolescent and Adult Literacy*, vol. 58, no. 2, 2014, pp. 123–33. https://doi.org/10.1002/jaal.323

Brooks, Peter. *Reading for the Plot: Design and Intention in Narrative*. Harvard UP, 1992.

Cardullo, Bert. "On the Road to Tragedy: Mice, Candy, and Land in 'Of Mice and Men.'" *American Drama*, vol. 16, no. 1, 2007, pp. 19–29. *ProQuest*, search.proquest.com.ez-proxy.library.uvic.ca/docview/2295640?accountid=14846

Chen, Mel Y. *Animacies: Biopolitics, Racial Mattering, and Queer Affect*. Duke UP, 2012.

Chivers, Sally. "Disability Studies and the Vancouver Opera's *Of Mice and Men*." *Disability Studies Quarterly*, vol. 23, no. 1, 2003, dsqsds.org/article/view/402/551

Derrida, Jacques. *The Animal That Therefore I Am*. Edited by Marie-Louise Mallet. Translated by David Wills. Fordham UP, 2008.

Fudge, Erica. *Pets*. Acumen, 2008.

Gates, Henry Louis. *The Signifying Monkey: A Theory of African-American Literary Criticism*. Oxford UP, 1988.

Goffman, Erving. *Stigma: Notes toward the Management of Spoiled Identity*. Penguin, 1990.

Halliwell, Martin. *Images of Idiocy: The Idiot Figure in Modern Fiction and Film*. Ashgate, 2004.

Haraway, Donna J. *When Species Meet*. U of Minnesota P, 2008.

Jensen-Moulton, Stephanie. "Intellectual Disability in Carlisle Floyd's *Of Mice and Men*." *American Music*, vol. 30, no. 2, 2012, pp. 129–56. https://doi.org/10.5406/american-music.30.2.0129

Keely, Karen. "Sexuality and Storytelling: Literary Representations of the 'Feebleminded' in the Age of Sterilization." *Mental Retardation in America*, edited by Steven Noll and James W. Trent Jr., New York UP, 2004, pp. 207–22.

Levant, Howard. *The Novels of John Steinbeck: A Critical Study*. U of Missouri P, 1983.

Liptak, Adam. "Texas Used Wrong Standard in Death Penalty Cases, Justices Rule." *New York Times*, Mar. 28, 2017. https://www.nytimes.com/2017/03/28/us/politics/texas-death-penalty-supreme-court-ruling.html

Long, Mia-Carré. "Of Mice and Men, Fairy Tales, and Legends: A Reactionary Ethical Proposal to Storytelling and the Briseño Factors." *Georgetown Journal of Legal Ethics*, vol. 16, no. 4, 2013, pp. 859–78.

McCullough, Jolie. "Texas Court Upholds Bobby Moore's Death Sentence, Rejecting Broadly Supported Claim of Intellectual Disability." *Texas Tribune*, June 6, 2018. https://www.texastribune.org/2018/06/06/texas-court-criminal-appeals-death-sentence-bobby-moore/

Moran, Rachel F. *Interracial Intimacy: The Regulation of Race and Romance*. U of Chicago P, 2003.

Morsberger, Robert. "Of Mice, Dogs, Wabbits, Ducks, and Men." *Steinbeck Quarterly*, vol. 14, nos. 3–4, 1981, p. 112. libx.bsu.edu/cdm/ref/collection/steinbeck/id/2454

Oswald, David. "Otherwise Undisclosed: Blood, Species, and Benjy Compson's Idiocy." *Journal of Literary and Cultural Disability Studies*, vol. 10, no. 3, 2016, pp. 287–304. https://doi.org/10.3828/jlcds.2016.25

Owens, Louis. "Deadly Kids, Stinking Dogs, and Heroes: The Best Laid Plans in Steinbeck's 'Of Mice and Men.'" *Western American Literature*, vol. 37, no. 3, 2002, pp. 318–33. www.jstor.org/stable/43022181

Perlin, Michael L. "Your Corrupt Ways Had Finally Made You Blind: Prosecutorial Misconduct and the Use of Ethnic Adjustment in Death Penalty Cases of Defendants with Intellectual Disabilities." *American University Law Review*, vol. 65, no. 6, 2016, pp. 1437–60.

Peterson, Christopher. *Beastial Traces: Race, Sexuality, Animality*. Fordham UP, 2013.

Pilkington, Ed. "Texas Executes Intellectually Disabled Killer Robert Ladd." *The Guardian*, Jan. 30, 2015. www.theguardian.com/us-news/2015/jan/30/texas-executes-robert-ladd-intellectually-disabled-prisoner

Quayson, Ato. *Aesthetic Nervousness: Disability and the Crisis of Representation*. Columbia UP, 2007.

Samuels, Ellen. *Fantasies of Identification: Disability, Gender, Race*. New York University P, 2014.

Shukin, Nicole. *Animal Capital: Rendering Life in Biopolitical Times*. U of Minnesota P, 2009.

Snyder, Sharon L., and David T. Mitchell. *Cultural Locations of Disability*. U of Chicago P, 2006.

Steinbeck, John. *Of Mice and Men*. Collier and Son, 1937.

Terada, Rei. *Feeling in Theory: Emotion After the "Death of the Subject."* Harvard UP, 2001.

Waggoner, Jess. "'Oh Say Can You ___': Race and Mental Disability in Performances of Citizenship." *Journal of Literary and Cultural Disability Studies*, vol. 10, no. 1, 2016, pp. 87–102. https://doi.org/10.3828/jlcds.2016.6

Part IV

The Matter of Memory

Informal Economies in Mexico City Transit

The Matter of Disappearance

Susan Antebi

A man in a wheelchair sits in the metro station of the Plaza de la Transparencia, Mexico City, at the base of two flights of stairs, each leading upward in opposite directions. There is no other entrance to the space he occupies. The athletic style of his chair with its angled wheels might suggest that he arrived at this floor on his own, somehow navigating the steep stairs, or he may have been assisted. But in either case, the presence of the wheelchair user in a jarringly inaccessible space cannot fail to command the attention of passing commuters, some of who respond to his requests for money as they reach the bottom of one flight of stairs, on foot, and then ascend towards the platform on the other side.

In December 2013, the cost of a one-way metro ride in Mexico City increased from three pesos to five, at the same time that the city enacted an explicit ban on informal commerce, or the presence of unlicensed vendors, in the subway cars. The anti-vendor policy appeared most visibly in an advertising campaign, featuring the photograph of a music CD vendor in a subway car, with the subtitle, "No les compres y desaparecen" [Don't buy from them and they will disappear] (Mora; Aristegui Noticias). Although there was no direct mention of disability in this ad campaign, it is well known that many disabled people in Mexico City participate in informal commercial practices; blind vendors in particular are well represented among those selling music or other products in the subway.

I begin the present chapter with the juxtaposition of these two scenes, in order to consider the circulation of social and corporeal vulnerability as materialized processes in the context of twenty-first-century Mexico City public transit. My reading in the pages to follow is based on the concept of

Fig. 1. The Mexico City campaign to ban informal commerce on the subway featured this advertisement, which states: "Don't buy from them and they will disappear. Informal commerce is prohibited on the metro. If you don't buy from them they won't come back to sell. With this action you will avoid the disturbance and excessive noise that the vendors generate. For more peaceful transit, tell them no! The metro is yours, take care of it!"

the "host," an ambivalent mode of psychically inflected intercorporeality suggestive of impairment, with reference to the novel *El huésped*, by Guadalupe Nettel, and on the politically charged uses of the projected threat of disappearance as central to the lived materiality of nonnormative and precarious embodiments. As I discuss further, "hosting" and "disappearance" become mutually implicated because the corporeal and economic dependency associated with the structure of the host-relation, in some analyses akin to parasitism, and also at times linked to repressed desire, implies the threat of extirpation, hence potential disappearance. In this argument, use of the term "disappear" also points toward an ongoing violence specific to Mexico, in which "the disappeared," including victims of organized crime and political targets, indicates a category of those who may or may not have been killed, for their absence is not fully explained. Yet first, I return to the scenes described above.

In the first episode, featuring a version of the classic image of the wheelchair user before the staircase, the presence of disability evokes a long and familiar history of nonnormative embodiment as the logical justification for begging, but with the key difference that here it is the body's incongruous presence in a seemingly inaccessible space that becomes the instigator of a financial transaction. In other words, rather than "selling" his physical impairment as signifying an inability to work, the disabled person sells a gesture toward the physical environment that he shares with other travelers. This material space and its failure to accommodate disability, rather than the body's failure to conform to established normativity, becomes the key marker of difference that now demands rectification, as if in a textbook rendition of the transition from the medical to the social model.

Our work in posthumanist disability theory throughout this volume emphasizes the limitations of the overused social model, in large part for its privileging of the environment over the specific materiality and agency of the body, and also, paradoxically, for the way in which in the social model, as Tobin Siebers notes, impairment—hence the body itself—remains key to the diagnosis of inaccessible environments.[1] The social model thus sustains itself through surreptitious, backward glances to the impairments that it nonetheless refuses to approach or interrogate further.

Here too, the wheelchair user as disabled body might appear as strangely reduced to a diagnosing function, as if structurally present yet viscerally absent in this scene of injustice, inaccessibility, and commercial exchange. But at this point, let us expand the field to incorporate the second scenario mentioned above, in which a transit price increase—one that created significant economic hardship for many users—coincided with the attempted exclusion of subway vendors, many of whom are disabled. In this way, I want to pay further attention to the dynamic, interactive mattering of disability, through the labor of nonnormative bodies as central to the public practices of both transit and financial transaction. The cited slogan, "Don't buy from them and they will disappear," is exemplary of the processes by which disability materiality circulates as a public threat, shadowed by its own potential disappearance, and integral to the workings of both affective and commercial exchange.

In making explicit a projected disappearance, the phrase suggests on one hand a collective desire to eradicate a vaguely defined plural subject, and on the other the power and supposed social responsibility of the ostensibly legitimate subway rider, whose decision to buy or not to buy will literally "disappear" the undesirable subject—the subway vendor. The use of a photograph accompanying this slogan gives specific, embodied form to the offending subject: he appears as male, young, and racialized as mestizo by his clothing and complexion. Also, despite being in an underground subway car, he wears dark sunglasses, which function in this image as an ambivalent marker of potential blindness, or alternatively as the projection of intimidation through a stylized social barrier. In this scene, the music vendor jeopardizes the comfort and tranquility of the other passengers, as potential blindness and potential threat mutually enact their indeterminate equivalences. The ambivalent slippage between disability and vaguely defined categories of poverty and criminality depend here on a history of their fluid cross-referencing. At the same time, the sense of threat, disturbance, or repulsion that the scene may elicit emerges instantaneously, thanks in large part to the ingrained familiarity of similar images. In this way, the advertisement cultivates rejection and dis-ease in the viewer as immediate and intimately experienced sensations.

Considered through this wider framework, the wheelchair user at the foot of the metro staircases gestures not only toward the inaccessibility of the space, as in a classic social model diagnosis, but also participates in a fraught affective and monetary economy, one that his material practices transform, and in which all transit users necessarily have a stake. The two additional pesos per trip that each passenger spends following the rate increase might previously have been invested in goods sold by subway vendors, or in charitable contributions. Now, the ad informs us, they have been channeled toward a more agreeable transit experience, contingent on the disappearance of vendors, beggars, or other transgressive bodies from the public space. In paying the additional transit fee, passengers "choose" to be complicit in the eradication of disturbances occasioned by the informal sector and the bodies associated with it.[2] In this context, the man in the wheelchair makes literal his paradoxical status as "matter out of place," in a dual sense—because there are no elevators or ramps through which he could enter or exit his location, and because the diversion of cash flow from the informal sector to the transit system has failed in its attempt to make him disappear via boycott.[3] Like the vendors who continue to work throughout the subway system, the wheelchair user remains undeterred, underscoring the continued economic viability of his localized, embodied position.

The scenes I have described here enact a series of close associations between disability and socioeconomic vulnerability, one that is consistent with a long and well-documented history of informal sector economics, and with contemporary statistics on disability in Mexico and worldwide. Nonetheless, my intention is not to propose a direct equivalence between these categories, but rather to engage their mutually constituting fluidity as a critical strategy, while remaining aware of the potential pitfalls of false equations. Reading disability and vulnerability as co-constitutive in specific instances allows for an approach that considers the organic, embodied quality of risk or investment that is often measured only abstractly in pesos and cents; and insists on the impact of nonnormative embodiment in public spaces as both affectively and economically transformative.

Histories of disability, labor, and public space offer key accounts of the dilemma of social vulnerability as continuous with nonnormative embodiment, even as these socioeconomic and corporeal categories still tend to enact the porosity of their boundaries. In Henry Mayhew's classic text, *London Labour and the London Poor*, the disabled people in the nineteenth-century urban center are defined as "those who cannot work," in order to distinguish them from "those who will not work."[4] These nomenclatures have always encountered ambiguity or flexibility in their practical application; work and disability are not mutually exclusive today, nor was this the case in the London that Mayhew described. In addition, the terms allow for the common suspicion that an immoral or criminal refusal to work in fact masquerades as the inability to work.[5]

In early to mid-twentieth-century Mexico City, disability, criminality, and begging were frequently associated as co-constitutive social ills.[6] Thus in 1935, José Casimiro Hernández, a sixty-two-year-old indigenous man, described as having a "mutilated leg," would be forcibly taken by public welfare officials to a shelter and held there against his will for at least seven months, on suspicion of begging in the streets. Yet Casimiro Hernández turned out to be a landowner who had worked all his life, hence the only evidence against him was his physical appearance, perhaps most notably the condition of his leg.[7] In this case and others, visual diagnosis is sufficient to confirm the inability to work, while not working, in turn, suggests possible laziness or illicit activity. Through this process, nonnormative embodiment, depicted as a form of vulnerability in need of rescue, becomes a social threat as soon as it enters public space, by virtue of its ambivalent status as potential labor force. This dilemma extends continually from individual to larger group, by casting suspicion on those of similar appearance. Those bodies that appear "not to work" in the physical sense are thus assumed to be incapable of work—that is, of performing labor.

In accordance with an alternative, contemporary model, described by

Argentinian social anthropologist Juan Pablo Matta, the pity that a vulnerable (read: visibly disabled) person in public space evokes forms part of the material binary of pity/charity. In this sense, the act of evoking pity, whether through one's physical appearance or through action, intentional or not, is an economic act, rooted in corporeal technique and in material and affective exchange. Moreover, the emergence of pity calls into question the legitimacy of such exchanges, as well as that of the broader and more established economy in which they occur. These models of disability as threat or as evocation of pity are perhaps excessively familiar, often overlap, and are not entirely unique to any locale or historical period. The point here, however, is to pay attention to forms of nonnormative embodiment as actively bound to the structure and performance of economic exchange. Disability materializes and goes to work within and across diverse economies, both evoking and engaging the risks of embodiment in these spaces. In this sense it does not simply emerge via the predetermined, discursive ascriptions of socioeconomic systems. In these scenarios, the evocation of pity in public spaces also links to a particular structure of ambivalent disgust and repressed desire. The tangibly materialized economic value of pity may, perhaps surprisingly, translate to the viewer's desire to embody the position of physical vulnerability, and hence to occupy the valued site of abjected matter, to be taken care of by others, and ostensibly freed from the market's continuous, oscillating demands. This dynamic emerges in particular in Guadalupe Nettel's novel, to be discussed at the conclusion to the present chapter.

In the context of contemporary neoliberalism in Mexico, social vulnerability derives in part from what Miguel Ángel Vite Pérez describes as a process through which what were previously considered rights of social protection become commodities (155–56). The same author also refers to the "rupture of established ties between work and state-sponsored social protection" (156) as an additional source of the new social vulnerability. Disability in Vite Pérez's reading relates directly to the ascription of social meaning and resulting processes of exclusion from the sphere of economic productivity. By the same token, disability as closely tied to the category of social vulnerability includes subjects in the process of "disaffiliation" from social and economic protection against market risks. In accordance with Carolina Ferrante it is through such processes that disabled people become "expendable bodies" (89). As Ferrante also notes, the ironic juxtaposition of the recent United Nations Convention on the Rights of Persons with Disabilities, with the increased presence of disabled people begging in public spaces, underscores the inadequacy of social rights discourse.

Vite Pérez and Ferrante both adhere to a notion of disability as determined by ascriptions of meaning, in overall accordance with the social model. Yet their emphasis on contemporary divisions between the sphere of the market and that of rights-based public welfare is nonetheless useful here for making apparent the increasingly ambivalent function of the roles of work and commerce in relation to social vulnerability. In this context, work as a concept expands to encompass multiple levels of formal and informal activities and interactions. Work and social vulnerability cease to be imagined as mutually exclusive categories, for even the most seemingly stable employment is at constant, heightened risk, while many forms of labor are completely devoid of worker protection. Hence forms of precarity cross freely into the labor market, at times imperceptibly. Through the same process, legislative guarantees of social rights have little to no bearing on the market value of labor power; for this reason, so-called rights-bearing citizens may still materialize as the "expendable bodies" to which Ferrante refers. The expanded, flexible, and often precarious marketplace within this model does not necessarily exclude nonnormative embodiments, but rather encompasses them on a noncontractual, fluid basis, allowing for their elimination at any time, or indeed, harnessing their unique qualities toward profitable ends.[8]

Shortly after the increase in Mexico City metro ticket fees, the photograph of a young man in a wheelchair passing over the metro turnstiles, with assistance from the metro personnel, began to circulate online, thanks in part to a Twitter campaign titled "#posmesalto."[9]

During this protest campaign, many metro riders showed solidarity in resistance to economic inaccessibility by jumping the turnstiles without paying. Initially, this sign of civil disobedience occurred without intervention from the authorities, who decided to respect the protest for a limited time. The activity of this popular protest effectively fused the issue of rights in the context of civil society with the marketplace dynamics made evident by the transit price increase. In other words, the protest opened a space of economic participation as a legitimate sphere through which to demand social rights, and in this way questioned the neoliberal separation between civil society and the marketplace.

The photograph of the wheelchair user as specific, individual protest participant is perhaps especially revelatory of the ironic and innovative qualities of this collective movement. Public transport in Mexico City is free for disabled people as well as for senior citizens, a fact that makes the wheelchair user's actions doubly symbolic. Jumping the turnstile in this case does not—on the surface—represent any direct savings, given that

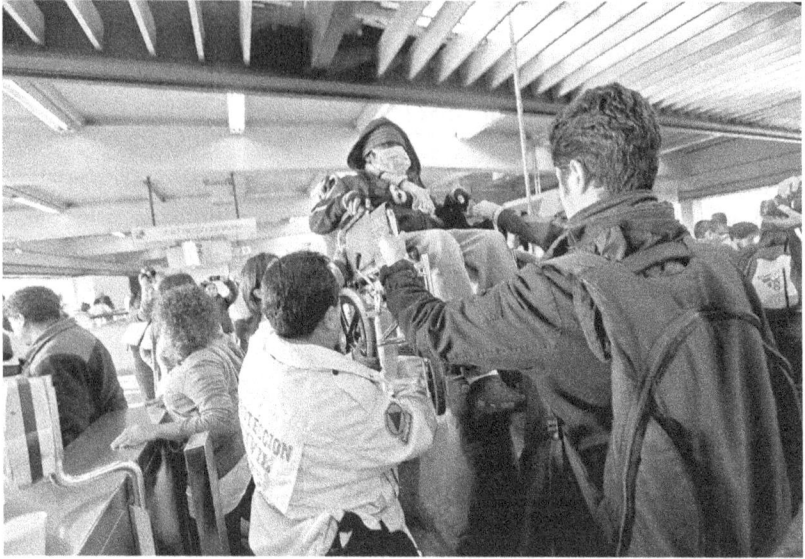

Fig. 2. A man in a wheelchair passes over the metro turnstiles with assistance from personnel, as part of the #posmesalto campaign. (Credit: Miguel Fuantos. Agencia Reforma. Consorcio Interamericano de Comunicación S.A. de C.V. All rights reserved. Reproduction in any manner in any language in whole or in part without prior written permission is prohibited.)

the young man's transit is always free. Yet this act underscores the fact that participation in civil society and in public spaces is inevitably an economic practice, an obligatory entry to the marketplace, and part of a collective action. And it signals that the ticket price and metro ride form part of a wider market, in which simply getting from point A to point B is never the whole story. As an "out of place" protest, the wheelchair user's turnstile jump demonstrates that the price increase, as in the case of other economic adjustments that impact daily life, transcends the individual and is distributed over a broad field of intersubjective interests, with effects that tend to express themselves more tangibly among the most vulnerable social sectors. It is of course ironic that the public protest originally imagined the participation of hypercapacitated subjects, those able to leap over a turnstile. The wheelchair user's solidarity with the broader movement, intentionally or not, draws attention to material embodiment as a condition of participation, and thus highlights both economic and other forms of exclusion.[10]

In the neoliberal labor market analyzed by Vite Pérez, financial interests are untethered from social protections and from the discourse of rights such protections imply; here, however, the fluid and collectively inhabited space of public transit tends to reiterate its complex web of links to both labor and consumer activity. In this photographed action, the disabled metro rider materializes in the public spaces of both metro and internet, literally suspended midair, and in this way performs the paradoxical embodiment of a commercial transaction. The effect is a simultaneous, cross-cutting disruption both of market logic, dependent on continuous price increases, and of social protections that are piecemeal, based on reductive categories, and falsely cordoned off from the material realities of the market.

Both the wheelchair user's protest in the photographed turnstile jump and the advertising campaign targeting subway vendors underscore the central relevance and material qualities of disability to the quotidian and contemporary issue of public transit in Mexico City, though in clearly distinct ways. In the case of the wheelchair, it is an easily recognized symbol of disability, yet here it appears in the air "out of place," thus indirectly emphasizing the issue of limited accessibility in many metro stations. In fact, despite Mexican legislation that guarantees accessibility in public transit and in other areas, it is common to witness the spontaneous cooperation of passengers who lift wheelchair users up and down staircases, due to lack of alternatives.

The ad campaign, in contrast, seems to at least partially sidestep the issue of disability, arguably increasing the efficacy of its message by minimizing controversy. According to the electronic publication *Dis-capacidad.com*, the group of vendors of pirated music CDs who circulate on subway cars carrying speakers on their backs—one of whom is represented on the advertisement poster—copied the model of a group of blind vendors who were the first to implement this practice. While most subway passengers would be unaware of this history and of the particular and complex workings of vendor groups, along with their practices and hierarchies, the specific agency of vendors who identify with a given cohort emerges explicitly in the internet publication with the insistence that blindness is indeed central to their collective identity and labor practices. In this context, the "disappeared" disability from the subway poster may easily go undetected yet remains sedimented in the histories of ambivalent social vulnerability and threat as intrinsic to informal, potentially illicit commercial practices.

Disappearance, and the action of disappearing with its dual meaning, suggestive of either the vanishing or departure of a given subject, or an action performed upon a human or nonhuman object, tends to evoke

238 | The Matter of Disability

magical or violent practices. In the Mexican context in which the poster appears, and indeed within an expanded trajectory of twentieth-century Latin American history, the term "disappear" frequently reverts to its past participle form, "the disappeared," in reference to political prisoners and other targeted individuals and groups, as well as victims of many forms of organized or state-sponsored crime.[11] Thus the future disappearance of subway vendors that the poster demands as inclusive in the increased transit fare cannot fail to summon a complex necropolitics, in which the violence of killing is carefully subsumed into the language of augmented personal space and reduced disturbance. The magic of disappearance works by simultaneously removing the offending body and erasing recognition of the unpleasant process by which that removal would take place. In this case too, focus on the desired disappearance of vendors from the informal marketplace might be said to momentarily shift attention away from the ongoing phenomenon of disappearance as an implied, partial synonym for murder.

The politically and affectively charged notion of disappearance acquired unprecedented weight in Mexico following the kidnapping and disappearance of forty-three students of the rural school of Ayotzinapa in the state of Guerrero in September 2014. Municipal police affirmed that the students, who had been involved in political protest, were turned over to members of a drug cartel, who then killed them. Investigation into the case has led to the discovery of many mass graves with human remains, but those of the Ayotzinapa students have not been definitively located. Mismanagement of the investigation called into question the veracity of some official testimony, and suggested the potentially illicit involvement of higher levels of government authority.[12] The case points to an intensified delegitimization of the state, and to the state's role in competition and collaboration with highly profitable criminal organizations within the paradigm of narcocapitalism.[13] Attention to the horror and corruption of the Ayotzinapa case also underscores a trajectory of violent disappearances in Mexico, many still unsolved, from those of political activists of the 1970s to the wave of femicides impacting Ciudad Juárez from the 1990s, to the nearly thirty thousand cases of disappearances since the 2006 initiation of the Mexican war against narcotrafficking.

In each of these contexts, the mechanism of disappearance bears a close relationship to structures of increasing socioeconomic inequality, through which gendered and racialized bodies become differentially expendable. In this way, the rise of factory production in the border location of Ciudad Juárez following the onset of NAFTA led to low-paying job opportunities for young rural women, many of whom had to travel to work at irregular shifts, through areas lacking street lighting or consistent public transit. Lack of public accountability, police corruption, and an easily replaceable, female workforce has arguably led to conditions in which gendered disappearance is a by-product of economic growth.[14] In the case of Ayotzinapa, as Rossana Reguillo has suggested, the students' political activism may have made them a potential threat to the capitalist interests of the cartels and their state affiliates. Moreover, as has arguably been the case in many other instances, their status as rural, poor, politically unruly, and racialized tends to define their expendability.

Use of the term "disappear" in the subway poster, in conjunction with the photograph of an anonymous music vendor with dark sunglasses, refers in one sense to a kind of straightforward market logic, dictating that products materialize and continue to exist only in response to demand. In the informal, improvised marketplace of the subway car, the product, vendor, and "shop" form a continuous, fluid unit, emerging and vanishing in accordance with the needs and desires of paying customers. From this perspective, the "disappearance" of the vendor is no different from that of the product. At the same time, the term "disappear" carries an inevitable political and affective charge that is specific to contemporary Mexico, evoking an ongoing history of targeted violence that remains painfully suspended, for the deaths of the disappeared are suspected but rarely if ever confirmed. In this poster, it is through the paradoxical fusion of the neoliberal marketplace's flattened affect with a threatening, indeterminate violence conditioned by vulnerability, that the imperative for disappearance achieves its full effects. In other words, the implied threat of the sunglass wearer, who both invades passengers' space and may remind them of his own precarious status, is veiled and contained by the economic framework in which he materializes, with clear instructions that grant agency to the potential buyer and explain the presence or absence of the vendor in terms of straightforward market logic. The market, in its informal sector iteration, thus appears to become host to the materiality of vulnerability and threat as continuous with the emergence and disappearance of nonnormative embodiment.

The concept of the host, and the act of hosting, is relevant here as a mechanism through which the public may observe human or nonhuman bodies in their environments as either conforming to expectations, or out of place, as in the case of wheelchair users before staircases, or jumping over turnstiles. Hosting defines a material, spatial, and economic relationship, suggestive of parallels with containment, dependency, and corporeal proximity. Needless to say, hosting does not necessarily suggest a welcoming or cooperative relationship, but instead may describe a form of parasitism, the dilemma of an unwelcome presence, or desire for extirpation, as in the case of the campaign to "disappear" subway vendors. The structure of hosting and parasitism at work in this scenario is further complicated when we consider the function of noise within the system, as Michael Serres discusses in his classic work *The Parasite*. In Serres's reading, the host, whether human or nonhuman, scares away the parasite by making noise, as in the case of an alarm system, or a bird singing, hence drawing attention to the parasitic relation, and attempting to drive out the offending element. Yet in this complex structure, noise itself is also the parasite, a disruption to the system, and its renewed beginning. The issue of noise in a literal sense is made explicit as central to the problem embodied by subway vendors in the ad campaign. The image of the man carrying a large speaker on his back as he sells music reminds passengers of the high volumes at which such music is regularly played in the subway cars. The noise emanating from the body of the vendor who transmits it is apparently, at least for a moment, the offending, parasitic element. In Serres's analysis, parasitism also functions as "white noise" and is defined as "the heart of relation" (52); thus singular (noisy) interruptions draw attention to the structure of relation, and in this case to its material inequalities, even as noise itself—as a kind of third term—is continuous with the evolving system itself.[15]

The dilemma of hosting/disappearance, or extirpation, materializes in repeated instances in the fraught, negotiated space of public transit discussed here, and in a broader economic framework in which corporeal affect jostles with market interests. *The Host* (*El huésped*) is also the title of a 2006 novel by Mexican writer Guadalupe Nettel, a text I now turn to for further exploration of the corporeal, affective, and monetary economies of the Mexico City metro, and of the circulation of nonnormative embodiment as central to the work of threat, desire, and vulnerability.

In Spanish, the term *huésped* (host) bears an ambivalent meaning, referring either to an invited guest, or to one who receives and houses the guest.[16] Nettel's novel appears to favor the first and more common definition, for the story centers around the narrator's inner experience of invasion by a strange being that gradually exerts power over her and transforms her existence. This transformation in turn corresponds to the narrator's process of vision loss, and to her growing identification with a community of blind people, through scenes that take place in the Mexico City metro, and in an institute for the blind in Mexico City's Colonia

Roma.[17] Yet here too, the "host" necessarily also reverts to its second meaning, through the increasingly blurred division between protagonist and "parasite," referred to in the text as "La Cosa" (The Thing).

The novel's associations between disability, including blindness, and the psychoanalytic notions of abjection and the uncanny are fairly direct, and tend to take advantage of familiar cultural scripts whereby the threat of invasive, nonnormative embodiment, in this case hovering between psychic and material manifestations, drive the plot and sustain readerly interest. Yet of particular interest here is the way this fictional exploration of disability, psychic transformation, and the space of public transit underscores a close interweaving of affective and monetary structures of "hosting" as key to the protagonist's experiences and projections of her changing world. As in the case of my discussion of the informal sector in the Mexico City metro, its historical underpinnings, and the campaign against subway vendors, in Nettel's novel too, informal commercial practices, including begging, link directly to representations of disability as materializations of threat and social vulnerability. In addition, it is particularly the case in the novel that disability evokes responses that trouble the division between disgust and desire; the narrator's encounters with social vulnerability become occasions for her intimate, visceral engagement with intercorporeal affect, as she navigates conflicting impulses to flee from or to succumb to the material provocation of nonnormative embodiment.

In *El huésped*, the space of the metro evokes both fear and a sense of liberation for the narrator, who begins to discover a world at odds with her prior concepts of financial transactions and corporeal affect, for in this fictitious metro, begging is a logical and legitimate mode of survival, directly equated with the affective performance of physical impairment. The text participates revealingly in an economy of social vulnerability, especially because the protagonist, in navigating between her attraction and disgust toward disability, frequently exemplified by blind people, implicitly questions herself about the aesthetic and social value of the Others she encounters. The following passage and its further unfolding are especially suggestive in this regard: "Apareció frente a mí un personaje de aspecto familiar, con esa inconfundible cara de beatitud, de quien lo merece todo, que tienen los miembros del grupo. Era un niño tullido. Me costó trabajo observarlo porque se arrastraba con los brazos a la velocidad de un torpedo más o menos a la altura de mis rodillas. Son una plaga, pensé, habría que detenerlos" [A familiar-looking character appeared before me, with that unmistakable beatific, all-deserving face, typical of the group members. It was a crippled child. I had trouble observing him because he dragged himself along with his arms at torpedo speed, passing at about the height of my knees. They are a plague, I thought. They should be stopped] (125–26).[18]

The protagonist's offensively expressed rejection of disabled people, as in this case, is complicated further upon her observation of the child's economic activity. The child's success in soliciting charity leads to further reflection: "Si alguien, por más mutilado que sea, sabe que cuenta con la lástima de los demás, deja de ser un absoluto desvalido" [If someone, no matter how mutilated, can count on the pity of others, he is no longer completely helpless] (126).[19] This train of thought certainly suggests the material binary of pity/charity, discussed earlier in reference to the work of Juan Pablo Matta, in which active, corporeal affect becomes inseparable from materially lucrative exchange, potentially leading to a sense that the disabled person has a kind of "unfair advantage." Moreover, in this instance, an abrupt transition occurs, as the narrator recognizes, perhaps with some irony, that the characteristics of the child—in this case, his relative "helplessness," and related implications—are determined by an evolving process of affective relations with all others with whom he comes in contact. In addition, these characteristics are not mere impressions, but actively transform the child's economic status. Although this realization may not actually change the narrator's disparaging view of disability and disabled people, it emerges here as a kind of begrudging admittance that human materiality in public spaces is inevitably fluid, determined by multiple and ongoing processes of interaction and exchange.

The eruption of pity in the space of public transport provokes not only an economic exchange, but also, from the narrator's perspective, the flourishing of an expanded intersubjective field. As she states: "Miré después a las señoras que abrían su bolso para dar unas monedas al muchacho. ¿Qué grupo sostenía a esas mujeres para lidiar con sus mutilaciones?" [Afterward, I looked at the ladies who opened their purses to give a few coins to the boy. What group supported these women in dealing with their mutilations?] (126). The "group" here refers within the novel to a collective of disabled people who live in the subway and survive by begging. In indicating that the ladies lack such a social collective, the narrator affirms the efficacy of the disabled people's group and their solidarity, while at the same time transferring her prior expression of disgust from the child to the charitable ladies, who now appear as metaphorically mutilated thanks to their participation in the observed exchange. The familiar use of disability as a charged metaphor through which to project discredit by association is clearly at work in this scenario; yet disgust appears to adhere only briefly to any given object and is primarily defined by its capacity to circulate and acquire new forms. In this way, the logic of economic exchange gives shape to affective responses that materialize but easily dissipate and emerge elsewhere. In a similar sense, the narrator's descriptions of her actions and of the world around her seem to suggest a certain remove, as if she were observing herself responding to others and then recounting the scene at a distance. From early on, we learn that the narrator as a child believes herself to be inhabited by The Thing, thus casting doubt on her responsibility for her actions and statements. As a narrative technique, the presence of the host fuses the indeterminate question of corporeal integrity with structures of affective exchange, with the result that rapidly shifting impressions of human and nonhuman others correspond to a transforming projection and materiality of the self as both within and beyond its familiar, tangible boundaries.

The role of The Thing in the narrator's intimate account of her psyche evidently parallels that of the vulnerable, disabled Others she encounters and describes in the space of the metro, as in her descriptions of the "crippled child." This link underscores the intensely material quality of the affective exchange, in which the narrator's impression of disgust shifts and implies a repressed desire to inhabit the ostensibly advantageous position of disability as social vulnerability. This form of desire or jealousy, in tandem with the narrator's more directly expressed disgust, is the mechanism through which the matter of corporeal otherness exerts its intimate force; it is a desire to escape the constant demands of the circuit of affective and economic exchange, to cede control, and to fully embody the materiality and value of abjected flesh.

Affective exchange in this work also relates closely to more literal financial transactions. The narrator makes this point explicit in her reflection on the situation of the blind people who inhabit the institute where she occasionally works, noting that the blind live in such institutions: "gracias a la hospitalidad de los videntes, a quienes, en el fondo, debían de odiar con toda su alma. Todos, de alguna u otra manera, soñaban con la autonomía, con abandonar su eterna condición de huésped" [thanks to the hospitality of the sighted, whom, at bottom, they should have hated with all their soul. All of them, in one way or another, dreamed of autonomy, of abandoning their eternal condition of "host"/guest] (109). Being a "host" in this case specifically means depending economically on others for one's survival. The narrator's disgust, expressed in response to forms of nonnormative embodiment at various points in the novel, is also directly tied to the question of economic dependency, the abjected condition of the host. The host is necessarily vulnerable, and equally capable of threatening or provoking pity or desire; it is a personal, embodied condition, while at once an expansive, interactive, and market-based social dynamic.

In this novel, the dilemma of socioeconomic inequality is materially expressed through the protagonist's body, experiences, and impressions of others, as an internalized fusion of hospitality and the threat of potential disappearance or extirpation. The materialization of inequality thus produces a constant preoccupation that is both social and corporeal, hovering around the dilemma of the aesthetic and economic values of embodiment as ambivalently intimate and foreign to the self. From here, one might return to the image of the sunglass-wearing music vendor, and the message of nonconsumption of his wares with the goal of "disappearance" of this offending embodiment from the subway. To some extent, the expression of nervousness surrounding the lived embodiment of inequality in this advertisement scene, and the wish to eradicate it by removing its alleged material cause, parallels the corporeal and affective structures at work in the novel. In both cases a form of hosting takes place, in which an economic relationship is posited in terms of an invasive embodiment within a confined physical space, one that calls into question the material contours and potential value of an implied subject, its vulnerability and its projection of threat to others. The hosting relationship also exerts specific demands on the viewer of the advertisement or the narrator of the novel, because the intimate, material encounter elicits both fear or disgust, and a repressed desire to embody extreme vulnerability. In this way, the matter of these subway encounters allows for the materialization of a highly charged structure of intercorporeal affect.

Ultimately, the question of whether any given, materialized subject is itself at risk of disappearance, or instead posited as an integral, valued self, to be defended from encroaching external—or internal—dangers, suggests potential ambivalence. This is not to imply that all bodies are equally at risk in the informal marketplace, nor in the broader economic framework of global capitalism, but rather that in this context, and in accordance with the logic of hosting and potential disappearance through which nonnormative embodiment circulates, it is the movement of transit, affect, and exchange that conditions risk, desire, and threat as intercorporeal processes of transformation.

In highlighting particular instances of vulnerable embodiment within the affectively and economically charged scenes of Nettel's novel, in the subway advertisement, in iconic instances of political protest, and in the evocation of quotidian metro encounters, part of my intention has been to frame these scenarios within a familiar and fluid marketplace. In these settings, movement and exchange triggered by notions of (non)normative embodiment and corporeal boundaries may pass unnoticed, because of an apparent continuity with standard practices of labor, consumption, and related social interaction. At the same time, prolonged attention to the materiality of such scenes serves to pull them momentarily from the circuits in which they repeat, thus isolating instances in which the ambivalent oscillation of vulnerability congeals to display the violent and materially specific conditions of radical inequality. At the conclusion of Nettel's novel, the protagonist, now united with The Thing that inhabits her body, listens to the passing metro trains as they come and go, "uno después de otro, pero siempre iguales, como un mismo tren que regresa sin cesar" [one after the other, but always the same, like one endlessly returning train] (189). In this ending, all trains become one and the same in their homogenous movement, reverting to a singular direction; the continuous return suggests, in these lyrical, compelling lines, a collapsing of tangible, corporeal distinctions, and the acceptance of exchange as always equivalent. Yet this seamless movement undoubtedly belies the particularity of the embodiments which the narrator has experienced, and the materialization of vulnerability—in fiction as in other scenes of transit—as specific to each traversal from there to here.

NOTES

This research was supported by the Social Sciences and Humanities Research Council of Canada.

1. Siebers further elaborates this point in his chapter in this volume; also see introduction.

2. It is worth noting here that the proposal for improved transit conditions does not explicitly include accessibility features, as these are not mentioned in the list of specific changes in service to be implemented following the rate increase; however, improved access for disabled people is mentioned in a more general sense as an area that was taken into account in the prior study (Mancera Espinosa 6).

3. "Matter out of place" is borrowed from Mary Douglas's classic *Purity and Danger*, in which she uses this phrase in her frequently cited definition of dirt (36).

4. Also see Martha Stoddard Holmes's reading of this text from a disability studies perspective (123–32).

5. As Henri-Jacques Stiker suggests, the notion of disability as imposture is already at work in the Middle Ages, and categories of marginality are ambiguous: "Between the authentic and the false disabled the boundaries are not so simple" (85).

6. See, for example, Urías Horcasitas, who argues that nineteenth-century dis-

courses of degeneration propose these associations, which also emerge in the Mexican penal codes of 1929 and 1931. In the postrevolutionary period, however, efforts shift toward normalization, rather than control of the population (66–67).

7. "Investigación para externación."

8. While the neoliberal model of social vulnerability discussed at length by Vite Pérez suggests similarity to Jasbir Puar's notion of debility, a useful distinction here stems from the fact that Mexican neoliberalism (from the early 1980s to the present) is read specifically in contrast to mid-twentieth-century Mexican structures of social protection as linked to the workplace, and typically associated with the legacy of Lázaro Cárdenas, president of Mexico from 1934 to 1940. Ferrante's analysis focuses on disability and begging in urban Buenos Aires, but is still relevant here for her emphasis on the paradoxical role of "rights" in relation to the marketplace.

9. As Andalusia Knoll explains, "#PosMeSalto loosely translates into, 'guess, i'll just jump'" in reference to those who jump the turnstiles rather than pay the increased fee. Knoll's article includes more detailed discussion of this protest movement. With thanks to Robert McRuer for suggesting the reference to this photograph and protest.

10. It is worth noting that many protest participants of a variety of ages and physical attributes did not actually jump over turnstiles, but opted to duck or crawl under, or assisted each other in climbing across barriers.

11. Within a broader Latin American context, the "disappeared" most frequently evokes the tens of thousands of victims of the Southern Cone Dirty Wars under the Plan Cóndor during the 1970s and 1980s. I am grateful to Patricia Brogna for her suggestion of the important link between use of term *desaparecen* in the advertisement and the political context of disappearance in Mexico.

12. See Andrea Noble for detailed discussion and analysis of this case and its repercussions.

13. Patrick Dove focuses in particular on the delegitimization of the state in the aftermath of Ayotzinapa. Rossana Reguillo reads the case in relation to complicity between organized crime and the state.

14. See Emily Bruce et al. for discussion of femicides in Ciudad Juárez in relation to economic transformation of the border region.

15. The concepts of host and parasite figure in many works of literary theory and philosophy. As Derrida writes: "Since there is also no hospitality without finitude, sovereignty can only be exercised by filtering, choosing and thus by excluding and doing violence" (55). Also see J. Hillis Miller, for his reading of the ambivalence of the host and of parasitism.

16. In its biological application, *huésped* refers to an organism that houses a parasite, but not the inverse. Note that J. Hillis Miller also refers to this dual meaning in the origins of the word, "host." As he writes: "The words 'host' and 'guest' go back in fact to the same etymological root: ghos-ti, stranger, guest, host" (442).

17. The author notes in an interview that the institute is based on a real one, which she has read about but has never visited (Hind 344).

18. All translations from Nettel's novel are mine.

19. Note that the word *desvalido* is also associated with *inválido*, meaning invalid, not valid, or disabled.

WORKS CITED

Aristegui Noticias. "No les compres y desaparecen. Campaña del Metro contra vagoneros." Dec. 12, 2013. http://aristeguinoticias.com/1212/mexico/no-les-compres-y-desaparecen-campana-del-metro-contra-vagoneros/

Bruce, Emily, Chelsea Fink, and Denise Lopez. "Maquiladoras, Misogyny and Migration: Exploring Femicide in Ciudad Juárez." *Human Rights in Latin America.* 31 May 2015. https://derechoslatinamerica.com/2015/05/31/maquiladoras-misogyny-and-migration-exploring-femicide-in-ciudad-juarez/

Derrida, Jacques. *Of Hospitality: Anne Dufourmantelle Invites Jacques Derrida to Respond.* Translated by Rachel Bowlby. Stanford UP, 2000.

Douglas, Mary. *Purity and Danger.* Routledge, 2002.

Dove, Patrick. "Ayotzinapa: Antes y después." *horizontal,* Jan. 19, 2016. http://horizontal.mx/ayotzinapa-antes-y-despues/

Ferrante, Carolina. "Mendicidad y discapacidad en la Ciudad de Buenos Aires: Un síntoma de nuevas formas de vulnerabilidad social." *Disability and the Global South: An International Journal,* vol. 1, no. 1, 2014, pp. 85–106.

Hernández, Libertad. "Se mantiene gratuidad en el metro del D.F. para usuarios con discapacidad; vagoneros ciegos, en riesgo." *Dis-capacidad.com,* Dec. 13, 2013.

Hind, Emily. *La generación XXX: Entrevistas con veinte escritores mexicanos nacidos en los 70.* De Abenshushan a Xoconostle. Eón, 2013.

Holmes, Martha Stoddard. *Fictions of Affliction: Physical Disability in Victorian Culture.* U of Michigan P, 2004.

"Investigación para externación." Oct. 14, 1935. MS. Fondo Beneficiencia Pública, Sección Asistencia, Departamento de Acción Educativa y Social. Archivo Histórico de la Secretaría de Salud. México, D.F.

Knoll, Andalusia. "'It's Not Just 2 Pesos; It's the Country': Mexico City's #PosMeSalto Movement Protests Rising Transit Costs." *Upside Down World,* Jan. 10, 2014. http://upsidedownworld.org/archives/mexico/qits-not-just-2-pesos-its-the-countryq-mexico-citys-posmesalto-movement-protests-rising-transit-costs/

Mancera Espinosa, Miguel Ángel. "Acuerdo por el que se emite Resolución que determina el importe de la tarifa aplicable al sistema de transporte colectivo (Metro)." *Gaceta Oficial del Distrito Federal,* no. 1750, Dec. 7, 2013. pp. 3–6. http://www.orden-juridico.gob.mx/Documentos/Estatal/Distrito%20Federal/wo88240.pdf

Matta, Juan Pablo. "Cuerpo, sufrimiento y cultura; un análisis del concepto de 'técnicas corporales' para el estudio del intercambio lastima-limosna como hecho social total." *Revista Latinoamericana de estudios sobre cuerpos, emociones y sociedad,* vol. 2, no. 2, 2010, pp. 27–36.

Mayhew, Henry. *London Labour and the London Poor. The condition and earnings of those that will work, cannot work, and will not work.* C. Griffin and Co., 1861.

Miller, J. Hillis. "The Critic as Host." *Critical Inquiry,* Spring 1997, pp. 439–47.

Mora, Karla. "Sube tarifa del metro a $5 el día 13 de diciembre." *El Universal,* Dec. 7, 2013. http://archivo.eluniversal.com.mx/ciudad-metropoli/2013/sube-tarifa-del-metro-a-5-el-dia-13-de-diciembre-971265.html

Nettel, Guadalupe. *El huésped.* Anagrama, 2006.

Noble, Andrea. "Introduction: Visual Culture and Violence in Contemporary Mexico." *Journal of Latin American Cultural Studies,* vol. 24, no. 4, 2016, pp. 417–33.

"No les compres y desaparecen. Campaña del Metro contra vagoneros." *Aristegui noticias*, Dec. 12, 2013.

Puar, Jasbir. "Coda: The Cost of Getting Better. Suicide, Sensation, Switchpoints." *GLQ: A Journal of Lesbian and Gay Studies*, vol. 18, no. 1, 2012, pp. 149–58.

Reguillo, Rossana."Ayotzinapa, el nombre del horror." *Anfibia*, Oct. 21, 2014. http://www.revistaanfibia.com/ensayo/ayotzinapa-el-nombre-del-horror/

Serres, Michael. *The Parasite*. Translated by Lawrence R. Schehr. Johns Hopkins UP, 1982.

Stiker, Henri-Jacques. *A History of Disability*. Translated by William Sayers. U of Michigan P, 2002.

Urías Horcasitas, Beatriz. "Degeneracionismo e higiene mental en el México posrevolucionario (1920–1940)." *Frenia*, vol. 4, no. 2, 2004, pp. 37–67.

Vite Pérez, Miguel Ángel. "La discapacidad en México desde la vulnerabilidad social." *Polis*, vol. 8, no. 2, 2012, pp. 153–73.

Posthumanist T4 Memory

David T. Mitchell and Sharon L. Snyder

Introduction: Alternative Genres of the Human and Nazi T4

At base, both disability studies and critical race studies attempt to usher in what black feminist materialist theorist Sylvia Wynter refers to as "different genres of the human" (McKittrick 9). Such recognition involves an enunciation of alternative ways of being human that are not based on qualities advocated in classical liberalism's hierarchical human-centered models of rationality, able-bodiedness, European/American exceptionalism, and the agency of a politically capacitated citizenship (Weheliye 5; McKittrick 109; Braidotti 24). Because these alternative genres of the human are grounded in a more active recognition of materiality's agency that is not overshadowed by discursivity (i.e., embodiment is more than the passively inscribed surface that social constructivism posits as "citationally iterative" [6]) those who embody alternative genres of the human find a relative comfort of inclusive (mis)fit beneath the elastic category of the new materialist methodologies loosely grouped together under the rubric: *posthumanism.*

The "new materialist" turn of posthuman theory (particularly the works of Rosi Braidotti, Asma Abbas, Alex Weheliye, Elizabeth Grosz, Diana Coole, Samantha Frost, and Sylvia Wynter) posits "the flesh" (i.e., material embodiment) as a site of critique for biopolitical concepts of expendability such as "bare flesh" (Agamben 8), "to *take* life or *let* live" (Foucault 136), "necropolitics" (Mbembe 39), and "social death" (Cacho 32). These theories of the state-sponsored destruction of lives tend to further abject the bodies in question by avoiding a more materialist grappling with the lives they represent (Weheliye 4). They all share a penchant for positing expendability as a discursive construct that makes the lives under

erasure somewhat abstract and, therefore, avoid a more materialist encounter with nonnormative being. Unlike many biopolitical theories of
the human, posthuman materialism does not strictly adhere to models of
resistance embedded in the agency of "politically sturdy citizens" (Abbas
40), persons who exercise their rights with a fictional ideal of full, self-
present, and coherent subjectivity. Why, as Asma Abbas asks in *Liberalism
and Social Suffering*, are formations of the oppressed deemed liberatory
only if they resist hegemony or exhibit the full agency of the oppressed
engaged in acts of civil disobedience?

Our key topic of analysis in this essay—contemporary scholarship and
memorializations of those killed by Nazi medical mass murder in German
psychiatric institutions during World War II—demonstrates the disas-
trous effects of transhumanist (read: eugenicist) approaches to rid society
of the "burden" of people with disabilities. This operation of the mass
murder of psychiatric patients is known as Operation T4 and began as an
extermination practice that corresponded with the invasion of Poland, beginning in the fall of 1939. Ultimately, by war's end, T4 culminated in the
deaths of three hundred thousand or more disabled people by bullets, gassing, lethal injection, and starvation (Müller-Hill 64–65; Knittel 43).
Scholarship on T4 has increasingly linked the killings of disabled people
in psychiatric institutions as leading directly to the Holocaust. For instance, Henry Friedlander refers to the euthanasia murders as "the first
chapter of Nazi Genocide," and his evidence supports a conclusion of "direct links" between the Holocaust and the euthanasia murders (*Origins*,
xii). Timothy Snyder argues that the euthanasia murders served as "pre-
cursor" to the development of "Nazi death factories" (*Bloodlands* 256–57).
Yet, as Suzanne Knittel points out in her book *The Historical Uncanny*,
"Despite the firmly established links between the 'euthanasia program'
and the 'final solution,' these people (people with psychiatric, cognitive,
and/or physical disabilities) are not commonly numbered among the victims of the Holocaust" (11).

While we don't believe an aporia between the T4 murders and the Holocaust exists, we do want to join Knittel and other memory studies scholars in contemplating why "their (disabled people's) memory does not form
part of the commemorative discourse about this period" (11). Up until recently the scholarship and memorialization of T4 have primarily pursued
a practice of exposing the killing psychologies, policies, and practices of
the perpetrators (Lifton xi–xii); this inclination of the findings result from
the fact that few records exist regarding how disabled people experienced
this murderous episode. Thus, T4 scholarship and memorialization have

continued to leave aside disabled people's points of view, meaning their material participation in this history. The existing body of work on T4 pursues the import of this information primarily as a cautionary tale to medicine, one that exposes the murderous results of medical overreaching and the danger awaiting professionals who cross the line of "First, do no harm" established by the Hippocratic oath (Agamben 143).

Our argument will consider how the intersection of disability studies and memory studies might come into posthumanist interactions with disability as an alternative to—or, at least, extension of—the fetishization of perpetrator mind-sets. Such a move might further open up questions of what to do about reading participant lives that fall short of what we reference as the liberal ideal of documenting the activities of a robust, capacitated counter-citizenry. How can we imagine alternative lives lived in zones of indeterminacy and social erasure such as the lock-down psychiatric wards or even the gas chambers of Germany in World War II? In taking up this question, our essay pursues an analysis of post-Holocaust contemporary memorialization practices of medical mass murder currently operating in Germany (with gestures toward parallel efforts in the United States, Austria, Poland, and Italy). Our explicit goal is to examine ways of imagining a "less agential" population navigating "unworthy" lives that does not inadvertently render such lives as meaningless and evacuated of historical weight.

This is not to claim an absence of resistance exercised among disabled participants, but rather that we might come to a more layered and improvisatory understanding of those who experience "extreme subjection" and "suffering." In order to accomplish this task we pursue the most radical promise of posthumanist memory studies in order to introduce a more visceral agency of materiality back into the equation. Such a practice can only happen if we don't begin by assuming what forms these state-authored memories may take from the start and how alternative forms of nonnormative living emerge in ways our current agential measures of resistance fail to record. Most importantly, we plan to show how recent memorialization efforts have begun to adopt a posthumanist, new materialist memory framework to their presentations in order to redirect attention from the perpetrators to the experiencers of the euthanasia murders (past, present, and future). This alternative direction of emphasis matters, we argue, because disabled people have been misrecognized in the historical erasure that was intended as the outcome of T4 as something less than liberal ideals of robust political citizens. We call this misrecognition a primary product of an encounter with "low-level agency."

Low-Level Agency

Before we get to our discussion of posthumanist alternatives emerging in the contemporary memorialization efforts around those who died in the Nazi T4 program, we want to theorize what we call "low-level agency." Our goal in doing so is to identify a pathway for the necessity of a further specification of the material lives of disabled people extinguished in the Holocaust. A reluctance to expose disability as the basis for one's determination as expendable by the Nazis, as we explain below, is an explicit product of encounters with what to do with individuals who experience their lives through periods of low-level agency. To keep these identities hidden—as was the case until very recently at German euthanasia center memorials and continues to some extent even today—is to further deepen the social stigma of disability that made T4 possible in the first place. This practice of avoidance of the materiality of disability leaves the lives of those living in nonnormative embodiments as a discomforting sidebar to the inhumanity of the murders.

As the editors point out in the introduction, the application of disability as a barometer for social oppression within the social model of disability suggests a somewhat monolithic methodology that requires further critique if the field is to ultimately engage a more robust encounter with disability as an alternative genre of the human. One of the courses we teach at university is a graduate seminar on crip/queer theory (with a healthy dose of critical race theory) and our readings begin with two important works that allow us to better understand the problems at the base of the social model of disability. Asma Abbas's *Liberalism and Human Suffering* and Alexander Weheliye's *Habeas Viscus: Racializing Assemblages, Biopolitics, and Black Feminist Theories of Embodiment;* both offer up an analysis of what we term "peripheral embodiment" in our book: *The Biopolitics of Disability: Neoliberalism, Ablenationalism, and Peripheral Embodiment.* "Peripheral embodiment" involves the analysis of those who could be characterized as experiencing lives of low-level agency (10–11). There are many gifts that Abbas and Weheliye's works offer to disability studies, but a key one for us is their serious turning to efforts at thinking peripheral embodiment at the level of subjective, embodied experience; they both refer to their work as part of the tradition of historical materialism at base. What this means is that even in the most leftist, progressive works of political theory there exists an overemphasis on the agency of "politically sturdy citizens" who, although experiencing significant levels of marginality, continue to exert a full degree of claims-based effort in pursuit of attaining equal rights (Abbas 40).

In part, this argument is based on a critique of Liberalism's over determination of the concept of "agency." What, they ask, do we do with people
who do not, or are incapable of, performing in the role of the robust,
sturdy, minority, rights-seeking citizen? Is there not, even in disability activist and academic circles, a preferential treatment we give to those lives
that exhibit the correct level of resistance as a matter of course?[1] Are we
not all culpable of excessively privileging (to one degree or another) those
who openly and actively challenge a discriminatory political system?
What of those who do not perform their opposition openly or even with a
working knowledge of themselves as oppressed? How might we get to the
significant question of identifying how disability and other minority citizens effectively navigate their embodied lives without only finding ways to
expose a discriminatory, oppressive politics? Is there anything out there to
be learned from those whose lives involve suffering, but do not appear to
qualify at the basic level of regard we give to our idealization of the "sturdy
political citizen"?

For instance, Abbas convincingly argues that liberal formulations of
personhood are founded on concepts of embodiment as commodity; to
seek one's "rights" in relation to embodiment must be expressed in terms
of damage, loss, or defacement of property (including one's body). So one
may have lost loved ones in Hurricane Katrina, for instance, but, in order
to effectively seek reparations within liberalism's property-based claims
system, one has to pursue the systemic recognition of harm in terms of the
loss of private property. Abbas draws many of her examples from damage
litigation related to Hurricane Katrina victims such as the loss of one's
house as a result of the levees breaking, or in the totaling of one's car by a
felled tree, or the closing of a business and the ensuing loss of profit which
results, or even the collapse of an entire economic way of life related to
fishing in the now contaminated Gulf of Mexico, etc. These all represent
serious harms to livelihood; they also involve translating harm into in-
fringements of property rights—there is no place in liberalism to define
and pursue justice on the basis of things without a property component.
Such a situation involves the necessity of turning harms into things we
possess and seeking reparations on their behalf. It is, at base, a substitution
of limited property rights for a vast range of experiential knowledge upon
which we have given up. We might think of hunger or starvation as Abbas's example of visceral experiences that cannot be adequately recognized
within liberalism's property-based logics (31).

Abbas and Weheliye would both argue that what is lost here is not the
consequences of power inequity leading to victimization in need of repa-
ration. That is merely the resurfacing of Liberalism's perpetual property

254 | The Matter of Disability

emphasis on claims to damages. Rather they both argue that our vocabulary of suffering is incredibly limited because we do not seek out the experience of those who undergo the labor of low-level agency (Abbas 31). We ask nothing of those who experience suffering because the point is to usher them into recognizable categories of harm (malpractice, a flooded house, defacing a public work of art) in order to move on to the next case (138). By taking up some matters of property damage Liberalism effectively silences the ways in which the experience of suffering might bring us new knowledge. There is a decided over-emphasis on perpetrators' motives, interests, and practices without a significant effort to access how those subject to the effects of harmful actions underwent the experience of harm and the creativity of navigating such circumstances.

The labor of being a patient at a psychiatric institution that significantly immobilizes one's freedoms goes silently underground and will not resurface unless we coax it into the world as significant. These experiences "undo" a person psychically and, in doing so, they radically alter the way one experiences the world. Low-level agency is often about the ways in which experiences of docility allow those who receive state sponsored supports to be denied a future of expanding agency. This is the meaning of living with suffering and the paucity of language/narratives we have for describing what experiences of material vulnerability bring into the world. Such embodied knowledge is due to the fact that Liberalism does not seek to know about the experiential side of these embodied situations.

In the historical cases of medical mass murder under examination in this essay we look at reasons for the perpetuation of silence about crip/queer lives and how that inclination in contemporary commemoration practices are giving way to more materially visceral encounters with disability. For instance, liberal courts' requirement of translating harm or loss into the terms of property value that Abbas discusses is pertinent to those murdered in the Nazi T4 program. Until recently compensation for victims' families has gone unrecognized in courts and thus the silence around victims' experiences has been doubly marginalized (Knittel 14). Rather than translations into monetary value posthumanist disability frameworks pursue the inclusion of biographical materials to make the individual lives of disabled people surface. This effort involves fighting back against a common argument about medical privacy that keeps the material nature of victims' conditions hidden and, for many years, off limits to researchers of T4. Further, our examination discusses the alternative pathways through which posthumanist disability frameworks make connections between the treatment of disabled lives during World War II and today in order to posit a transgenerational process of imagining disability into the future. Finally, we follow the tracks of the inhumane dumping of human remains during T4 (a gruesome investigatory undertaking at best) in order to make available ways of approaching questions of the endangerment of disabled lives and the alternative fashioning of crip/queer subjectivities in the present.

T4 Memorialization: Telling the Truth but Telling It Slant

In order to show how posthumanist disability theory proves necessary for making direct links between T4 and the Holocaust more explicit, we undertook a longitudinal research project involving fellow researchers, students, and German colleagues on visits to various T4 memorial sites (called euthanasia memorial centers in Germany) between the years 2002 and 2015. During these visits we actively pursued a desire to make the stories of the Operation T4 program materially emerge.

Our return visits brought posthumanist methodologies to bear on these public memory exhibitions by leading us to these sites with specific questions drawn from crip/queer studies. While we sought our own education in relation to the prepared content of German guides and exhibition directors alike, we also intended to productively question the pervasive resistance toward making direct links between T4 and the Holocaust. This identification of the continuing reluctance in some German memorial euthanasia centers about connecting disability mass murder to the Holocaust persistently emerged at several of the centers during multiple return visits. We use posthumanist theory as a basis for transforming ways of conceptualizing the historical relationship between the perpetrators of mass murders and those with low-level agency in order to make direct links more apparent to the public memory of disability history.

In other words, we went not just as visitors, tourists, or memorializers, but also as active shapers of the knowledge base that informs tour guide training and research at T4 memorialization centers. Our questions were as much about memorialization as a practice undertaken by contemporary institutions with respect to disability attitudes, for many of the memorials have been established at sites that were psychiatric facilities before, during, and after the war. One of the most striking experiences of visiting these euthanasia memorial centers after studying the history of T4 is the ways in which many visitors experience discomfort with the fact that several of the memorial sites still function on the campuses of active psychiatric hospitals. The irony of memorializing murder on the grounds of a lock down penitentiary space where such mass murders originally occurred causes visitors to do a double take with regard to whether such killings could recur in our own time.

The information we uncovered during these interactions proved critical to our growing understanding of medical mass murder in the sense that we wanted to apprehend attitudes about the targeted groups today as well as in the historical moment of their unfolding. Feminist memory scholar Marianne Hirsch refers to this expanded approach to the Holocaust as "postmemory"—"a generational structure of transmission" (114). We uncovered new information during each return visit and thus these memorial pilgrimages have proven rich as a way to track shifting information, attitudes, and presentation strategies over the past decade and a half. Our groups always include disabled people and, as a result, these site excursions have also played a hand in making the memorial sites more accessible: during the past five years each site has added an elevator, simple text versions of exhibition materials, and braille signage in an effort to expand access for a variety of disability groups.[2] Such interventions could be read through Abbas' theorization of low-level agency in that the materiality of disabled bodies entering inaccessible memorial spaces on multiple occasions resulted in the revision of public space through more inclusive accessible architecture and materials in the second decade of the 2000s. Such material imprinting on the space did not occur as a result of "political actions," but rather through a gradual recognition on the part of the memorial organizers that disabled people were going to use this history for their own ends and the site needed to integrate accessibility into their plans and practices.

Beyond these structural revisions of the space and guide practices, other materialist unearthings of T4 history also proliferated. For instance, at Bernburg we spoke with the director, Ute Hoffmann, who told us that her mother, who worked as a nurse at the psychiatric hospital during reunification, showed her the gas chamber when she was fourteen years old (Hoffmann). Later, as a young woman, Hoffmann was charged by institution staff (including the director and her mother) with the obligation of overseeing the opening of the memorial after the reunification of East and West Germany in 1989. Hoffmann continues as director to this day. It was also through Hoffmann's narration that we learned of the disposal of human ash from the crematoria ovens under a football field uncovered by a review of psychiatric hospital payment records to a man who transported ash in a horse-drawn wagon to a public dumping site in 1941 and 1942 (the primary T4 phase of gassings at Bernburg before the ovens were dismantled and moved to Dachau). The original location of the dump today exists below a community soccer field and a battle for excavating the remains is ongoing. The effort to explicitly track down the location of human remains serves as a posthumanist-based effort to make the material lives of these victims of Nazi mass murder surface—to literally expose the palimpsestic lives of our contemporary moment existing on top of the death-making processes of the past—as well as to fashion a more meaningful material burial of the remains that has yet to happen.

In each of these instances one can witness the ongoing efforts on the part of historians, researchers, and memorial staff to deepen their understanding beyond the necropolitics that informed the mass murder of disabled people interred in the German psychiatric system during the war. Their social marginality was physically approximated in their geographical isolation within psychiatric institutions located outside of major German city centers. This literal absenting of disabled people and the stripping of their citizenship rights by the state (yet, ironically, within an elaborate state bureaucracy that actively supervised and meticulously recorded the killings) made many crip/queer lives more susceptible to radical exclusion and, ultimately, mass murder. Their material presence prior to extermination was first absented geographically and the posthumanist disability turn makes their further absenting in the gas chambers and killing wards of these psychiatric institutions and hospitals more palpable as an encounter with the materiality of nonnormative lives. For instance, at the Brandenburg Euthanasia Center we discovered that the last disabled individual killed by the medical culture of murder was a young boy named Richard Jenne, who died of starvation on May 29, 1945, in Kaufbeuren-Irsee state hospital in Bavaria, Germany more than three weeks after US armies occupied the town and the German army had surrendered unconditionally. Brandenburg has allowed the biographical details of individual fates to emerge more viscerally as a contestation of their anonymity and a redress of the assumed stigma that would follow individuals diagnosed as disabled and exterminated in the gas chambers of Operation T4.

This posthumanist memorialization tactic also surfaces in the display of personal keepsakes recovered from victim remains. At the Sonnenstein Euthanasia Center, for instance, we learned of crematoria ash being dumped over the hill behind the gas chamber and into the town of Pirna that sits idyllically at the bottom of the hill. Archeological exhumation in the 1990s uncovered personal relics interred with human remains such as perfume bottles, "Frozen Charlotte" dolls, hair combs, pins, barrettes, and two charred leg braces during the exhumation. All of these items are powerful emblems of the lives that passed through them as they represent personal materials that victims were able to secret on their persons even after disrobing and undergoing medical examinations prior to their gassing. The objects are now displayed in a glass display case hung from the ceiling of the room that once housed crematoria chimney #2. This display of human artefacts may seem as if it could be completely contained within Liberal Humanist practices of the memorialization of individual lives lost, however, we argue that the belated nature of the effort to tell the story of T4 mass murder through the points of view of the victims exposes the degree to which those who occupy alternative genres of the human have been consciously left out of previous historical memorializations of the Holocaust. Their exclusion from the Western Project of the Human by Liberal Humanism speaks to the crip/queer recovery efforts that form the basis of posthumanist materialism.

While all of the euthanasia centers have traditionally told the story of T4 through the perspectives of the perpetrators, these alternative findings at Bernburg and Sonnenstein suggest that approaching the materiality of those in positions of low-level agency offer significant avenues for further imagining the events of T4 because they increasingly attempt to bring these nonnormative lives back into our contemporary memories through the materials, objects, and biographical details of the particularities of the lives that passed through them. Their recognition is not through the traditional channels of narrating instances of political resistance but rather through the display and presentation of mementos that signify the materiality of comfort sought by those who possessed them. Further the artefacts themselves speak of the materiality of lives lost and now sit abstracted in the numerical tallies that characterized the German killing bureaucracy. As Katherine Harrison explores in her essay, "What Remains: The Lure of Relics in a Faithless Age," to enter into an imagined relation with these lives across time and space does not mean abandoning their earthboundness—rather posthumanist materialism proves the opposite more true.

Perhaps one of the most striking posthumanist strategies of presentation occurs at the euthanasia center at Sonnenstein. Whereas medical secrecy and concerns about public shame have pressured other centers to keep identities hidden to a substantial degree, the Sonnenstein Euthanasia Center publishes the names of those killed in the mass extermination pro-

Fig. 1. Sonnenstein Euthanasia Center, Germany. A disrobing room where psychiatric patients were made to undress prior to moving to the gas chamber, disguised as a shower room next door. These are photos of some of the victims displayed on posts with individual biographies on the back of each portrait. Photography by Sharon L. Snyder.

gram on a series of frosted glass walls as one enters the basement area of the T4 memorial site.

This public display of names seeks to actively counter the stigma associated with inclusion in the Nazi killing program by refusing to recognize the medical histories of individuals in the T4 program as a source of devaluing revelation in need of protection and further state secrecy.

When we started this longitudinal project, one had to procure special permission from the German government to view the records of those killed in the T4 program. From our posthumanist perspective, not talking about disabled people's medical histories is a form of oppression rather than a form of protection. Such a vantage point recognizes the defining nonnormativity of bodies as a foundational premise of embodiment rather than its exceptional opposite. Whereas disability has been traditionally treated as evidence of something gone awry in individuals and therefore worthy of personal and generational shame and divestment of support from those bodies, the display of the names of those murdered at Sonnenstein refuses anonymity as substantive to the act of memorialization. Rather, the frosted glass walls of victim identities yield evidence of the curatorial refusal to participate in the stigma of disabled lives by hiding them away from view. They are openly recognized as worthy of commemoration, and even existing family members are not consulted for permission on their publication. This open display of the identities of those with low-level agency breaks a significant historical barrier of silence around the material lives exterminated in the T4 program. While this display of names and victim biographies may appear as a common humanist presentation tactic, the fact that their unveiling has taken so long and the institutional records treated as private medical information underscores an alternative posthumanist methodology at work.

Yet, as we show below, the euthanasia centers also shy away from efforts to explore any relationship between the Holocaust proper and the medical disability murders that preceded them. For example, during a visit in March 2014, our Sonnenstein T4 tour guide explained that "T4 was an experience for the later Holocaust—how to do it, how not to do it with these killing facilities in Germany, in this society itself. And so it went far and away into the Polish nowhere." The comment suggests a link between the two mass murder operations despite the fact that the Holocaust murders were exported out to lesser-known, rural locations. Yet this direct relationship between T4 know-how about mass murder and Holocaust implementation was interrupted whenever a question about the direct link between the two was proposed:

> VISITOR: Should we understand that the Holocaust could not have unfolded the way it did without these euthanasia killings?
> TOUR GUIDE: Yeah, I would be a little bit careful with that. And, of course, they used experience. Of course they learned about it, what is going to happen, what [one] was able to do and what [one] was not able to do. But these organizations in the background are not the same. So, of course, they talked about it, but it's not the Holocaust in a smaller way. Or it's also not a test for the Holocaust.
> VISITOR: Couldn't you say it's the germ or the first chapter of the Holocaust?
> TOUR GUIDE: Also, I would be careful with that because in the background the ideas have not this much to do with each other. Of

course, there was also the idea to clean the German people and society of the Jewish influence, of the Jewish people. And it's also
some way of racial hygiene, but it's not the center of racial hygiene.

Translation across linguistic boundaries always poses difficulties and instances such as those recorded here are no exception. Yet this circuitous
effort to avoid the identification of direct links between T4 and the Holocaust explicitly emerges in exchanges on the topic at many euthanasia centers, including Sonnenstein, Bernberg, Hadamar, and Hartheim Castle.
Brandenburg and Grafeneck both make more explicit connections between these two historical events, and the exhibition presentation materials display less tentativeness overall. Positing a relationship between the
two historical episodes of mass murder is assiduously avoided at the four
centers mentioned above. They bring the threat of nonnormative crip/
queer lives (a cause of killing that might be explained or rationalized to
some extent) into the world of the inexplicable meaning of killing Jewish
people en masse as an explicit objective of the state, Operation Reinhardt,
and so on. We would call this chronic dis-ease or trepidation about linking
one to the other yet another aspect of the ambivalence of contemporary
memory practices with regard to those with low-level agency. It is in the
avoidance of complicating a story of ethnic genocide with the mass killing
of those who were definitively defined as biologically and psychically nonnormative, abnormal, and avoidance of burdens on the state that threaten
the story of ethnic genocide most explicitly. The leakage of one minority
group's murder into the other is a highly regulated matter that has bor-
dered at various times on a concern about slander toward others killed on
the basis of the social construct of ethnicity.

During a tour of Bernburg in early 2015, our tour guide was queried in
a similar manner regarding whether the T4 murders could be considered
anticipatory of the Holocaust. While not severing the relationship as completely as the guide at Sonnenstein, our Bernburg tour guide made an explicit gesture toward the lack of consensus in Holocaust scholarship about
the ability to draw a connection between the two events:

TOUR GUIDE: That's a very difficult question (i.e., making direct links
between T4 and the Holocaust) because scientists nowadays have
different opinions. One group of scientists say the Holocaust was
planned from the beginning, and it first starts and it goes on and
on and on. And others would say it's radicalization. So it's really

> hard to say, "So this is the start and from this point on they start planning to do this on a bigger scale." So that's a question that I cannot answer.
>
> VISITOR: By using this word "radicalization" did they mean just size of the program, or did they mean radicalization in terms of moving from disability to ethnicity?
>
> TOUR GUIDE: The second one. Or there are some scientists who say the situation in the concentration camps got so much worse that they need to find a new solution to handle this bad situation in the concentration camps. There are different views. So that's why I cannot answer exactly your question.
>
> VISITOR: I think we're just looking for your opinion. Do you think the Holocaust could have unfolded without the euthanasia program in front of it?
>
> TOUR GUIDE: I guess if you really want to kill so many people there's always a way. I think they didn't really need these euthanasia centers at the beginning. I guess maybe sooner or later they would find another way to kill so many people. And they did find other ways: they shoot people, they let them starve or kill them by work, so I guess they would have find another way. So I guess they didn't really need euthanasia before.

One should give credence to the nuances of this argument in that it is qualitatively different to posit that the euthanasia program was part and parcel of the Holocaust and quite another to argue that the former was a necessary precondition of the latter. As the guide points out: to find another way of killing is always possible. However, the question of radicalization of Nazi ideas about how to eradicate Jewish people in Europe began with plans of slave labor or banishment to remote locations such as Lublin, Madagascar, and Siberia (Snyder, *Black Earth* 28). A posthumanist, new materialist approach asks what motivated these radical sequestering projects of labor and deportation into systematic mass murder of those living lives of low-level agency in nonnormative bodies? Does it matter that the mass extermination of Jews in the Holocaust ultimately occurred with an accelerated and expanded model of the killing procedures that unfolded during the T4 program?

Direct links between Operation T4 and the Holocaust abound, including the architects of the mass killing facilities who situated the process on a straight line of industrial, assembly line-like efficiency operated exclusively by physicians (Friedlander, "From 'Euthanasia' to the 'Final Solution'" 164), autopsy rooms to expand medical knowledge as a justification for the necessity of the killings (Burleigh, "Nazi 'Euthanasia' Programs" 151), the physical removal of crematoria ovens and the transfer of ninety-two T4 staff to the sites of the Holocaust (Snyder, *Bloodlands* 257), the elaborate ruse of transfers of disabled people from one facility to another (Burleigh, *Death and Deliverance* 144), and, finally, the administrators who creatively financed the cost of mass murder by delaying reports to their own state welfare agencies regarding the death of clients receiving public monies for their care or the pirating of family's private wealth to finance the killing of their own relatives (Aly 38; Friedlander, *Origins* 72). In other words, in the advent of the modern factory of death, the Holocaust depended on the workings of a system that effectively produced mass murder with great regularity due to earlier experiences in German psychiatric institutions (Bauman 17).

All of this information served to nuance our understanding of the overlaps and differences between T4 killing centers, the conduct of their deadly operations, and the nature of contemporary memorialization efforts. Some euthanasia centers are located in isolated castles, such as at Sonnenstein, Grafeneck, and Hartheim, while others are located in the centers of thriving cities such as Bernburg, Hadamar, and Brandenburg. The killing centers pursued their murderous work in full knowledge of the local residents: "The events in Grafeneck and elsewhere were widely known and had become a 'public secret'" (Friedlander, *Origins* 107). At each memorial we asked our guides if current medical staff were trained about the T4 program on site. We also queried our guides on whether or not patients were allowed to visit the center to learn of a history that might have well included individuals such as themselves now being treated at the same facility. These queries intended to get at the necessity of bringing a posthumanist framework to bear on T4 memorialization as they more explicitly make connections between generations of crip/queer people today. The euthanasia centers are becoming sites of radical political transformation in our understanding of nonnormative bodies as persisting across history, actively accessing T4 as part of their own histories, and recognizing disability as something other than deviant biology. At a wider social level, crip/queer lives are increasingly being encountered as evidence of materiality's intra-agency in the meaning-making process. Posthumanist disability theory can assist in effecting a cultural transformation of disability as an inevitable aspect of all material lives as they mutate, adapt, and rearrange our understanding of materiality. By recognizing disability as something other than failing bodies that prove a burden to families and/or the state, posthumanist crip/queer approaches endeavor to create bridges to contemporary modes of disability existence in order to promote a Nietzschean "transvaluation of value" where nonnormative embodiments are concerned.

All of the existing memorials openly claim ties to hosting training programs for professional, medical, and educational purposes. The exposure of the history of medical mass murder to patients was more haphazard and exuded traces of the persistent ambivalence toward T4. At Bernburg, for instance, we were told by one tour guide about patients who were addicted to drugs and happened to wander into the memorial site when their appointments were canceled in order to "waste some time" while awaiting a ride home. Dr. Hauer, one of the lead tour guides and T4 historians at the Brandenburg Asklepios Fachklinikum und Psychiatriemuseum, explained that prisoners in the psychiatric penitentiary on campus were often brought over to learn about the history of medical mass murder (Hauer). This was the only memorial site that argued it pursued an active education about the historical atrocities for patients on campus. Likewise, the T4 memorial center at Brandenburg has connections with local universities that bring medical students in training to the memorial site. In other words the memorials are slowly emerging as active education centers during preprofessional medical training rather than as reluctant memorializers of a barbaric past long gone. By drawing on posthumanist disability practices in their presentations, the euthanasia centers transition beyond facilities that had largely relegated one of their major functions to the role of serving as a cautionary tale to medicine.

Posthumanist T4 Memory

In order to build on the posthumanist arguments we have made to this point that both acknowledge and critique presentation modes of historical information about T4 at memorial sites, we want to extend our argument to include recent developments where one can witness posthumanist materialism coming into a fuller transformation of contemporary commemoration strategies. While many euthanasia centers demonstrate the slow emergence of a more posthumanist-based grappling with crip/queer materialities, as represented by decisions such as the open publication of twenty-two thousand names eradicated in the gas chambers at

Sonnenstein-Pirna, we want to point toward sites (both digital and physical) where the participation of nonnormative bodies is being made increasingly explicit. Such surfacings of posthumanist memorialization efforts evidence the degree to which T4 commemoration is being transformed from prior inclinations to fetishize perpetrators' mind-sets in order to move toward a more fleshy interaction with the crip/queer bodies in question.

For instance, the T4 website Gedenkort T4,[3] curated by German historian Robert Parzer, reflects the expanding body of posthumanist T4 materials slowly emerging on the contemporary memorialization and research of medical mass murder in Nazi Germany. Not only does this research and virtual memorial site contribute to the foundations of understanding laid by Holocaust studies, it also helps to make more explicit links between the T4 program and the mass murder of Jewish and Sinti people within and without the borders of Germany. The site offers a series of interactive nodes where visitors can uncover the hidden histories of T4 through investigations into the biographies of those killed. Significantly, contemporary disabled people participate in this unearthing of individual lives lost, as well as family members who desire to make clear that being murdered in the program is neither a stigmatizing revelation nor a matter of private dysfunction to be kept hidden. Instead, the biographies chart out the diversity of ways in which crip/queer individuals came to be included in the mass murder program, from participation in instances of petty crimes, to the espousal of political beliefs held untenable by the Nazis, to being identified by medical personnel as having a body excessively unfit to maintain oneself and others without burdening the state. This approach does not underplay disability, nor does it adopt the common tact of revealing that nondisabled people were caught up in the T4 dragnet; instead it recognizes that physical, sensory, and cognitive disabilities are expressions of nonnormative embodiment that do not lessen the value of the lives taken. Their crip/queer content is explicitly unearthed and addressed as an aspect of the alternative genres of the human these lives represent.

Further, as a participant in recent digital humanities projects that make historical materials more public, the Gedenkorte T4 website also makes materials previously available only in remote locations more visible. By housing these memorial details on an interactive website, the digital curators turn accessibility into a virtue and make travel to these remote locations less necessary. There is still something significant about physical participation in the locations of the killing centers, yet for many disabled people and the general public such travel is unavailable, inaccessible, and/

Fig. 2. Photography of the blue wall at the Berlin T4 memorial at Tiergartenstrasse 4, where the offices supervising Nazi medical murder once existed. In the background is the Berlin Philharmonic Opera House. Photography by Sharon L. Snyder (March 15, 2016).

or economically unfeasiable. Thus, the geographical barrier of remoteness is removed by the development of the Gedenkorte T4 online presence, and memorialization itself goes digital in its efforts to make this formerly disguised history more public.

Practices parallel to those on the Gedenkort T4 website are also employed at the Berlin T4 memorial located at the physical address of the former T4 headquarters at Tiergartenstrasse 4. The memorial was curated by a committee of disability professionals and advocates alongside disability studies scholars and cognitively disabled "citizens" (Fuchs). Despite Germany's open public commemorations of those killed in the Holocaust and its own state-sponsored tragic history, it has taken more than seventy years to include medical mass murder in the national conversation on Holocaust atrocities.

The physical memorial site includes a blue glass wall that represents the relationship of the past to the present and the necessity of seeing this intra-active connection more clearly. The blue wall separates the Berlin Philharmonic Building from an angled display that chronicles the history of those swept up in Operation T4. Importantly to the realization of post-humanist practices informing contemporary memorialization efforts, the exhibit includes the names of those who were transported on the Black Buses to the killing centers, stories of crip/queer people who wound up dying in the gas chambers, and the point of view of contemporary disabled people that begin the exhibit. One of the first quotations to open the exhibit by a disabled member of the Netzwerk People First Deutshland explains, "If we had been alive during the war, we wouldn't be here today. Then you would not be able to get to know us anymore." The comment may at first seem to represent a radical distance between the low-level agency of T4 victims and contemporary German disabled people. However, we would argue that the possibility of erasing disability today by various transhumanist objectives still informs the comment. Eradicating disabled people remains on the not so distant horizon of historical possibility, and doing so would mean a loss of exchange about disabled lives rather than a benefit. This frontloading strategy of including the perspectives of disabled community members living today emphasizes the fact that nonnormative lives persist and express chagrin at the attitudes of those who might will them not to exist. Further, the T4 memorial actively makes the disability conditions of those murdered in the program surface as the reason for their extermination, rather than de-emphasizing difference in order to make the killings seem more horrendous. The posthumanist rationale of what is at work in this choice of presentation regards a refusal to allow a simple strategy of identification between the viewer and the victim form the primary basis for bonding over the outrage of the killings. Instead, nonnormative embodiment is held out as a site of human diversity that is being honored in the memorial effort.

Prior to the web posting of Gedenkort T4 and the September 2014 opening of the T4 memorial, there was one other transitional exhibition space that explicitly employs a posthumanist framework to address direct links between the extermination of disabled people and the Holocaust: Otto Weidt's Workshop for the Blind on Rosenthaler Straße 39 in Berlin. The former broom-and-brush workshop is now transformed into a permanent exhibition with tours of a building that kept blind Jewish workers from being deported by the Nazi SS. The workshop was run by a man with a visual impairment, Otto Weidt, who cunningly used labor productivity arguments and bribes to preserve the value of his workers' lives despite their ethnic and disability embodiments. Weidt hid his workers in nearby neighborhoods and in the back of his workshop while he bargained with local Nazi SS officers and cajoled them into allowing his manufacturing plant to produce items for wartime consumption at various sites— including the Wehrmacht, disability institutions, Jewish hospitals, and deportation camps, where both groups were being exiled and systematically slaughtered. The effort to preserve blind and deaf lives, which finally fell through due to the deportation of many of the workers in 1943, explicitly indicates that disabled Jewish people were hunted down due to the hazardous liberal humanist intersection of ability *and* ethnicity.

Thus, we see these three recent memorialization efforts as posthumanist-based examples of the "politicization of memory" in regard to disability history. These sites all serve as important exceptions to a generalized ambivalence toward making direct connections between T4 and the Holocaust, but, more importantly, they go more directly to the existence of the materiality of crip/queer lives as a valuable aspect of contemporary encounters with difference. Rather than make the liberal assertion that these lives should be valued "because they are just like you and me" (an equation of homology as value), posthumanist disability exhibitions recognize nonnormative materiality as a basis for a contemporary revaluation of the lives lost. Thus, the terms of disability existence do not get set aside to be taken up at a later date or avoided due to fears of public stigmatization of relatives in future genetic lines of intimacy with the victims. Instead the nonnormative materiality of these lives is addressed directly in order to be recognized as a substantive loss within the terms of low-level agency. This approach, as we argue, does not require the fetishization of perpetrators' perspectives, nor does it rely on the robust tactics of an exceptional political citizenry. Rather, posthumanist disability frameworks allow a more earnest encounter with loss on the terms of material differences.

Conclusion: Of Moral Agents and Moral Patients

Perhaps the difficulty of maintaining disability history from the point of view of low-level agency comes most to the foreground in the experiences of Uta George, who formerly served as the director at the Hadamar Euthanasia Memorial. Ms. George explained to our group during a 2004 visit to the T4 archives that her role as director was largely that of "goalkeeper." She attended town meetings every few months where residents denounced the memorial as a stain on the community's reputation. The existence of the memorial was detrimental to local businesses because people did not want to shop in a place where so many thousands of people were killed and the killings were perpetually exhumed for beleaguered consciences. Ms. George, in turn, argued that the memorial was part of communal memory and a physical reminder not to forget the traumatic events or lives lost. She perpetually wrestled with the dilemma of how to explain that even severely disabled lives were worthy of support, caretaking, and love. The residents responded with arguments about how those who were killed would have asked for a peaceful death to remove them from their suffering. She, in turn, argued that "euthanasia" operated as a T4 euphemism for Nazi physicians seeking to promote death as a medical intervention desired by their patients. This, she explained, was the least successful of her tactics, as crip/queer lives remain heavily stigmatized within the borders of Germany.

In his book *What Is Posthumanism?* Cary Wolfe makes a further critique relevant to the theorization of low-level agency by drawing a distinction between "moral agents" and "moral patients" (58). If liberal humanist formulas posit that only those who are rational and autonomous as responsible (moral agents) and only interventions performed on agential citizens (by the state, for instance) have moral weight, then this explicitly leaves out groups such as disabled people in psychiatric institutions as well as nonhuman animals (moral patients). This passive assumption of exclusion effectively argues that what is done to those living lives of low-level agency occurs without a need for moral reflection or evaluation. They only possess a body from which things are to be extracted and thus are defined as static, passive, non-agential actors as a result of their status as those experiencing low-level agency. They cannot act within the terms of moral recognizability within liberal humanist conceptions of moral agents (i.e., robust political citizens).

For instance, in the United States the implementation of neoliberal austerity measures reference "access" to health care for all but falter at medical care as a right of individuals. They also have little say about quality of care, how and where one might receive said care, even the more critical question of what supports might make a life possible outside the walls of an institution. These are all part of the persistent terrain of social uncertainty regarding how much any crip/queer body can expect of the social order within which it must exist. To leave these questions as unanswerable, or to continue to perpetuate resistance to identifying the links between T4 and the Holocaust, which by now are deeply established in the scholarship even though only a partial historical reconciliation effort has been made. Tentativeness toward a fuller recognition of the value of crip/queer lives in relation to other forms of social devaluation has to cause us to ask questions of ourselves as scholars, memorializers, and advocates. In the resurfacing of refusals for recognizing a continuum between T4 and the Holocaust we also allow an avoidance of a general sense of material jeopardy to which disabled people continue to be exposed today within fully functioning states. Posthumanist new materialisms seek to make links between ethnicities, genders, sexualities, and disabilities that refuse to fetishize traditional forms of leftist resistance as the only activities worthy of memorialization— they resist applying the definition of robust political citizenries as a baseline determination of lives to commemorate, mourn, and celebrate. Rather than continue these refusals, hesitancies, and misfittings of disability within liberal humanist conceptions, posthumanist disability theory emphasizes alternative "genres of being human" that expand the terrain of political analysis to a wider range of abject bodies.

NOTES

1. For instance, a social media advertisement for a new play about T4, *All Our Children* by Stephen Unwin, circulated whose tag line reads: "Germany, 1941. A terrible crime is taking place. One brave voice is raised in objection."

2. When we initially visited the memorial sites in the late 1990s and early 2000s, no such accessibility existed. Our first visits to Hadamar and Bernburg necessitated sliding down to the gas chamber exhibition on our backsides after transferring to the floor from our wheelchairs. Thus, the changes documented in this article refer to architectural as well as informational and presentational alterations in concepts of disability history. Posthumanist T4 research involves not only a review of the research but, perhaps more importantly, a reclaiming of disability history by and on behalf of those who exist within disability materialities in the most literal sense.

3. http://blog.gedenkort-t4.eu/

WORKS CITED

Abbas, Asma. *Liberalism and Human Suffering: Materialist Suffering on Politics, Ethics, and Aesthetics.* Palgrave MacMillan, 2010.

Agamben, Giorgio. *Homo Sacer: Sovereign Power and Bare Life.* Stanford UP, 1998.

Aly, Götz. "Medicine Against the Useless." *Cleansing the Fatherland: Nazi Medicine and Racial Hygiene.* Edited by G. Aly, P. Chroust, & C. Pross, Johns Hopkins UP, 1994, pp. 22–98.

Barad, Karen. *Meeting the Universe Halfway: Quantum Physics and the Entanglement of Matter and Meaning.* Duke UP, 2007.

Bauman, Zygmunt. *Modernity and the Holocaust.* Cornell UP, 2001.

Braidotti, Rosi. "The Politics of Life Itself and New Ways of Dying." *New Materialism: Ontology, Agency, Politics.* Edited by D. Coole and S. Frost. Duke UP, 2010, pp. 201–19.

Burleigh, Michael. *Death and Deliverance: 'Euthanasia' in Germany, c. 1900–1945.* Cambridge UP, 1995.

Burleigh, Michael. "Nazi 'Euthanasia' Programs." *Deadly Medicine: Creating the Master Race.* Edited by D. Kuntz & S. Bachrach. University of North Carolina Press, 2004, pp. 127–53.

Butler, Judith. *Bodies That Matter: On the Discursive Limits of "Sex".* Routledge, 2011.

Cacho, Lisa Marie, editor. *Social Death: Racialized Rightlessness and the Criminalization of the Unprotected.* New York UP, 2012.

Coole, Diana H., and Samantha Frost, editors. *New Materialism: Ontology, Agency, Politics.* Duke UP, 2010.

Foucault, Michel. *The History of Sexuality*, vol. 1: *An Introduction.* Translated by Robert Hurley. Vintage, 1978.

Friedlander, Henry. "From 'Euthanasia' to the 'Final Solution.'" *Deadly Medicine: Creating the Master Race.* Edited by D. Kuntz & S. Bachrach. University of North Carolina Press, 2004, pp. 155–83.

Friedlander, Henry. *The Origins of Nazi Genocide: From Euthanasia to the Final Solution.* University of North Carolina Press, 2000.

Fuchs, Petra. Interview, Mar. 18, 2015.

Gedenkort-T4.eu. Edited by Robert Parzer. Europe for Citizens Program, 2010. http://www.gedenkort-t4.eu

George, Uta. Interview, Nov. 11, 2004.

Grosz, Elizabeth. *The Nick of Time: Politics, Evolution, and the Untimely.* Duke UP, 2004.

Harrison, Katherine. "What Remains: The Lure of Relics in a Faithless Age." *Harper's Magazine*, December 1995. Access on 9/20/2018. https://harpers.org/archive/1995/12/what-remains/

Hauer, Dr. Interview, Mar. 17, 2015.

Hirsch, Marianne. "The Generation of Postmemory." *Poetics Today* vol. 29, no. 1, 2008, pp. 103–28.

Hoffmann, Ute. Interview, Mar. 19, 2015.

Huffer, Lynn. *Mad for Foucault: Rethinking the Foundations of Queer Theory.* Columbia UP, 2009.

Knittel, Susanne. *The Historical Uncanny: Disability, Ethnicity, and the Politics of Holocaust Memory.* Fordham UP, 2014.

Lifton, Robert. *The Nazi Doctors.* Basic Books, 2000.

Mbembe, Achilles. "Necropolitics." *Public Culture*, vol. 15, no. 1, 2003, pp. 11–40.

McKittrick, Katherine, editor. *Sylvia Wynter: On Being Human as Praxis.* Duke UP, 2014.

Mitchell, David T., with Sharon L. Snyder. *The Biopolitics of Disability: Neoliberalism, Ablenationalism, and Peripheral Embodiment.* U of Michigan P, 2015.

Müller-Hill, Benno. *Murderous Science: Elimination by Scientific Selection of Jews, Gypsies, and Others, Germany 1933–1945.* Oxford UP, 1988.

Snyder, Timothy. *Black Earth: The Holocaust as History and Warning.* Tim Duggan Books, 2016.

Snyder, Timothy. *Bloodlands: Europe between Stalin and Hitler.* Basic Books, 2012.

Unwin, Stephen. *All Our Children.* https://www.facebook.com/profile.php?id=10001360
7079071&fref=nf&pnref=story.unseen-section

Weheliye, Alexander. *Habeas Viscus: Racializing Assemblages, Biopolitics, and Black
Feminist Theories of the Human.* Duke UP, 2014.

Contributors

SUSAN ANTEBI is Associate Professor of Latin American Literature and Director of the Latin American Studies Program at the University of Toronto. She has published on discourses of public health and architectural aesthetics in post-Revolutionary urban Mexico and on the production and circulation of disability in Mexican literature, film, and public space. Her work has appeared in the *Journal of Latin American Cultural Studies*, *Disability Studies Quarterly*, *Arizona Journal of Hispanic Cultural Studies*, and *Latin American Literary Review*. She is the author of *Carnal Inscriptions: Spanish American Narratives of Corporeal Difference and Disability* (2009) and coeditor, with Beth Jörgensen, of *Libre Acceso: Latin American Literature and Film through Disability Studies* (2016). Her book in progress is titled *Eugenics and Intercorporeality: Reading Disability in Twentieth-Century Mexican Cultural Production*.

PATRICK DURGIN teaches critical theory, art history, literature, and writing at the School of the Art Institute of Chicago. He is the author of two books of poetry and poetics: *PQRS* and *The Route* (a collaboration with Jen Hofer). His critical writing has appeared in journals such as *Disability Studies Quarterly*, *Jacket2*, and *Postmodern Culture*. Durgin is the editor of *Hannah Weiner's Open House*, a selected works.

CHRIS EWART has a doctorate with distinction in English and Disability Studies from Simon Fraser University. He teaches disability studies, humanities, and creative writing in the Faculty of Culture + Community at Emily Carr University of Art + Design. His publications include the novel *Miss Lamp*, short fiction in *Calgary Renaissance* and *West Coast Line*, poetry in *Open Letter, Canadian Literature*, and *Why Poetry Sucks: An Anthology of Humorous Experimental Canadian Poetry*, articles in the *Journal of Literary and Cultural Disability Studies* and *Shift: A Journal of Visual and Material Culture,* and chapters in *Global Rights and Perceptions* and *Disability, Avoidance and the Academy: Challenging Resistance.* His work often explores disability in literature, film, popular culture, art, and experience.

MATT FRANKS is an Assistant Professor of English at the University of West Georgia. He is currently working on a book manuscript entitled *Crip/Queer Modernisms* and has published articles in *Feminist Formations* and the *Journal of Modern Literature.* His research focuses on queer disability studies in British modernist and postcolonial literature.

JOSHUA KUPETZ researches, writes, and teaches on the intersections of critical disability theory, disability justice, and twentieth-century US literature at the University of Michigan. His work has been published in the *Journal of Literary and Cultural Disability Studies* and *The Cambridge Companion to American Novelists.* He holds a doctorate in English Language and Literature from the University of Michigan and an MFA in Poetry from Columbia University School of the Arts.

DAVID T. MITCHELL is a scholar, editor, history and film exhibition curator, and filmmaker in the field of disability studies. His books include the monographs *Narrative Prosthesis: Discourses of Disability* (2000); *Cultural Locations of Disability* (2005); *The Biopolitics of Disability: Neoliberalism, Ablenationalism, and Peripheral Embodiment* (2015) and the collections *The Body and Physical Difference: Discourses of Disability* (1997) and *A History of Disability in Primary Sources,* volume 5 of *The Encyclopedia of Disability.* He curated *The Chicago Disability History Exhibit* (Vietnam Veterans Memorial Museum, 2006) and assembled the programs for the Screening Disability Film Festival (Chicago, 2006) as well as the DisArt Independent Film Festival (Grand Rapids, MI, 2015). His four award-winning films include *Vital Signs: Crip Culture Talks Back* (1995), *A World without Bodies* (2002), *Self Preservation: The Art of Riva Lehrer* (1995), and *Disability Takes on the Arts* (1996). He is currently working on a new book and feature-length documentary film on disability and the Holocaust tentatively titled *Disposable Humanity.*

DAVID OSWALD teaches in the Department of English at the University of Victoria in British Columbia, Canada. His published writing appears in the *Journal of Literary and Cultural Disability Studies* and *The Goose: A Journal for Arts, Environment, and Culture in Canada,* and his main areas of research include twentieth-century US literature, disability studies, animal studies, biopolitics, and critical theory. In 2018, he successfully completed his SSHRC-funded dissertation, "Of Dogs and Idiots: Tropological Confusion in Twentieth-Century U.S. Fiction." This project elaborates his critical concept of tropological confusion vis-à-vis the literary-cultural habit of conflating caninity and idiocy, focusing on works by William Faulkner, John Steinbeck, Djuna Barnes, and Cormac McCarthy.

TOBIN SIEBERS (1953–2015) was born in Kaukauna, Wisconsin, and was diagnosed with polio at the age of two. He authored ten books, including the field-defining *Disability Aesthetics* (University of Michigan Press, 2010) and *Disability Theory* (University of Michigan Press, 2008). In 2004 Siebers was named the V. L. Parrington Collegiate Professor at the University of Michigan. In 2009, the University of Michigan Council for Disability Concerns presented Siebers with the James T. Neubacher Award in recognition of extraordinary leadership and service in support of the disability community. Siebers was selected for fellowships by the Michigan Society of Fellows, the Guggenheim Foundation, the Mellon Foundation, and the Institute for the Humanities at the University of Michigan.

ANGELA M. SMITH is Associate Professor in English and Gender Studies and Director of the Disability Studies Initiative at the University of Utah. Her research focuses on body politics in American literature, cinema, and popular culture, and she has published in the journals *Post Script* and *College Literature* and in the essay collections *Horror Zone* and *Popular Eugenics*. Her book *Hideous Progeny: Disability, Eugenics, and Classic Horror Cinema* (2011) studies the ways classic American horror cinema exploits and alters eugenic understandings of disability.

SHARON L. SNYDER's career includes a range of work as an author, artist, activist, and filmmaker. Her books include *The Body and Physical Difference: Discourses of Disability* (1997); *Narrative Prosthesis: Disability and the Dependencies of Discourse* (2000); volume 5 of *An Encyclopedia of Disability in Primary Sources* (2005); *Cultural Locations of Disability* (2006); *The Biopolitics of Disability: Neoliberalism, Ablenationalism, and Peripheral Embodiment* (2015), as well as more than thirty-five journal articles and chapters. She has curated a museum exhibit on disability history at the National Vietnam Veterans Memorial Museum, done disability film and arts programming for festivals and conferences, and created four award-winning documentary films: *Vital Signs: Crip Culture Talks Back*

(1995), *A World without Bodies* (2002), *Self Preservation: The Art of Riva Lehrer* (2005), and *Disability Takes on the Arts* (2006).

OLGA TARAPATA holds a doctorate in English from the University of Cologne. Her dissertation, *Extraordinary Bodies in the Work of William Gibson*, reads Gibson's representations of the human body from the late 1970s until today in parallel with disability history. Olga specializes in North American literature with an emphasis on contemporary fiction. Her research and teaching interests include disability studies, literary theory, cultural constructivism, literature and law, science fiction, and zine and comic culture. She is the guest editor of "Bodies on the Line: Intersections between Gender and Dis|ability," the spring issue of *Gender Forum: An Internet Journal for Gender Studies*.

SAMUEL YATES is a doctoral candidate at George Washington University, where he researches disability aesthetics and theatrical performance in his dissertation "Cripping Broadway: Neoliberal Performances of Disability in the American Musical." His project was awarded the 2017 Helen Krich Chinoy Dissertation Fellowship from the American Society for Theatre Research. He received his M.Phil in Theatre and Performance Studies from Trinity College Dublin as a Mitchell Scholar and his BA from Centre College as a John C. Young Scholar. Samuel holds a Humanity in Action Senior Fellowship for his work on performance and body politics and has previously collaborated as a dramaturg, playwright, and performer with theaters such as the Abbey Theatre, the Eugene O'Neill Theater Center, the Samuel Beckett Centre, and New Harmony Theater, among others. His recent work is published or forthcoming in *Radical Contemporary Theatre Practices by Women in Ireland* (Carysfort Press), and *Studies in Musical Theatre*, among others.

Index

Note: Page numbers appearing in italic refer to an illustration on that page.

www.ingramcontent.com/pod-product-compliance
Lightning Source LLC
Chambersburg PA
CBHW020339270326
41926CB00007B/239